re W

chandising: nciples
and practices.

28098

Oakton Community College
Morton Grove, Illinois

Food Merchandising
Principles and Practices

Food Merchandising
Principles and Practices

Theodore W. Leed
Department of Agricultural and Food Economics
University of Massachusetts

Gene A. German
Food Industry Management Program
Cornell University

CHAIN STORE AGE BOOKS
An Affiliate of Lebhar-Friedman, Inc., New York

Printing   5   4   3   2   1

Library of Congress Catalog Card Number: 73-88739
Internation Standard Book Number: 0-912016-15-9

Contents

v

Preface

There is one marketing innovation that is uniquely American—the self-service supermarket. The supermarket and its attendant self-service selling revolutionized not only food distribution but all types of distribution in the United States and throughout the world.

The self-service supermarket was a creative response to the needs of a growing and more highly urbanized population for a method of distribution that could significantly reduce operating costs and selling prices as well as provide a wider assortment of merchandise under one roof.

As the self-service method of selling food and grocery products gained wide acceptance by the public and grew in importance, merchandising methods rapidly became more sophisticated. New methods and concepts were tried, and many of them have become established merchandising principles in the relatively infant supermarket industry. It is these principles, along with related practices, many of them unique to food merchandising, that provide the basis for this text.

We believe that this text represents the first attempt to describe and analyze the basic principles and practices of food merchandising comprehensively in one source. It is our sincere hope that we have succeeded in providing students and others interested or already engaged in the exciting and challenging food industry with a reference that will lead to greater knowledge, understanding, and advancement of food merchandising.

For valuable assistance in reviewing the manuscript, the authors wish to acknowledge the following individuals and companies: Kenneth G. Abrahams, Holyoke Food Marts, Inc.; Ralph J. Lordi, Stop & Shop, Inc.;

Milton Segel, First National Stores, Inc.; Jack Faulkner and William Howard, Star Markets, Inc.; The Grand Union Company, Inc. (especially Harry Flynne and H. F. Kronewitz); The Kroger Company, Inc.; Edward M. Harwell; Charles Mallowe, Academy of Food Marketing, St. Joseph's College; and William O. Haynes, Food Distribution Program, Western Michigan University.

Also, for their invaluable assistance in typing the manuscript, the authors wish to recognize Mrs. Dorothy Leahey and Mrs. Gloria Pidduck.

A special note of thanks to Patrice Sobin for an excellent job in both editing and designing this book.

Theodore W. Leed
Gene A. German

July 1973

Food Merchandising
Principles and Practices

1

Food Merchandising and the Consumer

DEVELOPMENT AND HISTORY OF MERCHANDISING

Service to Self-Service

The concept of merchandising as we know it today is the product of the self-service store and the development of name brands and trademarks. Self-service was a feature of food stores as early as 1912. The most famous proponent of self-service food retailing was Clarence Saunders, the founder of the Piggly Wiggly Stores. Saunders opened his first store in Memphis, Tennessee, in 1916. The real significance of this first breakthrough in self-service retailing is that Piggly Wiggly Stores, which opened after 1916, were designed and built specifically for self-service. By the early 1900s, food chains and independents had begun to experiment with the self-service concept, but it was not until the growth of the supermarket beginning in 1930 that self-service was adopted on a widespread scale.

Self-service marked the beginning of a new era in food retailing and food merchandising. This was, in fact, the first major change in retailing since the days of the general store. Although certain refinements had been made in the small service stores of the early 1900s—more merchandise was available on the shelves, and the stores were cleaner and more attractive—they still followed the same selling techniques employed by the general store of the 1880s. It took the advent of self-service to bring about significant changes in assortment, pricing, displays, store layout, advertising, and packaging.

Consider the reaction of an owner of a general store in the 1800s if he were suddenly placed in the "modern" self-service store of the 1920s. What changes would have impressed him most? Even though by today's standards the 1920 store is extremely antiquated, great strides had been made, and many changes would have been evident to him.

The pricing of grocery items would have been one particularly evident change. The most radical change in pricing brought about by self-service was that all products on the shelves were marked with a retail price. In the old general store, the selling price was not established until a customer indicated an interest in purchasing the items. Even then, the price might not have been in dollars and cents.

Barter was an important means of transacting business in the 1800s. The store owner had to be a quick judge of character and had to have a ready knowledge of the resale value of items such as butter, eggs, and even home-brewed whiskey, which the customers would bring to trade for his merchandise. Self-service, however, did not allow for bartering, and standardized prices were necessary because of the use of newspaper advertising and floor displays that were introduced with self-service retailing.

The general-store owner would also have been impressed with the method in which the merchandise was displayed in a self-service store of the 1920s. Self-service required that the merchandise be placed on open display so that customers could help themselves. Those who experimented with self-service in its early days found that special displays of merchandise greatly increased the sale of a product. By contrast, merchandise in the general store was seldom accessible to the customer. A sales clerk was needed to get the item from shelving behind the counter. The sales clerk was also needed to weigh, measure, and wrap food items, such as sugar, flour, and molasses, that were available only in bulk quantities.

The layout of the self-service store would have presented a striking contrast to the retail establishment of the 1800s. Not only was merchandise displayed out in the open where customers could help themselves but dry groceries occupied the center of the 1920 store. The merchandise replaced the pot-bellied stove that once served as the focal point of the informal meeting room that filled the center of the general store. Also gone were the barrels of crackers, vinegar, and whale oil and the wooden boxes of raisins, prunes, and coffee.

There was little or no order to the old general store. Heavy items were usually dropped off close to the front door. Many items hung on nails or pegs on the walls. The organization and planning required for the placement of merchandise in the self-service store was a sharp contrast to this. Products were grouped by commodities and displayed in separate compartments. The 1920s saw the beginning of the "combination store," which offered fresh produce, dairy products, and even fresh cuts of meat along with dry groceries. The array of merchandise and the layout would certainly have been an impressive sight to the general-store owner.

Bulk to Packaged

In the early days of the general store, a large proportion of merchandise was sold in bulk and packaged by the storekeeper at the time of sale. Those products that were packed by a food processor or canner were sold more as commodities than as branded items. Canned peas, beans, and other products seldom carried the name of the packer, and consumers had little help in determining quality before they opened the can.

Government purchasing agents, however, began to specify that the name of the packer appear on all products. This enabled them to identify the higher quality products by the packer that stressed quality. As packer names became more and more prominent, food manufacturers sought trademark protection so that they could advertise and promote their own brand of merchandise.

An early example of brand promotion was the advertising campaign conducted for Uneeda Biscuits. This was perhaps the first real success story for national advertising. It may also have had a significant impact in eliminating the cracker barrel from the old general store. Uneeda was the first branded soda cracker in the United States. It was introduced at a time when bulk crackers were the rule—the cracker barrel was a reality. A national advertising campaign utilizing newspaper, magazine, and printed signs introduced Uneeda as the first soda cracker that customers could buy in a store as a branded item. Customer response was extremely favorable, and the success of this campaign encouraged other food manufacturers to develop and establish brand names.

Brand names, which were practically nonexistent in the general store's line of commodities, were an essential element in the self-service store. The general store sold products as *commodities*; the self-service store sold *brands*.

Advertising, packaging, and branding would all have been new concepts to our general store owner. Advertising was almost as nonexistent as prepackaged items from food manufacturers, and of course brand-name products could not have been found in the old general store.

Even though these merchandising practices associated with self-service were unknown to the general-store owner, he did carry on a form of retail merchandising. His own private blend and custom grinding of coffee, the open cracker barrel, and sometimes even a special display of a product on which he had made a special buy were the extent of his merchandising activities, however. Merchandising practices that are important to us today did not grow out of the general store. They had their origin in the development of the self-service food store.

Since the days of Uneeda Biscuit, name brands have played a key role in the marketing and merchandising of food products. They denote quality and instill consumer trust. Branding has been an essential ingredient of the self-service concept. Self-service eliminated the sales clerk, who might have suggested certain products or often verified the quality of a specific product. With self-service, the products had to sell themselves. Branding, advertising, packaging, and display became important elements in the merchandising plan.

The general-store owner of the 1800s would surely have been impressed with a self-service store of the 1920s. The features of the store that would have impressed him are the retail merchandising principles that we will examine in this book. We will look at retail pricing, displays, advertising and promotion, store layout, packaging, and buying practices not from an historical standpoint as the general store owner might have but from the point of view of their application to the food industry today.

WHAT IS FOOD MERCHANDISING?

Merchandising—Art or Science?

Is food merchandising an art, based upon skill and ingenuity, or is it a science, based upon a systematized body of knowledge or general principles?

Few, if any, would insist that food merchandising is a science based upon a body of knowledge that enables us to predict the outcome of any merchandising strategy with little or no error. There is much that we do not know about merchandising food, especially in the area of consumer motivation and behavior. Food merchandising is characterized by trial and error, intuition, and skillful manipulation based upon past experience.

However, even though food merchandising cannot be classified as a science, it can become more scientific. In other words, it can become more like a science as our knowledge becomes more organized and extensive and as we learn to predict consumer behavior more accurately.

In order to develop a systematized body of knowledge concerning food merchandising, it is necessary to utilize the scientific method, which involves the recognition and formulation of a problem, the systematic collection of data through observation and experimentation, and the formulation and testing of hypotheses (tentative assumptions). The scientific method provides us with an approach to merchandising that is much more likely to result in correct decisions than mere intuition or guesses. This is not to say that ingenuity and creativity should not play an important part in food merchandising; to the contrary, this is what lends excitement to food merchandising. Many innovations have come about as a result of someone having an idea and then being willing to risk trying it. But the use of the scientific method brings problems into focus and results in decisions that are based on the organized use of the best information available.

Thus, we can conclude that food merchandising is not a true science but that it is becoming more scientific through the application of knowledge gained from scientifically conducted research studies. We can also conclude that the skills and intuition of experienced and creative individuals are also important elements and must be considered in the study of food merchandising.

Three Concepts

In order to study and understand food merchandising, it is important to have a firm grasp of what it entails. *Merchandising,* as it relates to food or any other commodity, can be approached from several vantage points.

Each approach contributes to an understanding of merchandising.

First of all, there is the *institutional* concept, which explains merchandising in terms of the organizations and methods involved. In food merchandising, the organizational institutions include manufacturers, wholesale suppliers, brokers, and supermarkets and other types of retail food stores. The institutional methods involved in food merchandising include self-service, prepackaging, advertising and promotion, and national brand and private-label products. This list of food merchandising institutions is not complete but is intended to illustrate the kinds of organizations and methods that are the focal point of the institutional concept.

Another approach to merchandising is the *functional* concept, which is based upon defining the groups of related activities that make up merchandising. The functional concept places merchandising within the broader context of marketing.

Marketing includes *all* the activities involved in the movement and handling of goods from the point of production to the point of consumption or use. The following is a list of the basic functions involved in the marketing process:

> Standardization and grading
> Transportation
> Buying
> Risk bearing
> Assembling
> Financing
> Selling
> Storage

This list groups the activities that appear to be most important and common to the marketing process. Product planning is also sometimes considered a basic marketing function. These functions are not mutually exclusive; that is, they overlap. For example, risk bearing is involved in practically all the other marketing functions.

Merchandising is that part of the marketing process which deals primarily with the buying and selling functions. The selling function, as it applies to merchandising, includes pricing and presentation. Presentation includes such activities as packaging, display, space allocation, and advertising and promotion. Therefore, the functional concept views food merchandising as that part of the marketing process which deals with buying, pricing, and presenting food products to the consumer.

A third approach to merchandising can be termed the *consumer satisfaction* or *value* concept, which concentrates on the needs of the consumer as the basis of the marketing process, and merchandising as part of the total marketing process that creates and satisfies consumer needs. This view of marketing is referred to as the *total marketing concept* or *market orientation*. The following is a good description of the total marketing concept:

Marketing is not just a collection of functions such as product planning, market research, pricing, advertising and distribution. Nor can marketing properly be defined as selling. Selling concentrates on the needs of sellers while marketing concentrates on the needs of the customers. Marketing emphasizes customers, not products, processes or services.

Marketing is learning, creating and satisfying customers' needs at a profit. It is the total process of creating customers efficiently.[1]

The "total marketing concept," then, focuses on the consumer rather than on institutions or functions. The entire marketing process, including merchandising, begins with the identification of consumer needs, and the production and distribution of goods and services are only means for achieving the ultimate objective—satisfying consumer needs. Merchandising is that part of the marketing process which provides customer satisfaction or value through the development, procurement, pricing, and presentation of goods and services.

The three approaches to merchandising are all useful in defining what merchandising really is. They help to place merchandising in the broader framework of marketing so that it becomes apparent that merchandising is an integral part of a total process. It also becomes apparent that merchandising involves certain types of facilities and methods and requires the performance of groups of activities that constitute certain functions. However, the institutions and functions only facilitate the identification and satisfaction of consumer needs, which is the true role of the marketing process.

The definition of *food merchandising,* as used in this text, is based primarily upon the consumer satisfaction or value concept of marketing. However, the definition specifies functions because it is necessary to separate food merchandising from the broader field of food marketing. Thus, *food merchandising is maximizing customer satisfaction or value profitably through buying, pricing, and presenting food and grocery products and related services.*

The definition includes nonfood grocery products because the combination of food and nonfood products has become a well-established consumer purchasing pattern. Therefore, it is virtually impossible to separate food and many nonfood products when studying food merchandising. The major emphasis, however, will be placed upon food products. *Food merchandising,* as defined here, includes food products purchased for consumption off the premises and does not include meals or snacks purchased for consumption in restaurants, drive-ins, hotels, or other establishments.

This text deals primarily with food retailing because the retail food store is the point at which food and grocery products are presented to the consumer and the merchandising process is completed.

Therefore, this text will include an analysis of the institutions (methods and facilities) and functions (groups of activities) involved in maximizing

---

[1]Clinton B. Reeder, Marketing Management Specialist, Extension Service, Oregon State University. From a talk presented at a conference on "Growth Opportunities for Agriculture and Forestry Businesses," March 28, 1968.

consumer satisfaction (value) from the purchase of food and grocery products and related services.

Value to the Consumer

If food merchandising is the process of fulfilling consumer needs for food and grocery products and related services through buying, pricing, and presentation at the retail level, what kinds of needs are fulfilled? Looking at it another way, what kinds of values to the consumer are provided by food merchandising?

Perhaps the best way to identify consumer values provided by food merchandising is to analyze the reasons why consumers select one food store over another. In this manner, the consumer is identifying what is actually important to him and, therefore, is identifying the components of value.

In an analysis of surveys of consumer food-shopping habits and attitudes, two researchers concluded that "a food store does not simply sell food but rather merchandises a complex attribute mix made up of various components which have different values to different people."[2] This analysis went on to identify the attribute mix as made up of three major components: the values associated with convenience, the values associated with the food products themselves, and the values arising out of the behavior of the business as a going concern (see Table 1-1).

It is apparent from Table 1-1 that consumer value in food stores is composed of many attributes from which consumers may receive varying degrees of satisfaction.

The Values of Convenience

The *convenience values* are those things that save time and effort for the consumer. The location of the store with respect to the consumer's home, highway access, and nearness to other types of stores are perhaps the most important attributes associated with the values of convenience. The physical facilities are also important convenience attributes. Attributes such as ease of parking (including entrance and egress), ease of shopping, and checkout facilities that lead to convenient and prompt checkout service are important components of values of convenience. A congested highway or dangerous intersection could seriously interfere with ease of entrance or egress from the parking lot. The parking lot could be too small or arranged improperly for smooth traffic flow. The store layout or aisle width might interfere with customer shopping, and cartons or hand trucks might block aisles and prevent smooth customer traffic flow. Checkout facilities may be inadequate to accommodate customers reasonably promptly during peak sales periods. These physical conditions can be responsible for reducing

---

[2]R. L. Kohls and John Britney, *Consumer Selection of and Loyalty to Food Stores,* Research Bulletin No. 777, Purdue University, Agricultural Experiment Station, March 1964.

TABLE 1-1   The Salable Attribute Mix of a Food Store

I. The Values of Convenience
(Factors of time and effort saving in some form)

A. Location of store with respect to:
   Customer's home
   Customer's routes of travel
   Customer's desire for other types of store facilities (shopping center)

B. Physical layout of store:
   In-store features as wide aisles, shelf access, checkout facilities, bottle return arrangements, rest rooms
   Out-of-store features as parking facilities, automatic doors, parcel pick-up

C. The product mix as it contributes to one-stop shopping for other lines of goods such as drugs, health and beauty aids, housewares, etc.

D. Services available:
   Carry-out
   Check cashing, utility bill payment
   Store hours
   Well-arranged stock, store directory

II. The Values of Products
(Factors of the physical products and their mix)

A. Prices
   Both for the over-all product mix and for the individual product groups (meats, produce, groceries)
   As to level such as high, moderate, low, or wide range

B. Quality
   Both for the over-all product mix and for individual product groups
   As to level such as high, moderate, or wide range

C. Variety as to:
   Selection of merchandise; brands, items, and sizes
   Completeness of product lines
   Methods of merchandising (bulk, prepackaged, etc.)

III. The Values of Behavior of the Business
(Factors of consumer satisfaction from the services, behavior, and atmosphere of the managerial unit)

A. Personnel relationships:
   With each other and with customers
   Shopper assistance in selection and use of products

B. Physical and aesthetic features:
   Cleanliness and neatness
   Decor; design, color, fixtures
   Lighting
   Odor
   Special features such as music

C. Ethical bahavior
   Honesty and integrity of management
   Involvement in civic affairs

D. Methods of salesmanship:
   Advertising methods
   Promotional techniques such as trading stamps, premiums, games, discounts, price specials
   Consumer education

Source: Adapted from R. L. Kohls and John Britney, *Consumer Selection of and Loyalty to Food Stores*, Research Bulletin No. 777, Purdue University, Agriculture Experiment Station, March 1964, p. 3.

customer value in food stores and, depending upon their seriousness, could result in some customers selecting one store in preference to another.

The product mix with respect to lines of merchandise handled is also a convenience attribute. Some consumers like to fill all their shopping needs in as little time as possible and with a minimum of travel. Therefore, an assortment of products such as health and beauty aids, housewares, drugs, and house and garden supplies in addition to food and conventional grocery items can result in an important convenience value.

Services such as check cashing and accepting payment of utility bills are a great convenience to some consumers. Carry-out, long store hours, and the arrangement of merchandise (see Chapter 7) are other convenience-value attributes.

The Values of Products

Product values concern price, quality, and variety. These separate dimensions may apply to a specific item, such as canned peaches; to a product group, such as all canned fruit items carried in the grocery department; and to the overall product lines of a store. It is in the product area that a store may attempt to establish a general image of high, moderate, or low prices, assortment, and quality or choose to establish the image that it handles a wide range of prices, quality, and products.

It is quite likely that price is associated not only with individual products but also with the total attribute mix of the food store. The consumer undoubtedly compares the total set of values offered by the store to the total amount of money that he must spend to fulfill his shopping needs.

The product quality attribute is very difficult to define because quality is highly subjective; it depends on the individual as well as the food product. For example, the quality of a head of lettuce is judged by a different set of factors than is the quality of a steak or a can of whole tomatoes. In addition, the quality of any item depends upon individual tastes and preferences. However, there is a group of characteristics that are generally involved in consumer evaluation of quality; these include color, odor, texture, flavor, and uniformity. Perhaps the most meaningful test of quality is the degree to which products meet the expectations of the purchaser. If this is true, the retailer must determine consumer expectations if he expects to achieve a high degree of consumer satisfaction (value) from product quality.

Variety is also an important product value. The completeness of the assortment with respect to merchandise lines and the assortment of items within each line are variety attributes, as are methods of merchandising and the sizes of units and packages available. Thus, variety attributes include not only the number of product lines and items available but also the manner in which merchandise is presented. For instance, the product values in the produce department depend upon the extent of bulk versus prepackaged food, and the product values in the meat department depend upon the availability of clerk service in relation to self-service. In addition, product values are affected by the variety of package sizes made available, especially for the store-processed and packaged perishable items.

The Values of Behavior of the Business

Behavior of the business values include personnel relationships, physical and aesthetic features of the store, ethical behavior, and selling methods. These values make up the shopping "climate," that is, they determine the degree to which the store is a nice place to shop.

The conduct of the store personnel with respect to other employees and to customers is very important in creating a favorable shopping climate and in contributing to customer value. Bickering in public among store employees or indifferent or discourteous treatment of customers can easily discourage customer patronage. Conversely, high employee morale and polite and considerate treatment of customers constitute positive values that can lead to greater customer patronage. Likewise, personal services that assist customers in shopping and selecting merchandise are attributes that can increase customer value. These services might include clerk service in certain departments, such as meat, delicatessen, or bakery, and consumer information provided by store hostesses on the selection, handling, and preparation of foods.

Physical and aesthetic features include those characteristics that give each store its physical appeal. These attributes are highly subjective because they depend on the tastes and preferences of the individual, but they are part of the bundle of attributes that makes up total value to the customer. Each store creates an impression upon each customer, and that impression can be good, bad, or indifferent depending upon the physical and aesthetic features. The impression that the customer receives can be conditioned by cleanliness and neatness, interior decor, music, lighting, and even the odor inside the store.

Ethical behavior values concern the reputation of the owner or owners and the employees of the store for being honest and concerned citizens of the community. The reputation of the owner, be it an individual, a partnership, or a large corporation, is influenced by the manner in which he conducts his business and relates to his employees and the public. Honesty and fair play in pricing, advertising and promotion, handling complaints, and hiring practices are determining factors. Involvement in civic affairs and support of service clubs and charities also influence the reputation of the business and, consequently, the ethical values.

Methods of salesmanship provide values other than those associated with the reputation of the businessman. The type of advertising utilized can provide value depending upon the degree to which it offers information, excitement, or interest to the customer. The use of promotional techniques such as trading stamps, premiums, games, discounts, and price specials can also add to total customer value provided by the retail food store. Furnishing educational information to customers on the selection, handling, and preparation of foods in advertising or point-of-sale materials is another value related to the methods of salesmanship employed by the food store operator.

The three types of value described provide us with a framework or model for analyzing and discussing food merchandising because they help to identify ways in which the consumer may be satisfied. As one study states, "The fact that food stores sell food and services at a price is not a useful analytical framework. Obviously, all food stores do sell food and services, but it is equally obvious that the attribute mix that makes up the package individual stores offer to their customers may vary widely."[3]

Why Consumers Select a Particular Store

What is the relative importance of various attributes in the consumer's choice of a food store? Table 1-2 shows the results of consumer surveys conducted in more than 30 urban and suburban market areas throughout the country. Of the three major dimensions of the total store operation, product-related reasons, including quality, prices, and selection, were ranked most important. Convenience factors combined made up the second most important consideration in selecting a favorite supermarket, and these included location, checkout service, ease of shopping, and parking facilities. Business-behavior values were the third most important set of factors and included attractiveness and cleanliness of the store, friendliness of store people, and trading stamps.

TABLE 1-2   Factors Considered Most Important by Consumers in Selecting a Favorite Supermarket (In Selected Years)

	1971	1967	1963	1958	1954
Quality and freshness of meats	20%	18%	20%	16%	16%
Low prices on groceries	19	18	15	12	15
Attractiveness and cleanliness of store	12	10	11	11	11
Quality and freshness of fruits and vegetables	12	11	12	12	15
Convenient location	10	12	11	14	16
Variety and selection of grocery merchandise	10	11	9	13	13
Fast checkout service	5	4	4	6	—
Good store arrangement—ease of shopping	5	5	6	2	1
Friendliness of store people	4	6	6	7	8
Better parking facilities	2	3	3	5	4
Trading stamps	1	2	3	2	1

Source: Adapted from *1971 Food Shopping Habits Study* (Cincinnati, Ohio: Burgoyne, Inc., 1971), p. 21.

It is apparent from Table 1-2 that the relative importance of factors influencing consumer selection of a favorite supermarket may vary over time. For instance, it appears that meat quality, grocery prices, and store arrangement have become relatively more important, while store location,

---

[3]Kohls and Britney, p. 2.

variety and selection of grocery merchandise, friendliness of store people, and better parking facilities have become less important since 1954.

The crucial problem for the food store operator is to identify the relative importance of the factors that provide value to his prospective customers. These may change over time, depending upon the competitive situation and customer tastes and preferences. Each operator should attempt to differentiate his store or stores by offering something unique or in some way providing greater value to the customer than his competition provides.

THE CONSUMER DEMAND FOR FOOD

The development and implementation of a successful food merchandising program or strategy requires a knowledge of consumer demand. After all, merchandising strategy is the offering of a set of attributes that hopefully will provide greater value to the consumer than the attribute mix offered by competitors. The success of any particular merchandising strategy, or the amount of value it provides, depends upon how well it fulfills consumer needs and desires or "value sets." It becomes important then to understand what determines and influences consumer needs and desires in order to develop a merchandising strategy that will offer the greatest possible value to the consumer and the greatest profit to the store.

Individual Consumer Demand

Consumer demand refers to the quantities of goods or services that will be purchased at given prices and under a given set of economic conditions. A brief review of basic economic theory will help to clarify the concept of consumer demand.

Figure 1-1 shows a demand schedule that illustrates the nature of demand for two consumers in response to changes in the price of sirloin steak. The curve D_A shows the expected behavior of Mr. A in terms of the quantity of sirloin steak that he will purchase at various prices. Curve D_B shows the same relationship for Mr. B.

TABLE 1-3   Hypothetical Demand Schedule for Sirloin Steak

Price per Pound	Pounds Purchased		Total Revenue	
	Mr. A	Mr. B	Mr. A	Mr. B
2.25	1	0	2.25	—
2.00	1½	0	3.00	—
1.75	2	1	3.50	1.75
1.50	2½	1¼	3.75	1.83
1.25	3	1½	3.75	1.88
1.00	4	2	4.00	2.00
0.75	6	2¾	4.50	2.06
0.50	-	4½	—	2.25

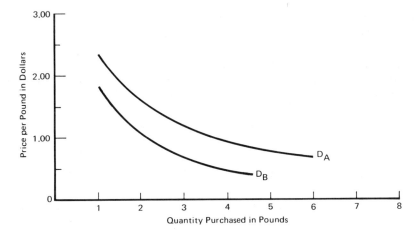

FIGURE 1-1 Hypothetical demand schedule for sirloin steak for Mr. A and Mr. B (based on data in Table 1-3).

The demand schedule shown in Figure 1-1 illustrates a basic economic principle of demand, and that is that consumers will take increasing quantities of a good or service as price declines, and vice versa. This does not mean that all consumers will react the same, however. As shown in Figure 1-1, Mr. A and Mr. B react quite differently to changes in the price of sirloin steak. For example, at a price of $1.00 per pound Mr. A will purchase four pounds of steak, but Mr. B will purchase only about two pounds. Thus, we can say that Mr. A has a greater demand for sirloin steak than does Mr. B. This could be due to one or more factors, such as differences in personal tastes and preferences or in income.

The nature of demand also varies widely among commodities, as shown in the hypothetical demand schedule for fresh whole milk (Figure 1-2). Here again, it is apparent that Mr. A, for some reason or reasons, has a greater demand for whole milk than does Mr. B because Mr. A is willing to purchase more milk at any given price.

The examples of the demand schedules for sirloin steak and milk illustrate another important economic principle of consumer demand—the quantity purchased is more responsive to changes in price for some goods and services than for others.

TABLE 1-4 Hypothetical Demand Schedule for Fresh Whole Milk

Price per Gallon	Gallons Purchased		Total Revenue	
	Mr. A	Mr. B	Mr. A	Mr. B
2.50	1½	-	3.75	—
2.00	1¾	1	3.50	2.00
1.50	2	1¼	3.00	1.93
1.00	2½	1½	2.50	1.50
0.50	3	2¼	1.50	1.13

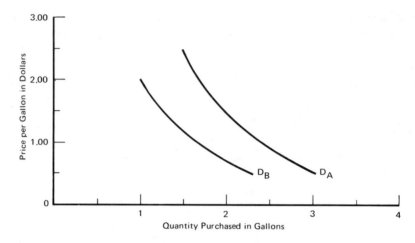

FIGURE 1-2   Hypothetical demand schedule for fresh whole milk
for Mr. A and Mr. B (based on data in Table 1-4).

Price Elasticity

The relationship of changes in quantity demanded to changes in price
is called *price elasticity* of demand. The greater the change in quantity
relative to the change in price, the more elastic the demand.

The demand for sirloin steak by both Mr. A and Mr. B is elastic because
the changes in price are accompanied by more-than-proportionate changes
in quantity purchased (see Figure 1-1 and Table 1-3). This relationship
between price and quantity results in greater total expenditures for the
purchase of steak as price decreases because Mr. A and Mr. B will increase
their consumption of steak substantially as the price is lowered, up to the
point at which their appetite for steak is reasonably well satisfied. Steak
is a highly desirable food for most people but is expensive relative to other
beef items and other meats. Consumers will tend to substitute less-expensive
beef items, such as hamburger, or other meats, such as pork or chicken,
for steak when the price of steak rises. Likewise, when the price of steak
declines they will substitute steak for the less-desirable, cheaper cuts of
beef or other meats. For this reason, the quantity of steak consumed is
quite responsive to changes in steak prices, and the demand is therefore
elastic with respect to price.

The price elasticity of demand for items for which there are close substitutes is generally greater than that for items that have no close substitutes.
The demand for fresh whole milk by Mr. A and Mr. B is inelastic with
respect to price because changes in price are accompanied by less-
than-proportionate changes in quantity purchased (see Figure 1-2 and Table
1-4). This relationship between price and quantity results in lower total
expenditures for the purchase of whole milk as price decreases. This happens
because consumers will not change their purchases of milk very much regardless of price. There is no close substitute for milk, and consumers do not

tend to switch to other beverages when the price of milk increases or vice versa. Therefore, the quantity of milk consumed is not highly responsive to changes in milk prices—the demand for milk is price inelastic. The price elasticity of demand for items for which there are no close substitutes is generally less than that for items having close substitutes. Foods that are important in the diet and have no close substitutes are referred to as *staples*. These include items such as milk, bread, sugar, and coffee. The price elasticity of staple items is generally inelastic. Studies have indicated that the demand for food in general is inelastic with respect to price except for certain food commodities.

The concept of demand and the determination of demand schedules are based upon the rigid qualifying assumptions that consumer income, consumer tastes and preferences, prices of alternative goods, time, and all other factors are held constant. Because this is unrealistic, the basic demand theory is best used as a general explanation of the nature of the relationship between price and consumption rather than as a precise measurement. If the theory explains consumer behavior in principle, then it is practical inasmuch as it can help us to predict changes in consumer purchases in response to changes in price in an approximate way.

One researcher put the value of demand theory this way: "Clear theoretical concepts and correct theory are basic to progress in any field. A correct theory is 'practical.' It explains in principle how prices are actually made, and how consumers actually respond to changes in prices and in their incomes."[4]

Product Utility

Why do consumers purchase more of a good as the price decreases? Theory tells us that a consumer's choice of goods is based upon the *utility* or *satisfaction* furnished by the goods being consumed or in anticipation of being consumed. Utility refers to a general sense of satisfaction and not a precise measure.

Marginal Utility. Consumers are not able to fulfill all their desires for goods and services, and therefore must make choices among alternatives in order to maximize satisfaction from their incomes, which are limited. As a consumer purchases more of a good, he tends to receive progressively less utility. This is called diminishing *marginal utility* and means simply that the consumption of each additional unit of a good adds less satisfaction (has less utility) than does the previous unit.

As the marginal utility of a good declines, the consumer is likely to purchase other goods that provide greater utility than additional purchases of the same good. The consumer will purchase that combination of goods and services which will maximize his total satisfaction from his allocation

---

[4]Frederick V. Waugh, *Demand and Price Analysis*, Economic Research Service Technical Bulletin No. 1316, U.S. Department of Agriculture, Washington, D.C., November 1964.

of income. At this point, he has allocated his income in such a way that the marginal utilities of a unit of money's worth of all commodities purchased are equal. For example, at the point of maximum satisfaction, one dollar's worth of steak will provide the same marginal utility (increase in satisfaction) as one dollar's worth of any other good or service purchased.

The Indifference Approach. The marginal-utility approach to the explanation of consumer choice assumes that the consumer has some way of measuring marginal utility or satisfaction. The indifference approach explains consumer choice in terms of the various combinations of goods that will yield a consumer the same total satisfaction. It does not require that the consumer measure utility but merely that he rank his preferences for alternative combinations of goods and services. The optimum allocation of income according to the indifference approach is expressed in terms of the rates of substitution of various goods for one another. As the price of a commodity falls, the consumer will buy more of it because its price is more favorable relative to other commodities, and he will buy more of the lower-priced commodity to replace units of other commodities.

TABLE 1-5 Hypothetical Consumer Indifference
Combinations for Bananas and Cupcakes

Choice	Number of Bananas	Number of Cupcakes
A	6	1
B	4	2
C	2	4
D	1	6

An indifference combination based upon choices between bananas and cupcakes with a given expenditure is shown in Table 1-5. Each of the combinations shown—A, B, C, and D—yields the *same* amount of satisfaction. In other words, the consumer is indifferent concerning which combination he chooses because each one will satisfy him equally well. The combinations depend upon the rate of substitution of one commodity for the other. As the number of units of one commodity increases, it takes proportionately less of the other commodity to replace units of the first in order to maintain the same level of satisfaction. This rule is known as the *marginal rate of substitution* and is related to the rule of diminishing marginal utility.

The indifference combinations shown in Table 1-5 are illustrated graphically in Figure 1-3. These combinations make up an indifference curve that shows the combinations of bananas and cupcakes that give the same amount of satisfaction. Other sets of combinations could also be drawn, each one representing a different amount of total satisfaction. The nature of the indifference curves for two commodities depends on the extent to which the commodities are substitutes for each other and on the prices of each. If the price of either commodity changes, then the indifference combinations would change because price affects the amount of the commodity that can be purchased with a given expenditure.

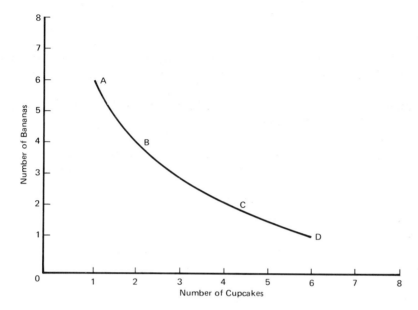

FIGURE 1-3   Consumer indifference curve for bananas and cupcakes (based on data in Table 1-5).

According to indifference theory, the consumer will choose that combination of goods which will provide the greatest total amount of satisfaction given the indifference relationships, the prices of the goods, and the total expenditures to be made. This theory is a simplification of actual consumer behavior, but it is useful in explaining, in concept, how people make choices among alternatives based upon the relative utility or satisfaction provided.

Both the marginal-utility and indifference approaches to consumer choice are based upon rigid assumptions, including consumer awareness of all possible alternatives, no change in tastes or preferences, no changes in the quality of available goods and services, and that there are rational consumers who will not only be able to identify utility or rates of substitution but who will always select that combination of goods and services which provides the greatest total utility. In spite of the assumptions involved, demand theory does help us to explain why consumers behave as they do with respect to consumption in relation to price changes.

Cross Elasticity.   Indifference analysis explains consumer choice in terms of combinations of goods based upon rates of substitution of one good for another. The rate of substitution depends upon the prices of the goods and consumer preferences for the goods. The term *cross elasticity* of demand describes the responsiveness of the purchase of one good to changes in the price of another good. This relationship is expressed as a ratio.

$$\text{Cross-elasticity ratio} = \frac{\%\text{ change in quantity purchased of good A}}{\%\text{ change in price of good B}}$$

If the ratio is positive, goods A and B are called substitutes for each other because a change in the quantity of A purchased is directly related to the percentage change in the price of good B. For example, steak is a substitute product for hamburger, and oleomargarine is a substitute for butter. As the price of steak increases, the quantity of hamburger purchased also increases because the consumer will substitute hamburger for steak. Likewise, if the price of steak decreases, the sales of hamburger will also decrease as the consumer substitutes steak for hamburger. The higher the ratio of cross elasticity, the greater the substitutability.

If the value of the cross elasticity is negative, it indicates that the goods may be complementary, that is, the use of one is tied to the use of the other. For example, the use of butter is related to the use of sweet corn, and an increase in the use of sweet corn is accompanied by an increase in the use of butter. As the price of sweet corn decreases, the purchase of sweet corn will increase and will result in an increased purchase of butter. Likewise, an increase in the price of sweet corn will reduce the quantity purchased and will result in a decline in the use of butter, unless there is an offsetting or compensating demand for the use of butter.

The concepts of marginal utility, indifference, and cross elasticity help to explain why the demand for various food products and services are interrelated so that changes in the price of one commodity can lead to changes in the quantities of other commodities purchased.

The Effect of Income

The demand theory discussed so far concerns the relationship between price and quantity. Income is also a major determinant of consumer demand with respect to both the choice of goods and services and the intensity or level of demand for goods and services. The *level* of demand refers to the quantities of a commodity that the individual will purchase at various prices and is represented by the relative location of the demand curve. For example, in Figure 1-1 (see page 13) Mr. A has a more intense or a higher level of demand for sirloin steak than does Mr. B because Mr. A is willing to purchase more steak at any given price, and this is represented by the location of the two curves—Mr. A's demand curve is above and to the right of Mr. B's demand curve.

Income Elasticity. Mr. B and Mr. A might also represent consumers in low-income areas and high-income areas, respectively. Consumers with high incomes are able to satisfy their wants more fully and purchase more of the goods that are classified as luxury items than can consumers with low incomes. This observation simply tells us that as income changes, the shopping habits and purchase patterns of the consumer also change. The term used to describe changes in shopping patterns that are related to changes in income is *income elasticity*. This is expressed as a ratio:

$$\text{Income elasticity} = \frac{\% \text{ increase in quantity of a specific product purchased}}{\% \text{ increase in income}}$$

This formula for income elasticity is used to measure the effect of changes in income on purchases of various products. When a change in income results in an increased purchase of a specific product that is greater than the percentage increase in income, the ratio will be positive. For example, a 10 percent increase in income that results in a 20 percent increase in the purchase of steak would result in a positive ratio of 2 (or 2 to 1). The ratio would be negative if an increase in income were accompanied by a decrease in the rate of purchase of a specific product. For example, an increase in income might result in a consumer purchasing more steak but less hamburger. Products that are purchased at a rate greater than the increase in income are referred to as *superior* goods. Products that are purchased at a rate less than the increase in income are referred to as *inferior* goods.

In the case described above, steak is a superior good, and hamburger is an inferior good. This, of course, in no way reflects product quality but simply designates the preference that the consumer has for specific products. These terms are used to indicate which products are purchased at a rate in excess of the increase in income and which products are purchased at a rate less than the increase in income.

Changes in consumer income influence the way in which consumers distribute their expenditures among various types of goods and services, such as food, clothing, housing, recreation, and so on. In general, as income rises, the proportion of income spent on food drops, or in other words, the demand for food is inelastic with respect to income. This relationship was first stated by Ernst Engel, an English statistician, and is known as *Engel's Law*. However, as in the case of the price elasticity, expenditures for some individual food commodities are elastic with respect to income even though total expenditures for food are inelastic. In other words, when a consumer's income increases he purchases more expensive, or luxury, foods, but the total amount of food purchased does not increase. So, as income increases, consumers do spend more total dollars for food, but as a percentage of total income their food expenditures become smaller.

Tastes and Preferences.   Economic theory of consumer demand is concerned with the relationships of prices, income, and quantities of goods and services taken off the market. Consumer tastes and preferences are assumed by economic theory to be constant, which of course is an unrealistic assumption. We know that consumer tastes and preferences are changing constantly and influence both consumer choice of goods and services and the intensity or level of demand for goods and services.

The major factors that influence consumer choice of goods and services can be classified into three general categories: economic factors, market and product factors, and tastes and preferences (see Table 1-6).

TABLE 1-6   Factors Influencing Consumer Choice of Goods and Services

Economic Factors	*Market and Product Factors*
Size of income	Past experience (favorable/unfavorable)
Debts and savings	Merchandising factors
Expected income	Convenience
Anticipated expenses	Product quality and selection
Credit	Business behavior
Price	

Tastes and Preferences	
Social factors	Personal characteristics
Family influence	Ethnic origin
Cultural influence	Sex
Education	Age
Occupation	Marital status
Urbanization and region	Motivational factors
Reference groups	Needs (physical and psychological)
Family	Values
Friends	Beliefs
Associates	Attitudes
	Habit
	Perception
	Expectations

Market and product factors are closely related to the purely economic factors of income, both current and anticipated, and price. The values provided by merchandising determine the price consumers are willing to pay, which in turn is related to the amount of income.

The values provided through merchandising and the price consumers are willing to pay for goods and services are conditioned or influenced by tastes and preferences. Tastes and preferences are formed on the basis of many social and psychological factors. The social influences include family, friends, business associates, education, culture, and place of residence with respect to region and type of neighborhood. Personal characteristics that are involved in forming tastes and preferences include ethnic origin, sex, age, and marital status.

Motivational factors involved in the formation of personal tastes and preferences include needs, both physical and psychological, values, beliefs, attitudes, habits, perceptions, and expectations. These factors are obviously different for each individual, so each individual has different tastes and preferences. Each of your customers has certain physical needs, such as hunger and thirst, that must be fulfilled. Beyond the physical needs, they have other kinds of needs, such as the needs to be recognized, to belong, and to be fulfilled as a person. In addition, habits, values, attitudes, perception or the ways people see things, and expectations play an important role in forming tastes and preferences.

Thus, the kinds of food people buy, the place in which they buy it, and the price they are willing to pay are all influenced by many factors. Individuals may tend to behave like their parents with respect to food purchasing, or they may try to emulate their friends and associates in order to achieve a certain social status. The role of many of the factors influencing the formation of personal tastes and preferences for food and other commodities is not well understood. More research is needed to identify these relationships and to predict changes more accurately.

We do know that tastes and preferences are not static, they are ever-changing, and that these changes influence consumer food shopping behavior. Some of these changes will be described in the next section and in Chapter 2.

The factors that influence consumer choice of food and other goods and services are interrelated—they influence each other. For example, market and product factors both influence and are influenced by tastes and preferences. Advertising and promotion, as part of the merchandising mix, can influence tastes and preferences, which in turn influence consumer choice. There are many other such interrelationships too numerous to describe.

However, we do have some knowledge of the factors influencing consumer food shopping behavior, which is useful in developing and carrying out a food merchandising program.

What We Know about Consumer Demand for Food

Thus far, we have been discussing consumer demand in terms of the behavior of individual consumers. From a practical standpoint, it would hardly be possible to identify or satisfy the tastes and preferences of each individual for food. However, it is possible to identify the total or market demand for the major food product categories and to determine the relationships between total demand and some of the factors influencing total demand. This can be accomplished by studying consumers as a single group or by studying groups of consumers classified according to an economic factor, such as income, or a taste and preference factor, such as age, size of family, urbanization, and so on.

Furthermore, we can study changes in food consumption and shopping practices over time, which provides us with some insights into changes in tastes and preferences.

Knowledge relating to consumer food consumption and shopping behavior is essential to planning and carrying out a merchandising program that will appeal to as many consumers as possible.

Income and Food Consumption

Disposable personal income is the amount that people have left from their incomes after paying federal, state, and local taxes. It is the amount available to spend for goods and services, to save, or to invest. By using one year as a base or reference, it is possible to show percentage changes over time in personal disposable income. The percentages are referred to as index numbers (see Figure 1-4). For example, disposable income was $350.0 billion in 1960 and $687.8 billion in 1970. Thus, the index or rate of change in disposable income in 1970 based upon or relative to 1960 is calculated as follows:

$$\frac{687.8 \text{ (1970 disposable income in billions of \$)}}{350.0 \text{ (1960 disposable income in billions of \$)}} \times 100$$

$$= 1.97 \times 100 = 197\%^5$$

The index of disposable personal income in 1970 was 197 percent based upon 1960 as 100 percent. In other words, disposable personal income was almost twice as great in 1970 as in 1960. Not only has *total* disposable personal income in the United States more than doubled since 1960 (see Figure 1-4) but disposable income *per person* has also increased substantially since 1960.

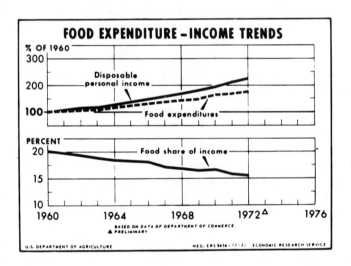

FIGURE 1-4

Although expenditures for food have increased considerably over the years, the increase has not matched the gain in disposable income. As a result, the percentage of income spent for food has declined over the past several decades. In 1929, the first year that data of this type were recorded, 23 percent of disposable income was spent for food. This percentage dropped to 20 percent in 1942 and rebounded to a record high of 26 percent in 1947. Since then, the percentage has declined to 20 percent in 1960 and to a record low of less than 16 percent in 1972. The decline in the percentage of income spent for food is the direct result of the inelastic nature of the total demand for food relative to changes in income.

---

⁵We must multiply by 100 in order to express the quotient as a percentage.

The percentage of income spent for food varies widely among families of different sizes and income. Data from the 1960-61 *Survey of Consumer Expenditures,* conducted by the U.S. Department of Labor and the Department of Agriculture, showed that the percentage of income spent for food varied from about 12 percent for families with annual incomes of $15,000 and over to more than 50 percent for families with incomes below $1,000. The percentage of income spent for food varied from 19 percent for two-person families to 26 percent for families with six or more persons.[6]

The amount of family income is related not only to the proportion of income spent for food but also to the types of food consumed. A nationwide survey of household food consumption made by the U.S. Department of Agriculture during the spring of 1965 identified some of the relationships between income and food consumption (Table 1-7). The higher income families used larger quantities of milk and milk products; meat, poultry, and fish; bakery products; vegetables and fruit; and soup and baby-food mixtures. The higher income families used less flour and cereal, eggs, and sugar and sweets.

TABLE 1-7   Consumption of Foods per Person per Week by
Income Group, 1965

| | | Income Group | | |
Food Group		$1,000-1,999	$5,000-5,999	$9,000-9,999
Milk, cream, cheese	(quarts)	3.67	4.23	4.53
Fats, oils	(pounds)	.84	.84	.79
Flour, cereal	(pounds)	2.31	1.32	1.05
Bakery products	(pounds)	1.83	2.36	2.58
Meat, poultry, fish	(pounds)	4.08	4.61	4.61
Eggs	(dozens)	.62	.56	.49
Sugar, sweets	(pounds)	1.25	1.10	.97
Potatoes, sweet potatoes	(pounds)	1.48	1.66	1.70
Other vegetables, fruit	(pounds)	6.64	7.36	8.61
Soup, other mixtures	(pounds)	.39	.63	.67

Source: *Food Consumption of Households in the United States, Spring 1965,* U.S. Department of Agriculture, Agricultural Research Service, Washington, D.C., 1968.

For example, the consumption of beef per person in families with annual incomes of $15,000 and over is 123 percent of the U.S. average, or 23 percent greater per person than the national average (see Table 1-8). It is apparent that the per capita consumption of beef; fresh, frozen, and canned fruits; fresh and frozen vegetables; and processed potatoes (canned, frozen, dried) increases considerably as income increases. On the other hand, the per capita consumption of pork, chicken, and fresh potatoes is greater at the lower than at the higher income levels.

[6]*Food–Consumption, Prices, Expenditures,* Agricultural Economic Report No. 138, U.S. Department of Agriculture, Economic Research Service, Washington, D.C., July 1968, p. 41.

TABLE 1-8 Indexes of Consumption per Person, Selected Foods, by Family Income, Spring 1965

Income Group (dollars)	Meat and Poultry			Fruit			Vegetables			Potatoes and Sweet Potatoes	
	Beef	Pork	Chicken	Fresh	Canned	Frozen	Fresh	Canned	Frozen	Fresh	Processed
U.S. average	100%	100%	100%	100%	100%	100%	100%	100%	100%	100%	100%
Under $1,000	66	97	102	79	63	34	95	71	36	95	40
1,000–1,999	72	99	107	93	67	40	103	80	48	100	31
2,000–2,999	76	99	96	85	77	52	93	79	59	102	68
3,000–3,999	83	103	100	82	84	46	87	91	55	106	64
4,000–4,999	95	101	106	92	93	59	92	101	86	115	86
5,000–5,999	102	102	97	98	102	90	94	107	86	102	97
6,000–6,999	108	101	101	104	106	105	100	114	91	101	107
7,000–7,999	111	104	97	107	109	113	102	102	127	99	133
8,000–8,999	114	99	96	103	121	141	101	106	124	96	139
9,000–9,999	111	91	97	107	129	166	109	107	138	99	135
10,000–14,999	114	97	100	126	117	182	110	107	166	89	148
15,000 and over	123	93	99	125	115	200	143	102	193	76	132

Source: Food–Consumption, Prices, Expenditures, Supplement to Agricultural Economic Report No. 138, U.S. Department of Agriculture, Economic Research Service, Washington, D.C., January 1970, Table 119.

Food Prices and Consumer Income

The Consumer Price Index measures the changes in the prices of all goods and services purchased by urban wage earners and clerical worker families as well as single workers living alone (see Figure 1-5).[7] *The Consumer Price Index* is based upon about 400 commodities and services, including about 100 food items, priced in retail outlets in 56 metropolitan areas and cities.

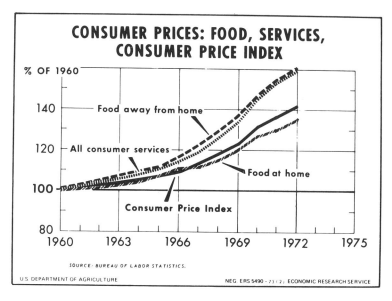

FIGURE 1-5

The prices of all goods and services (including food) have increased more than the prices of all food since 1960, and the prices of food purchased away from home—in restaurants or institutions—increased considerably more than the prices of foods purchased at retail for home consumption.

Even though the prices of food purchased for home consumption have increased by about 30 percent since 1960, the increase in disposable income has been even greater (see Figure 1-4). Thus, the purchasing power of the consumer's dollar has increased with respect to food. In other words, the proportion of consumers' income required to purchase an identical or fixed quantity of food at the retail store has declined since 1960, continuing a trend that began at the end of World War II.

The price of food increased sharply in 1972 and 1973, reflecting strong demand for meat in the face of shorter supplies and inflationary increases in marketing costs. This situation prompted strong public reaction and placed

[7]*The Consumer Price Index* is published monthly by the Bureau of Labor Statistics, United States Department of Labor, Washington, D.C.

the food retailer in the difficult position of trying to maintain a reasonable level of net profit in view of higher operating and merchandising costs.

Region and Urbanization

The preferences for food used at home varied considerably among consumers in the four regions of the United States based upon the food consumption studies made by the United States Department of Agriculture in 1955 and 1965. Some foods used in markedly larger quantities in certain regions of the continental United States than in others were:

Region	Foods
Northeast (Maine, New Hampshire, Vermont, Massachusetts, Connecticut, Rhode Island, New York, New Jersey, Pennsylvania)	Fresh whole milk, butter, lamb, veal, shellfish, fresh fruit, fruit juice
North Central (Ohio, Indiana, Michigan, Illinois, Wisconsin, Minnesota, Iowa, Missouri, North Dakota, South Dakota, Nebraska, Kansas)	Fresh whole milk, cheese, butter, beef, pork, lunch meat, fresh white potatoes, canned fruit, frozen fruit
South (Texas, Oklahoma, Arkansas, Louisiana, Kentucky, Tennessee, Mississippi, Alabama, West Virginia, Delaware, Maryland, Virginia, North Carolina, South Carolina, Georgia, Florida)	Evaporated milk, lard, vegetable shortening, pork, chicken, fish, sweet potatoes, rice, cornmeal, hominy grits, self-rising flour, syrup, molasses
West (California, Oregon, Washington, Montana, Idaho, Wyoming, Utah, Nevada, Colorado, Arizona, New Mexico)	Skim milk, cheese, beef, fresh fruit, canned fruit, dried fruit[8]

The U.S. Department of Agriculture food-consumption studies also showed that shifts occurred in the quantities and types of foods used by households between 1955 and 1965. Changes tended to occur in all four regions in use of the same foods and in the same direction, although not always to the same extent (see Table 1-9). Household food expenditures were highest in the Northeast and lowest in the South.

The U.S. Department of Agriculture food consumption studies also revealed some differences in food consumption among urban (city) and farm families. In both the North and South, urban families tended to select more commercially prepared foods and farm families more ingredients for home-prepared foods.

In both the North and South, farm households tended to use more of each of the major groups of food per person than either urban or rural nonfarm households—milk and milk products; fats and oils; grain products;

[8]*Food Consumption of Households in the North Central, Spring 1965,* U.S. Department of Agriculture, Agricultural Research Service, Washington, D.C., July 1968.

TABLE 1-9   Household Food Expenditures in 1965 and Percentage Change in Household Consumption of Selected Food Items, by Region, 1955 to 1965

Food	Percent Change by Region 1955 to 1965			
	Northeast	North Central	South	West
Increases				
Nonfat dry milk	140	100	138	129
Salad and cooking oils	92	100	117	19
Bakery products (except bread)	64	66	79	48
Beef	30	22	56	14
Chicken	20	27	21	37
Frozen potatoes	150	375	1300	250
Frozen vegetables	30	21	62	25
Potato chips and sticks	140	60	83	46
Fresh fruit juice	381	267	167	575
Soft drinks	86	77	68	96
Fruit drinks	1036	764	756	457
Peanut butter	50	57	67	45
Decreases				
Fresh fluid milk	12	18	23	24
Evaporated milk	23	42	40	46
Butter	26	34	54	40
Shortening	30	35	37	49
Flour	31	31	50	42
Sugar	7	20	15	22
Fresh white potatoes	18	18	15	25
Fresh vegetables	18	17	19	15
Fresh fruit	5	21	11	15
Frozen fruit	64	50	43	38
Household Food Expenditures				
Weekly value of food purchased for home consumption, Spring 1965	$31.01	$27.06	$23.39	$27.69

Source: *Food Consumption of Households in the North Central, Spring, 1965,* U.S. Department of Agriculture, Agricultural Research Service, Washington, D.C., July 1968, pp. 1-3.

meat, poultry, and fish; eggs, sugar, and sweets; and vegetables and fruits including potatoes and sweet potatoes. The only exceptions occurred in the South, where urban households used more vegetables and fruit and meat, poultry, and fish than did farm households.

Demographic Characteristics

Tastes and preferences of consumers vary not only among regions and according to the amount of urbanization but also among neighborhood areas served by food retailers. Buying patterns—the kinds and amounts of products that people buy—vary among neighborhood areas depending upon the characteristics of consumers living in those neighborhoods. The study of populations with respect to size and density as well as vital statistics, such as age, race, sex, income, education, and so on, is referred to as a *demographic study*. Demographic studies can be related to food shopping and buying patterns in order to identify some of the relationships between social and economic characteristics of groups of consumers and the types and amounts of food that they buy.

One of the early studies of consumer food-buying behavior and demographic characteristics was conducted by *Progressive Grocer* magazine in cooperation with the Reuben H. Donnelly Corporation and the Kroger Company.[9]

The study was conducted in Cleveland, Ohio, and included fairly detailed sales audits in ten Kroger stores as well as consumer research conducted through telephone and personal interviews and a consumer panel.[10]

Five types of neighborhoods in the city of Cleveland and surrounding suburban areas were selected for study. They were identified as upper-middle-income, white-collar families (professional); middle-income, blue-collar families (industrial); young, married, middle-income families with young children; black families; and small-town families. Although the groupings are not mutually exclusive, and although the breakdowns could have been more extensive, each type of neighborhood did have dominant characteristics that reflected its individuality and influenced buying patterns. The population characteristics analyzed included education, income, family size and composition, race, and occupation.

The food shopping and buying behavior of consumers in the five neighborhoods varied considerably with respect to expenditures, shopping patterns, and preferences and therefore types of food purchased. It is apparent that there were differences among neighborhoods with respect to stability of the neighborhood, family size, food store and supermarket expenditures, weekly income, and occupational type (see Table 1-10).

Also considered in this study was how the average family in each type of neighborhood spent its food-store dollar (see Table 1-11). Some of the differences shown are probably related to income, but most of the differences reflect tastes and preferences to some degree.

It is interesting to note the wide variations in the sales of foods within major product groups among the neighborhoods (see Table 1-12). For example, in black neighborhoods the sales of frozen meat and fish were 14 percent above average; the sales of frozen cakes, pies, and pastries were 75 percent below average.

These data do not give a precise measure of differences in tastes and preferences among the various neighborhood groups of consumers, but they do provide us with a general indication of the effects of differences in tastes and preferences among groups of consumers with differing demographic characteristics. The *Consumer Dynamics* study illustrates the fact that consumer demand for food can be analyzed and broadly defined in terms of

---

[9]*Consumer Dynamics in the Super Market* (New York: Progressive Grocer, 1966).

[10]The Kroger Company is the fourth largest retail food chain in the United States. It operates over 1400 supermarkets in 24 states.

groups of consumers who possess similar social or economic characteristics. These groups, which often congregate in the same neighborhood, tend to exhibit similar tastes and preferences with respect to food shopping. It is extremely important for the food retailer to identify the characteristics and shopping preferences of the consumers whom he intends to serve so that he can provide the kinds of goods and services that will appeal to, and satisfy, as many consumers as possible.

TABLE 1-10   Characteristics of Consumers by Neighborhood Type, Cleveland, Ohio

| | | | Neighborhood Type | | | |
Characteristics	Average	High Income	Industrial	Black	Young Married	Small Town
Average number of years at present location	9.7	8.8	13.1	16.3	5.9	12.6
Average number of persons per household	3.8	4.3	3.7	3.7	5.0	4.7
Average weekly number of trips to food stores	3.1	2.9	3.2	3.3	2.8	3.2
Total amount spent in food stores per week	$26.69	$28.00	$24.67	$25.08	$29.04	$25.48
Percentage spent in supermarkets	77	84	76	71	71	78
Average age of housewife	41	44	47	43	33	44
Average weekly income	$179	$238	$138	$127	$155	$144
Occupation						
White collar	54	70	19	20	49	37
Blue collar	40	24	66	70	50	52
Retired	6	6	15	10	1	11

Source: *Consumer Dynamics in the Super Market* (New York: Progressive Grocer, 1966), pp. K143, K173, K199, K222, K254.

TABLE 1-11   Family Food and Grocery Product Expenditures by Neighborhood Type, Cleveland, Ohio (in percentage of total expenditures)

| | Neighborhood Type | | | | |
Product Group	High Income	Industrial	Black	Young Married	Small Town
Meat	28.5	28.4	23.9	25.9	27.2
Produce	9.9	10.0	10.2	9.1	9.9
Dairy	14.1	10.8	9.6	8.9	9.7
Frozen foods	5.8	3.2	4.0	4.1	3.2
Grocery	37.8	44.2	49.1	49.0	45.2
Nonfoods	3.9	3.4	3.2	3.0	4.8
Total	100.0	100.0	100.0	100.0	100.0

Source: *Consumer Dynamics in the Super Market* (New York: Progressive Grocer, 1966), pp. K149, K190, K214, K243, K270.

TABLE 1-12   Sales Indexes of Food Products by Type of Neighborhood,
(in percentage of 10-store average sales)

| | Neighborhood Type | | | | |
| | High | | | Young | Small |
Food Product	Income	Industrial	Black	Married	Town
Dairy					
Milk	81	113	121	80	70
Margarine	108	96	96	89	119
Eggs	96	137	122	96	99
Noncarbonated drinks	81	95	162	103	54
Frozen foods					
Vegetables	176	74	87	91	88
Meat and fish	79	104	114	111	92
Pot pies and dinners	130	97	74	76	90
Cakes, pies, and pastry	148	59	25	83	79
Grocery					
Baking mixes	85	79	109	79	123
Bread and rolls	109	88	112	91	123
Cereals	115	78	80	116	114
Coffee	83	105	85	95	93
Cookies	109	99	78	· 130	103
Canned fish	113	69	114	77	89
Canned fruits	102	81	93	64	131
Jams, jellies, and spreads	110	71	105	98	113
Canned juices	114	94	145	51	106
Dry macaroni products	64	110	76	107	115
Shortening and oils	49	118	146	88	111
Canned and dry soup	95	91	55	94	111
Tea	131	83	60	76	105
Canned vegetables	72	107	107	93	106

Source: *Consumer Dynamics in the Super Market* (New York: Progressive Grocer, 1966), pp. K126-27.

Trends in Food Consumption

In addition to the differences in consumer tastes and preferences for food among regions, urbanizations, and demographic groups, there have been some general trends or changes in food consumption that apply to the entire population.

First of all, there has been a considerable increase in the total demand for food since 1960 in the United States. Most of the increase has been due to the increase in population.

Aggregate demand analysis shows that per capita food consumption is relatively unaffected by changes in retail food prices and consumer incomes. Total food consumption increased by more than 20 percent from 1960 to 1970 while per capita food consumption increased by slightly more than 6 percent, which shows that most of the increase in total food consumption during this period was due to population increase (see Figure 1-6).

The most important changes in the demand for food during the last 20 to 30 years have been associated with shifts in food preferences, not with changes in the per capita amount of food consumed.

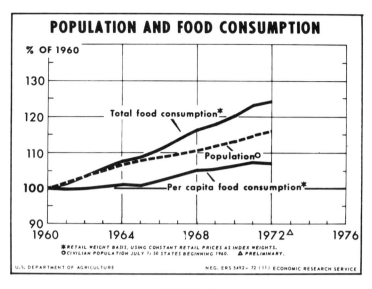

FIGURE 1-6

Figures 1-7 and 1-8 show the per capita consumption of livestock and crop products from 1960 to 1970. Increases in the consumption of beef, veal, and poultry have been primarily responsible for the increase in consumption of animal products. Pork consumption has been erratic but is slightly higher than it was in 1960. In general, per capita consumption of both eggs and total dairy products has declined since 1960 (see Figure 1-7).

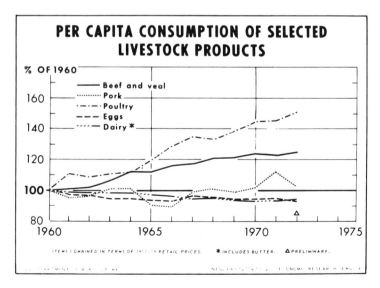

FIGURE 1-7

The trend in consumption of crop products has been influenced strongly by the switch from fresh to processed products (see Figure 1-8). The largest increases have been in the consumption of frozen vegetables and citrus concentrate. Consumption of fresh fruits and vegetables has declined, but the decline has leveled off during recent years.

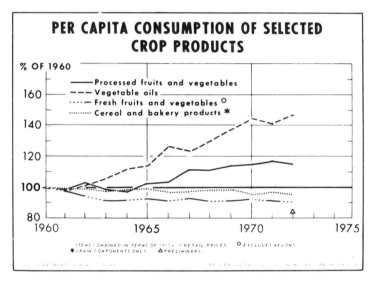

FIGURE 1-8

Per capita consumption of potatoes has been increasing since 1960. Consumption of fresh potatoes has continued to decrease, but consumption of processed products, principally chips and frozen french fries, has increased sharply and is largely responsible for a net upturn in consumption of total crop products since 1960.

Consumption of total fats and oils has remained relatively stable since 1950, but consumption of vegetable oils has increased. Strong upward trends in consumption of margarine and cooking and salad oils have about offset the decline in consumption of butter and lard.

Some of the changes in food consumption reflect a shift to foods requiring less preparation by the homemaker. Consumers are purchasing more "built-in services" along with the food products. This trend is illustrated by the decrease in the quantity of fresh citrus juice used; the increase in frozen and chilled juices used; and the shifts from fresh to frozen vegetables, from fresh to processed potatoes, and from flour and mixes to purchased bakery products. Use of all breakfast cereals rose, but the increase in the use of ready-to-eat cereal was greater than the others.[11] The growth in use of frozen convenience foods such as boil-in-the-bag vegetables, TV dinners.

---

[11]*Food Consumption of Households in the United States, Spring, 1965,* p. 3.

and prepared entrees also demonstrates the trend towards the consumption of foods that require less preparation by the homemaker.

Some of the changes in food consumption may reflect increased concern about consumption of fats or particular kinds of fat. Consumption of fresh whole milk and cream, evaporated milk, butter, and shortening decreased while that of fresh skim milk, nonfat dry milk, margarine, and vegetable oil increased.

Another trend is indicated by the greater popularity of foods associated with snacking. This trend may be related to the increased proportion of children and especially youths in the population. From 1955 to 1965, consumption increased for soft drinks, punches and ades, potato chips, crackers, cookies, doughnuts, ice cream, candy, lunch meats, and peanut butter.

Summary

Personal income in the United States has increased faster than the prices of food purchased for home consumption since 1960. The proportion of disposable income spent for food declined to a record low in 1972 due to the increased purchasing power of the dollar with respect to food and to the inelasticity of demand for food relative to changes in income.

The proportion of income spent for food and tastes and preferences for food vary according to income level, where people live, and other demographic characteristics.

Even though the proportion of income spent for food is at an all-time low, the consumption of processed convenience foods and meat has increased.

It is important to keep abreast of the general trends in tastes and preferences for food so that merchandising decisions will be consistent with consumer demand. Although it would be impractical to identify and attempt to satisfy the demand of each individual consumer for food, it is possible to identify the characteristics of groups and how these traits influence the demand for food. Consumers can be grouped according to factors such as income, ethnic background, age, and neighborhood, all of which influence the demand for food. The demand for food with respect to expenditures and types of food preferences can then be identified so that a merchandising strategy can be developed that will best satisfy the needs and preferences of the particular group of consumers that is to be served.

MERCHANDISING STRATEGY AND OBJECTIVES

Return on Investment

The first step in establishing a merchandising program for a retail food store is determining a realistic sales objective. The sales objective, in turn, depends on the company's profit objective.

A retail food business, like any other business, is operated in anticipation of earning a profit. Although there may be related goals, such as growth in size and prestige, share of market, or public service, most would agree that the profit motive is paramount in today's business enterprise. The profit earned in food retailing should be adequate to provide a return on the investment of the owners that is at least equivalent to the returns that could be earned on investments in other types of businesses. The major investment in food retailing consists of equity in building and land (if owned), equipment, supplies, and inventory.

The company's profit objective depends upon its merchandising policies, its competitive situation, and the management skills available. As we have already stated, the minimum profit objective of a food retailing firm is usually that rate of profit which will yield a return on investment that is equivalent to the returns on investment available in similar business enterprises. The maximum profit objective will depend upon competition, merchandising policy, and the ability of management to satisfy consumer needs and preferences.

Because investments in retail food stores represent long-term commitments—usually 10 to 20 years—investors are concerned with earning an adequate return over the life of the investment. Declines in yearly profits are not necessarily serious, as long as the total profits earned over the life of the investment are adequate to yield a satisfactory return on that investment.

Because profits are the difference between sales and expenses, it is obvious that an adequate profit depends upon the achievement of a certain level of sales not only on an annual basis but over the life of the investment.

The importance of sales in achieving an adequate return can be illustrated by analyzing how return on investment is calculated. Return on investment can be expressed in more than one way, depending upon whether total assets or owner's equity is used as a measure of investment and whether net profit before or after taxes and interest on loans is used as a measure of return. Owner's equity, or net worth, relative to net profit after taxes and interest is perhaps the most meaningful way of appraising earning power of the ownership investment.

First of all, net profit is expressed as a percentage of sales. This is done by dividing net income by net sales[12] for whatever period of time we are concerned with.

$$\frac{\text{Net income}}{\text{Net sales}} \times 100 = \text{Net profit \%}$$

Let's say that we are dealing with the financial results of the most recent year for **Big Bag Supermarket, Inc.** Sales were $1 million, and net income

---

[12]*Net sales* represents the amount of money received from customers less refunds for merchandise or returnable bottles.

(sales less expenses, taxes, and interest) was $15,000. Therefore, the net-profit percentage would be:

$$\frac{\$15,000}{\$1,000,000} \times 100 = 1.5\%$$

In other words, 1.5 percent or 1.5 cents of net income was realized on each dollar of sales during the year.

In order to calculate the return on owner's equity, we need to determine the turnover of owner's equity, or in other words, to determine the amount of sales per dollar of owner's equity. Owner's equity is the difference between total assets and total liabilities. Let's say that it amounted to $125,000 at the end of the year in Big Bag Supermarket. Owner's equity turnover is calculated by dividing net sales by owner's equity.

$$\frac{\text{Net sales}}{\text{Owner's equity}} = \text{Owner's equity turnover}$$

The equity turnover for Big Bag Supermarket was:

$$\frac{\$1,000,000}{\$125,000} = 8 \text{ times}$$

In other words, there were eight dollars in sales for every dollar of owner's equity in Big Bag Supermarket during the year. Now, by multiplying the net-profit percentage by the equity turnover, the overall return on owner's equity can be determined.

1.5% (net profit %) × 8 (owner's equity turnover) = 12% return on owner's equity

The example shows the importance of the volume of sales in determining the rate of return on investment. The more dollars of sales realized per dollar of owner's equity, the higher the rate of return, assuming the same rate of net profit on sales.

Sales volume also influences the amount of net income earned, and therefore net income as a percentage of sales (net profit). The net-profit percentage in turn affects the return on owner's equity.

Therefore, it is very important to achieve sales objectives in order to realize satisfactory returns on investment. This is especially true in food retailing because of the relatively low rates of net profit. In other words, the amount of net profit per dollar of sales in food retailing is lower than in most other kinds of business so that adequate returns on owner's equity depend upon a relatively large sales volume.

In the final analysis then, the sales objective in the retail food firm must be adequate to yield a return on investment that compares favorably with that earned in other types of businesses.

Estimating Sales

Sales objectives should be established for short-run periods, such as monthly, quarterly, and yearly, as well as for long-run periods—five to ten years and longer. Sales objectives should also be set for each major department in the food store.

The sales objective must be realistic, that is, it must be in line with the amount of business that is available. For established stores, past performance provides a good basis for making future estimates.

Setting sales objectives for new stores is much more difficult. One of the most critical decisions that has to be made by food retailers is that of how much sales volume is available in any particular location. If the estimate is too high, the resulting sales may not be adequate to yield a satisfactory return on the investment. Also if the estimate is too low, the store may be too small to serve the needs of the customers adequately. To make a reasonably accurate estimate of the sales that can be expected from a specific location requires an evaluation of several market factors: trade-area boundaries, accessibility, population, competition, and economic stability.

> The trade area of a store is that area from which a store gets its business—where the customers come from. A store's trade area is determined by the convenience of the location and by what the store sells, the manner in which it sells, the shopping habits of its customers, existing competition and the type of location (shopping centers or free standing, for example).[13]

The Trading Area

The initial step in assessing the sales potential of a new food store is to define, at least approximately, a trading area. This step requires careful analysis of the several factors mentioned above.

Once a trading area has been defined, the next step is to determine the total amount of business available from consumers within the area and the proportion of that business that can be captured by the new store.

The total amount of food store business available from consumers within a trading area depends upon the size and characteristics of the population. As already pointed out, family expenditures for food depend upon income, family size, and urbanization, so it is necessary to identify these characteristics as well as the size of the population.

Population Statistics

Population statistics are available from a variety of sources. The most comprehensive source of information is contained in the United States Census of Population and Housing, which is taken every ten years by the Bureau of the Census. Census statistics are available for the entire country, regions,

---

[13]William Applebaum and others, *Guide to Store Location Research,* ed. Curt Kornblau (Reading, Mass.: Addison-Wesley Publishing Company, 1968), p. 33.

individual states, counties, SMSA's (Standard Metropolitan Statistical Areas—a fairly new category that recognizes core cities and the surrounding smaller towns as one unit), cities, and various smaller breakdowns. Census tracts and city blocks are the smallest areas for which data published by the Bureau of the Census are generally available. Census tracts are small areas within and around large cities and are usually quite similar to each other with respect to population characteristics.

The most serious limitation of the U.S. Census as a source of population information is that it is conducted only every ten years. Also, it may not be possible to obtain census data for a specific trading area because it may not coincide with a census reporting area. In spite of its limitations, the census is useful as a basis for identifying population size and characteristics in or near a particular trading area, especially when other sources are used to update the census information. [14]

Such other sources include the following agencies:

State and local planning agencies

State departments of commerce

State industrial development commissions

Local or regional industrial development agencies

School boards or committees

Colleges and universities

Real estate boards

Chambers of commerce

Newspapers, radio, and television companies

Local government agencies and officials (assessor, clerk, engineer, board of elections, and so on)

Banks

Utility companies

Many of the sources listed above assemble current information and projections for the future on population growth and characteristics in local areas. Both current and projected population data for local areas are very useful in estimating food-store business or expenditures in a trade area.

Food Expenditures

Once population size and characteristics have been identified for the trade area, food store expenditures can be estimated. One of the most comprehensive sources of information on consumer expenditures for food is the *Survey of Consumer Expenditures* made by the Bureau of Labor Statistics in 1960 and 1961. This survey was conducted in 66 cities selected to represent urban areas and also included a sample of consumers selected to represent

---

[14]For further information and a list of reports and data available, contact the Bureau of the Census, Washington, D.C. 20233.

rural nonfarm areas. The expenditures for food are reported by several population characteristics including family size and income.

Another, more recent source of consumer expenditures for food is the *Household Food Consumption Survey* made by the U.S. Department of Agriculture in 1965 and 1966. This study reports food expenditures by urban, rural, and rural nonfarm families during one week in the spring, 1965. Expenditures for food were reported by family size and income, region, and several other population characteristics (see Table 1-13).

TABLE 1-13   Expenditures for Food for Home Consumption, per Household per Week, by Urbanization and Income, United States, Spring 1965

Urbanization and 1964 Money Income After Taxes	Household Size [a] (persons)	Expenditures for Food at Home (Dollars)
All Urbanizations		
All households [b]	3.29	26.95
Under $3,000	2.57	15.10
3,000-4,999	3.39	23.91
5,000-6,999	3.59	29.71
7,000-9,999	3.60	33.45
10,000 and over	3.63	38.42
Urban		
All households [b]	3.16	27.83
Under $3,000	2.26	15.39
3,000-4,999	3.19	23.79
5,000-6,999	3.44	30.02
7,000-9,999	3.53	33.63
10,000 and over	3.56	39.10
Rural Nonfarm		
All households [b]	3.50	25.77
Under $3,000	2.85	14.35
3,000-4,999	3.70	25.29
5,000-6,999	3.90	29.71
7,000-9,999	3.80	33.81
10,000 and over	3.83	37.81
Rural Farm		
All households [b]	3.99	21.32
Under $3,000	3.81	15.43
3,000-4,999	4.00	20.76
5,000-6,999	4.16	25.36
7,000-9,999	3.95	26.83
10,000 and over	4.41	28.86

[a] *In equivalent persons; 21 meals at home equal one person.*
[b] *Includes households not classified by income.*

Source: *Food Consumption of Households in the United States, Spring 1965,* U.S. Department of Agriculture, Agricultural Research Service, Washington, D.C., 1968.

Similar statistics are available for each region in the United States, so the expenditure data from the region in which the trade area is located can be used as a general approximation of food expenditures.

Because food expenditure data from most sources are based upon food prices at that particular time, it is necessary to adjust for food price changes, especially if the data are a year or more old. This adjustment can be made on the basis of the food (at home) component of the *Consumer Price Index*, which measures changes in food prices in major metropolitan areas and in the United States as a whole. The indexes of retail food prices in the United States increased gradually in the early 1960s and rapidly from 1965 to 1972 (see Table 1-14). These indexes are also available for 23 SMSA's in the United States, so the appropriate index can be used to adjust food expenditures in the trading area being analyzed.

TABLE 1-14   Retail Food Price Indexes, United States, 1960-72 (1967 = 100)

Year	Retail Food Price Index (food used at home)
1960	89.6%
1961	90.4
1962	91.0
1963	92.2
1964	93.2
1965	95.5
1966	100.3
1967	100.0
1968	103.2
1969	108.2
1970	113.7
1971	116.4
1972	121.6

Source: *National Food Situation,* February 1973; and *Food–Consumption, Prices, Expenditures,* Supplement for 1971, U.S. Department of Agriculture, Economic Research Service, Washington, D.C.

The method for adjusting food expenditure data for changes in retail food prices can be illustrated by using the data in Tables 1-13 and 1-14. For example, let's say that we want to estimate the weekly food expenditures in 1972 of urban families in the United States with incomes in the $7,000 to $9,999 range. From Table 1-13, we see that the level of expenditures was $33.63 per week in 1965. However, from Table 1-14 we find that retail food prices in the United States were higher in 1972 than in 1965. By determining the percentage change in the retail food price index between 1965 and 1972 and multiplying it times the family food expenditures in 1965, we can adjust for the price change. Therefore:

$$\frac{1972 \text{ Index} - 1965 \text{ Index}}{1965 \text{ Index}} = \begin{array}{l}\% \text{ change in retail food} \\ \text{prices from 1965 to 1972}\end{array}$$

$$\frac{121.6 - 95.5}{95.5} = \frac{26.1}{95.5} = .273 \times 100 = 27.3\%$$

Thus, food prices increased by 27.3 percent from 1965 to 1972, or, food prices in 1972 were 127.3 percent of prices in 1965.

Now, to calculate the change in family food expenditures from 1965 to 1972 due to price changes:

Retail food prices in 1972 as a % of food prices in 1965	×	Weekly family food expenditures in 1965	=	Weekly family food expenditures in 1972
127.3	×	$33.63	=	$42.81

Based upon the overall increase in retail food prices, an urban family in the $7,000-$9,999 income range would have to spend $42.81 per week in 1972 for the same foods that cost $33.63 in 1965. To make this calculation, we must assume the following: (1) that urban families in the $7,000-$9,999 income range bought the same foods in 1972 as in 1965; and (2) that the price indexes measured accurately changes in prices actually paid. Although these factors may not have remained constant, this method is still useful in estimating current family food expenditures when recent expenditure data are unavailable.

Nonfood Expenditures

Once current family food expenditures per week are estimated, expenditures for nonfood items purchased in food stores must be considered in order to arrive at an estimate of total food store sales potential in the trade area. The data reported in the sources discussed so far include expenditures for food only and do not include nonfoods purchased in food stores. It is apparent that nonfoods comprise an important part of grocery store sales and that they have increased in importance since 1959; their sales have

TABLE 1-15   Nonfood Sales as a Percentage of Total Grocery Store Sales, 1959 and 1969

Product Type	Year	
	1969	*1959*
Food sales [a]	77.8	85.0
Nonfood sales		
Household supplies	5.3	5.2
Pet foods	1.2	0.8
Tobacco products	4.0	4.0
Health & beauty aids	3.4	2.3
Other nonfoods [b]	8.3	2.7
Total nonfoods	22.2	15.0
Total	100.0	100.0

[a] *Includes meat, produce, dry groceries, dairy products, bakery products, and frozen foods.*
[b] *Includes greeting cards, household glassware, other housewares, magazines and newspapers, phonograph records, toys, pet accessories, women's hosiery, and miscellaneous items.*

Source: "Annual Consumer Expenditure Study," *Supermarketing,* September 1969.

gone from 15.0 to 22.2 percent of total store sales (see Table 1-15). Therefore, some adjustment must be made to account for the amount of money spent weekly for nonfood items in food stores. The adjustment will depend upon the selection of nonfood items available in the store and an estimate of the proportion of total family food store expenditures that will be devoted to the purchase of nonfood items. Once the estimate is made, it is added to the weekly food expenditure in order to arrive at an estimate of the total weekly food store expenditure.

The fact that some of the weekly food expenditures will not be made in food stores must also be taken into account. For example, home-delivered foods, roadside stands, and specialty stores will account for some portion of family food expenditures each week.

By using the estimating procedures previously described and applying them to the appropriate population, price, and expenditure data, the weekly food store expenditures for a trade area can be estimated. Multiplying by 52 will convert weekly estimates to annual expenditure estimates, if they are desired.

Expenditure estimates calculated on the basis of average figures are only approximations, and the characteristics of the population in the particular trade area should be considered carefully. Sources of information that provide localized data on food store expenditures are often helpful in making more accurate estimates for a particular trade area. [15]

Share of the Market

The next and most difficult step is to determine how much or *what share* of total food store expenditures can be captured by the new store. As mentioned previously, this depends on several market factors and requires careful analysis based upon store-location research techniques. One factor of great importance is how well the store is able to satisfy the tastes and preferences of consumers in the trade area compared with competitors, both large and small. Thus, it is of great importance to determine the characteristics of the trade-area population, the tastes and preferences associated with them, and make a thorough evaluation of the strengths and weaknesses of competitors with respect to their ability to satisfy consumer tastes and preferences.

When all the data associated with the sales estimate has been accumulated, it is often convenient to use a simple form to calculate the sales estimate for a new store for at least two years (see Figure 1-9). This form makes computation easy and provides those persons making the decision on whether or not to construct a new store with clear and concise data that can be compared easily and analyzed quickly.

---

[15]There are market-data yearbooks published and sold commercially that estimate current buying income and food store sales by countries, SMSA's, and cities. One that is frequently used is the "Survey of Buying Power," published annually by *Sales Management,* 630 Third Avenue, New York City.

	First Year	Second Year
Average income per household		
Weekly food expenditures per household		
Weekly household expenditures for nonfood items		
Weekly food store expenditures per household		
Number of households in trade area		
Total weekly food store expenditures available		
Estimated share of market (% of total food store ..... expenditures)		
Total estimated weekly sales		

FIGURE 1-9   New store sales estimate for a trade area.

When all factors have been considered, sales estimates for a proposed new store must be made in order to determine whether the expected sales volume is adequate to justify the investment in the store facilities, merchandise, and equipment, at least by the end of the second year of operation.

Merchandising Strategy

As pointed out in the discussion of merchandising definitions and consumer demand, people buy goods and services because of the utility or satisfaction that they furnish and not because the food retailer wishes to earn a profit. Therefore, the food retailer must have a plan, or strategy, for providing a set of values to the consumer that will result in the achievement of his financial objectives (sales, profit, and return on investment). How does the retailer go about maximizing consumer satisfaction or value through buying, pricing, and presenting food and grocery products and related services in order to reach the financial objectives?

A plan or strategy must be developed that expresses the retailer's intentions or policies with regard to providing specific values or attributes to prospective consumers. The strategy should be tailored to the tastes and preferences of the consumers who live in the trade area that has been selected.

A merchandising strategy, then, involves a set of decisions as to what kinds of values the retailer intends to offer the consumers and how he plans to offer them. The values he plans to offer should be based upon those values identified by consumers as important in their selection of a food store. For each value that he plans to offer, there are several decisions that must be made concerning the specific activity or method necessary to implement that value.

There are ten major decisions that must be made in order to properly plan and carry out an effective merchandising program once the location decision has been made (see Table 1-16).

The first decision that must be made concerns the *products* that are going to be offered. This decision involves not only selecting product groups, such as produce, meat, dry groceries, dairy, bakery, frozen foods, and non-

TABLE 1-16   Food Merchandising Strategy

Major Decisions	Considerations and Activities
Product line	Commodity groups; selection of brands and sizes; quality; buying practices; selection of new items.
Inventory control and quality maintenance	Ordering sequence and methods; display conditions and rotation.
Processing and packaging	Extent and methods of in-store trimming, cutting, preparation, and packaging.
Selling price	Margins on commodity groups and individual items.
Store layout	Location of departments; arrangement of selling fixtures.
Display	Location of commodity groups and individual items; space allocation; methods of display, policing displays; price marking.
Advertising and promotion	Media; point-of-sale; use of premiums or other promotional techniques.
Customer services	Types of customer services, educational, informative or convenience; methods of providing services.
Housekeeping	Cleaning of equipment, merchandise, and facilities.
Employee appearance and behavior	Attire, grooming, and behavior.

foods, but also the brands, sizes, and items within each product group and the quality of the merchandise. For example, the food retailer must decide whether to handle a complete line or a limited line of products. Assuming that he decides to handle a complete line of product groups, as a conventional supermarket, he must then decide upon the extent of the assortment within each product group as to brands, items, and sizes. He must also decide upon the quality of the products he wishes to offer. In the case of perishables, the quality offered may be U.S. Prime or Choice meats, or U.S. Fancy or U.S. Number 1 produce, whenever grades exist. In the absence of government grades, the retailer must decide upon the specifications that the merchandise must meet.

Once the merchandise mix and quality standards have been established, it is necessary to establish procedures to ensure proper levels of *inventory control and quality maintenance*. The method and sequence of ordering and receiving in relation to the amount of merchandise on display and in reserve storage are the critical factors with respect to inventory control. The control of product quality involves display conditions, such as temperature and humidity and rotation method, especially for highly perishable products.

The extent and methods of *processing and packaging* is another important decision that must be made. This decision includes the amount of product preparation and packaging that will occur in the store and the methods that will be utilized, especially for highly perishable products like fresh meats, produce, bakery, and delicatessen items. The packaging methods, materials, and sizes must be chosen along with the extent of in-store product preparation.

Selling price policy is a major decision that must be made by the food retailer. He must decide upon the margin that he wishes to realize on the overall volume of sales as well as for each product group and item. Price specials, promotions, and reactions to competitors' price changes are other elements of price strategy that must be specified.

The *layout* of the store requires decisions concerning the location of each major department as well as the arrangement of the display fixtures within each department.

In addition to store layout, the food retailer must decide upon merchandise *display* with respect to the location of commodity groups and individual items on display, the amount of space allocated to each item, the methods of display, and the method of identifying the selling price for the customer.

Advertising and promotion strategy involves decisions concerning the amount and kind of advertising and promotion within the store (point-of-sale) as well as outside the store in newspapers, circulars, direct mail, radio, television, and so on.

The nature and extent of *services* provided to the customer is another major merchandising strategy decision. Included in this decision are the kinds of services to be offered, such as carry-out, check cashing, store hours, shopper assistance in the selection and preparation of products, and the method for handling customer complaints. The other part of the decision is how extensive the offering of services should be, that is, how many checkers and carry-out personnel should there be, and how many other service personnel and facilities should be provided, and for how long each day or week.

The definition of *housekeeping* requirements in terms of cleaning methods and frequency is important to maintaining a clean, sanitary, and attractive shopping environment. Provision should be made for maintaining clean facilities, equipment, and merchandise.

Employee behavior and appearance decisions involve method of attire, grooming, and the behavior with respect to dealing with each other and with customers.

The above list indicates the major decisions necessary to define and carry out a merchandising strategy in a retail food store in order to achieve financial objectives. The merchandising strategy specifies the value to the customer that the firm intends to provide. Each food retailer attempts to "differentiate" his offerings, that is, to make his goods and services unique or different from those offered by competitors.

The duties or merchandising activities that must be performed in order to maintain the desired set of customer values are identified by the merchandising strategy. Most of the merchandising activities concern the presentation of merchandise. Presentation includes all the major merchandising-strategy decisions except *product line* and *selling price,* which are basically buying and pricing functions.

Most merchandising activities, then, are those duties that must be carried on in the retail food store on a day-to-day basis in order to implement the merchandising strategy. Some of the major strategy decisions do not involve day-to-day activity. For example, once the layout of the store has been established, there is little or no change or adjustment involved on a day-to-day or week-to-week basis.

Customer service, housekeeping, and employee appearance and behavior may not appear to be merchandising activities inasmuch as most of them do not involve the physical handling or presentation of merchandise. However, value to the consumer is a combination of many attributes including services, cleanliness, and employee appearance and behavior. Therefore, activities relating to customer service, housekeeping, and employee appearance and behavior are a part of the presentation function and are considered merchandising activities.

Store location and design, a vital part of food merchandising strategy, are not included in this discussion because the highly specialized nature of the store location and design decision requires a text of its own. In addition, once the location decision has been made and the store constructed, it becomes a fixed part of merchandising strategy, and no additional location or design decisions or activities are possible as long as the store continues to operate or until the store is remodeled.[16]

This text will deal with the major components of merchandising strategy other than store location. The principles and practices concerned with each major decision and the specific merchandising activities necessary to carry out the strategy successfully will be the primary focus of the remainder of the text.

WHO HAS THE RESPONSIBILITY FOR MERCIIANDISING?

Who bears the responsibility for planning the retail merchandising strategy and carrying out the merchandising activities in the stores? Basically, there are two groups who share the responsibility. The first group includes those who are not directly employed by food retailing firms but who are engaged in the business of supplying retail food stores with merchandise, equipment, or supplies. This group includes food and grocery product manufacturers; brokers; rack jobbers; wholesaler fieldmen or counselors; and manufacturers and suppliers of shelving, refrigerated cases, cash registers

---

[16]Additional information on store location may be obtained from references on the subject. One of the most recent sources of information is William Applebaum and others, *Guide to Store Location Research.*

and checkstands, packaging materials, price-marking equipment, and other supplies and equipment required for the operation of retail food stores. The second group includes those who are directly engaged in food retailing and are part of the retailing team. This includes top management of the retail firm, the middle management or supervisory level, the store management team, and all the full-time and part-time employees in the retail food store.

Manufacturers' Representatives and Brokers

The food and grocery product manufacturer has a vital interest in retail merchandising because his very existence depends upon the sale of his products in retail stores. Therefore, the manufacturer takes an active role in the merchandising process either through a broker or through his own personnel.

A person who is employed directly by the manufacturer to promote the sale of the manufacturer's products in the marketplace and to represent him in dealing with the buyers of his products is known as a *manufacturer's representative*. A *food broker* is an independent sales agent who performs the services of negotiating the sale of food and/or grocery products for the seller, is not employed or affiliated with any trade buyer, and whose compensation is a commission or brokerage paid by the seller.[17] A food broker may represent many manufacturers (principals) of processed foods or grocery products; the manufacturer's representative is concerned only with the products of his employer.

Manufacturers' "reps" and brokers usually cover a specific market or market area and become involved in merchandising in several ways. First of all, the broker or rep calls on the buyers associated with retail food chains, independents, and wholesale suppliers. The broker or rep is responsible for acquainting the buyers with new products, upcoming deals and promotions, and any other important information or problems concerning the manufacturer's products. They also attempt to assist buyers and merchandisers in planning merchandising strategy with respect to product line, pricing, display, and advertising and promotion decisions. Naturally, the brokers or reps try to gain advantages for the products that they represent in order to increase sales and gain a larger share of the market.

Brokers and manufacturers' reps also play an active role in carrying out merchandising activities at store level. This role includes planning and erecting point-of-sale promotional materials and special displays, checking product rotation and inventory levels, removing outdated and damaged merchandise, and assisting in maintaining well-stocked, orderly, clean displays of correctly priced merchandise on the shelves. The extent to which brokers and reps actually assist in the physical handling of merchandise depends upon the merchandising conditions in the stores, the time available,

---

[17] Official definition used by the National Food Brokers Association.

and the policy of the retail firms or labor union contract requirements concerning the performance of merchandising functions by nonemployees.

Brokers and manufacturers' representatives perform a valuable service and make many contributions to improving the merchandising of food and grocery products in retail food stores. They are specialists in merchandising the products that they represent and are part of the team effort required to plan and carry out a successful merchandising program in the retail food store.

Wholesalers

Wholesale distributors of food and grocery store products provide important services that contribute to more effective in-store merchandising. There are three types of wholesalers that supply retail food stores—the specialty or limited-line operator, the rack jobber, and the complete-line or full-service wholesaler—and each normally provides merchandising services to his customers.

The Specialty Wholesaler

The specialty wholesaler specializes in only one or a few grocery product lines, such as spices and condiments, gourmet foods, snack foods, candy, pickles, olives, and relishes; nonfoods, such as cards or light bulbs; or perishable foods, such as dairy products or frozen foods. In addition to direct store delivery, the specialty wholesalers usually provide merchandising assistance in the form of point-of-sale materials; suggestions for pricing, display, and shelf allocation; and, in some instances, will service the displays by rotating the product, restocking the shelves, and removing damaged or outdated merchandise.

The Rack Jobber

The rack jobber is also a specialty wholesaler who deals in a limited line of merchandise, but, instead of providing some merchandising assistance to the retailer, he assumes complete responsibility for the in-store merchandising of the products that he supplies. The rack jobber assumes full responsibility for ordering, displaying, point-of-sale promotion, rotation, price marking, and, in some instances, setting retail selling prices. The costs of these services are included in the cost of merchandise to the retailer. Rack jobbers are most commonly used by chains and independents in merchandising lines such as health and beauty aids, housewares, toys, records, or other types of nonfood merchandise that have handling and merchandising requirements that differ substantially from the requirements for the usual line of food and nonfood products. If rack jobbers assume full responsibility for handling and merchandising certain lines, it also relieves the retail organization of the warehousing and distribution functions for the items included. For these reasons, many retailers believe that rack jobbers can do a better and more profitable job of handling and merchandising general nonfood lines than can their own staff.

The Full-service Wholesaler

The full-service wholesaler generally makes available to retailers the same merchandising services as the corporate chains provide to their stores. A full-service wholesaler is one who offers a complete line of grocery food and nonfood merchandise and usually provides one or more of the following lines: general merchandise, dairy, bakery, frozen foods, fresh meats, and fresh produce.

Although a complete-line wholesaler may not supply all the merchandise required by independent retailers, they usually provide all the services needed by the retailer. For example, some full-service wholesalers do not warehouse fresh meat or produce but they do provide assistance to the retailer in procuring, advertising, and merchandising both fresh meat and produce.

The merchandising services available from full-service wholesalers usually include retail accounting, site selection, store design and interior layout, personnel training, selection and procurement of display equipment, shelf allocation, display and promotion, advertising, suggested retail selling prices, and advisory assistance in projecting and controlling sales, gross margin, expenses, and net profit. In addition, the wholesaler often makes available to the retail clients a private or controlled brand.

Large full-service wholesalers usually provide merchandising services through a headquarters staff of specialists, as well as field representatives or counselors who assist retailers in the stores much the same as the corporate food chain supervisors function. The important difference between the wholesaler field counselor and the chain store supervisor is the organizational relationship. The chain store supervisor has line authority over store personnel, but the wholesaler field counselor can only advise the independent store owner and personnel unless the wholesaler has a controlling financial interest in the store.

The extensive merchandising assistance programs developed by full-service independent wholesalers have been an important reason for the success and growth of voluntary and cooperative groups of independent retail food stores. When many independent retailers voluntarily become affiliated with a single wholesaler or a group of retailers cooperatively own the wholesale facility, the resulting scale of operation makes it possible for each retailer to realize merchandising assistance that he could not otherwise afford and consequently to achieve success in an increasingly competitive and sophisticated industry.

Equipment and Supply Manufacturers and Distributors

Many manufacturers and distributors of food store equipment and supplies provide merchandising assistance to the retail food industry. The types of firms that often provide merchandising assistance to chain and independent food stores include manufacturers and distributors of cash registers, scales, refrigerated cases, shelving, materials handling equipment, work tables and benches, processing and packaging equipment such as meat saws and produce tables, light fixtures, price-marking and packaging materials, and other store equipment such as flooring and signs.

The merchandising activities provided by manufacturers and suppliers range from store planning and layout to packaging and display methods and customer service, and in some cases personnel training. These services are very helpful to food retailers, especially to those who are not large enough to employ their own merchandising specialists.

Marketing and Trade Associations

Another source of merchandising assistance for retail food stores is the marketing or trade association representing producers, processors, or distributors of food products.

There are many national and regional associations that represent agricultural producers and attempt to promote the sale of certain commodities. These efforts usually include advertising directed to the consumer and the retail food industry in order to increase the demand for the product, the distribution of point-of-sale promotional materials to the retailer, and in some cases field representatives who visit large supermarkets and offer assistance in merchandising the products that they represent. Occasionally, contests are sponsored by some of these associations with prizes awarded to the department manager or store manager who does the best job of promoting the product. Marketing associations frequently publish information on the nutritional value, handling, and storage requirements of their products, along with recipe ideas, that is available to retailers for distribution to consumers. Some of this material is very attractive and informative and is a valuable asset to the retailer in providing greater value to the customer through his merchandising activities. A partial list of marketing associations sponsored by agricultural producers includes the following:

> The American Dairy Association
> The National Livestock and Meat Board
> The National Apple Institute
> The Poultry and Egg National Board

In addition to the marketing associations that represent food producers, there are those that represent processors, brokers, and distributors of food products. The food trade associations, as they are also known, provide a wide range of services and activities designed to improve the merchandising of food and grocery products. Some of the associations specialize in providing educational opportunities for their members, others concentrate on legislative matters that affect the food industry in general and their members in particular. Other activities and services may include research, public relations, and special efforts to resolve industry-wide problems through voluntary cooperation. A partial list of trade associations that represent processors, brokers, and distributors includes the following:

American Meat Institute
American Frozen Food Institute
Grocery Manufacturers Association
National American Wholesale Grocers Association
National Food Brokers Association
National Food Distributors Association
Cooperative Food Distributors of America
National Association of Convenience Stores
National Association of Food Chains
National Association of Retail Grocers of the United States
Super Market Institute

Retail Personnel

Everyone in the retail organization, whether it be a large chain or a single independent store, shares in the responsibility for merchandising. Some personnel, such as checkout operators and stock clerks, are more directly involved in the merchandising process than behind-the-scenes personnel, such as an office secretary or computer programmer. However, because merchandising is providing the greatest possible value to the customer at a profit, everyone in the food retailing company shares in the responsibility for merchandising, depending upon the particular activities or function performed.

In individual stores or small retailing companies with only a few stores, each individual is likely to be responsible for several merchandising functions. For example, the owner-manager of a single supermarket might be responsible for buying, pricing, advertising and promotion, training, managing, and supervising the people working in the store. He assumes the responsibility for making merchandising-policy decisions and also shares in the responsibility for carrying out those decisions. In effect, the owner-manager wears several hats, one for top management, one for middle management, and one for store or operating-level management. This simple type of organization is depicted in Figure 1-10.

In companies with more than one store, however, it becomes necessary to specialize, that is, to assign responsibility for the various merchandising functions to different individuals. Specialization becomes necessary because it is physically impossible or inefficient for one man to assume responsibility for several merchandising functions. The organization chart shown in Figure 1-11 illustrates how responsibility for merchandising might be delegated in a small retail food chain. In the example, a general manager is responsible for directing the merchandising activities in the stores based upon overall policy established by the owner-president. The general manager is assisted

FIGURE 1-10 Example of organization chart for an independent food store.

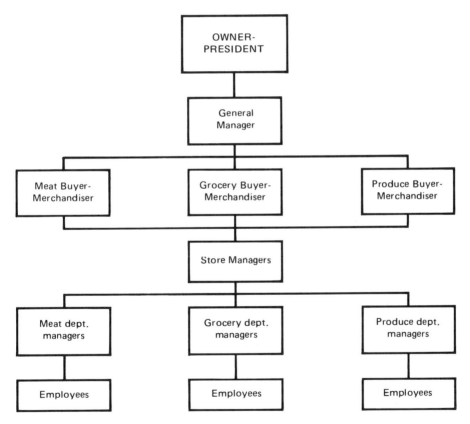

FIGURE 1-11 Example of organization chart for a small retail food chain.

by three buyer-merchandisers for meat, groceries, and produce, respectively. The buyer-merchandisers are responsible for buying and setting the selling prices as well as for supervising the merchandising activities in the stores.

The store managers are responsible for supervising department managers, who in turn are responsible for all merchandising activities in their departments.

A large retail food chain may have a high degree of specialization in assigning responsibility for merchandising, as shown in Figure 1-12. In this example, there is a treasurer and four vice-presidents who are responsible to the president for specific merchandising functions or matters that relate directly to merchandising, such as personnel and real estate. In large companies, the primary responsibility for making merchandising policy and seeing that it is carried out in the retail stores is often shared between the heads or vice-presidents of operations and merchandising.

The vice-president of operations is usually responsible for the people, inventory, equipment, and facilities required to carry on merchandising activities. The vice-president of operations is held accountable for expenses and net profit, and consequently has line authority over store managers. This authority over store managers is exercised through district or zone managers and, in some cases, supervisors that may be responsible for certain departments or the entire store.

The head or vice-president of merchandising, on the other hand, is usually responsible for buying, setting retail selling prices, advertising and promotion, and displaying merchandise. He is held accountable for sales and gross margin. Merchandising assistance is provided to store managers and department managers by specialists, who are accountable to the vice-president of merchandising. The specialists usually have a staff (advisory) relationship with store and department managers.

The division of responsibilities into operations and merchandising in larger retail companies results in a need for close coordination if the merchandising objectives, including net profit, are to be achieved. For example, when the merchandising vice-president recommends a particular method for displaying products, the responsibility for the labor and equipment costs required to put the recommendation into effect is borne by the operations vice-president. Therefore, close cooperation between operations and merchandising is essential if the display method is to create the desired sales impact at a reasonable operating cost. Cooperation and coordination between operations and merchandising is required in all matters because of the shared responsibility for planning and conducting merchandising activities successfully.

Perhaps the most critical role in successful food merchandising is assumed by the store manager, department managers, and personnel. The retail food store is "where the action is," because the ultimate test of a merchandising program is consumer acceptance as indicated by store sales. The store management team and store personnel are responsible for the day-to-day merchandising activities, and the manner in which they perform these activities has a major impact upon ultimate success. The current trend seems to favor granting more authority to store managers for making deci-

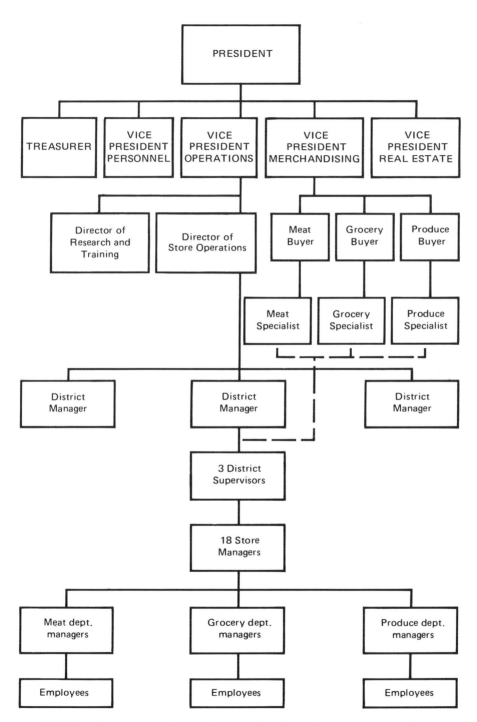

FIGURE 1-12   Example of organization chart for a large retail food chain.

sions and carrying them out. Many believe that the key to successful retail food merchandising is the store manager and that he must have greater authority in order to meet consumer needs and adjust to the fast-changing competitive situation.[18]

---

[18]For a comprehensive description of methods for effective management in the retail food firm, see Edward M. Harwell, *Personnel Management and Training* (New York: Chain Store Publishing Corporation, 1969).

2

Buying

INTRODUCTION

One of the important merchandising functions is the wholesale procurement of goods to be sold at the retail level. The importance of buying the right product in the right amount at the right price at the right time has long been recognized as a vital ingredient to a successful merchandising program.

Although scientific methods and computer programs now supplement the buyer's ability to make routine purchasing decisions, the role of the buyer is still an important one in the chain of merchandising activities. In this chapter, we will examine large-scale buying at the food distribution center; the buying and ordering activity as it affects the individual store; the demand that new items place on the buyer and the marketing system; and the importance of buying allowances and how they apply to merchandising programs.

BUYING AT THE DISTRIBUTION CENTER

The grocery buyer for a corporate food chain or a wholesaler is not just a buyer in the traditional sense of picking out an item and paying for it. The procurement of merchandise is an important aspect of the buyer's job (see the section on new items later in this chapter), but additional considerations such as how much to buy and when to buy are even more vital. In addition to these considerations, the buyer is often called upon to determine how to *sell* the product. The term *buyer-merchandiser* is often used to describe this job, and the word *merchandiser* carries with it the connotation of sales or sales promotion.

A job description for a buyer-merchandiser might include these areas of responsibility:

1. Arrange for the routine buying to be done with clerical assistance and the utilization of electronic data processing equipment where possible.
2. Assist in the development of creative merchandising plans as follows:
   a. Work with the advertising manager in the development of advertising programs for all grocery products for which the buyer is responsible.
   b. Suggest the introduction of new items where appropriate.
   c. Discontinue slow-moving items as required.
   d. Work with manufacturers in coordinating promotional efforts on national brands and private labels.

Although many other areas of responsibility are covered in this job description, the inclusion of the duties of (1) the purchase of products and (2) the responsibility for the sale of products clearly points out the dual responsibility of the buyer-merchandiser.

How Much to Order

The buyer knows *what* merchandise to order on the basis of the present items carried in stock or listed in the order book, and he adds new items on the recommendation of the buying committee (see page 84). With the problem solved of what to order, he can turn his attention to the other vital questions: How much? When?

The answer to the first question—how much—actually determines the answer to the second—when. For example, if the buyer orders a small quantity of an item, he will have to order more frequently than if he ordered a larger quantity of the same item. Therefore, the first question that must be answered is: How much of any given item must be purchased?

From the buyer's point of view, the easiest solution to his problem would be to buy approximately one year's supply of each item. This would reduce his buying job to a once-a-year decision for each item he is responsible for purchasing.

There are two factors, however, that make this both impractical and impossible. The first is the cost factor. For each dollar in sales taken in by a supermarket company, it must spend 78.5 cents just to buy the merchandise. In other words, it costs a food retailer about 80 cents for each dollar's worth of merchandise he sells. This is called the *cost of goods sold*.[1]

With this much investment required, it would be impractical to stock a year's supply of merchandise. The investment required for a single supermarket with annual grocery sales of $1 million with a cost of goods sold of 78.5 percent would be $785,000. Multiply that by the number of stores in a chain, and the dollar investment tied up in inventory is formidable.

The second factor that makes buying in this large a quantity impossible is the physical size of the distribution center. A distribution center for a

---

[1]See Chapter 3 for a discussion of the importance of the cost of goods sold and the part it plays in the pricing function.

typical food chain or wholesaler would not be able to store this much merchandise.

If once-a-year purchasing is impractical, what is practical? Should a company strive for maximum turnover of grocery products? Is this the most efficient and economical method of doing business? The answer is *no*. Turnover is important, but there are other cost considerations.

There are four principal costs associated with the purchase of grocery products. These are:

1. The purchasing cost—the cost of actually making out the order, processing the order, and paying for the merchandise, or in other words the cost of internal record keeping.

2. Handling cost—the cost of physically handling and storing the merchandise once it has been received at the distribution center.

3. Cost of lost sales—this cost results only when a firm is out of stock. However, no grocery distribution center will be in stock on 100 percent of its items at any specific time; therefore, there will always be a few items that are "out of stock." The lost sales that result represent a cost or a profit loss to the firm.

4. Opportunity costs—the cost of capital that is tied up in inventory and therefore cannot be invested in some other manner. A firm that maintains a $5 million inventory is incurring a minimum opportunity cost of 5 percent (or $250,000)—the amount they could receive if they put this money in a savings bank for a year.

In buying merchandise, all these costs must be considered. Our discussion in the next section will cover costs (1) and (2)—purchasing and handling costs—and the cost of lost sales will be taken up later in the chapter. It is sufficient to say that if the inventory level is kept at an optimum, then the opportunity costs will be kept to a minimum.

Purchasing Cost versus Handling Cost

For the purpose of illustration, let's assume that it costs one dollar every time an order is placed with a vendor and that it costs 10 percent of the value of the merchandise to keep it in inventory for one year.

Let's also say that an item moves through the warehouse at the rate of 100 cases per month (or 1200 units per year). If the buyer chooses to purchase in lots of 200 and orders every other month, he would incur purchasing costs of six dollars per year. If usage is at a constant rate and the buyer knows how long it takes to receive the goods, he can plan for a new shipment to arrive just as he runs out. The inventory movement for this item is plotted in Figure 2-1.

Beginning inventory is 200 units. The average inventory during this period is 100 units and is equal to one-half the beginning inventory (or the reorder quantity). This average inventory is commonly known as *cycle stock*.

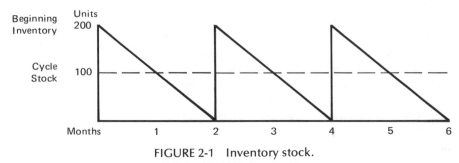

FIGURE 2-1   Inventory stock.

Because cycle stock is one-half the order quantity, the buyer has available a direct means of controlling total inventory (and the number of purchases) by controlling order quantity. By ordering additional products, the average inventory increases, and by reducing the order quantity, the average inventory decreases (assuming the stores continue to order the same quantities from the distribution center.)

In Figure 2-1, the order quantity is 200, and the cycle stock (average inventory) is 100. If the unit cost is $1 and the maintenance cost is 10 percent of the unit cost ($100), the maintenance cost for the year would be $10. Assume that the cost of ordering is $1; at six purchases per year, $6 is the annual purchase cost.

The total annual cost of ordering 200 units would be:

$$\$6 \text{ (Purchasing cost)} + \$10 \text{ Maintenance cost)} = \$16$$

If the buyer decided to order at different intervals, such as quarterly, monthly, or semimonthly, a different annual cost would result. Considering all the alternatives mapped out in Figure 2-2, a buyer who orders $200

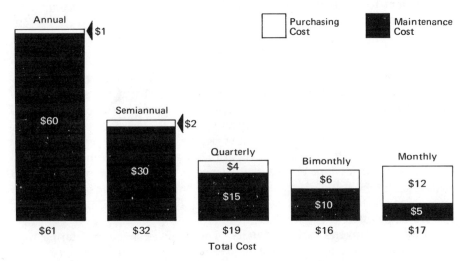

FIGURE 2-2   Total annual costs of various ordering strategies for unit cost = $1.

worth of merchandise (200 units at $1 each) bimonthly would incur the lowest total cost ($16).

If the unit cost were 10 cents, the $200 order would consist of 2,000 units, which would have the same total cost of $16. If the unit cost were $10, the $200 order would cover 20 units, and the total cost would again be the same. Some companies have adopted a rule that says, "order all items every two months," but they could operate more economically.

Let's now say that unit cost is $10, and all other conditions remain the same (annual usage 1,200 units, purchase cost $1, maintenance cost 10 percent). Test the same alternatives tried before.

In this case, the lowest total cost is obtained when the buyer orders 500 units twice a month (see Figure 2-3). The least-expensive ordering strategy is related to the annual sales in dollars (annual usage x unit cost) as long as the purchasing and maintenance costs remain the same. Fortunately, such costs tend to remain constant for relatively long periods of time in any given company.[2]

Frequency	Order Quantity	Cycle Stock	Maintenance Cost	Number Orders	Purchase Cost	Total Cost
Annually	$12,000	$6,000	$600	1	$1	$601
Semiannually	6,000	3,000	300	2	2	302
Quarterly	3,000	1,500	150	4	4	154
Bimonthly	2,000	1,000	100	6	6	106
Monthly	1,000	500	50	12	12	62
Semimonthly	500	250	25	24	24	49
Weekly	250	125	12.50	48	48	60.50

FIGURE 2-3   Total costs of various strategies for unit cost = $10. Source: Reprinted by permission from *IMPACT*. © 1967 by International Business Machines Corporation.

The Principle of Least Cost in Buying

All grocery buyers should be familiar with the principle of least cost and know the most economical buying periods for the products they buy.

There are two important factors that relate to the principle of least cost in ordering (see Figure 2-4).

1. As a buyer orders more frequently (in smaller quantities), he incurs increased purchasing costs.
2. As he purchases less frequently (in larger quantities), maintenance costs increase because the cycle stock is larger. (Recall that cycle stock is one-half the order quantity.)

The total cost of buying is the sum of the purchasing cost and the maintenance cost, and this total is the lowest when these two costs are

---

[2]Adapted from *IBM, IMPACT* (White Plains, N.Y.: International Business Machines Corporation, © 1967). p.10. Reprinted by permission.

equal. Notice, in Figure 2-4, that between points *A* and *B* there is a range of choices in which the total cost does not greatly change with minor changes in buying strategy. In this example, the best buying strategy would be to purchase merchandise 20 times a year, yielding a total annual cost of $20. However, the buyer could purchase from 16 to 25 times per year (the area between *A* and *B*) without exceeding a total cost of $22. This means that the buyer could continue to buy the most convenient quantities—carload or truckload lots and in full pallets—as long as he purchased within the range of 16 to 25 times per year, without affecting the total cost of buying.

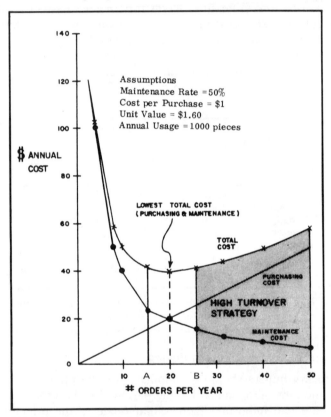

FIGURE 2-4   Total inventory costs versus ordering strategy. Source: Reprinted by permission from *IMPACT*. © 1967 by International Business Machines Corporation.

Note the shaded area to the right of line *B*. This is an area of high-turnover strategy, where the buyer places 25 or more orders per year. Many buyers consider high turnover the best standard for judging the effectiveness of their buying practices, but Figure 2-4 shows that turnover alone does not yield the lowest total cost. Turnover is certainly important, but it must be kept in mind that a very high rate of turnover will actually increase the total cost of buying. Also remember that the cost of buying includes purchasing and handling costs. Handling costs for most products will far exceed purchasing costs. Obtaining high turnover may result in abnormally high handling costs. Rapid turnover for some products is desirable in the distribution center and in the supermarket. For example, daily turnover of such items as fluid milk, ground beef, and bakery products is desirable in the supermarket. But replenishing all the items sold in the store every day is an impossible task. Therefore, the manager reorders only a portion of the total items in the store on each order. Because only 10 percent of all the dry grocery items in the supermarket sell in quantities of a full case or more a week, 90 percent of the items do not need to be replenished on a weekly basis.

The distribution center must operate on the same basis. All items cannot be replenished each day or each week. Although some items may be purchased several times a week, some others may be purchased only three or four times a year.

Other Quantity Considerations

We have discussed the principle of least cost in buying as it affects the purchase of grocery products. Stated very simply, this principle says that the smaller the quantity purchased, the more frequently the buyer will have to reorder, and the larger the quantity purchased, the less frequently the buyer will have to reorder (at any given sales volume). The principle of least-cost buying attempts to balance the cost of purchasing with the cost of handling or maintaining the merchandise once it has been received, given that the handling cost will usually be greater than the purchasing cost.

A grocery buyer can seldom, however, order the exact amount that he needs. A specific quantity must be adjusted for factors such as (1) number of units per case or master container; (2) number of cases per pallet; (3) full truckload requirements, or full rail-car requirements; (4) available warehouse space; and (5) total vendor order. A grocery buyer seldom orders a single item from a vendor. More typically, he will order a composite of items such as a rail-car of canned soup from the Campbell Soup Company. In this case, he must take into account all the above items in placing his order.

First of all, because the number of units per case varies with different varieties of soup, the buyer must take into account the pack size in ordering. Second, he should order in full pallets in order to facilitate the handling of merchandise in the warehouse. Less than full-pallet quantities may be ordered, but they do not allow warehouse employees to take full advantage of materials-handling equipment. Quantities that are received in less than pallet loads usually require extra hand stacking, which becomes an added cost to the total operation. The total order placed with Campbell Soup should equal the cube of the rail car. Most food manufacturers provide this type of information to grocery buyers for their ease in placing full truck or car orders. The buyer must also be aware of available warehouse space, particularly if the order is larger than usual. (For example, merchandise that is ordered for a special promotion or for a weekly sales feature will usually require extra storage space.) In most cases, buyers tend to "over order" to meet the requirement of full-pallet size or full truckload or carload requirements. The principle of least-cost buying is, therefore, influenced by cost considerations other than buying costs.

When to Order

Up till now, we have been discussing how much to order and how many times a year a buyer should reorder merchandise to minimize total buying costs. With these general guidelines in mind, the buyer must then determine exactly *when* to buy. This is referred to as the *order point*. The question of when to order, or where to set the order point, is usually answered in the form "when stock is reduced to 100 units, it is time to buy." This number of 100 (or any other appropriate number) is the order point.

Although this discussion deals with the procedures that a grocery buyer at a distribution center would follow, the same principle would apply to orders placed at the supermarket. For example, the grocery manager must determine when to reorder an item based on the number of units still on the shelf or in the back room. When this quantity reaches a certain level, an order must be placed so that the new merchandise will arrive before the shelf stock or store inventory is depleted.

The order point is set so that merchandise is ordered while there is still stock on hand. During the time it takes the new shipment to arrive, the stock that was on hand will be depleted. The order point is set to plan for this depletion, recognizing that to wait until an item is actually out of stock is undesirable. To set the order point, the following factors must be taken into account:

1. Lead time
2. Review time
3. Forecast of sales
4. Safety stock
5. Level of service

Very simply stated, *lead time* is the amount of time between the written order and the receipt of the merchandise. In includes the time it takes to process a purchase order (or to place the order) and the time for the order to travel to the distribution center. In addition, it includes vendor processing time, transit time for shipment, and the time it takes for the distribution center to receive the merchandise and make it available for delivery to stores.

Under ideal circumstances, the grocery buyer would like to have the new shipment arrive just as the last case of merchandise is being sold. In determining when to order, it is necessary to know (1) the weekly selling rate of the product and (2) how much lead time is required. So, for our purposes at this point, the definition of *order point* is:

Order point = Lead time in weeks × Weekly selling rate

Assume that the product A sells 100 cases a week and requires two weeks lead time. Using the formula, the buyer could easily figure that he must order when the stock gets down to 200 cases. If lead time were four weeks, the order point would be 400 (4 x 100) instead of 200. If the lead time could be reduced to one week, the order point would be 100 (1 x 100). In other words, the longer the lead time, the higher the order point for a given selling rate. A change in selling rate would also affect the order point. If the selling rate increased, the order point would be higher; and conversely if the selling rate decreased, the order point would be lower. (See Figure 2-5.)

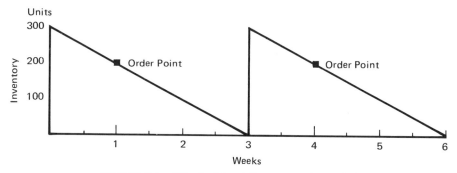

FIGURE 2-5 Effect of lead time on order point.

In determining when to order, a grocery buyer compares the amount of available stock with the projected order point. Through this comparison, he will know whether it is time to place the order. Most buyers review their available stock on a periodic basis—usually each week. This is often done through a computer printout, which provides this information to the buyer. Some products may be scheduled for a monthly review.

Therefore, the *review time* is defined as the number of days between reviews. For products that are reviewed on a weekly basis, the review time would be one week. Because the buyer does not follow the inventory level of a given product between reviews, some allowance must be made for the sales that will take place during this period. If this is not done, sales during the period between reviews could deplete the inventory to a level below that which is required to cover the normal demand during lead time. This would, of course, result in an out-of-stock situation.

Assume that the grocery buyer reviews the available stock of product A each Monday morning. On this particular week, when he reviews the amount of available stock, his report indicates that he has 250 units available. He knows, however, that during the succeeding week the normal sales of product A will reduce the available stock by 100 units, bringing it to a level of 150 by the next review period. This, of course, is below the order point; if he places an order the following week, an out-of-stock situation will develop before the new stock is received because lead time is two weeks.

To avoid this sort of out-of-stock situation, a fraction of the review time must be added to the lead time to calculate the order point. The order point could be reached on any day between successive reviews; it will usually be reached at the midpoint of a review period. Therefore, it would be appropriate to add one-half the review time to the lead time. So, revising our order-point formula:

Order point = (lead time + ½ Review time), in weeks, × Weekly
selling rate

Using our previous example, with lead time of two weeks and estimated sales on product A of 100 units per week, the order point is projected as 250 (see Figure 2-5).

In calculating lead time and establishing order points, we have assumed up to this point that the rate of sales was a known factor. In actual practice, *the buyer must forecast* how rapidly each product will sell. By collecting sales data over a period of time, it is possible to predict with some degree of accuracy the average turnover for each product in stock. This forecast, however, is subject to error due to seasonal buying habits, weather conditions, and holidays.

Because of the difficulty in accurately forecasting sales, some allowances must be made to compensate for errors that may result. It can be safely assumed that the forecast of sales will be too low about half the time and too high about half the time. Although either a too-high or too-low error results in certain problems, the buyer is most concerned about a forecast that is too low because it would result in an out-of-stock situation and therefore lost sales. To allow for this contingency, the order point should be raised to create a buffer or *safety stock*. Adding this safety stock to an order point increases the average inventory and raises the order point (see Figure 2-6).

Safety stock can be defined as the amount of additional inventory it is necessary to carry to compensate for errors in forecasting sales. Let's assume that during the past year the average sales for product A were 200 units per month. The maximum sales for any one month during the entire year were 300 units. It would be reasonable, therefore, to forecast that typically product A will be used at the rate of 200 each month, but that occasionally usage may increase to as much as 300 units. Therefore, if inventory is increased by 100 units as a safety stock, it will provide merchandise for any forecast error up to an additional 100 units per month.

If customers purchased with clock-work regularity and if stores ordered in exact quantities each week, no safety stock would be necessary, but this of course does not happen in reality. In Figure 2-6, the old order point and the new order point have been plotted. Without the safety stock, the order point is located so that merchandise will be reduced to zero at the exact time the new order arrives. When safety stock is introduced, the

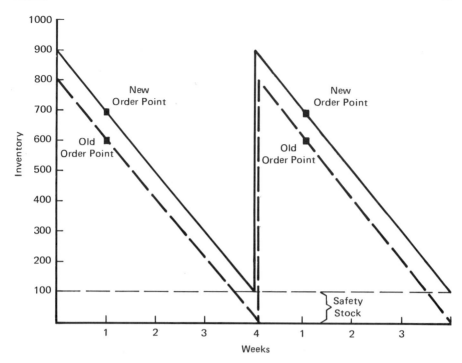

FIGURE 2-6 Adjusted order point with safety stock.

level where safety stock would be used is just reached when the shipment arrives. However, safety stock is available in case errors occur in forecasting sales.

The introduction of the safety-stock concept can be shown by adding it to our order-point formula as follows:

Order point = (Lead time + ½ Review time) × Forecast of sales per time unit + Safety stock[3]

Safety stock is therefore introduced as another factor that raises the order point.

The grocery buyer in a distribution center measures the *level of service* that he is providing to the stores by the percentage of orders, measured in dollars, that can be supplied from existing inventory. Grocery buyers are often supplied with weekly or periodic computer printout reports that indicate the level of service that they are providing the stores. This report is usually presented as a negative report in that it indicates the dollar amount of items that were "scratched" from store orders or that were out of stock when the store order was prepared. This dollar figure is then converted

---

[3]*IMPACT*, p. 24.

to a percentage of dollar inventory shipped to the stores. At the retail store, it becomes more difficult to determine with any degree of accuracy the level of service being provided to customers, but the same concept applies.

Most grocery wholesalers and food chains strive for a level of service between 95 and 98 percent. It would be unrealistic from an investment standpoint to have a service-level goal of 100 percent due to the many variables that enter into the supply picture, which principally include:

1. *Fluctuating consumer demand.* Even with accurate sales-forecasting tools and the use of safety stock, it is impossible to provide sufficient stock at all times to meet unanticipated consumer demand. This demand may result from unusual market situations, seasonal fluctuations, or weather conditions. For example, the manufacturer of product A may embark on an extensive advertising and promotion campaign that may increase the consumer demand for the product far in excess of that anticipated by the grocery buyer. A warm spell, early in the spring, may increase the sale of charcoal and picnic supplies before the buyer has had the opportunity to increase warehouse stocks to a level that can satisfy this increase in demand. The first snow or ice storm, in colder climates, often catches the stores with an insufficient stock of the rock salt or ice-melting chemicals that are demanded by customers. The warehouse also may not have a sufficient stock to supply the stores in this circumstance. In the examples mentioned, it would be impractical at either the store or the warehouse to attempt to carry a sufficient stock at all times to preclude an out-of-stock condition.

2. *Ordering errors.* Grocery buyers and persons ordering merchandise at the retail store are subject to inadvertant ordering errors. These errors typically take the form of ordering the wrong item or the wrong quantity. This, of course, creates an out-of-stock condition and reduces the level of service.

3. *Manufacturer's inability to supply a product.* The supplier often contributes to out-of-stock conditions because he is faced with internal problems. Labor problems that cause a slowdown or sometimes a strike make it impossible for food manufacturers to fill all customer orders. On the demand side, customer orders often exceed the manufacturer's projected sales volume and force the manufacturer to supply part orders only or to delay shipment until production can catch up with demand.

4. *Delays in transit.* Although the food industry has made great strides in improved transportation methods, delays still occur between producer and retailer. Trucks do break down, railroad cars do get lost on the wrong siding, and weather conditions often play an important part in the speed with which the transportation system operates. When merchandise is delayed beyond its expected arrival time, safety stocks are used up, and out-of-stock situations are created.

5. *Clerical errors.* The human element at both the warehouse and the store often contributes to out-of-stock conditions and lowers the level of service to customers. At the warehouse, merchandise may be in stock but

placed in the wrong picking slot by a warehouse operator. Even though the merchandise is on hand, if it cannot be located, the store's order cannot be filled and the customer cannot be served. Similar problems present themselves at the retail store. Merchandise may be placed in the wrong shelf location or buried in a reserve area, and therefore customers and clerks are unable to locate the desired product. Here again, the merchandise may be in stock, but the customer is not being served. Also, merchandise that is in the back room of the store but not priced or placed on the shelf represents an out-of-stock condition to the customer looking for that item.

These five variables indicate the problems associated with providing a high level of service to customers. It is impractical to maintain enough reserve stock to provide a 100 percent service level under all these conditions; in fact, in those cases where the merchandise is actually on hand but not available to the customer, additional inventory would not be the answer. A reasonable warehouse service level of 95 to 98 percent is realistic and being achieved by many grocery companies today.

Inventory Movement Reports

Buyers at food chain headquarters and wholesale distribution centers also make use of interindustry reports that are a compilation of the product movement of many retailing and wholesaling firms to assist them in their buying activities. These reports are designed to show the movement of individual products and commodity groups within specific marketing areas. The most widely used reports are a product of SAMI (Selling Areas-Marketing, Inc.), a subsidiary of Time Life Incorporated. The A. C. Nielsen Company also produces food industry product movement reports on a national basis, although they are not as widely used or accepted by food industry buyers as the SAMI reports.

The basic purpose of the report is to record the movement of individual products and product groups that are distributed by the major food wholesalers and retailers in a specific marketing area. This information provides retailers and food manufacturers alike with sales data for an entire marketing area. It indicates, for example, the market size of various commodity groups (that is, the number of dollar sales that is attributed to baking supplies, canned vegetables, tobacco products, as well as other individual product groups) for a specific marketing area, such as Boston or Los Angeles.

Product movement is measured by "warehouse withdrawals." That is, the amount of merchandise shipped out of each warehouse during a specific time period (for example, one week or four weeks). This, of course, does not reflect specific retail sales, but only those products that were shipped to the retail stores to be offered for sale. However, as product movement is analyzed over a four-week period most retailers and manufacturers agree that warehouse withdrawals accurately reflect the sales picture at the retail level.

The SAMI reports are prepared for both food retailers and food manufacturers. Although the same basic information is used in the preparation of both reports, it is presented in slightly different format for each audience. For example, the report that is prepared for food manufacturers includes the following information about all national-brand products sold in a given marketing area; the item size, case pack, average shelf price (from all companies selling that product), and both the case volume and the measured dollar sales for 4-week periods and 52-week periods. In addition, the report tells the manufacturer what share of the market his product represents. It also breaks down the share of the product group that is represented by each individual item (for example, the share of Del Monte 16-ounce sauerkraut is reported separately from those of all other sizes of Del Monte sauerkraut). An additional subcategory would tell the dollar contribution of Del Monte 16-ounce sauerkraut to all other brands and sizes of sauerkraut sold in the marketing area. The report to the manufacturer indicates a number of food operators who have shipped each product during the past 4-week period as well as a list of new and discontinued items that have entered or left the market system during the previous 4-week period.

The manufacturers' report also includes a separate category for private-label products. The category indicates the sales by commodity groups for all private-label items sold in each marketing area. Specific private label names are not used so that individual company sales are not disclosed.

The manufacturers' report of product movement as prepared by SAMI describes the movement of individual national-brand items within specific marketing areas. This, of course, assists the marketing and sales people of these food manufacturing firms who are responsible for product movement in various parts of the country and in individual marketing areas.

Whereas the manufacturers' report tends to describe product movement in a total marketing area, the report prepared for retail buyers is more specific in nature and tends to relate product movement of the individual company to the total marketing area. In other words, the retailer reports focus on the performance of individual products by specific companies. For example, the report for Chain A in the Baltimore-Washington marketing area would include the following information about each individual national-brand product:

1. Total case movement of product in the marketing area.
2. Share of the market of each product by average retail price (by 4-week and 52-week movement).
3. Share of the market accounted for by Chain A for each product as measured by case movement for previous 4-week and 52-week period.

Summary Reports

Additional summary and exception reports are also provided to retail buyers. These reports include such summary information as a listing of the sales totals of the 42 major commodity groups (for example, baking mixes, canned vegetables). This report tells the retailer the total dollar sales for each major commodity group as well as the retailer's share of that commodity group within the retailer's specific marketing area.

Exception Reports

SAMI provides retailers with several "exception" reports, which are designed to pinpoint critical buying and merchandising situations within their own company. One such report provides retailers with information on the top 200 products from grocery, health and beauty aids, and frozen and refrigerated products. This report compares present case movement of these 200 items with similar 4-week and 52-week periods from the previous year. It also compares the dollar sales ranking of these products for the current year with the previous year. This is an indication to buyers of changes in sales patterns of the fastest moving items they carry. Buyers are provided with other exception reports that include product movement within a specific marketing area on items that the retailer does not carry. This report helps buyers keep abreast of products with sales potential that are carried by other retailers in the marketing area.

Another exception report pinpoints those items for which the food chain or wholesaler accounts for 30 percent or more of the total market share (these would normally be items that only one or two retailers in a marketing area now carry).

In retailing and wholesaling firms where private label is important, "the private label comparison report" provides important information to the buyer. This report tells what the total market is for each private-label product and product group and what share of the private-label market is represented by their own company sales. In other words, this report compares the sales of each private-label item distributed by the firm receiving the report with the total private label market sales for that item (or product group).

Food chain buyers and buyers for wholesale distribution centers find these market area product movement reports extremely helpful and useful in making sound merchandising and buying decisions. Most buyers agree that the use of these reports will increase in the years to come.

ORDERING AT THE STORE— INVENTORY CONTROL

Most of our attention thus far has been focused on the grocery buyer's job in placing routine orders. The same principles that affect the ordering decisions made by the grocery buyer also affect the grocery manager or the person who does the ordering at the retail store. Just like the buyer at chain headquarters, so must the store manager be concerned with the principle of least cost. The larger the store's inventory relative to sales, the greater the cost of doing business. Therefore, the manager, like the buyer, strives to keep his inventory as low as possible but must avoid out-of-stock situations, which are also costly in terms of lost sales. Therefore, he is really balancing the cost of holding extra merchandise in reserve (opportunity costs) against the cost of ordering and lost sales that result from out-of-stocks.

In principle, this is the same function that is performed by the buyer at the warehouse level. The primary difference is that the buyer must *procure* the merchandise from a multitude of manufacturers and suppliers, and the manager *orders* several thousand items from a central warehouse and from suppliers who deliver direct to the store. So, in this section, we will examine the specific systems that are used by food retailers in store ordering, with the emphasis placed on controlling inventory to match retail sales requirements.

Inventory control has become a more important aspect of in-store ordering because supermarkets today are placing less emphasis on reserve storage of surplus merchandise and greater emphasis on improved delivery systems to the stores. This trend is designed to reduce store inventory and improve turnover and increase sales by reducing out of stocks. The goal of increased turnover has been achieved by few companies in recent years. Statistics indicate that typical store turnover has declined from 12.85 turns per year in 1962 to 11.09 turns per year in 1968-69. Turnover has increased during the past few years—12.51 turns were recorded for 1971-72.[4] The drop in turnover appears to be due primarily to an increase in the number and type of items carried by the typical supermarket (especially nonfoods, which have lower turnover rates) and not due to inefficiencies in the operating system. Had there not been some attempt to improve inventory control at the store, the slight gain in turnover rate would probably not have been realized in 1971-72.

Picture a supermarket with 22,000 square feet of selling space and only 1,000 square feet of back-room space for storage. Sound like a store manager's nightmare? Actually, it is just the opposite. It is one of the advanced features of Red Owl's QRP (Quick Recovery Program) shelf restock system and a highlight found in many of their new stores.[5]

This emphasis on more of the total store space devoted to selling area and less for back-room reserve stock is typical in many supermarket companies today. Why this trend to small back rooms? The principal reason is to reduce store operating costs by reducing reserve inventory.

In order to maintain an adequate supply of merchandise, avoid out of stocks, and reduce excess merchandise and handling to a minimum, the manager of a supermarket must order as close to customer demand as possible. In the past, many managers were able, through experience, to anticipate customer demand. These managers developed a "feel" for their stores and knew how much of each item to order and were able to keep large back-room

---

    [4]Wendell Earle and John Hughes, *Operating Results of Food Chains* (New York: The Progressive Grocer Company, 1973), p. 12.

    [5]"But Where's the Backroom?" *Chain Store Age Supermarket Executive Edition,* November 1967, p. 3.

inventories to correct their errors. As both the size of new stores and numbers of items handled have increased, it has become too costly to have large reserve inventories and more and more difficult to predict customer demand and keep it all in one's head with any degree of accuracy.

To assist the store manager in the ordering process, many firms have adopted programs that incorporate order control and inventory control into a single system.

The SLIM System

One of the original inventory systems developed for the retail store is SLIM—Store Labor and Inventory Management. In widespread use and frequently copied or modified by many supermarket companies to meet specific local conditions, this system provides the store manager with an important tool for controlling inventories and reducing the need for back-room storage of most grocery items. Moreover, SLIM results in substantial labor savings in ordering and stocking.

Making this system work requires a team effort on the part of the personnel from the store, warehouse, data-processing department, transportation, and buying office. According to Edward M. Harwell, who created the acronym SLIM, and who has worked with numerous supermarket chains in installing the system, in order to work effectively, SLIM, like most of its counterparts, requires that the total system comply with these six conditions:

1. Of paramount importance to the success of this program is the correct allocation of shelf space. Basically, this requires a minimum shelf capacity of one full case for each grocery item carried plus space for the item's average weekly movement.

2. Orders are placed for items only when a *full case* will go on the shelf at the time the order is written.

3. The time lag must be reduced between the placement of the order and the receipt of the merchandise from the food distribution center from a few days to a few hours. Fast replenishment of stock is absolutely necessary for this program to be successful.

4. Order and delivery dates must be rescheduled to provide full trailer loads of merchandise for each store. Also, it is desirable to set delivery dates so that there is equal sales distribution between grocery orders.

5. Merchandise must be segregated by commodity groups for movement to specific aisles within the store. This segregation of merchandise may take place either at the warehouse when the order is being selected or in the back room of the store when the merchandise is being delivered.

6. When the merchandise is received at the store, it must be moved directly to the shelf for price marking and stocking. Night stocking is desirable if day stocking causes congestion in the aisles, especially during heavy customer traffic periods.

Space Allocation

If correct space allocation is the most important ingredient to the success of this program, how is space allocated? A careful study of the movement of each item in the store is necessary to correctly allocate space. A minimum of 13 weeks is required for collecting this movement data. However, 26 weeks provide a more accurate data base. Because the primary goal of a correct space allocation program is to eliminate the possibility of running out of an item between orders, the formula for providing enough space is that of a full case of merchandise plus the average weekly movement of the item.

It is possible to draw up a space allocation formula for a specific store in a specific company (see Table 2-1). This data would have to be modified for each store's or company's requirements.

One general exception to the space allocation rule is fast moving items. In a typical store, it is necessary to carry reserve inventory on only a handful of the fastest moving items, such as five-pound bags of sugar, certain

TABLE 2-1   Space Allocation Ground Rules
(For stores requiring two or more loads per week)

Case Pack	Movement in Units per Week	Minimum Space Allocation
12	0-4	16
	5-18	12 plus M*
	19-24	30
	25-36	36
	37-60	M*
	61-80	60
	More than 80**	75% M*
24	0-6	30
	7-36	24 plus M*
	37-48	60
	49-72	72
	73-120	M*
	121-160	120
	More than 160**	75% M*
48	0-8	56
	9-72	48 plus M*
	73-96	120
	97-144	144
	145-240	M*
	241-320	240
	More than 320 **	75%M*

*M—Movement in units per week.
**These items automatically require reserve inventory; in a store requiring one load per week, they represent 2 to 3 percent of all items carried; in a store requiring two loads per week, they represent less than 1 percent of all items carried.

Source: Edward M. Harwell, "Store Labor and Inventory Management," *Chain Store Age Supermarket Edition*, June 1965, p. 79.

paper products, cereals, or liquid bleach. With these items, it usually would not be realistic to allocate enough shelf space to eliminate the chance of running out of the product without restocking between orders. Sufficient inventory of these items will have to be carried in the back room to replenish the stock between deliveries.

Another consideration that is important in allocating shelf space is the location of the product on the shelf. Information derived from various industry reports such as the McKinsey Studies on direct product profit and *Chain Store Age*'s Cifrino Space Yield Study show that moving an item from the bottom shelf to an eye-level position may increase sales and directly affect the number of facings and amount of space allocated to the product. Conversely, moving an item from an eye-level position to a less-accessible location on a bottom shelf may slow down movement on that item and thereby reduce the shelf space requirement.

Two in-store controls are necessary to maintaining a proper shelf allocation program:

1. Some type of control tags attached to the molding of the grocery shelving. These tabs should indicate the item, the item code, and the number of facings for that particular item. This will assure that the item is not lost if an out-of-stock condition occurs and another item is "filled in" on the empty shelf space. It will also assure that the correct number of facings are maintained for each item.

2. Some type of master list on which the space allocation for each item is recorded. This might be the printout of item movement from the 26-week report. When space allocations change, they should be changed in the master list as well as on the shelf control tag. The master list is an important check and must be kept current.

Ordering

Once the shelf space for each item has been correctly allocated, the reordering system provides a sure-fire control of the store's inventory. The key to the reordering system is *order only when a full case will go on the shelf at the time the order is written.* By following this rule except for the few items that require reserve inventory, there is little back-room stock. However, because the space allocation program has allowed for a full case *plus* enough merchandise to carry through between orders, there should be no need to restock. This not only reduces back-room inventories but eliminates the labor involved in restocking as well.

SLIM and similar systems require that the manager reorder stock from the shelf and not from the order book. There are several obvious advantages to ordering in this manner.

First of all, it is a time-saving feature. The manager simply walks down the aisle and orders only those items whose shelf space can accommodate a full case of merchandise. This eliminates the need to review each specific item in the order book and compare it with shelf stock or in some cases, back-room stock.

A second advantage is that it simplifies the ordering procedure and makes it possible for less-experienced personnel to do the ordering. Ordering in this manner requires that the shelf control tags contain the item code and case pack. Some companies now include this information on a unit-pricing shelf control strip. This has the advantage of combining unit-pricing and reordering information on one tag. However, this combination may confuse the customer by introducing numbers that have no meaning for him.

Ordering under the SLIM system requires that the manager not anticipate future product movement but order only when a full case will go on the shelf. The question invariably comes up, what do you do if only 23 cans will go on the shelf and there are 24 cans in the case? Do you order? The answer is *no*. Remember, the shelf allocation provides for one full case plus enough additional merchandise to insure no out of stocks between orders. Therefore, when there is room for only 23 cans there is still enough merchandise to last until the next order is received.

Placing and Receiving Orders

The placing of orders is handled the same way for both the SLIM system and variations of SLIM. After the manager makes out the order, it is transmitted to the data processing office at the warehouse or headquarters. The order is sent to the warehouse, where it is selected and loaded for delivery to the store. In most SLIM companies, the ordering, transmission, selection, delivery, and stocking cycle takes place in less than 24 hours. By reducing the amount of time lag from a few days to a few hours, ordering becomes more accurate and the replenishment process is greatly facilitated.

Unloading and Restocking

As indicated in the previous section, order receiving at the store requires the use of carts or skids to move the merchandise to the selling area. Before the merchandise can be moved to the selling area, it must be segregated by commodity group so that the stock crews, working in specific aisles, have the necessary merchandise for their aisle. This segregation may take place at the warehouse when the merchandise is selected or in the back room of the store when the merchandise is unloaded from the truck. Each pallet, skid, or cart should contain the merchandise for a specific aisle or section of an aisle. If the order is delivered before the stocking crew is available, it is temporarily stored in the back room. If the stocking crew is available when the order is delivered, merchandise is moved directly to the sales area.

Control versus Merchandising

Programs, such as SLIM, that attempt to control inventory at store level are not always accepted by merchandising people because shelf depletion is generally greater with SLIM. The traditional thinking of many grocery merchandisers is that more merchandise is sold when shelves are full than when partially depleted. However, this personal bias has never been proved by scientific research and, in fact, the experience of companies using SLIM has refuted this argument.

Inventory control systems, such as SLIM, are possible now because of the computer and are a natural outgrowth of the trend to do our merchandising in a more scientific way to achieve greater sales volume and profits. They have also resulted from the inability of the manager to cope with larger stores and the rapidly increasing number of new products being introduced in the market place. The manager is incapable of accurately forecasting the sales of all items in the store. A scientific approach is needed, and the type of inventory control systems described in this section are an answer to this need.

Disadvantages of SLIM

One of the concerns often expressed about the SLIM system is that because there is no reserve stock in the store, the store is more likely to be in an out-of-stock position if the warehouse is out of stock on an item. However, the experience of companies using the SLIM system is that out of stocks are reduced by approximately 75 percent because the shelf control tag ensures that the position will not be lost if the item is out of stock for any period of time.

A more realistic objection to SLIM is that it frequently requires the use of night stocking crews, which can lead to laxity in controls unless there is good supervisory personnel on hand.

A second disadvantage of SLIM is that when the order-delivery-stock cycle is compressed, delays in delivery are more likely if there is a breakdown at any stage of the cycle. For example, if there is a computer breakdown, there will be little if any time cushion to make up for that delay and each succeeding step in the cycle will be delayed.

Despite these two disadvantages, SLIM companies agree unanimously that the advantages of this system far outweigh any possible disadvantages. The economics of operating a successful business are forcing more and more retailers to take a scientific approach to controlling inventory at store level, and many of the systems being used today are adaptations of SLIM.

As stores continue to grow in size and as more and more new products are introduced into the supermarket, the need for inventory control will become even more pressing. Automatic reorder systems utilizing electronic checkout equipment are a likely possibility in the future. With greater utilization of computers and electronic scanning systems, scientific methods of inventory control will probably become an accepted way of life.

Computers and Inventory Control

Inventory control at the point of sale—the checkout—is one of the most significant developments in supermarket retailing in the 1970s. In 1973, the Universal Product Code Committee adopted a symbol that can be read by optical scanning systems. (See Figure 2-7.) The symbol, with its code structure, represents the ten-digit numerical code previously adopted by the Universal Product Code Committee. The first five digits identify the manufacturer, and the second five, the item, so that each item will have a unique code.

FIGURE 2-7   Universal product symbol.

Although the primary advantages of the optical scanning system are labor savings at the checkstand and better service to the customer as a result of increased productivity and greater accuracy, one of the byproducts is the availability of movement data by item, which facilitates automatic ordering and inventory control.

The optical scanning system is tied into a minicomputer at the store. As each item is scanned, the price of the item is looked up by the minicomputer and flashed back to a customer display window at the checkstand. This process takes place in a matter of milliseconds. As the price is being looked up, the minicomputer records a sale for that particular item. At the end of the day, the minicomputer has in its memory the quantity of each item sold in the store that day. This information is then transmitted over normal telephone lines to a central computer at headquarters. The central computer has the capability of maintaining the quantity on hand of each item in every store on the system. Thus, automatic reordering becomes a possibility. However, certain problems in maintaining accurate data must first be solved. For example, some means must be found to ensure accuracy in identifying the individual items and quantities delivered to the store so that adjustments can be made for warehouse selection and delivery errors. In addition, periodic inventories must be taken by individual item at store level to correct errors in current item inventories in the computer that are caused by pilferage or breakage that may have occurred since the previous physical inventory. Assuming these problems can be overcome, automatic reordering is a viable possibility in the future. However, automatic reordering will always require some adjustment by personnel either at store or headquarters level for exceptions, such as items to be advertised or given special promotions or displays.

The complete changeover to the computerized inventory control system described will take some time. These systems are initially very expensive and demand a radical change in thinking and work methods on the part of those people whose experience has been limited to mechanical registers and manual inventory control.

NEW ITEMS AND NEW LINES

What is a New Item?

To the casual grocery shopper, the word *new,* when associated with a food product, is certainly an overused and in many cases meaningless label. Laundry detergents are always "*new* and improved"; your favorite drink comes in a *new* one-way bottle; a beauty care product is found in a *new* family size; there are *new* colors and prints in facial tissue; and the list goes on and on. How many of these products are really *new*?

Basically, "new" products can be grouped into three classifications:

1. A line extension—a new size, flavor, color, or package that has been added to an existing product line or group of products. Most "new" products are line extensions.

2. A new, but duplicate product—a product that is new for the company that makes it, but duplicates a competitive product.

3. An entirely new product—a product that is unique because of its natural ingredients or its manufacturing process. Of all the new products presented to food store buyers during any given period, those falling into this classification are the fewest in number.

Importance of New Items

How important are new items in food retailing today? Take a look around the grocery and frozen-food departments. Over half the products on the shelves and in the frozen-food cabinets were not there ten years ago. According to a recent study by *Progressive Grocer,* the total number of items handled in the grocery and frozen-food department in 1967 was 4,657, as compared with 3,675 in 1957—or a net increase of 982 items. During this ten-year period, 2,540 new items were added and 1,558 were dropped for the net increase of 982 items.

TABLE 2-2   Shifts in Items Handled, 1967 vs. 1957
(Grocery and Frozen Food)

Number of items handled, 1957	3,675
Number of 1957 items dropped since 1957	1,558
Number of items handled in 1967 not handled in 1957	2,540
Number of items handled in 1967	4,657

Source: *Progressive Grocer,* June 1967.

The study also pointed out that these new items represent 52 percent of dollar sales and earn 57 percent of dollar margin of all grocery and frozen-food products.

This spectacular increase in the number of new items handled not only points out their importance but brings to the surface a number of problems for the supermarket retailers who handle these products.

New Items Affect Stockturns

Individual companies have watched their grocery inventories grow with guarded concern. Harry Beckner of the Jewel Companies states in a report to the National Association of Food Chains: "Our grocery assortment has increased by upwards of 200 to 300 items each year for the last five."

Noting a similar growth at Hillmans, Gardner H. Stern, Jr., reported, "Today, we carry approximately 4,250 items in the warehouse. Contrast that figure with the 3,900 items we carried only five years ago."[6]

Super Market Institute, a trade association composed of firms with stores of supermarket size ($1 million or more in annual sales), reported that their typical member handled 5,000 dry grocery items in 1968. The total number of items carried by member firms had increased by 1,000 items from 1966 to 1969, moving from 7,000 to 8,000 items during this three-year period.

As the number of items increases each year, so does the size of the supermarket. Although stores have expanded over the years, they have not increased in size at a rate to keep pace with the introduction of new items. SMI reported that new supermarkets constructed in 1959 had a median size of 20,000 square feet for the total store, which included a selling area of 13,300 square feet. Supermarket size remained about constant until 1967 and 1968. New stores constructed in 1968 had typical selling areas of 15,000 square feet in a total store area of 21,000 square feet (a net increase of only 500 square feet for the total store).[7] According to SMI, store size remained virtually unchanged through 1971 (for new stores opened during that year).[8] With the number of products increasing at a faster rate than the size of the supermarket, selling areas are being pressed for space.

More products and greater variety have also had an effect on inventory turnover for supermarket companies and wholesalers. Average stockturns for food chains in 1962 was 12.85. This represented an all-time high. The trend in stockturns has been declining since then and reached an all-time low of 11.09 for the 1968-69 period.[9]

A reduction in the number of stockturns seems to be directly associated with the increase in new items being introduced and the tendency for food retailers and wholesalers to increase the total number of items in their inventories.

---

[6]"Assortments vs. Inventory," *Chain Store Age Supermarkets,* November 1966, p. 65. An adaptation of the panel discussion of Monday, October 24, 1966, NAFC Annual Leadership Forum.

[7]Curt Kornblau, *Facts about New Supermarkets Opened in 1968* (Chicago: Super Market Institute, 1969), p. 5.

[8]Willard R. Bishop, Jr., *Facts about New Supermarkets Opened in 1971* (Chicago: Super Market Institute, 1971), p. 9.

[9]*Operating Results of Food Chains,* p. 12.

Assimilating New Items

There are four main problem areas that must be considered at store level whenever a new item is added to the inventory. The type of product being introduced has a direct bearing on how each of these problems is met.

Where to Stock. Finding the right location for a new item is an easy decision when it is an extension of an existing line. It becomes more difficult when the product is truly a new item, such as a powdered dessert-topping mix. In this case, it must be decided if the product belongs with frosting mixes, with the powdered desserts, or in some other section.

In many cases, the manufacturer will suggest where the product should be displayed in order to obtain maximum sales. This recommendation is usually based on the results obtained from the test market in which the product was first introduced.

Shelf Space. Making room in the appropriate department and in the appropriate location within that department for the new item is no simple task because of the physical labor involved and, as previously mentioned, the number of items carried in today's supermarket is increasing at a faster rate than is store size.

Lack of shelf space has become such a problem in many stores that new items are often looked upon as a source of irritation and not as a source of greater sales and profits.

The new-product increase is a benefit primarily to new stores constructed during this period or stores that were or can be enlarged. Smaller stores have the greater problem of trying to find room for this net increase of nearly 1,000 items on their already planned, and crowded, shelves, unless they have a SLIM-type operation. A SLIM operation affords a built-in flexibility that allows the store to accommodate new items. This is accomplished by adding additional facings or rows (beyond the minimum allocation called for in the space allocation formula) to carefully selected, high-profit, high-turnover items. These cushions, which are an integral part of the SLIM system, serve two purposes: (1) they enable the store to increase profits, through an improved product mix, by increasing the sales of these high-profit, high-turnover items; and (2) they provide space to accommodate new items that are anticipated to be added in the future in each commodity group.

Informing Employees. Product information must be provided to employees who order and stock the new item. Employees must be told where to locate the product—in what family grouping and in what shelf location. In some cases, it is important to tell employees how the product is to be used by consumers, so that they can answer questions intelligently.

Order Quantity. Another problem that must be solved is how much to stock and how much to order during the introductory period for the new item, and how to anticipate the normal weekly movement. This becomes critical when the manufacturer advertises heavily or offers coupons on the item. Customer demand may be very heavy because of this initial promotional activity and may drop off sharply thereafter. Providing the stock initially needed to meet the demand is important, and then it is important to know when the demand will fall off so that overstocking does not occur. With the SLIM system, the minimum space required in relation to the case pack is allocated on the shelf, and off-shelf displays are used during the initial promotional period to meet customer demand.

How New Items Are Introduced

Thousands of new items are presented to food chain and wholesale buyers each year. Naturally, not all items are accepted. In fact, most new items presented to buyers are turned down. In a *Progressive Grocer* study, a small sampling of new-items presentations indicated that only 23 percent of those items presented to food chain buyers were accepted.[10] Most buyers feel that even this estimate is high, and that over a full year in which many seasonal items, such as picnic supplies, Easter candy, and Christmas decorations, are presented, the percentage of new items accepted would be only about 10 percent. If only 10 percent of all new items presented to food buyers are accepted, what happens to the rejected 90 percent? In many cases, they are dropped by the manufacturer or the processing firm completely, or they are sent back to the manufacturer's marketing department for further research and development.

However, many items that are dropped or rejected by one food retailer are accepted by another, and so the product does not really die. The rest of the rejected new items that do not fit into any of these categories do die—they are just quietly and completely dropped by everyone involved.

Presentation of New Items to the Food Buyer

When the food manufacturer or processor has prepared his final marketing plan for the new item, the company's sales staff is called together to review the plan and to determine how and when it will be presented to the retail food trade. Sales representatives are provided with detailed information on all aspects of the program, including a detailed breakdown of the advertising program: How much advertising will be done, what type of media will be used—newspapers, magazines, radio, television, or direct mail—and the use of coupons or other promotional devices. The sales representative must also know all the details of the sales and advertising allowances available to the wholesale customer, as well as order quantities and freight rates.

The New-item Form.   These details must then be written out on the grocery product information form required by the food chain or wholesaler

---

[10]"Nielsen Research Underscores Power of New Items," *Progressive Grocer,* June 1967, p. 70.

(see Figure 2-8). The purpose of this form is to give the buyer the facts concerning the new item at a glance. This form is much like an application-for-employment form—just as an interviewer looks over an employment form to determine if the job applicant possesses the necessary qualities for the job, so the food buyer reviews the product information form to determine if the new product and the marketing program contain the qualities that will make it a success.

The Sales Presentation. The product information form is given to the buyer at the same time that the manufacturer's rep or broker presents the new product. Most food buyers limit their interviews with sales representatives to about 15 minutes. With this short a time allocated to a sales presentation, it is imperative that the rep or broker be well prepared and organized. As the old saying goes, he needs to "know the territory." He certainly must know the policies and practices of the companies on which he calls, as well as those of his own company.

There are several key points that the food buyer wants to hear from the manufacturer's representative during the sales presentation:

1. Product characteristics—such as size, weight, grade or quality, ingredients, and pack and pallet size. The buyer also wants to know about product liability insurance, as well as warrantees and guarantees. The buyer appreciates a salesman who knows these facts and can answer questions about his product quickly and accurately.

2. Suggested shelf locations—where the product is likely to reach maximum sales. Also, promotional ideas and suggestions of related items that can be promoted with the product are welcome.

3. Test market results—especially important if the item has no previous sales history. These test market results should be projected by the sales representative to the local market area to show what results can be expected.

4. Suggested retail price—as well as the projected markup are helpful guides for the food buyer. The food manufacturer may not, of course, "tell" the retailer what he *must* charge for the product, but he can *suggest* a fair retail. This suggested retail price is usually based on a fair markup or on the current retail price of similar items.

5. Advertising program—that will back up the introduction of the new item is very significant in the buyer's evaluation. Of special importance are the dates the advertising will appear, the types of media to be used, the message to be carried in the ad copy, and any special coupons or introductory offers.

6. Special allowances—on new items result in extra profit on the product, and are designed to encourage retailers to stock the item. Such allowances also provide the retailer an inducement to feature the new item either at a special retail, or at regular retail (buying allowances are covered more fully later in this chapter.)

7. Product handling methods—important to food retailers who are striving for greater efficiencies in this area in order to cut costs and improve profit. The salesman must be prepared to give detailed answers to questions about the method of shipment, unitized loads, type and size of pallet used, and the pallet patterns.

NEW PRODUCT INFORMATION FORM

Presented To: _____ Company Name _____ Buyer's Name

Manufacturer: _____ Telephone: _____

Address: _____ Zip: _____

Representative: _____ Telephone: _____

Address: _____ Zip: _____

Purchase Order Mailed To: _____ Representative _____ Manufacturer

F.O.B. Point: _____ Freight to Whse. Delivery: _____ Shipping Point: _____

Handling or Hauling Allowance _____ C/L - T/L - P/C Allowance _____

ITEM	Size	Pack	Regular Cs. Cost	Regular Unit Cost	Suggested Retail	Profit %	Profit ¢	Est. Wk. Cs. Sales
Regular								
Deal								

Case Weight: _____

Case Dimensions in inches: _____
   (Length, Width, Height)
Case Cube: _____

Pallet Pattern: Tie _____ High _____

Special or other pack: _____

Type of Container: _____

Normal Delivery Days: _____

Min./Max. Shipments: _____

Fair Traded: _____ Yes _____ No

How Shipped: _____

Guaranteed Sales: ____ Warehouse _____ Store

How Long: _____ Does Vendor Pay Freight: _____

Price Protection: ____ Yes _____ How Long _____ No

Trade or Other Discounts: _____

Cash Terms: _____

Guaranteed to Conform to FFDA _____ USDA _____

Quantity Discount: _____

Coop. Adv. Allow. _____

STORE HANDLING CONSIDERATIONS: Shelf Stocking _____ Good _____ Fair   Spot for Retail Price: ____ Yes ____ No

Tear Strip Case: _____ Yes _____ No   Merchandise Pre-Priced: _____ Yes _____ No

Damage: _____ Warehouse _____ Retail   Describe: _____

(B.F.B.A. Form # 1 - May 1971)

FIGURE 2-8

8. Samples of the new item—should be left with the buyer. According to a survey conducted by the Food Trade Marketing Council of *Family Circle* magazine, three samples will satisfy eight out of ten chains and seven out of ten wholesalers.

Name Insurance Co. _____ Address _____

Amount Product Liability Carried: _____ Vendor Coverage _____ Yes _____ No

Are there any ingredients in this product which are suspect and under investigation by any government agency? _____

If so, describe: _____

Introductory Offer: _____

_____

Promotional Allowances: _____

_____

Advertising by Supplier — Describe: _____

_____

Competitors Handling Product	Test	Regular	Retail Price	Competitors Handling Product	Test	Regular	Retail Price

Is this item offered to similar distributors on proportionately equal terms: _____ Yes _____ No

Salesman's Signature _____ Date Submitted _____ Date Available _____

(DO NOT WRITE BELOW THIS LINE)

FIGURE 2-8   (Cont.)

The Buying Committee

After the food buyer has obtained the necessary information and facts from the sales representative, he may accept or reject the new item immediately. However, in most companies, policy dictates that the new item be referred to the buying committee for further consideration and a final decision on its acceptance or rejection.

Most food chains and wholesalers have a buying committee, which is set up to pass judgment on all new items, promtoions, and deals. The justification for the buying committee is that "two heads are better than one." Actually, the buying committee is usually made up of four to six buyers who meet once a week to discuss new offerings from food manufacturers.

Another rationale for a buying committee is that it provides a more analytical approach to the selection of new items. Many companies feel that the buyer is often placed under undue pressure by some salesmen who have a "hot new item," and that the atmosphere is not always conducive to sound business decisions. Some companies feel that their buyers may be led to make hasty decisions, based more on emotion than on sound facts, when confronted by an eloquent salesman.

The buyer, after hearing the salesman's presentation, will set aside the new-item proposal until the weekly buying committee meeting. Sometimes the buyer will make a specific recommendation on the acceptance of an item to the buying committee. However, the entire buying committee must decide if the new item should be accepted or rejected.

By providing for group action in the decision-making process, the buying committee offers these advantages:

1. Permits a wider range of ideas and experience to come to bear in the decision-making process.
2. Takes the buyer "off the spot" in his face-to-face relationship with the salesman.
3. Allows for a decision to be made in a more scientific atmosphere.

There are, of course, certain disadvantages to the buying committee. These include:

1. The delay in making the decision to accept a new item—and the subsequent delay in getting the item stocked in the stores. It is important to have the item stocked in the stores when the major advertising programs break.

2. Committee meetings that take up valuable time of *all* buyers—even those who are not specifically involved with the product being presented.

3. A disadvantage to the food manufacturer and the sales representative because the buyer does not always present all the facts and sometimes he presents them incorrectly. Also, the buyer does not usually present the new item with the same enthusiasm to the buying committee that the salesman would have in making his original presentation to the buyer.

Why New Items are Rejected

There are many and varied reasons why new items are rejected. The following is a list of factors that affect the acceptance of a new item.

1. Duplicates a present item—when a new item is presented that is a duplicate of an item already on the shelves, there must be evidence to indicate a sufficient demand to justify both items.

This is a particularly difficult decision for a grocery buyer or a buying committee when a new size or a new color of a product is under consideration. For example, if a buyer receives a new-item request from a food manufacturer to carry a "large economy size" of a present product, he must decide if sufficient sales can be generated by the addition of this new size to justify the costs of adding the new item and its shelf space in the store. If a new size shifts sales from one size to another and does not result in a sales gain, there is no benefit to either the food manufacturer or the retailer.

2. Wrong line or brand—often a new item is rejected because the food retailer does not carry the particular line to which the item belongs.

Logistics often plays an important role in this decision. The buyer must take into consideration order size and shipping arrangements. When a buyer orders a full truckload of an item, he receives a bigger discount and gets better service than when he orders less than truckload quantities. A full rail car usually qualifies him for a bigger discount than a truck load. Therefore, in order to receive the highest discount, buyers traditionally order merchandise from a food manufacturer in the largest quantities possible in line with buying practices that fit into the least cost strategy.

For example, when a buyer places an order with the Scott Paper Company he orders the quantities he needs of all Scott's products carried by the retailer in order to fill a truck or a rail car and thereby qualify for the greatest freight and purchase discount.

If a new item is not part of a line of products now carried by the company, it may present some logistics problems—in ordering and shipping—that make it impractical for the firm to carry that particular item without carrying the entire line of items (that is, the whole line of Del Monte, Stokley, Libby, and so on).

3. Seasonal or limited sales potential—the basic lack of sales potential or consumer demand is probably the major factor in rejecting a new item. A seasonal item with a short selling period and a limited use might not be accepted by the committee.

4. Inconsistent with present merchandising policies. Certain nonfood items may be rejected when they are not consistent with present merchandising policies, even when they have demonstrated sales potential. For example, motor oil might be sold by some food retailers and not by others in their nonfood departments, depending on their merchandising policies.

5. Poor sales presentation—the sales representative plays an important role in the acceptance or rejection of a new item. According to Franklin H. Graf, executive vice-president of the Nielsen Company, the greatest

deterrent to the sales presentation is the "unprofessional selling" approach used by many sales representatives. The two factors that damage the sales presentation to the greatest extent are lack of formal sales presentation and an apparent lack of enthusiasm for the product or the task of presenting it.[11]

Distribution to the Store

After the new item has been accepted by the food retailer or wholesaler and before it arrives at the distribution center, plans must be made for its distribution to the stores.

The initial distribution to the stores is made in one of two ways:

1. Predetermined order written by the grocery manager or the store manager.
2. Automatic distribution based on store size and volume.

By using the first method, the store personnel have the opportunity to order the quantity that they feel they can display and sell. If this method is used, store employees must be properly informed about the advertising program and special merchandising plan (if any), such as coupons, cents-off deals, and so on, that may be used during the introductory period.

With the second method, the quantity to be delivered to the store is determined by the merchandiser or the buyer and is usually allocated to the various stores on the basis of their sales volumes and store sizes. The merchandiser is usually aided by the manufacturer's rep in his decision on the quantity to ship to each store.

Stocking New Items at the Store

Once a new item reaches the retail store, the way it is displayed or presented will have a great bearing on its success. It is important to point out here that many new items that are introduced by food manufacturers, accepted by buying committees, and placed in retail stores are rejected by consumers. The management-consulting firm Booz, Allen & Hamilton estimates that approximately half the products that are market tested and reach the retail outlet become failures.[12]

One chain buyer put it this way: "It usually takes about a year for an average item to complete its life cycle. The manufacturer's introductory fanfare lasts anywhere from three to four months before all the sales results are measured and the item is dropped.[13] This makes it evident that there are not only new-item casualties at the buying-committee stage, but also

[11]"Nielsen Research Underscores Power of New Items," p. 71.

[12]*Management of New Products* (New York: Booz, Allen & Hamilton, 1961), p.11.

[13]*1969 Supermarkets Sales Manual* (New York: Chain Store Age, July 1969), p. 43.

at the retail store. However, once the store is is committed to a new item, the investment in inventory and shelf space demands that proper treatment be given the item at the retail level.

Today, there are three principal methods of displaying new items in the supermarket:

1. Shelf display (normal shelf space)
2. Special floor display
3. Display in a special "new item" section

Each method is workable, but is predicated, to some extent, on the type of item being introduced and the promotional program behind the introduction.

Factors Affecting the Method of Display

There are a number of factors that affect the presentation and display of a new product at the store; these can be grouped under two basic classifications.

1. The *characteristics* of the new item.
2. The *marketing program* behind the new-product introduction.

The characteristics of the new item affect the method of display for the introductory period. If the new item is an addition to a present line, or a line-extension item, it would probably be displayed in the normal shelf position for that line. If the product is new in that it does not duplicate a present item, it would justify space in a floor display or a special display in a new-item section.

The *perishability* of the product may also dictate its method of display. Certain items, frozen foods for example, must be displayed in refrigerated cases. There are also limitations to how pies and cakes can be displayed due to their high perishability.

The *size and shape* of the item is often the key factor to where it is displayed. When a new item is especially bulky, such as a 25- or 50-pound bag of dog food, it must, of necessity, be given a special floor display. Small items, however, such as spices and vanilla extract, do not lend themselves to large floor displays.

The marketing program for the new item will also affect the type of display that will be required in several ways.

Strong *advertising and coupon* support from a food manufacturer would require a floor display so that a sufficient quantity of the new item would be available when consumers redeemed their coupons.

Supermarket operators may not want to change their shelf facings and arrangements if a new item is only to be *test marketed* in their stores for a short period of time. On the other hand, the test market program may require that the item be sold only from the normal shelf space. Therefore, the specific requirement of the marketing program may dictate the method of display for the new item.

The method of display for each new item should be analyzed in view of the foregoing merchandising principles. The display should fit the needs of the new-product merchandising program and be functional for the product itself. If these goals are met, the retailer will have done his part in helping to make the new item a success in the market. The success of new products in turn adds to the retailer's success by contributing greater sales and profits —a benefit for the manufacturer and retailer alike, as well as for the consumer who benefits from a variety of new and exciting products.

BUYING ALLOWANCES

When the grocery buyer decides how much of an item to purchase, the decision may be influenced by some type of buying or promotional allowance. A manufacturer institutes a buying or promotional allowance to encourage a grocery buyer or the customer to purchase more of the manufacturer's product. Allowances fall into five basic categories: (1) quantity discounts; (2) special purchase allowances; (3) manufacturer's promotions to consumers; (4) manufacturer's promotions to retailers; and (5) cooperative advertising allowances. In this section, we will examine each type of allowance to see what effect it might have on the buyer's decision regarding how much to purchase.

Quantity Discounts

Quantity discounts provide an incentive for the buyer by reducing the unit price for large-quantity purchases. Figure 2-9 shows a typical quantity discount schedule for a grocery product.

This schedule is designed to encourage the buyer to purchase a fairly large minimum quantity. It provides additional price discounts at higher quantities (above 500 units). The minimum price for a case of 24 two-ounce boxes of Dream Whip Dessert Topping Mix is $5.54. If the buyer purchases 3,500 pounds, this price per case drops to $5.51. There is an additional savings of three cents per case if the buyer purchases in quantities of 40,000 pounds or more. In this quantity, any combination of two-ounce, four-ounce, and eight-ounce boxes that exceeds in total 40,000 pounds would qualify the purchaser for a price of $5.48 per case (see *Bracket 1* in Figure 2-9.).

Quantity discounts are often directly related to cost savings that the manufacturer can realize by handling and shipping merchandise in full pallets, full truckloads, or full carloads. By passing these cost savings along to the purchaser, the manufacturer helps improve the efficiency of the entire marketing system. The retailer benefits by lower wholesale costs. The lower unit price that results when a buyer purchases in carload lots rather than less-than-carload lots (LCL) is primarily the result of savings in freight

THIS IS NOT AN OFFER TO SELL

PAGE 8 (SEE BELOW)

JELL-O DIVISION
GENERAL FOODS CORPORATION

DREAM WHIP
DESSERT TOPPING MIX

Price List As Of August 7, 1972

A) Denotes change since last issue dated February 7, 1972

ALL PROVISIONS OF THIS PRICE LIST, INCLUDING PRICES, ARE SUBJECT TO CHANGE WITHOUT NOTICE

PRODUCT	PRODUCT CODE	CASE CONTENTS	GROSS SHIP'G WEIGHT LBS.	CUBIC FOOT DISPL.	NO. OF CASES PER PALLET	BRACKET 1 40,000 LBS. AND OVER		BRACKET 2 22,000 LBS. TO 39,999 LBS.		BRACKET 3 3,500 LBS. TO 21,999 LBS.		BRACKET 4 BASE PRICE MINIMUM 500 LBS.	
						CASE	PKG.	CASE	PKG.	CASE	PKG.	CASE	PKG.
DREAM WHIP DESSERT TOPPING MIX	2 5910	24-2 OZ. PKGS.	4.40	.35	136	$ 5.48	A) $.2283	$ 5.51	A) $.2296	$ 5.51	A) $.2296	$ 5.54	A) $.2308
	2 5920	24-4 OZ. PKGS.	8.10	.66	60	9.75	A) .4063	9.81	A) .4088	9.81	A) .4088	9.87	A) .4113
	2 5950	* 12-8 OZ. PKGS.	8.20	.53	85	8.91	A) .7425	8.97	A) .7475	8.97	A) .7475	9.03	A) .7525

DISTRICTS: ALL DISTRICTS.

* *8 OZ. DREAM WHIP NOT AVAILABLE FOR SALE IN NEW YORK.*

A) *REVISED DUE TO PRICE ADVANCE.*

FIGURE 2-9

89

costs. Lower freight costs are often an important factor in the buyer's decision regarding how much to buy. A buyer who knows that 900 cases from a particular vendor are all he needs at the present time may increase his order to 1,200 cases because it represents a lower freight cost per unit than the 900-case shipment. This same buyer may decide to increase the order from 900 to 1,200 cases more on the basis of convenience than on the economics of freight costs. If he knows that he will have to share a car with other customers when he orders only 900 cases and he knows that other deliveries cause him delays in receiving his shipment, he may prefer the convenience of purchasing the additional merchandise over the disadvantage of holding or warehousing the excess stock. A buyer will seldom purchase additional merchandise on the basis of the quantity discount alone. Instead, he strives to balance his purchase against the value of his investment.

Another form of quantity discount that also relates to a freight savings involves pooling shipments in one section of the country for delivery to another section. The pooling of shipments, also known as "pool cars," is a common practice of East Coast retailers and wholesalers who buy fruits and vegetables from West Coast canners and frozen-food packers. The buyer will arrange for a car to start in one section of California and move across or down the state adding additional merchandise at each food plant until the car is filled. The railroad then ships a full car of product to the buyer's warehouse for distribution to the stores. The pool car acts as a quantity discount on each of the products shipped because the freight rate on each product is reduced.

Special Purchase Allowances

As fruits and vegetables come into season, certain processors provide a special buying allowance in order to (1) clean out old inventory from the previous season, or (2) move through as much new pack as possible while their plants are in full production during the peak of the season. This procedure allows certain efficiencies and economics in the plant operation. It enables the processor to fill orders directly off the processing line and avoid warehousing the merchandise until later in the season when it may be ordered. This type of special purchase allowance encourages the retailer to do the warehousing of the product because the retailer has the opportunity to own the product at a reduced price. Some buyers shy away from purchasing large quantities of merchandise at so-called special new-pack prices because the special price often becomes the regular new-pack price and there is in reality no special purchase allowance.

Campbell, for example, gives a special purchase allowance on its tomato soup at the peak of its tomato season. In general, this type of allowance is smaller than other types and therefore less likely to influence the retail price of the product and the buyer's purchasing activities than are other types of buying allowances. Buyers often use this type of allowance to increase gross margins rather than to lower retail prices.

Manufacturer's Promotions to Consumers

Manufacturers direct their promotional activities toward two primary audiences—the ultimate consumer of the product and the wholesale and retail trade that must stock and sell the product to the ultimate consumer.

The promotional activities directed to the ultimate consumer are designed to attract the customer to a particular product by offering a special incentive to buy that product.

Premium Pack

An incentive that is commonly used by manufacturers is known as the premium pack. This type of promotion offers two or more of the same product banded together at a special price, or a special related premium attached to or enclosed in the product that the manufacturer is promoting. For example, two tubes of toothpaste might be offered for the price of one or at a price lower than the cost of two tubes; or, a toothbrush might be attached to a tube of toothpaste, or a toy enclosed in a box of ready-to-eat cereal.

Premium packs are usually offered for very short periods of time. The goal of the premium pack that offers two or more items of the same product is to encourage the consumer to "stock up." This promotion has the effect of taking the customer out of the market for competing brands of the same product. The goal of the premium pack that attaches a different item to the product being promoted is to get new customers to sample the manufacturer's product; in this case, the manufacturer is content with a single sale to many new customers.

Near Pack

A manufacturer's promotion that offers a completely different product free with one purchase of the product he is promoting is known as a near pack. For example, a free dish might be offered with each purchase of a new laundry detergent. In this case, the retailer is expected to build a display of both products, placing the display of dishes next to the display of detergent. The customer would then be able to pick up a dish when he purchased a package of the detergent at the regular price.

Cents-off Label

In recent years, one of the most frequently used manufacturer promotions to consumers has been the cents-off label. In order to offer this type of promotion, the manufacturer reduces the invoice price to the retailer by at least the amount of reduction offered on the label of the product. The product is usually imprinted with something to the effect of "three cents off regular price." In some cases, the invoice from the manufacturer to the retailer is reduced by an amount greater than the reduction listed on the label of the product because the manufacturer wants to encourage the retailer to lower the price more than the cents-off label indicates. The manufacturer is, in effect, encouraging the retailer to use the product as a leader (see Chapter 3) or as a feature item in his weekly newspaper advertisement.

Retailers have never been fond of this type of promotion because they feel that it creates many more problems than benefits. They cite the fact that they must carry duplicate inventory in their warehouses—the cents-off label stock and the regular stock for the same item. Stores, too, must carry this double inventory because once the cents-off merchandise is placed on the shelf customers will not purchase the regular stock at the higher price. This duplicate inventory creates problems for the retailer and wholesaler throughout the system—from the accounting department, which must provide two item numbers and two warehouse slots, to the retail store, which must set aside the regular merchandise until the special merchandise is sold. Retailers also claim that this type of promotion adds to the possibility of error in posting the unit price at the retail store.

Customers, however, generally like this type of promotion because it does represent an actual cash savings for them. However, the recent push toward unit pricing may discourage the use of cents-off promotions. Not only does the cents-off label create additional work at both headquarters and the store in correctly pricing and identifying the merchandise under unit-pricing conditions but it creates confusion for customers making weekly pricing comparisons. These problems may eventually eliminate the cents-off promotion as an effective sales device.

Coupons

Manufacturers use coupons as a means of reducing the price to the customer on a specific product. Coupons are used primarily to introduce a product to new users as opposed to encouraging present customers to stock up or use more of the product. In fact, coupons generally prevent consumers from purchasing more than one item at the special price—both retailers and manufacturers often impose limits on coupon use by stating on the coupon "only one per customer." The fact that it is inconvenient to obtain more than one coupon has a limiting effect on their use.

Coupons, classified by method of distribution, can be divided into five types:

1. *Coupons inside package.* Coupons packed inside a retail package are intended to encourage the customer to buy another unit of the same product or to purchase a related product. These coupons offer a savings on a product that the customer will buy in the future. From the retailer's viewpoint, this type of coupon has little or no promotional effect. Also, it may cause confusion at the checkstand by looking like a cents-off package.

2. *Coupons outside the package.* This approach is used less frequently than the coupon inside the package because although it may have a greater promotional impact, it also creates greater problems at the point of sale. Redeemable coupons that are part of the label or package and are visible to shoppers encourage the defacing of the product. Many customers will

attempt to remove the coupon in order to redeem it during their shopping tour. This in itself is no problem if the person removing the coupon is buying the product, but often a shopper who has no intention of purchasing the product removes the coupon, which exposes the product and reduces its shelf life or quality, or renders it completely unsalable.

3. *Coupons that are mailed to consumers.* Manufacturers use this method primarily when introducing a new product. The value of the coupon is usually quite high, which encourages new users to try the product. Retailers prefer this method of introducing a new product over the method of sending a free sample of the product directly to the household because the customer must come to the store to redeem the coupon. This means a sale for the store when the customer redeems the coupon for the product as well as another method of introducing customers to the store.

4. *Coupons that appear in manufacturer's ads.* Food manufacturers periodically include coupons redeemable on specific products in their news-paper and magazine advertisements. These coupons are valid for specific periods of time. This method is another means of introducing nonusers to a product or introducing a new product to the public at large.

5. *Coupons that appear in retailer ads.* Many food manufacturers prefer to have their coupons appear in the retailer's ads rather than in their own because it gives the manufacturer a much broader exposure to customers at a smaller advertising cost. Coupon redemption is much higher when the retailer includes the coupon in his ad because a retailer ad gives a specific location—the retailer's store or chain of stores—where the consumer can redeem the coupon, as opposed to a manufacturer's ad, which tells only that the coupon is being offered. Although higher redemption means higher costs to the manufacturer, he knows that his product will be given a stronger promotional push at the retail level, and he does not have to pay for the ad space. Most retailers prefer to control the coupon in their own ad because this provides them with a greater degree of flexibility in advertising and promoting the product. Retailers, of course, often include their own coupons in their weekly newspaper ads.

Who Pays for the Coupon. When a food manufacturer uses a coupon through any of these methods, the entire cost of the coupon is absorbed by the manufacturer. Manufacturers also pay the retailer a fee of 3 cents a coupon to cover the cost of collecting, sorting, and returning the coupon to the manufacturer. Coupons have become such a big business that many retailers turn over the job of sorting and returning coupons to an outside agency.

Several agencies provide this service, most notably the A.C. Nielsen Company. The redemption agent assumes responsibility for sorting all the store coupons from a given retailer, distributing them to each manufacturer, and collecting the amount due from the manufacturer. They charge the retailer a percentage of the redemption fee for this service. The retailer, however, eliminates all the work involved with this function and receives a single check from the redemption agent as soon as the coupons have been processed. Although most retailers agree the collection fee provided by the manufacturer to the retailer to collect and handle coupons is satisfactory, they do not prefer coupons as a method of promoting a manufacturer's product.

In a study of 229 companies, the Food Trade Marketing Council of *Family Circle* magazine found that 37 percent of the firms contacted ranked manufacturers' coupons as the least popular of all types of manufacturers' deals. In particular, they disapproved of "special label merchandise with coupon to be returned directly to the manufacturer for cash or premium." Of all types of manufacturers' promotions to consumers, this was the one that was least preferred.[14]

Consumers appear to approve of this type of merchandising activity on the part of the manufacturers. In a recent survey conducted by the A. C. Nielsen Company, it was revealed that 58 percent of all households found coupons helpful and useful in their food shopping experience.[15] In this nationwide survey, consumers were asked to indicate the reason why they used coupons. Nearly all the respondents (99 percent) said they used coupons "to save money." Eighty-six percent of those using coupons said they did so to "try a new product." Therefore, manufacturers who use coupons to support a new-product introduction are making effective use of this promotional technique—at least among the 58 percent that use coupons.

Two out of three persons who use coupons are using more at the present time than they did a year ago.

Even though manufacturers' coupons are not popular with food retailers, they are popular with consumers. Manufacturers, therefore, will continue to make use of this form of promotional activity that reaches a large number of consumers in an inexpensive and effective manner.

Manufacturer's Promotions to Retailers

When a manufacturer offers a promotion to the retailer, he gives the retailer the responsibility for promoting the item to the ultimate consumer. A manufacturer knows that any type of promotional activity will cost money. The cost of consumer promotions may be the redemption of coupons or the lower profit obtained from a cents-off label item.

Promotions aimed at retailers also have a cost. These costs vary from one type of promotion to another, but the manufacturer eventually gets a return on these costs because retailer promotions are designed to give the retailer an incentive to promote the manufacturer's product.

Manufacturer promotions to retailers fall into two basic categories: (1)

[14]John J. Sheehan, *Marketing Practices and Preferences in the Food Industry,* (New York: Family Circle Magazine), Chart 14, p. 36.

[15]Frank Soltan, "Nielsen Study Finds Coupons Liked by 58 percent of Households," *Supermarket News,* February 12, 1973, p. 6.

free goods; and (2) cash allowances. In order to qualify for these allowances, the retailer must perform some type of advertising or promotional activity, so the incentive is very favorable to the manufacturer. No promotional activity is required of the retailer for manufacturer promotions to the consumer. The type of promotional activity required for each type of retailer promotion varies greatly from one manufacturer to another.

Free Goods

Free goods to the retailer may be in the form of additional merchandise at no cost when the retailer purchases a certain amount of the same merchandise, such as one free with five or one free with ten, and so on. In other words, if the retailer purchases five cases of the product involved in the promotion, he will be given one case at no extra charge. This in effect gives the retailer a lower unit cost, which enables him to sell the merchandise at a lower retail price to his customers.

Another form that free goods take is that of premiums that are offered with the purchase of the manufacturer's products. These premiums may be television sets, stereos, or other merchandise of this nature. Premiums to the retailers are usually used as prizes or give-aways at new-store openings and special store sales.

The need to promote a new item is usually greater than the need to promote existing items. Therefore, the allowance offered, in this case free goods, is also greater.

Cash Allowances

A retailer may receive a cash allowance for performing advertising or promotional activities for a given product. The performance of these activities is a legal prerequisite to receiving the allowance. An example of a cash allowance agreement is shown in Figure 2-10, and it shows not only the allowance but also the activities required of the retailer to receive it. Because of the requisites involved, cash allowance agreements are often called merchandise performance agreements.

Cash allowances are paid to the retailer in one of two ways: as a reduction in the invoice or by the "bill back" method. Retailers generally prefer that the cash allowance be deducted from the original invoice because it reduces the internal accounting operation of the firm. The bill-back approach requires that records of the amount of merchandise eligible for an allowance be kept, an invoice or statement must then be sent to the manufacturer for the allowance, and then the retailer must establish a follow-up procedure to insure the collection of the allowance.

Cash allowances are generally the most popular type of manufacturer promotion to retailers. In a study conducted by the Food Trade Marketing Council of *Family Circle* magazine, 43 percent of the respondents to the survey indicated that they preferred this type of promotion over all others.[16]

---

[16]*Marketing Practices and Preferences in the Food Industry,* Chart 13, p. 34.

Boston Region
Louisville Region   MERCHANDISING PERFORMANCE AGREEMENT
Detroit Region
NY-2, 3
AT-2
CH-1, 2(Except Fargo)
KC-1, 2(Except
        Des Moines)

Items-Amounts Per Case: Check (√) items to be featured:

☐	24/1F	Dole Fancy Sliced P/A Juice Pack	.35 per case
	48/1F	Dole Fancy Sliced P/A Juice Pack	.70 per case
☐	24/1F	Dole Fancy P/A Chunks Juice Pack	.35 per case
	48/1F	Dole Fancy P/A Chunks Juice Pack	.70 per case
☐	24/1F	Dole Fancy Crushed P/A Juice Pack	.35 per case
	48/1F	Dole Fancy Crushed P/A Juice Pack	.70 per case

Effective Date: September 20 on orders through November 5 for shipment
                         from mainland warehouses by November 12, 1971.

Performance Alternatives: Check one (√)

☐   Authorization to stores for the purchase of these items.

☐   Display, other than shelf position, in a majority of stores. Copy of the bulletin
    sent to participating stores, requiring display performance, must be attached to
    the performance certification.

Performance Period: Through November 26, 1971.

Payment Options: Check one (√)

☐   a. Automatic payment off-invoice

☐   b. Bill-back

Performance Certification:
    Wholesalers and co-ops must certify that:
        (1) All my customers have been notified of the availability of Dole's promotion
             program and are being treated equally.

        (2) Allowances have been passed on to our customers who have expended these
             allowances solely for the purpose for which they were given.

    Wholesalers and co-ops may disregard 1 and 2 for their customers and chains whom they
    represent by an agency agreement.

Proof of Performance:
    Proof of performance must be attached to the canary copy of the signed performance
    agreement, and yellow payable copy of promotion monies available, Form DP-6703A,
    and returned to Dole no later than December 17, 1971.

I certify performance will be accomplished as required by this agreement. In the event
the allowances have been paid by off-invoice option and are not earned because of
non-performance, I agree to reimburse Dole for the amount of allowances received but
not earned.

Date   Customer's Name

Broker Name

Signature of Dole Representative   Signature of Customer

Distribution: 1. White   - If off-invoice, mail to Dole Co., San Jose, Calif., Sales
                              Administration, prior to effective date of program.
              2. Canary   - Dole Co., San Jose, Calif., Sales Administration
              3. Pink   - Buyer's Copy
              4. Goldenrod - Broker's Copy

FIGURE 2-10

Count and Recount. Count and recount is not a special type of allowance—rather, it is the procedure commonly used to determine the cash allowance due the retailer. As the name implies, the retailer's or wholesaler's warehouse inventory is counted before the promotion period begins and then recounted at the conclusion of the period. The difference between the beginning and ending inventory is added to the total purchases during the promotional period (or the ending inventory is subtracted from the total inventory for the period) to determine the number of units on which the cash allowance will be paid. This type of procedure provides a protection for the retailer in that it guarantees that he will be compensated for all the merchandise distributed to the stores during the promotion. There is also protection for the manufacturer; if the retailer or wholesaler increases warehouse stock during the promotion and does not move the merchandise through the stores to the consumer, the manufacturer is not committed to provide a cash allowance for the unused stock.

For example, let us assume that a manufacturer of chocolate cake mix is offering a 50 cents per case allowance on all merchandise purchased between June 1 and June 30. The manufacturer's sales representative takes a physical inventory of the retailer's warehouse stock just prior to June 1 and finds that there are 110 cases of the mix in stock. During the period between June 1 and June 30, the retailing firm purchases 850 cases of chocolate cake mix. At the conclusion of the special buying period, the sales representative again takes inventory. At this time, the count comes out to 70 cases. To determine the total cash allowance due the retailing firm, ending inventory is subtracted from beginning inventory (see Figure 2-11). The difference between beginning and ending inventory is 40 cases. This amount is added to the 850 cases that were ordered during the allowance period, giving a total of 890 cases distributed to the retail stores. The cash allowance is then calculated by multiplying the 50 cents per case times the total number of cases distributed to the stores (890), resulting in a total cash allowance payable to the retailer of $445.00. This is then handled as a bill back, and the retail firm would therefore submit a statement or invoice to the manufacturer for this amount.

Beginning inventory	110 cases
Ending inventory	− 70
Difference	40
Amount ordered	+ 850
Total distributed	890 cases
Cash allowance	× .50
	$445.00

FIGURE 2-11 Figuring cash allowance by count and recount method.

Cooperative Advertising Allowances

In theory, a cooperative advertising agreement between a food manufacturer and a food wholesaler or retailer is mutually beneficial, that is, it provides benefits to both parties concerned. In reality, the agreements are seldom beneficial to either party involved.

These agreements, which are primarily used by soap companies and cookie companies, require the wholesaler or retailer to advertise the manufacturer's product periodically. The extent of the advertising required may vary greatly from one advertising agreement to another. It may be as frequent as once a week or as infrequent as once a year. A typical co-op agreement might require that the retailer "devote a minimum of one column inch per quarter" to the manufacturer's product in the firm's regular retail ad. A specified size of ad is usually included in the agreement, such as one column inch or two column inches.[17] If the retailer or wholesaler complies with these advertising requirements, the firm becomes eligible for a cash payment from the manufacturer.

Payment is made on one of three bases: (1) a fixed amount is paid to the retailer on each case of merchandise purchased during the specified period. (2) A percentage of total purchases during the specified period is repaid; this procedure is used by firms who carry a variety of products in their line that may have different unit prices, such as a cookie or cracker company. These firms might specify a 3 percent discount on the total dollar figure of merchandise purchased during the specified time period. (3) Payment for space may be quoted at national line rates. This means that the manufacturer agrees to pay the retailer the equivalent of rates charged by national magazines for each one column inch of advertising. The retailer buys space in his local newspaper at rates far below national line rates. The difference between national line rates and local rates therefore represents income to the retailer.

The manufacturer does, of course, require proof of performance, such as copy of the ad in which the manufacturer's product appeared. The manufacturer pays the retailer the amount indicated by their agreement by a bill-back method. Because these agreements are continuous in nature, the bill-back procedure becomes automatic. The advertising rebate becomes a permanent discount to the retailer, or at least as permanent as the agreement.

The inclusion of manufacturer's products in a retailer's weekly ad as specified under co-op agreements has become more automatic than promotional. In most companies, these agreements are turned over to the director of advertising, and it becomes his job to see that a column inch ad appears for each product covered in the agreement whenever it is scheduled. Many firms do not include these ads with their regular weekly ads but rather

---

[17]One column inch is the width of one newspaper column and one inch long. Two column inches can run either the width of one newspaper column and two inches long or the width of two columns and one inch long.

insert a special ad as often as necessary in the major newspaper in their area to comply with the agreement. Merchandise listed in this manner is usually presented at regular retail prices. No special effort is made at store level to display or sell more than the normal weekly movement of the product. In fact, store managers are seldom notified of the items to be included.

Retail merchandising and advertising people accept the fact that co-op advertising does little to increase their sales, but they are willing to devote newspaper space to this nonproductive purpose to obtain the added income for their firms that the agreements afford. Manufacturers also recognize the weakness of co-op advertising, but many keep using the method as a means of maintaining good trade relations rather than as a means of increasing sales. Co-op advertising has apparently been kept alive because manufacturers believe that retailers like the income it produces and that a discontinuance of the practice may therefore damage good will and lose customers.

Other Savings Afforded to Retailers

There are two other major savings that food buyers can take advantage of: the back haul and cash discounts. These are not buying allowances in the same sense as the other allowances discussed in this chapter. They are not directly related to a particular product or group of products, and they are not promotional in nature. However, they are similar in that back hauls and cash discounts are incentives to change or modify buying behavior in order to save money.

Back Hauls

Back hauls provide the retailing or wholesaling firm with an opportunity to reduce freight costs. When a truck from a food distribution center delivers its merchandise to the retail store, it can make a back haul by stopping to pick up an order of merchandise at a supplier's warehouse or plant and then delivering the merchandise back to the distribution center. This saves the supplier from delivering the merchandise himself, so the back haul generates savings and therefore income for the food retailer or wholesaler in two ways: (1) If the merchandise is billed FOB plant, the supplier will pay the retailer the commercial rates for hauling the merchandise. It is a generally accepted fact that commercial rates are higher than the actual cost of picking up this merchandise and returning it to the distribution center. (2) If the merchandise is billed FOB destination, the supplier reduces the invoice by an amount equal to the commercial rate for delivering the merchandise to the retailer's warehouse from the plant; in other words, the freight charge has already been deducted from the price of the merchandise. Both methods represent a freight savings for the retailer or wholesaler.

Cash Discounts

Cash discounts are available from most manufacturing firms as an incentive to the retailer to pay for the merchandise promptly. Cash discounts usually amount to 2 percent of the total invoice price and are available only if the merchandise is paid for within a specified time period—usually ten days. This 2 percent can provide important additional income to the retailing and wholesaling firm.

It is important to note that cash discounts do not contribute to the gross profit of the firm but are considered as "other income" (see Chapter 3). Also, the cash-discount savings is initiated by the retailer, in that the accounting department must act to realize this savings. The back haul must also be initiated by the retailer, in that he must arrange to pick up the merchandise. So, although both savings can be great, the retailer must show more initiative to realize them than he must to realize a savings through regular buying allowances.

Summary

All buying allowances do not affect gross margins even though they afford the retailer a savings. Gross margins are affected only by quantity discounts, special purchase allowances, and manufacturers' promotions to retailers. In each of these categories, the actual price of the merchandise to the retailer or wholesaler is reduced. A lower purchase price does afford an opportunity for greater gross margins, but the retailer often lowers the retail price by more than the amount of the purchase allowance in order to feature the product in a weekly ad. Therefore, he actually realizes a lower gross margin.

Manufacturers' promotions to consumers do not contribute to the retailer's gross margin even though the retail price of the product may be reduced. Cooperative advertising allowances also do not affect the gross margins on most products. The accounting structure of most retail firms credits income from cooperative advertising allowances to the advertising department and not to the buying or merchandising department, and therefore not to the product itself. This would be categorized as other income and not as a reduction in the purchase price. Accounting systems do vary, however, and some firms take the cooperative advertising allowance into consideration when pricing their products. Most wholesalers pass this advertising allowance along to the retailers they service, so in this case the co-op allowance would be a source of revenue to the retailer and could lower the purchase price of the product.

3

Pricing I

INTRODUCTION

Pricing is probably the most important decision that the food retailer has to make because there is a critical relationship among prices, sales, and net profit. If prices are too low, the retailer cannot cover his expenses despite high sales volume, and he will incur a net loss. If prices are too high, sales will decline to the point at which expenses cannot be covered, and a net loss will occur. Thus, the food retailer must be careful in pricing merchandise if he is to realize a net profit adequate to achieve the desired return on investment.

In theory, in order to maximize his profit the retailer would price his merchandise so that the increase in total cost that results from selling an additional unit equals the increase in total sales or revenue resulting from the sale of that additional unit. As long as additional revenue exceeds additional costs, it would pay to sell more merchandise because it would continue to contribute to net profit.

However, in practice, is is virtually impossible that a food retailer know what his marginal costs are because he is handling thousands of products and it is difficult to identify the cost of selling an individual product, especially when many of the costs in food retailing are common to all the products. In addition, price theory assumes that the retailer has perfect knowledge of the demand for his products—that he knows the exact quantity that he can sell at any given price. These and other limitations severely limit the use of price theory in explaining price behavior in food retailing.

Pricing in food retailing is far from a science, and the exact outcome of any particular pricing policy is not predictable. One author stated the problem of retail food pricing this way:

> The establishment of supermarket pricing policies and techniques remains more an art than a science. The complicated and intricate number of variables and their interactions are all but too much for the supermarket operator to control.

> Imperfections in the market mechanism, plus the imperfections in the price setter's own knowledge, forces him to rely heavily on his experience and merchandising skill, plus his intuitive knowledge of the pricing situation.[1]

In spite of the unscientific or inexact nature of retail food store pricing, there are some general rules and considerations that seem to inflence pricing objectives, methods, and policies.

PRICING FUNDAMENTALS

In order to understand the pricing objectives, methods, and policies used by food retailers, it is first necessary to understand the relationship among sales, gross margin, expenses, and net profit in the operation of the retail food store.

The Profit and Loss Statement

The profit and loss or income statement is a basic financial tool used to forecast and evaluate operating results in the retail food firm. It is used to project or forecast the desired amount of net profit and also to determine what results have actually been obtained at the end of an operating period. Profit and loss statements are usually prepared for one year, but may also be prepared for shorter periods of time, such as monthly or quarterly.

The basic profit and loss (P-L) statement includes sales, cost of goods sold, gross margin, operating expenses, and operating net profit in terms of dollars and percentage of sales (Table 3-1).

TABLE 3-1   Basic Elements of the Retail Food Store Profit and Loss Statement

	Dollars	Percentage of Sales
Sales	1,000,000	100
Cost of goods sold	800,000	80
Gross margin	200,000	20
Operating expenses [a]	180,000	18
Operating net profit	20,000	2

[a] Expenses and costs will be used synonymously in this text.

Sales represent the net volume of business on which a profit (or loss) is earned during the period of time covered. It is a key figure because it is needed to calculate the rest of the statement.

The *cost of goods sold* represents the amount paid by the retailer for the merchandise that was sold during the period. The cost of goods sold is determined by adding the value of the inventory at the beginning of the

---

[1]Rom J. Markin, *The Supermarket,* Economic and Business Studies Bulletin No. 36, Washington State University Press, January 1963, p. 83.

period to the purchases during the period, and subtracting the value of the inventory at the end of the period.

Cost of goods sold = Beginning inventory (at cost) + Purchases (at cost)
    − Ending inventory (at cost)

Based on the figures in Table 3-1, the cost of goods sold is determined as follows:

Beginning inventory	$700,000
Purchases	+ 1,100,000
Total	$1,800,000
Ending inventory	− 1,000,000
Cost of goods sold =	$ 800,000

If the beginning and ending inventories are taken at retail value, they must be converted to cost value in order to accurately determine cost of goods sold for the entire store and individual departments. This can be done by using the average cost-of-goods-sold percentage to adjust the retail value of inventory. The cost-of-goods-sold percentage is the difference between sales (100 percent) and the gross-margin percentage.

Based upon previous P-L statements, the gross-margin percentage for the store and departments can be determined. This percentage subtracted from 100 percent yields the cost-of-goods-sold percentage because cost of goods sold plus gross margin equals sales. For example, if the gross margin in a food store has been averaging 20 percent, the cost-of-goods-sold percentage would be 80 percent (100% - 20% = 80%). In other words, 80 percent or 80 cents of each sales dollar is required to pay for merchandise. Thus, if the inventories are taken at retail value, 80 percent of the inventory at retail value would equal the value of inventory at cost.

In calculating the cost of goods sold, let us suppose that the beginning and ending inventories were taken at retail instead of cost value.

Beginning inventory	=	$875,000 (at retail)
Purchases	=	$1,100,000 (at cost)
Ending inventory	=	$1,250,000 (at retail)

To convert the retail values to cost values, we multiply by the cost-of-goods-sold percentage (80 percent).

Beginning inventory at cost = Beginning inventory at retail × 80%
    = $875,000 × .80
    = $700,000

Ending inventory at cost = Ending inventory at retail × 80%
    = $1,250,000 × .80
    = $1,000,000

Now the cost of goods sold can be calculated accurately.

Dollar *gross margin* is derived by subtracting the cost of goods sold from sales. It is a key figure because it shows the amount of money remaining after the merchandise sold has been paid for, and therefore it indicates how much is available to cover all operating expenses and net profit. Gross margin is important as a control over pricing and net profit, and the pricing policy must be geared to achieve a gross margin that is adequate to cover both operating expenses and the desired net profit.

Operating expenses include all those classifiable costs directly related to the food retailing activity. These are:

Salaries

Wages

Laundry and supplies

Depreciation on equipment

Utilities (heat, light, power, water, and telephone)

Repairs and maintenance

Rent

Advertising and promotion

Taxes and insurance

Accounting and legal

Interest

Miscellaneous (such items as donations, service fees, window washing, snow removal, shopping service, security, and other expenses not included in the other categories)

A few of these expenses can be directly attributed to the operation of individual departments within the food store, and these are sometimes referred to as direct expenses. These include the department manager's salary; department personnel wages; supplies; and depreciation, repairs, and maintenance of equipment utilized in the department. It is possible to allocate accurately certain other expenses to individual departments when adequate records exist. For example, most electrical power expenses can often be allocated to departments based on the power usage by equipment within the departments. Likewise, the major portion of the depreciation expense can be allocated to the individual departments based upon the use of the equipment being depreciated.[2] In both cases, however, there will be some part of the power and depreciation expense that cannot be allocated to any one department, but is common to all departments—for example, the power and depreciation associated with the operation of checkout equipment. These expenses that are common to the entire food store operation and cannot be allocated directly to the operation of individual departments with-

---

[2]*Depreciation* refers to that portion of the original cost of a fixed asset charged against current sales.

out arbitrary judgments are sometimes referred to as indirect expenses. These common expenses include the store manager's salary; store occupancy; advertising and promotion; taxes and insurance; accounting and legal; miscellaneous expenses; wages of personnel who are not assigned to a specific department, such as front-office, checkout, and carryout personnel; and as we have already pointed out, most utilities and depreciation.

Operating net profit is the difference between gross margin and operating expenses. It is the amount of profit earned from the operation of the retail food business after all operating expenses have been paid.

In addition to operating net profit, there are usually other sources of income available to the food retailing firm that, when added to operating net profit, make up total net profit, or earnings. Two common sources of other income are: (1) cash discounts for prompt payment of bills and (2) earnings from real estate owned by the firm. Neither of these sources of income is directly related to the operation of the retail food store, and they are not included in operating net profit.

Total earnings or net profit is the amount available to the owners of the business, after paying federal, state, and local income taxes, that may be distributed to the owners or may be reinvested. Total net profit compensates the owners of the business for risk and constitutes a return on capital invested in the business.

Gross Margin and Markup

Gross margin, as mentioned previously, is an important consideration when pricing to achieve the desired amount of operating profit. It is very important to understand gross margin thoroughly in order to understand and practice profitable pricing in food retailing.

Gross margin can be expressed in dollars or in percentage of sales.

$ Gross margin = Sales in $ - Cost of goods sold in $

$$\% \text{ Gross margin} = \frac{\text{Sales in \$ - Cost of goods sold in \$}}{\text{Sales in \$}} \times 100$$

For example, let's calculate the dollar and percentage gross margin for Big Bag Supermarket for one month based on the following information:

Sales	$200,000
Beginning inventory (at cost)	$180,000
Purchases (at cost)	$210,000
Ending inventory (at cost)	$230,000

First of all, we must determine the cost of goods sold during the month:

Beginning inventory + purchases − ending inventory = cost of goods sold
$180,000 + $210,000 − $230,000 = $160,000

Then, we can calculate the gross margin in dollars:

$$\begin{aligned} \text{\$ Gross margin} &= \text{Sales - Cost of goods sold} \\ &= \$200,000 - \$160,000 \\ &= \$40,000 \end{aligned}$$

Next, we can calculate the gross-margin percentage:

$$\begin{aligned} \text{\% Gross margin} &= \frac{\text{Sales} - \text{Cost of goods sold}}{\text{Sales}} \times 100 \\ &= \frac{\$200,000 - \$160,000}{\$200,000} \times 100 \\ &= \frac{\$40,000}{\$200,000} \times 100 \\ &= 20\% \end{aligned}$$

We know that during the month we realized a gross margin of $40,000 or 20 percent, based on a sales volume of $200,000. In other words, after the merchandise was paid for, we had left $40,000 or 20 cents from *each* dollar of sales from which to pay all operating expenses. The difference between gross margin and operating expenses equals operating net profit. If gross margin is inadequate to cover all operating expenses, a net loss will result.

Gross margin always indicates the amount or percentage of the selling price that remains after the cost of the merchandise sold has been deducted. Gross margin can be calculated for total store sales, departmental sales, or the sales of an individual item, using the method described above. Figure 3-1 shows that each sales dollar is divided between cost of goods sold and

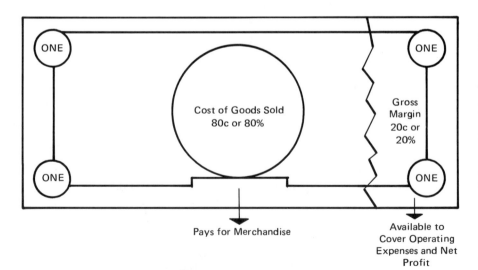

FIGURE 3-1   Retail sales dollar.

gross margin. In other words, the amount of each sales dollar remaining after the merchandise has been paid for is the gross margin—the amount available to apply towards operating expenses and operating net profit. In the illustration, 80 cents or 80 percent of the sales dollar represents the cost of the goods, and the remaining 20 cents or 20 percent represents the gross margin. Therefore, out of each sales dollar, 20 cents or 20 percent is available to apply towards operating expenses and operating net profit.

The difference between cost of goods sold and selling price (dollar gross margin) is sometimes referred to as the markup. When the difference between cost and selling price is expressed as a percentage of *selling price,* it is always called gross margin. When the difference is expressed as a percentage of *cost,* it is always called the markup. Markup percentage indicates the percentage of cost that is added to the cost in order to arrive at the selling price. For example, 12 nonreturnable quart bottles of carbonated soda costs the retailer $3.50 and is priced at 2 for 73 cents, or a total retail value of $4.38 for the case. The dollar gross margin, or markup is:

$$\text{\$ Gross margin or markup} = \text{Sales (selling price)} - \text{Cost of goods sold}$$
$$= \$4.38 - \$3.50$$
$$= \$0.88$$

$$\text{Gross margin \%} = \frac{\$0.88}{4.38} \times 100 = 20\%$$

$$\text{Markup \%} = \frac{\$0.88}{3.50} \times 100 = 25\%$$

Thus, we find that we must add a markup of 25 percent to the cost of the case of carbonated soda in order to realize a gross margin of 20 percent on the sales or selling price. (Percentages to the nearest whole percent.) In other words, gross-margin percentage is always a percentage of sales whereas markup percentage is always a percentage of cost; therefore, the gross-margin percentage is always a smaller figure than the equivalent markup percentage.

Calculating Selling Prices

How is merchandise priced in order to realize the desired gross margin? For example, if we wished to realize a gross margin of 33⅓ percent on a case of 24 units of an item that cost $2.40, what would the selling price have to be? Although we do not know the selling price, we do know that 66⅔ percent of two-thirds the selling price will equal the cost of the merchandise. This is true because:

$$\text{Sales (or selling price)} - \text{Cost of goods} = \text{Gross margin}$$

Therefore:

$$\text{Sales (or selling price)} - \text{Gross margin} = \text{Cost of goods}$$

and 100 percent is the selling price.

So we know that 66⅔ percent (66.7 percent) of the selling price will be equal to the cost of goods, which is $2.40. If we express this relationship mathematically, it becomes:

$$66.7\% \times X = \$2.40$$
$$X = \frac{\$2.40}{.667}$$
$$= \$3.60$$

where X is the selling price.

Therefore, in order to realize a gross margin of 33⅓ percent on a case of merchandise that costs $2.40, we must price it so that we receive $3.60 for the contents of the case. Because there are 24 units in the case, we can sell each unit for 15 cents ($3.60/24) in order to realize $3.60 from the sale of the entire case.

We can check to see whether or not the selling price of $3.60 is adequate to return a gross margin of 33⅓ percent by using the formula for determining gross-margin percentage.

$$\text{Gross-margin }\% = \frac{\text{Sales} - \text{Cost of goods}}{\text{Sales}}$$
$$= \frac{\$3.60 - \$2.40}{\$3.60}$$
$$= \frac{\$1.20}{\$3.60} \times 100$$
$$= 33⅓\%$$

Now we know that a total selling price of $3.60 for a case of merchandise costing $2.40 will result in the desired 33⅓ percent gross margin.

The markup necessary to yield a gross margin of 33⅓ percent is calculated by using the markup formula:

$$\text{Markup }\% = \frac{\text{Sales} - \text{Cost of goods}}{\text{Cost of goods}}$$
$$= \frac{\$3.60 - \$2.40}{\$2.40}$$
$$= \frac{\$1.20}{\$2.40} \times 100$$
$$= 50\%$$

It is apparent that we must mark up the case of merchandise by 50 percent, or we must add 50 percent of the cost in order to arrive at a selling price that will result in a 33⅓ percent gross margin.

There is a simple pricing formula that can be used to calculate the retail selling price when the cost of the merchandise and the desired rate of gross margin are known. Based upon the example:

$$
\begin{aligned}
\text{Selling price} &= \frac{\text{Cost of goods}}{100\% - \% \text{ gross margin desired}} \\
&= \frac{\$2.40}{100\% - 33\frac{1}{3}\%} \\
&= \frac{\$2.40}{.667} \\
&= \$3.60
\end{aligned}
$$

Another common method for calculating selling price is to apply the markup percentage necessary to achieve the desired gross margin. A margin conversion table can be used to indicate the markup on cost equivalent to the gross margin on selling price (see Table 3-2). From the conversion table, we find that a 50 percent markup on cost is equivalent to a 33⅓ percent gross margin. We can use the following formula to calculate the selling price when a gross margin of 33⅓ percent is desired on an item that costs $2.40:

$$
\begin{aligned}
\text{Selling price} &= \text{Cost of goods} + 50\% \times \text{Cost of goods} \\
&= \$2.40 + .50 \times \$2.40 \\
&= \$2.40 + \$1.20 \\
&= \$3.60
\end{aligned}
$$

Converting Gross Margin and Markup

Even though gross margin and markup tables (and pricing wheels and slide rules) are available, it is sometimes useful to know how to convert gross margin to an equivalent markup, and vice versa.

When the gross-margin percentage is known, the equivalent markup-on-cost percentage can be determined as follows:

$$
\begin{aligned}
\text{Markup \%} &= \frac{\text{Gross-margin \%}}{100\% - \text{Gross-margin \%}} \\
&= \frac{33\frac{1}{3}\%}{100\% - 33\frac{1}{3}\%} \\
&= \frac{33\frac{1}{3}\%}{66\frac{2}{3}\%} \\
&= \frac{.333}{.667} \times 100 \\
&= 50\% [3]
\end{aligned}
$$

---

[3]Rounded to the nearest percent.

TABLE 3-2   Gross Margin and Markup Conversion Table

Gross-margin Percentage of Selling Price	Markup Percentage of Cost	Gross-margin Percentage of Selling Price	Markup Percentage of Cost
5.0	5.3	28.0	39.0
6.0	6.4	29.0	40.9
7.0	7.5	30.0	42.9
8.0	8.7	31.0	45.0
9.0	10.0	32.0	47.1
10.0	11.1	33.0	49.3
11.0	12.4	34.0	51.5
12.0	13.6	35.0	53.9
13.0	15.0	36.0	56.3
14.0	16.3	37.0	58.8
15.0	17.7	38.0	61.3
16.0	19.1	39.0	64.0
17.0	20.5	40.0	66.7
18.0	22.0	41.0	70.0
19.0	23.5	42.0	72.4
20.0	25.0	43.0	75.4
21.0	26.6	44.0	78.6
22.0	28.2	45.0	81.8
23.0	29.9	46.0	85.2
24.0	31.6	47.0	88.7
25.0	33.3	48.0	92.3
26.0	35.0	49.0	96.1
27.0	37.0	50.0	100.0

When the markup percentage is known, the equivalent gross margin can be determined as follows:

$$\text{Gross-margin \%} = \frac{\text{Markup \%}}{100\% + \text{Markup \%}}$$

$$= \frac{50\%}{100\% + 50\%}$$

$$= \frac{50\%}{150\%}$$

$$= \frac{.50}{1.50} \times 100$$

$$= 33\frac{1}{3}$$

PRICING OBJECTIVES

Basically, there are three types of pricing objectives that may be used by businessmen: profit-oriented pricing, sales-oriented pricing, and status-quo pricing.[4]

---

[4]E. Jerome McCarthy, *Basic Marketing, A Managerial Approach,* 3rd ed. (Homewood, Ill.: Richard D. Irwin, Inc., 1968), pp. 511-19.

Profit-oriented pricing involves setting a profit goal that the firm attempts to achieve. The target profit might be in terms of net profit on sales or return on investment and might be a short-run or long-run objective. The target return might be specific, such as an annual profit of 2 percent of sales or 12 percent return on net worth, or it may be stated as a range, such as 1.5 to 2.5 percent of sales or 10 to 15 percent return on net worth. Usually in food retailing, however, the target is based on gross margin, which is easier to project than is return on investment at the retail level. Although large firms may have a corporate objective of 12 percent return on net worth, they translate this into a gross-margin objective for the retail store. The overall store gross margin is derived from the gross margins of the various departments. Each department within a store will in turn have a gross-margin target that it is expected to meet. For example, the meat department gross-margin objective may be 24 percent; the produce gross-margin objective, 32 percent; the grocery gross-margin objective, 18 percent; and so forth.

Instead of a target return, a firm may attempt to earn as much profit as possible or as much as the traffic will bear. Although this kind of profit objective may seem desirable, most retail food firms realize that there is a practical limit to the amount of profit that can be earned in a competitive situation and therefore establish a realistic target return based upon competitive conditions.

Sales-oriented pricing involves setting a sales rather than profit objective. The sales objective may be expressed in terms of a particular volume of sales that the firm hopes to achieve, such as $10 million during the current year. The sales objective may also be stated as a share of the market, such as 20 percent of retail food store sales in the market area by the end of the year. The share-of-market objective can be translated into dollars once the total sales in the market area are known; however, the primary intent of a share-of-market objective is not a specific volume of sales but a certain percentage of sales in a particular market area. This share-of-market objective is often found in market areas where price competition is intense. It is usually initiated by one firm that cuts prices; other firms then follow suit to maintain or increase their share of the market. This often results in losses or reductions in earnings.

The sales-oriented pricing objective is really an indirect form of a profit-oriented objective because it is intended to build a sales base or market position upon which a desired profit return can be earned. The sales objective may be considered more important initially because a certain level of sales enhances a firm's ability to earn a profit. However, a sales objective must be tied to a profit objective, or the results could be disastrous, especially in the long run.

Status-quo pricing objectives are intended to maintain prices as they are, or simply to meet the prices set by competition. The firm may not wish to engage in price competition any more than necessary and is willing to let competitors set the pace. Firms that have status-quo pricing objectives are probably aggressive in nonprice competition; that is, they attempt to build customer acceptance by providing a more pleasant shopping experience through broader convenience, product, and business-behavior values than do competitors. If they are highly successful in nonprice competition, these firms may not even try to match competitors' prices but may decide to price merchandise a certain percentage above prices established by one competitor who is regarded as the "price leader" in the market area.

All three types of pricing objectives are employed, to some extent, in food retailing. However, it appears that profit-oriented objectives are the most common. Sales-oriented objectives may be important to some firms in the short run, but it is quite probable that a profit-oriented objective is the ultimate aim in the long run. Even where status-quo pricing objectives prevail, the firm usually has a profit objective as an overall goal. The extensive use of budgets that specify sales, gross-margin, and expense objectives seems to support the conclusion that profit-oriented objectives are the most common within the retail food industry. Although we recognize that other objectives are important at certain times and under certain conditions, we will assume for the balance of this discussion that pricing is profit oriented in food retailing.

PRICING METHODS

Variable-markup Pricing

The basic pricing method used in the retail food industry is known as variable-markup or margin pricing. Variable-markup pricing involves pricing individual products and product categories at varying rates of markup and margins. The margins resulting from variable-markup pricing vary not only among major commodity groups, such as groceries, meats, and produce, but also within product categories, such as canned vegetables.

According to a *Chain Store Age* survey, margin percentages range from a low of 4.7 for regular coffee to a high of 36.0 for cleaning implements and lightbulbs (see Table 3-3). The analysis also indicates that there is a wide variation in gross-margin rates within product categories although the variation is not generally as great as that among categories. For example, within the canned vegetable category, the margins range from 14.7 percent for tomato sauce and paste to 27.6 percent for sauerkraut.[5]

This method of pricing is similar to average-cost or cost-plus pricing, which involves adding a standard markup percentage to the total purchase cost of each item. The variable-markup method of pricing, however, involves markup rates that vary among and within product categories depending primarily upon two factors: (1) cost factors (selling costs); and (2) demand factors (consumer demand).

---

[5]Chain Store Age, *1972 Sales Manual,* July 1972, p. 162.

TABLE 3-3 Average Gross Margin and Percentage of Total Supermarket Sales for Selected Supermarket Grocery Product Categories

Grocery Product Category	Average Gross Margin	Percentage of Total Supermarket Sales
Canned vegetables	20.0	2.38
Canned fruit	19.1	1.32
Canned and dry soup	14.2	1.15
Breakfast foods	14.6	1.73
Frozen foods	25.5	4.61
Butter	9.1	0.70
Regular coffee	4.7	1.56
Bakery foods	21.7	4.46
Cookies and crackers	23.6	2.30
Sugar	6.1	0.80
Oil and shortening	10.4	0.59
Spices, extracts, and seasonings	31.5	0.45
Peanut butter	16.1	0.38
Pet products	17.6	1.68
Candy and gum	27.7	1.42
Baby food	7.6	0.74
Nuts	26.5	0.32
Tobacco products	8.6	4.51
Health and beauty aids	27.7	2.97
Soaps and detergents	13.0	2.18
Housewares	32.3	1.26
Magazines and stationery	32.2	0.56
Cleaning implements and light bulbs	36.0	0.59

Source: Chain Store Age, *1972 Sales Manual,* July 1972, p. 71.

Cost Factors

There are differences in the costs of handling and selling the various commodity groups and individual products that are usually reflected in markup and margin rates.

As previously pointed out, most food retailing costs are common costs, that is, they are necessary for the sale of all products in the retail mix and are not attributable to the sale of one or a few products or departments. These indirect costs are known as *overhead costs*. There are also *direct expenses* that can be easily allocated to individual commodity groups. (See pages 104-5).

There are important differences among the major commodity groups and departments in the retail food store with respect to direct expenses, and some of these differences are reflected in the margins. Table 3-4 shows the relationship between gross margin and direct expense for the major commodity groups in two supermarkets. Although the results shown for these supermarkets may not be typical of other food stores in terms of specific figures, the relationships among commodity groups are rather typical.

Except for health and beauty aids and other nonfoods, the food groups with the highest gross margins (produce, meats, and frozen foods) also have the highest direct-expense rates (see Table 3-4).

TABLE 3-4   Gross Margins and Direct Expenses for
Major Commodity Groups in Two Supermarkets

Commodity Group	Gross Margin (in % of sales)	Direct Expenses[a]
Groceries	16.7	2.2
Dairy	15.2	2.4
Baked foods	16.1	1.3
Frozen foods	25.7	7.8
Health and beauty aids	32.1	2.4
Other nonfoods[b]	26.0	1.7
Meats	18.3	9.1
Produce	28.9	12.0

[a] *Includes depreciation on equipment, repairs and maintenance, personnel, and supplies.*
[b] *Includes housewares, soft goods, stationery, magazines, records, toys, and miscellaneous items.*

Source: *The Colonial Study* (New York: Progressive Grocer, 1962), pp. C 77-80.

Produce shows the highest direct-expense rate and gross-margin percentage of any *food* commodity group. This relationship reflects both cost and demand factors. The merchandising of produce involves a higher labor expense than any other commodity group and also requires relatively expensive refrigerated storage and display equipment. Produce is a bulky commodity and is often handled several times from the time it is received until it is selected by the consumer. A considerable amount of preparation and packaging is also involved in most retail produce departments. Handling and preparation equipment and supplies such as hand trucks, skids, wrapping tables, wrapping materials, and weighing and pricing devices are required.

In addition to the high labor, equipment, and supply expenses, most produce is highly perishable, and the risk of deterioration is greater than it is for most other commodities. Therefore, markups are higher in order to compensate for shrinkage losses, and higher gross margins may be achieved. The actual gross margin realized is affected by the amount of shrinkage, and this aspect of merchandising perishables will be explored in detail in Chapter 4.

Produce gross margins, therefore, reflect the relatively high direct costs associated with operating retail produce departments.

The meat department in retail food stores is also a high-cost department. It is similar to the produce department inasmuch as it involves handling and processing a bulky commodity, which incurs relatively high labor, equipment, and supply costs. The operation of the meat department usually involves even more processing and packaging than does the operation of the produce department. Due to the higher sales volume and more efficient use of labor and equipment, however, the direct expenses as a percentage of sales are often lower in the meat than in the produce department. Meats are also highly perishable and are marked up more than nonperishable food commodities in anticipation of shrinkage.

Unlike produce and meats, frozen foods do not require a relatively high labor cost in retail food stores. However, the cost of operating frozen-food display equipment is very high, because the equipment must maintain temperatures of 0° Fahrenheit or below. (Although it is not included as a direct expense, in the Colonial study, the utility expense is quite high in merchandising frozen food because of the high electric-power requirement in operating frozen-food storage freezers and display cases; this is another cost factor that is reflected in frozen-food pricing and margins.) Thus, the depreciation, repair, and maintenance cost is relatively high in frozen-food merchandising.

The costs of merchandising dry grocery, dairy, and bakery products are usually less, relative to sales, than for produce, meats, and frozen food, and the lower margins for these commodity groups partially reflect these lower merchandising costs. Bakery products as well as dairy products, particularly fluid milk, are high turnover items, and those items with the highest turnover generally have the lowest gross margins. Fluid milk is a prime example in this case. Therefore, the low gross margin associated with fluid milk tends to reduce the overall gross margin of the dairy department because fluid-milk sales represent such a large share of total dairy department sales.

The costs of merchandising health and beauty aids are very low in relation to the gross margins, which are among the highest of any commodity group handled in the supermarket. The relatively high margins in these nonfood categories are due to demand factors, which will be discussed in the next section of this chapter.

The costs of handling and merchandising individual products can vary considerably depending upon the bulkiness and other handling characteristics, the amount of display space, and the sales volume of the product; and therefore the margins of individual products in one commodity group will vary. The amount and type of processing and packaging also affects merchandising costs. For example, in the meat department the cost of handling and merchandising beef steaks and roasts, which must be cut, packaged, weighed, and priced, is higher than the cost of handling prepackaged, prepriced luncheon meats, which need only be placed upon display. In the produce department, it is more costly to bag or tray-wrap, weigh, price, and display bulky citrus fruit than to simply display carrots or broccoli that are received already wrapped and need only to be priced and displayed.

In product groups where little or no processing and packaging are done, there are still cost differences due to handling requirements, display-space requirements, and sales or turnover. In the frozen-food department, for example, large frozen pizza requires more display space per package than most other products and must bear a higher space cost per unit than other items. A high rate of sales may help to offset the space cost, however. In the grocery department, bagged pet food, flour, and paper towels are examples of products that are bulky and relatively costly to handle and display.

As stated previously, it is difficult to determine the true cost of merchandising in the retail food store because of the many indirect, or overhead, expenses. For individual products, however, it is even difficult to allocate direct expenses because these are usually attributable to the entire commodity group. It is more likely, in determining merchandising costs for the individual products, that supermarket operators are aware in a general way of the products that have relatively high costs of handling and merchandising and, whenever possible, attempt to obtain higher margins for those items.

Thus, variable-markup pricing does reflect cost factors, such as handling, processing, and display costs, as well as the anticipated rate of shrinkage. Costs may or may not be fully reflected in pricing margins, depending upon how accurately the true costs are known and upon the importance of demand factors.

Demand Factors

Velocity. A relatively high cost of merchandising does not by itself provide a sufficient reason for pricing a commodity at a higher-than-average gross-margin percentage. In setting prices, the food retailer must also consider the velocity of sales, or demand, for the item.

The velocity or rate of sales of food store items is most affected by price when the demand for the items is elastic, that is, close substitute products exist. The greater the elasticity of consumer demand, the greater the effect of selling price upon the sales of an item. Rather than trying to maximize the sales dollars of an item, the food retailer is more concerned with getting as many gross-margin dollars as possible from the sale of an item. Because the operating expenses and net profit must be covered by gross margin, it is to the retailer's advantage to obtain as many gross-margin dollars as possible *as long as expenses do not increase more than gross margin.* Because most operating expenses are fixed from week to week in the retail food store, an increase in gross-margin dollars will usually add to net profit.

Greater sales velocity can more than compensate for both a lower selling price and a lower gross-margin percentage. In the example given in Table 3-5, the gross-margin dollars are greater at a selling price of $1.33 per unit than at $1.54 per unit because of a much higher rate of sale at the lower selling price. It is to the retailer's advantage to sell the product at $1.33 as long as the gross-margin dollars increase more than operating expenses.

TABLE 3-5   Example of Weekly Sales and Gross-margin Potential
of a Food Store Product Offered at Two Different Selling Prices

Cost per Unit	Selling Price per Unit	% Gross Margin	Weekly Units	Sales $	$ Gross Margin
$1.00	$1.54	35	50	77.00	26.95
1.00	1.33	25	90	119.70	29.92

Another consideration is the effect of the sales of one item upon the sales of other items. If a lower price on one item results in a reduction of sales of items that contribute more gross-margin dollars, then the net effect may be a reduction in gross-margin dollars realized from total product category and store sales.

Competition. In addition to the price-sales-gross-margin-dollar relationship, the food retailer must be aware of his competition. Prices of individual items as well as the overall price levels among competitors are important in attracting customers and achieving the sales and profit objectives. Although it is not known exactly how consumers form their judgments concerning the prices charged by competing stores, the results of several studies make it clear that consumers are aware of price differences within and among supermarkets.[6]

Because an average of 8,000 items is handled by supermarkets, it is understandable that consumers are not able to identify prices of specific items. The critical question concerns the extent to which consumers are able to make meaningful price comparisons among competing stores. Can consumers remember prices so that they are aware of both price changes and price differences among competing stores?

One study that sheds some light on this question was conducted by Progressive Grocer in cooperation with Colonial Stores. Consumers were asked to state the prices of 60 items that executives of the Colonial food chain "considered as frequently advertised and on which prices were generally highly competitive."[7] The results of the study showed that, with the exception of Coca-Cola, most consumers could not name the exact prices for the 60 food store items. (Eighty-six percent of the consumers identified the correct price for Coca-Cola six packs.) The correct price identification for the remaining 59 items ranged from 39 percent for Camel cigarettes to only 2 percent for Colonial private-label shortening. However, a much higher proportion of the test consumers was able to come within 5 percent above or below the correct price. The proportion of customers who were able to do this ranged from 91 percent for Coca-Cola six packs to 12 percent for one-pound Nestle Quick.

All in all, there were 26 of the 60 items for which consumers could come within 5 percent of the actual retail price (Table 3-6). Most of the items were national or regional brands that were available in most food stores, although five of the items were chain private labels that were available only in Colonial stores.

The results of this study do not indicate consumer awareness of price for all the 8,000 different items carried by food stores. As the report concludes: "These, however, are the types of product that are generally consi-

---

[6]An unpublished study conducted by Peter Ryan in partial fulfillment of the requirements for the Master of Science degree, Department of Agricultural and Food Economics, University of Massachusetts, Amherst, Mass., 1965, indicated that when consumers rated the prices in grocery, meat, and produce departments in four competing supermarkets they could identify differences in price levels among competing stores and among departments in the same store. Another study (Marion, Simonds, and Moore, *Food Marketing in Low Income Areas,* Cooperative Extension Service, The Ohio State University, Columbus, Ohio, 1969) showed that consumers were able to rate accurately the relative prices of six out of nine stores in Columbus, Ohio. Prices were collected for a sample of 37 items that were estimated to represent nearly half the food expenditures of low-income families.

[7]*The Colonial Study* (New York: Progressive Grocer, 1962), pp. C104-6.

TABLE 3-6   Customer Estimates of Actual Retail Prices of Highly Advertised
Food Store Grocery Items

Item	% of Customers within 5% of Exact Price	% of Customers Naming Exact Price
Coca-Cola, six pack	91	86
Domino sugar	67	20
Colonial apple sauce	57	30
Camel cigarettes	54	39
Ballard biscuits	53	20
Tide, large size	52	24
Pillsbury flour, 5 lb.	51	13
Campbell tomato soup	49	30
Pet milk	49	23
Colonial canned milk	45	20
Kleenex 400s	44	34
Land-O-Lakes butter	43	17
Red Band flour	42	18
Dixie Crystal sugar, 10 lb.	42	5
Cut-Rite wax paper	41	28
Texize cleaner	38	31
Colonial frozen orange juice, six pack	38	27
Duke's mayonnaise	38	21
Tide, giant size	35	10
Colonial shortening, 3 lb.	34	2
Carnation milk	33	25
Kraft mayonnaise	32	18
Ivory bar soap, large size	32	17
Clorox, one-half gallon	31	25
Kellogg's corn flakes	31	19
Colonial fruit cocktail	30	22

Source: *The Colonial Study* (New York: Progressive Grocer, 1962), p. C105.

dered as price competitive, those used to make a low-price impression via advertising and display. It is a safe assumption, therefore, that consumers have less knowledge of retail price in the total range of merchandise than these figures indicate."[8]

In view of the thousands of items available in food stores and the frequent price changes, perhaps it is remarkable that the degree of price recognition is as great as shown by the Colonial study. The study does indicate that a substantial percentage of food shoppers has a reasonably accurate understanding of the prices of some of the frequently advertised and price-competitive items in food stores. These items also represent some of the highest velocity items in food stores, as one would expect.

On the other hand, it is probable that there are ways by which consumers evaluate the prices in competing firms other than memory or recall at point of sale. It is possible that newspaper advertisements provide an important basis for making price comparisons and shopping decisions. The consumer may form an opinion on the basis of newspaper price advertising that may, in turn, influence shopping behavior, even though he may not be able to recall accurately the actual prices that were advertised. The Burgoyne annual study of supermarket shoppers in eight market areas indicated that nearly

[8]*The Colonial Study*, p. C106.

78 percent of all shoppers read food store newspaper advertisements and more than 80 percent of the shoppers read two or more different food store ads.[9] The common food store practice of advertising prices in weekly newspaper ads provides another opportunity for shoppers to make price comparisons among stores, on at least a few items.[10]

The Burgoyne study also showed that 90 percent of the shoppers interviewed shopped in more than one supermarket each month during 1971.[11] This figure has been increasing steadily since 1954, when only 59 percent of the respondents said that they shopped in more than one store. The fact that a high proportion of food shoppers regularly visit more than one store indicates that most shoppers have the opportunity to compare prices between at least two stores.

Another possibility is that consumers may be able to assess rather accurately the relative prices of items in competing stores. Through shopping experience, the consumer may know which of two or more competing stores usually has the lowest price on items that are important to him, even though he may not be able to recall the actual price of most of the items.

Regardless of how shoppers form price impressions, the important fact made clear by these studies is that they are aware of price differences within and among stores, and this fact must be considered by the food retailer when establishing selling prices for the merchandise he offers. In addition to the demand items for which consumers can identify prices, there are also specific items for which certain consumers are extremely price sensitive. For example, the shopper who owns a cat or dog will be sensitive to cat or dog food prices. Those consumers who must buy dietetic products will be especially sensitive to the prices of these products, which they purchase on a regular basis. However, it appears that the demand items, those that are purchased frequently by a high proportion of consumers, are most price sensitive. Demand items are usually nationally branded items that are carried by most food stores and are the most important in influencing consumers' price impressions of food store offerings. This conclusion is supported by the relatively low average gross margins realized on national brands of coffee, sugar, peanut butter, baby food, soups, and tobacco products (see Table 3-3). Many other high-turnover (or demand) items such as hamburger, fresh whole milk, butter, and fresh broilers or fryers are also frequently advertised and are usually priced competitively so that gross margins are lower than for most items in the respective product categories.

Prices and margins are not always lower on demand items than on less-frequently purchased items, however. This is especially true for many highly perishable and nonfood commodities.

Most products in the fresh meat and produce departments are not as highly standardized as grocery and nonfood products, and there are often

---

[9]*1971 Food Habit Shopping Study,* (Cincinnati, Ohio: Burgoyne, Inc., October 1971), pp. 25 and 26.

[10]An *item* refers to each different product, brand, size, or type of package.

[11]*1971 Food Habit Shopping Study,* p. 10.

qualitative differences in these products from store to store. A can of Maxwell House coffee or Cambell tomato soup and a carton of General Electric light bulbs are exactly the same quality regardless of the store where they are purchased. A sirloin steak or a head of lettuce, however, may be quite different from store to store, depending upon the original quality and the handling and merchandising practices employed after the product reaches the store. Even when highly perishable products are branded, such as Sunkist oranges, Chiquita bananas, or Armour Star beef, the quality can vary from store to store because of some of the differences in original condition as well as store handling and merchandising practices. Qualitative differences tend to make pricing less competitive, as indicated by the fact that gross margins for fresh meat and especially produce are generally higher than for most other food commodity groups (see Table 3-4). There are exceptions, such as broilers, fryers, and hamburger, that are used frequently as advertised items and are quite competitive with respect to price.

The pricing of most nonfoods is such that gross margins are higher than for most food product categories (see Table 3-4).[12] Even though nonfoods tend to be highly standardized, they are not priced as competitively (with the exception of price specials) as are most food items. One reason for this is that many nonfoods, including health and beauty aids, housewares, and soft goods, have been added to the food store product mix as impulse items in order to bolster gross margins, and food retailers have probably been reluctant to shave margins on them. Although supermarkets generally sell nonfoods at lower prices than conventional drug, variety, specialty, or department stores, the margins are still highly favorable compared with most food and grocery items. Perhaps supermarket operators are more concerned with being competitive with conventional nonfood retailers than with each other in the case of nonfood merchandise.

Another reason for high margins on nonfoods is the existence of state fair-trade laws, or voluntary adherence to manufacturers' suggested retail selling prices. Under state fair-trade acts, a producer or distributor can prescribe by contract either a minimum or stipulated resale price for his product in states where fair-trade regulations exist.

The higher margins on nonfoods compared with food products have resulted in greater emphasis on nonfood items by food retailers through greater selection and merchandising emphasis. This increased emphasis has resulted in a growing proportion of total sales accounted for by nonfoods, which has been responsible for some of the increase in overall gross margins. The higher margins on nonfoods have helped to offset rising operating expenses because of their increasing importance in the retail food store product mix.

---

[12]The term *nonfoods* as used here refers to nongrocery items, including health and beauty aids, housewares, magazines and stationery, soft goods, records, toys, and automotive and hardware supplies. Grocery nonfoods include paper products, soaps and detergents, household and laundry supplies, pet foods, and tobacco products.

Psychological Pricing

Velocity and competition are demand factors that strongly influence pricing methods. Conversely, there are several established pricing methods that are effected by food retailers (as well as by other types of retailers) to create demand, or influence consumer buying habits, through some kind of psychological appeal. Research tends to confirm certain kinds of psychological pricing, but for the most part, the effectiveness of psychological pricing has not been well established for retail food stores.

Odd-cent Pricing

A common practice in food retailing is to use odd-number prices, especially prices ending in "9," such as 29, 59, 99, and so on. This practice is based upon the assumption that consumers will buy more at odd prices, like 29 cents, than at even prices, like 28 or 30 cents. Odd-cent pricing also assumes that consumers will relate 29 cents to 20 cents more frequently than they will relate it to 30 cents; psychologically (again supposedly), 29 cents seems much lower than 30 cents, and in fact gives the impression of being a 20-cent item.

This practice is so widespread in the food industry that it can be considered customary. One study showed that 57 percent of the advertised prices of the leading food chains in 23 market areas ended in "9."[13]

The validity of this pricing method has not been proven conclusively, although many people in the food industry are convinced that it is effective in selling more merchandise.

Multiple-unit Pricing

Another commonly practiced food retailing method is pricing merchandise in multiples—such as 3 for 29 cents, 4 for 99 cents, 2 for 25 cents, and so on. Multiple-unit pricing usually incorporates the odd-cent pricing concept as well. The rationale of multiple-unit pricing is that consumers will buy more in multiples than they would at single-unit prices because they feel they are getting more for their money.

Merchandising studies conducted by Progressive Grocer indicate that multiple-unit pricing is highly effective in stimulating the sale of food store products.[14]

The sales of five items that were normally single-unit priced increased an average of 27 percent when they were multiple-unit priced (see Table 3-7). It is interesting to note that the greatest increase occurred for Libby tomato juice, the item for which the multiple-unit price offered no savings over the single-unit price. In the case of each of the other four items, a

---

[13]Dik Warren Twedt, "Does the '9 Fixation' in Retail Pricing Really Promote Sales?" *Journal of Marketing,* Vol. 29, No. 4 (October 1965), p. 55.

[14]*The Colonial Study,* pp. C128-32.

savings of one cent was provided by the multiple-unit price. These results raise the question of whether consumers will buy more at the multiple-unit price even when the price per unit is higher than at the single-unit price. The Progressive Grocer research did not provide any answers to that question.

TABLE 3-7   The Effect of Multiple-unit Pricing on the Sales of
Five Grocery Items

Item	Regular Price	Test Price	Normal Unit Sales	Test Unit Sales	Change in Unit Sales No.	%
Del Monte catsup, 14 oz.	23¢	2/45¢	52	67	+ 15	+ 29
Libby tomato juice, 46 oz.	33¢	3/99¢	33	56	+ 23	+70
Underwood deviled ham	21¢	1/41¢	63	92	+ 29	+46
Reynolds aluminum foil, 25 ft.	33¢	2/65¢	194	233	+ 39	+ 20
Pillsbury Deluxe pancake mix	21¢	2/41¢	30	35	+ 5	+ 17
Total	—	—	372	473	+101	+ 27

Source: *The Colonial Study* (New York: Progressive Grocer, 1962), p. C131.

The sales of five items that were normally multiple-unit priced declined an average of 37 percent when they were single-unit priced (see Table 3-8). One of the five items tested, Del Monte golden cream style corn, increased in sales when changed from multiple-unit to single-unit pricing. For each of the five items tested, the single-unit price was one-half cent higher than the multiple-unit price per unit.

TABLE 3-8   The Effect of Single-unit Pricing on the Sales of
Five Grocery Items

Item	Regular Price	Test Price	Normal Unit Sales	Test Unit Sales	Change in Unit Sales No.	%
French's mustard	2/23¢	12¢	87	62	− 25	− 29
Welch's grape jelly	2/49¢	25¢	31	23	− 8	− 26
Whitehouse apple sauce, 16 oz.	2/33¢	17¢	243	144	− 99	− 41
Green Giant peas, #303	2/45¢	23¢	78	33	− 45	− 58
Del Monte corn, golden cream style	2/39¢	20¢	30	34	+ 4	+ 13
Total	—	—	469	296	−173	− 37

Source: *The Colonial Study* (New York: Progressive Grocer, 1962), p. C131.

The study also indicated that the higher the multiple, the greater the sales. When regular unit prices of "3 for" and "2 for" were changed to

"6 for," unit sales increased by an average of 31 percent for five grocery items.

Presumably, multiple-unit pricing appeals to customers because of the savings, either real or imagined, that are associated with buying in larger quantities. Multiple-unit pricing probably has the same psychological effect on the consumer as the larger size unit of a commodity—the association of quantity with economy.

In order to assess the net effect of multiple-unit pricing, it would be necessary to determine whether the additional sales were short-run, were simply substitutes for other items, or were transfer purchases from competing stores. In other words, consumers may buy more at one time when items are multiple-priced but may buy less often so that total consumption of the item does not really change. Another possibility is that consumers shift their purchases from a substitute item to an item that is multiple-priced and appears to be a better buy. Still another possibility is that consumers will shift their purchases of an item from one store to another depending upon which store appears to have the most favorable price. The existing research does not permit an evaluation of these possibilities so that the net effect of multiple-unit pricing upon sales and profits in food stores is really not known. However, because multiple-unit pricing does seem to be effective in stimulating the sales of merchandise, at least on a week-to-week basis, it has become a widely accepted industry practice.

One of the problems associated with multiple-unit pricing concerns the customers who buy less than the multiple. The checker must either mentally calculate the price or refer to a price chart (both of which are time consuming and can slow the checkout operation). In either case, the possibility of error in charging the customer is greater than when the multiple price, which is marked on each unit, can be charged. For example, if an item is priced at 6 cans for 49 cents and the customer buys less than 6 cans, the checker must determine how much to charge, which is difficult to do mentally, and, even when there is reference to a fractional-price chart, may lead to a mistake. Whether the mistake is in the store's favor or the customer's favor, it can be equally serious. If the error favors the customer, it means that the store is losing money on the product being sold, which will in turn adversely affect the gross margin and net profit of the store. If the error is in the store's favor, it does not necessarily mean the store is making more money. The store may benefit from the few cents error, but this is a very short-run benefit. When the customer realizes that a mistake has been made, he will be dissatisfied and may not return to the store to shop. Therefore, the store loses even more in the long run.

Another problem with multiple-priced items concerns the necessity for product grouping at the checkout counter. The checker must determine whether or not the entire multiple has been purchased before ringing the price. Fortunately, most customers seem to have become conditioned to sorting and grouping their merchandise when placing it upon the checkstand in stores that do not have personnel available to unload customer's purchases from the shopping cart.

Perhaps the most difficult decision concerned with multiple-unit pricing is what items respond best and what multiple prices are most effective. The Progressive Grocer study concluded that the most effective prices are those that are relatively easy to comprehend and are within the one-dollar structure. When units are priced in multiples exceeding one dollar, or if it becomes too difficult to determine whether a real savings is available, customers tend to buy with greater restraint.[15]

In conclusion, there is evidence that multiple-unit pricing does increase the sales of merchandise in food stores, at least in the short run. Although the net effect on sales and profits is not known, multiple-unit pricing has become a widely accepted practice in the food industry. It is possible that the use of multiple-unit pricing, which consumers associate with economy, may be an important ingredient in establishing a total store low-price image.

Prestige Pricing

Another pricing situation involving consumer psychology is prestige pricing. Assuming that consumers associate quality with price, at least for some merchandise, they may actually buy *more* at higher prices. Although prestige pricing is more common in fashion goods and high-value durable goods, there are instances in which it may be applied to the pricing of food store commodities. The best example is the pricing of certain brands of canned and frozen foods, which are often limited in distribution to one or a few food store firms in each market area. The brand is priced higher than any other similar products, and the advertising, labeling, and display are all focused on creating a prestige image. The prestige brand will often include specialty products in addition to the conventional food items.

Although the consumer's association of price with quality has been established for some kinds of merchandise, there is no clear indication of how effective prestige pricing can be for food store items, especially with increasing acceptance of low-price private labels (see page 129).

In summary, psychological pricing is based on the assumption that there are special or unique kinds of consumer demand that require unique pricing methods. There is some evidence to support the concepts of psychological pricing, especially multiple-unit pricing. However, little is known about the long-run effects of psychological pricing relative to sales and profits of the food retailing firm. Perhaps the greatest advantage of psychological pricing is that it requires the retail operator to at least consider various demand factors in pricing.

Leader Pricing

One of the most common practices in food retailing is the use of price "specials" or "leaders." "A price special is a temporary low price used to promote the store which is not justifiable in terms of the economics

---

[15]*The Colonial Study,* p. C129.

of cost or demand for the individual product.''[16] In other words, price specials or leaders are items that are sold at reduced prices for a short period of time, regardless of cost or sales considerations, in order to attract customers and promote greater overall sales and profit for the store. This is accomplished by (1) providing attractive values for the customer on the items being specialed; and (2) creating an overall low-price image for the store.

Specials are most frequently used on weekends, when most food shopping is done, but they are also used at other times. For example, first-of-the-week specials, which are available only on Monday and Tuesday or Monday through Wednesday, are somteimes used in an attempt to increase customer traffic and sales during the early part of the week.

The practice of using price specials on a widespread, regular basis was one of the strategy components of the supermarket pioneers. Michael Cullen, one of the pioneers of the supermarket, in a letter outlining his concept of the supermarket to a food chain executive in 1930, set forth the following price strategy:

I want to sell 300 items at cost.
I want to sell 200 items at 5% above cost.
I want to sell 300 items at 15% above cost.
I want to sell 300 items at 20% above cost.

Cullen went on to say the following:

Can you imagine how the public would respond to a store of this kind? To think of it—a man selling 300 items at cost and another 200 items at 5% above cost—nobody in the world ever did this before. Nobody ever flew the Atlantic either, until Lindberg did it.[17]

The use of specials has become a permanent part of supermarket pricing strategy ever since the days of Michael Cullen and other pioneers in the development of the self-service supermarket.

In a study of prices in three supermarket chains in a large city, the National Commission on Food Marketing found that more than one half of 105 food items were specialed at some time during an eight-week period. The list of items was chosen to represent the typical sales mix of a supermarket.[18]

What kinds of items are usually specialed, and how much are prices reduced from the "regular" or "normal" shelf price?

One study concluded that only 200 to 300 items out of a store's total offerings of several thousand are normally used in specials, and that items with high turnover rates and high margins are selected for specials. Out

---

[16]*Organization and Competition in Food Retailing,* Technical Study No. 7, National Commission on Food Marketing, Washington, D. C., June 1966, p. 175.

[17]M. M. Zimmerman, *The Super Market* (New York: McGraw-Hill Book Company, 1955), p. 33.

[18]*Organization and Competition in Food Retailing,* p. 174.

of 4,000 items in the grocery department, fewer than 150 usually meet these requirements.[19]

"Many meat items make attractive price specials," according to the National Commission on Food Marketing.

> During a 14-week period studied by the Commission over two-thirds of the retail cuts of beef were specialed at one time or another. The price cuts ranged from 6.3 percent to 34 percent of regular retail price. On the average, price specials reduced the gross margin for beef by 6 percentage points or by about 26 percent. During the week of the most extensive price specialing, however, gross margins on beef were reduced 45 percent below gross margins obtained with no beef specials. Due to frequent specialing of meat products, the meat department in the supermarket may not cover its share of costs. The loss of revenue is viewed as a cost of promoting the store generally and is made up by other departments.[20]

Price specials do not always cover the cost of merchandise, let alone the costs of handling and merchandising. When the special selling price is inadequate to offset the cost of goods, it is known as a *loss leader*. If the price of a special is too low to cover handling and merchandising costs, it can also be regarded as a loss leader, but, as already stated, it is difficult or practically impossible to determine accurately the cost of selling any one item in the food store mix because of the many common costs. Therefore, the term *loss leader* will be defined as an item with a selling price below the purchase cost of the item delivered to the store.

Based upon the available research and observation of newspaper advertising, it appears that food stores usually select items for price specials that are most important in the consumers' grocery budget. Therefore, fresh meats, which account for nearly 30 percent of the consumers' *food* dollar, are used frequently as price specials. In the grocery department, the relatively fast selling items that are used frequently by a high proportion of customers are specialed more often than less-important items. For instance, coffee, canned tuna, and margarine are frequently specialed grocery food items. Detergent, pet food, and paper goods are frequently specialed nonfood grocery items.

In produce, lettuce, bananas, and potatoes are frequently used as price specials. In the frozen-food department, frozen orange juice concentrate is a commonly specialed item.

The effectiveness of price specials depends upon the items specialed, competition, and other aspects of the store's offer. Price specials do seem to be effective in increasing the sales of the items on special.

Several studies of meat price specials indicate that the tonnage movement of meat items on special is greater than when the item is not on special. The studies also show that total meat tonnage can be increased by the use of specials, and the effect upon total tonnage depends upon

---

[19]*McKinsey-Lever Promotion Study,* Lever Brothers Co., October 1965, p. 27.
[20]*Organization and Competition in Food Retailing,* p. 176.

the particular meat item specialed and the extent of the price reduction. In general, the more important the product on special is in the normal meat-department mix, the greater the effect upon total meat tonnage.

Fryers seem to be especially effective as price specials, resulting in large increases in both fryer tonnage and total meat tonnage during the period of the special.[21]

The effect of price specials on total store sales is much more difficult to determine than the effect on sales of the price specials. The specials may result in more customers shopping the store who will buy merchandise in addition to the specials. However, whether or not they will buy enough other merchandise to offset the gross-margin loss on the specials is the important question, and one that is difficult to answer. It is also possible that the specials will not attract additional customers, and the "regular" store customers will stock up at the special prices. In this case, the specials may only reduce the gross margin and net profit of the store. On the other hand, it may be necessary to offer specials in order to maintain the customer traffic and sales volume because regular customers may go elsewhere to shop unless their regular store makes some attempt to match the specials offered by competitors.

Certainly, the effectiveness of specials is influenced by the products chosen and the extent of the price cuts. Price specials on products with a highly elastic demand will be more effective in attracting customers than specials on products that show little response to change in price. Staple products such as coffee, bacon, eggs, potatoes, and ground beef are frequently used as price specials and apparently show a highly elastic demand for the individual food store even though the overall demand for these products is inelastic. Staple products are used regularly and constitute an important part of the family food budget; probably for this reason, consumers respond to price reductions on staple products. The increase in sales of staple products on special probably does not result in an increase in consumption. It merely means that consumers are buying ahead and storing the items for future consumption.

So, the individual firm is faced with an elastic demand for many staple products both because of more customers buying and those customers buying more. This is a short-run response, and it is doubtful if staple items would continue to exhibit an elastic demand for a store if specialed for two or more consecutive weeks. There is a limit to how much of a product consumers will store, and this limit is likely reached rather quickly for most staple items, especially for perishable foods. As one food chain merchandiser put it when trying to estimate the sales of fryers on special, "peoples' freezers are only so big."

---

[21]*Economic Effects of Price Specials for Meat,* National Association of Food Chains, Washington, D.C., January 1959; Marion, Ott, and Walker, *Meat Department Labor Requirements,* Research Bulletin 982, Ohio Agricultural Research and Development Center, Wooster, Ohio, June 1966; and Leo R. Gray, *Effects of Price Specials on Volume of Sales of Frying Chickens,* Agricultural Economic Research, Vol. 16, No. 3 (July 1964).

Other types of products frequently used as price specials include items that are not staples, but that do respond to price reductions. These items may be luxury-type foods such as steak or rib roast, or seasonal foods such as fresh strawberries. It is likely that the total demand as well as the individual store demand for these foods is elastic with respect to price.

It is clear that the more important the product in the family diet or the more appealing it is to consumer tastes and preferences, the greater the sales response to reductions in price. Products that are less-frequently purchased or are purchased by only a few consumers, anchovies and artichokes for example, are not highly responsive to changes in price and are rarely used as price specials. The demand for these products is generally inelastic both overall and with respect to the individual store.

The price special is only one aspect of competitive behavior or strategy in food retailing. If other components of value to the customer are lacking, price specials cannot be expected to compensate for them. Also, it may be very difficult to create a low-price image by the use of specials in a highly competitive market. The NCFM study concluded that it is possible to identify the store with the "lower price" only in the most simple, clear-cut cases. The study indicated that price levels are rather unstable among competitors so that the lowest price for a shopping list of items is likely to vary among major competitors from week to week.[22] Whether or not price specials are effective in creating a low-price image in the consumer's mind, regardless of whether it actually exists, is hard to say because little is known about how consumers formulate judgements about relative price levels among competing firms.

It is apparent that the wise use of price specials must involve judgment based upon a knowledge of customer demand, the actions of competitors, and a careful analysis of the likely effects upon customer traffic, sales, and gross margin. A record of past experience can be most helpful.

The indiscriminate use of price specials can have a disastrous effect on gross margin and net profit. A planning procedure for controlling the effect of price specials will be discussed in Chapter 8.

Promotional Pricing

Food retailers advertise and promote the sale of items other than price specials or leaders. Often items are featured in advertising or in-store displays because they provide an opportunity for increasing sales and gross margin. Unlike price specials, promotional items are sold at or near the regular retail selling price and are used to help compensate for the gross margin foregone on price specials.

Two studies[23] verify the fact that items accorded the most prominent

---

[22]*Organization and Competition in Food Retailing,* pp. 169-74.

[23]*Organization and Competition in Food Retailing,* p. 174; and Lee Preston, *Profits, Competition and Rules of Thumb in Retail Food Pricing* (Berkeley, Cal.: Institute of Business and Economic Research, 1963), pp. 49-50.

positions in newspaper advertisements are not always markdowns from regular prices. Some prominently featured advertised items are promotional rather than leader items.

Promotional items are usually selected on the basis of their customer appeal and sales and margin potential. The promotional item should be a good value for the customer and should have a reasonably high sales potential. The promotional items should also contribute to the store's image of price, selection, and quality.

Items selected for promotion usually include seasonal products, new items, tie-in items, items that are heavily advertised by the manufacturer, or items that carry an advertising or promotional allowance.

For example, the first fresh native sweet corn or peaches of the season may be used as a promotion. New items, especially those that are heavily advertised, make good promotions because they attract customer interest. Tie-in items, items that complement or are tied to the sale of other items, are frequently promoted in combination with price specials. For instance, salad dressing or another salad item like fresh tomatoes can be tied in with a fresh-lettuce price special. Tartar sauce or lemons might be promoted in combination with a fresh-fish price special. Items that carry advertising or promotional allowances from the manufacturer are frequently promoted in order to meet the requirements for receiving the allowance. Furthermore, these items make good promotions because of the favorable gross margin. The retailer can offer the item below the regular retail price and still realize a higher-than-normal gross-margin contribution because of the reduction in the cost of goods and increased sales.

Merchandise that is seasonal is well suited for promoting at certain times of the year. Charcoal briquets, frankfurters and luncheon meats, frozen lemonade, and picnic supplies during the summer months are good example of seasonally promoted items.

Items that are frequently specialed are also promoted on occasion depending upon the supply and price situation. For instance, when beef supplies increase and wholesale prices decline, the retailers may promote steaks or roasts at slightly reduced prices and still realize the same or even higher gross margins than usual. The same is true of other perishable items like head lettuce, which may be promoted when quality is especially good and wholesale prices are lower than usual. Certain canned items, such as fruits or vegetables, juices, fish, or shellfish, may be used as promotional items when the supply is unusually large and wholesale prices are relatively low.

The use of promotional pricing in retail food stores is closely related to price specialing and requires careful planning in order to be effective in achieving sales and profit objectives. The planning of promotional items in combination with price specials will be discussed in Chapter 8.

Private-label Pricing

An important development in food distribution that has influenced pricing at the retail level is the growth of private-label products.

Private label, or distributor's label, refers to "merchandise packaged mainly to a distributor's specifications either by a distributor or a manufacturer for resale only by a distributor, under a brand name owned by a distributor." An advertised label, or national or regional brand, refers to a "manufacturer's or producer's brand of merchandise having wide distribution and supported by heavy advertising and/or promotion regionally or nationally to the public. Advertising is paid for by the manufacturer."[24]

The NCFM study of private labeling showed that the private-label products are concentrated in a small number of categories. Among the most important categories are:

1. Canned fruits and vegetables
2. Diary products, particularly eggs, oleomargarine, and ice cream
3. Bakery products
4. Coffee
5. Salad dressings and mayonnaise

In addition to these product categories, there were a few individual products frequently mentioned such as evaporated milk and peanut butter. Most of the private-label products are standard products; they have been on the market for a relatively long period and are frequently purchased by consumers.[25]

In addition to the food products sold under a private label, several nonfood products are also handled by many distributors. Laundry detergents and supplies, paper products, and household supplies were among the nonfood products most frequently mentioned by retailers as being private-labeled.[26]

Although the large chains were the primary initiators of private labeling, independent food stores have been able to obtain private-label products through their voluntary, cooperative, or independent wholesale supplier. The private-label products available to both chain and independent operators are becoming more numerous and include most product categories in the food store. The private label has been extended to practically all grocery food product categories and even to some meat and produce categories. Private-label products are also available in a growing number of nonfood categories.

The primary reasons given by food retailers for carrying private-label products were, in order of importance, consumer loyalty, competition, and greater profitability. Retailers apparently believe that private-label products enable them to develop consumer loyalty to an exclusive line of products.

---

[24]*Special Studies in Food Marketing,* Technical Study No. 10, National Commission on Food Marketing, Washington, D.C., June 1966, p. 1.

[25]*Special Studies in Food Marketing,* p. 44.

[26]*Special Studies in Food Marketing,* p. 45.

Second, because competitors stock private-label products, retailers feel that it is necessary to carry a private label to remain competitive. The third most important reason given was that private-label products return a greater profit than do manufacturer's-label products.[27] It is the profitability aspect of the private label that involves special pricing considerations. A detailed study of 13 product categories carried by a selected sample of chain retailers indicated that prices were lower and gross margins higher for private-label than for advertised brands.[28]

Table 3-9 shows that the retail prices for ten private-label products were 20 percent lower, on the average, than the prices of the advertised brands with which they competed. Thus, private-label products offered consumers substantial savings over advertised brands in this study.

TABLE 3-9   Average Retail Prices[a] per Case for Selected Products by Type of Label

Product	Private Label[b]	Advertised Brand[c]	Differences as a % of Private Label
Frozen orange concentrate, 6 oz.	$8.74	$11.84	+35
Frozen cut green beans, 9 oz.	4.94	6.42	+30
Canned cut green beans, No. 303	4.57	6.09	+33
Canned green peas, No. 303	4.76	5.52	+16
Canned sliced cling peaches, No. 2½	6.24	6.46	+ 4
Canned Bartlett pears, No. 2½	10.86	12.93	+19
Canned applesauce, 25-oz. glass	3.29	3.64	+11
Catsup, 14 oz.	4.46	5.10	+14
Tuna fish, light, chunk, 6½ oz.	12.72	15.81	+24
Evaporated milk	6.52	7.48	+15
Average	$6.71	$8.13	+20

[a] *Prices are averaged over 12 weeks and include specials.*
[b] *Best quality private label is compared.*
[c] *Includes prices for three advertised brands.*

Source: *Special Studies in Food Marketing,* Technical Study No. 10, National Commission on Food Marketing, June 1966, p. 66.

Table 3-10 shows that for 13 products the average gross margin was 2.4 percent higher on private-label than on the advertised brands. The largest difference was for frozen green beans, for which the private-label margin was 6.7 percent higher. At the other extreme, private-label applesauce had an average gross margin 1.1 percent lower than the advertised brands. The variation demonstrates the high degree of flexibility in pricing and merchandising practices among retailers.[29]

It is apparent that food retailers are pricing private-label merchandise lower than competing advertised brands and that they are realizing higher

[27]*Special Studies in Food Marketing,* p. 57.
[28]*Special studies in Food Marketing,* pp. 60-76.
[29]*Special Studies in Food Marketing,* p. 74.

TABLE 3-10   Average Gross Margins on Selected Products by Type of Label

Product Category	Private Label	Advertised Brands
	Percent Margin	
Frozen orange juice concentrate	22.0	23.0
Frozen strawberries	27.3	26.4
Frozen green beans	37.2	30.5
Frozen french-fried potatoes	32.5	29.1
Canned green beans	26.8	23.7
Canned green peas	25.8	21.2
Canned cling peaches	18.5	18.1
Canned pears	28.7	24.0
Canned applesauce	22.2	23.3
Catsup	17.3	16.5
Spaghetti	28.3	25.6
Tuna fish	23.8	19.2
Evaporated milk	12.6	11.2
Average	24.8	22.4

Source: *Special Studies in Food Marketing,* Technical Study No. 10, National Commission on Food Marketing, June 1966, p. 73.

gross-margin percentages on private labels. It is difficult to determine the relative profitability of private-label and advertised brands, however, for two reasons.

First of all, it was not possible to obtain the true cost of private-label or advertised brands in the NCFM study. Advertising and promotional allowances, which are often available for advertised brands, were not deducted from the invoice cost so that the gross profits of the advertised brands are somewhat understated. On the other hand, the cost to the retailer of advertising private-label products, which normally is not offset by an allowance, was not included, so the gross profits for these products were slightly overstated.[30]

Second, even though gross-margin percentage is an indicator of profitability, other factors such as merchandising costs and sales velocity must be considered in making an evaluation of the true profit contribution of a product. Merchandising costs are approximately the same for both private-label and the competing advertised brands for any particular commodity because the physical product characteristics and handling requirements with respect to size of container, case size, price marking, and display practices are nearly identical. The sales velocity may vary considerably, however, so that the total amount of gross-margin dollars is a better indicator of relative profitability than is gross-margin percentage. In addition, the amount of display space allocated to each product has to be considered because space represents a cost. The NCFM study included a comparison of gross-margin dollars per facing for 13 private-label products and competing advertised brands. The comparison showed that there was a wide variation among

---

[30]*Special Studies in Food Marketing,* p. 63.

products but the average gross-margin dollars per facing for all 13 products were equal for private-label and advertised products.[31]

The profitability of private-label merchandise is also affected by merchandising philosophy, which in turn determines the pricing strategy for private labeling. There are two primary philosophies of private-label merchandising that concern the gross-margin objectives for private-label products compared with competing advertised brands. One point of view is that private labels should be priced so that they realize a higher percentage gross margin than do advertised brands. The other philosophy contends that the percentage gross margin should be the same on both private-label and advertised brands. In both cases, the private label is priced below the advertised brands, but the price difference would be greater when the latter point of view prevails. Table 3-11 illustrates the effect of these two philosophies on the pricing and gross margins for private-label and advertised brands. *Example A* shows that a selling-price differential of two cents a can less for the private label, based upon a 15 percent lower cost of merchandise, would result in a gross margin 6 percent greater for the private-label item. In *Example B,* the second private-label merchandising philosophy is illustrated. In this instance, the private-label item can be priced three and one-half cents less than the advertised label and still result in a gross-margin percentage that is approximately the same as that realized on the advertised brand. The gross-margin dollars from each case of private-label product would be less in *Example B* because of the lower selling price. However, some retail operators believe that increases in total store sales plus increased sales of the private-label merchandise due to the greater price differential will more than offset the lower gross-margin dollars per case.

TABLE 3-11   Illustration of Pricing Strategy Effect on the Prices and Gross Margins of a Private-Label and Advertised Brand Canned Fruit Item[a]

Type of Brand	Cost Per Case	Selling Price		Gross Margin Per Case	
		Per Case	Per Can	$	%
Example A					
Advertised Brand	$4.80	$6.00	25¢	$1.20	20.0
Private Label	4.08	5.52	23	1.44	26.1
Example B					
Advertised Brand	4.80	6.00	25	1.20	20.0
Private Label	4.08	5.16	21.5 or 2/43	1.08	20.9

[a] *Twenty-four cans per case.*

In conclusion, the relative profitability of private-label and advertised brand merchandise seems to be inconclusive. However, the use of private-label products is intended to build customer loyalty and meet the offers

[31]*Special Studies in Food Marketing,* p. 76.

of competition as well as to increase the profit earned on individual products. Therefore, private label must be evaluated and incorporated into the competitive strategy of the retail food firm on the basis of its contribution to the achievement of the overall sales and profit objective of the firm.

Summary of Pricing Methods

Variable-markup pricing best describes the pricing method used in retail food merchandising. It involves the application of varying rates of markup to products and product categories based upon cost and demand factors, so gross-margin percentages also vary among products and product categories.

Pricing of individual products and product categories reflects differences in handling and merchandising costs as well as differences in sales velocity, competition, consumer psychology, and other demand factors, such as consumer response to price specials, promotional items, and private-label products.

In view of the complexity of retail pricing, the variable-markup pricing method may provide the best means of achieving the overall profit objective of the firm because it does take both cost and demand factors into consideration and is not based upon the addition of an arbitrary or standard markup to each item. As one authority states:

> A profitable price structure for a retail firm is likely to be one in which percentage markups over cost are not constant among products. Only in the rare case in which sales of each product are equally responsive to changes in price would a policy of pricing each product at the same percentage markup over cost prove most profitable. Even in this case, such a policy would neglect the distinguishing characteristics of retail pricing—the ability of the firm to increase sales of many products by offering attractive prices for a few.[32]

---

[32]*Profits, Competiton and Rules of Thumb in Retail Food Pricing*, p. 70.

4

Pricing II

PRICING POLICY

Each firm must decide upon the pricing strategy that will enable its store or stores to achieve the profit objective. The strategy should specify the level of prices in relation to competition as well as the pricing methods that will be used. The pricing strategy defines the pricing policy, which should be based upon an analysis of the tastes and preferences of the clientele and the image or appeal that the firm wishes to project. The establishment of price policy involves judgment based upon the best information available.

Pricing to Achieve Profit Objectives

There is a planning tool that can help choose the most advantageous price policy by providing estimates of the most profitable of several price-level alternatives. This planning tool is referred to as volume-cost analysis.

Volume-Cost Analysis

Volume-cost analysis involves making estimates of what a firm's cost will be at different levels of sales and the relationship among sales volume, cost, and profit. Volume-cost analysis can assist the management of a firm in making decisions by providing estimates of (1) the minimum sales volume required to prevent a loss; (2) the minimum sales volume necessary to reach profit objectives; (3) the probable profit or loss at any realistic sales volume; and (4) the effect of changes in price strategy and costs upon net profit.

The Break-even Point. One of the most common uses of volume-cost analysis by food retailing firms is to determine the minimum sales volume necessary to prevent a loss. This is called the break-even point.

The use of volume-cost analysis in determining the break-even point, or for any other purpose, requires an accurate estimate of sales, gross margin, and expenses. This information can be prepared in the form of an estimated (pro forma) profit and loss statement (see Table 3-1). The estimated P-L statement is also referred to as an operating budget, and it can be prepared for any period of time. Usually the complete operating budget is prepared annually or quarterly (four 13-week periods.)

Operating expenses must be itemized in order to calculate the break-even point for a food store (see Chapter 3). Then, each item of expense must be classified according to its relationship to sales—variable, fixed, or semivariable (see Figure 4-1).

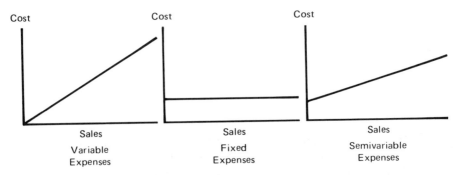

FIGURE 4-1 Behavior of expenses with respect to sales volume in retail food stores.

Variable expenses are those that change in direct proportion to changes in sales. The cost of goods, supplies such as paper bags, and trading stamps are examples of variable expenses. Wages are usually considered a variable expense because the amount of labor required depends mostly upon the volume of sales, and retailers try to adjust labor hours according to anticipated sales.

Fixed expenses are those expenses that do not change with changes in sales. Fixed expenses are commitments that must be met regardless of the amount of business that is transacted. Depreciation on equipment, managers' salaries, licenses, real estate taxes, and insurance premiums are examples of fixed expenses.

A third type of expense is the *semivariable expense*, which lies somewhere between a variable and a fixed expense. A semivariable expense changes with changes in sales, but not in direct proportion to sales changes. Examples of semivariable expenses include utilities, repairs, and maintenance. Semivariable expenses must be classified as either fixed or variable in order to determine the break-even point. Usually, the classification will depend upon whether the semivariable expense most closely resembles a fixed or variable expense. However, some prefer to classify all semivariable expenses as fixed, which is a more conservative approach and results in a higher break-even point. Actually, the practice of classifying all semivariable expenses as fixed is realistic because most expenses in the retail food business are relatively fixed commitments and are difficult to adjust on a quarterly and even annual basis, regardless of sales.

Some expenses in the retail food store can be either fixed or variable depending upon management policy or financial arrangements. The advertising and promotion expense may be budgeted in terms of a fixed amount, in which case it is a fixed expense. On the other hand, the amount budgeted may be based on a certain percentage of sales, in which case it becomes a variable expense.

The classification of the rent expense depends upon the financial arrangement between landlord and tenant. In some cases, the food store operator pays a fixed rent, so the expense is fixed. The fixed rental expense is usually based upon the size of the store or the selling area. For example, a rental arrangement might be based on an annual charge of $2.50 per square foot of floor space. In other instances, the rent consists of a certain percentage of sales, such as 2 percent, in which case the expense is variable. Food chains, which often have real-estate divisions that locate and build stores, will usually assess each store a certain percentage of sales for a rental charge, which means that rent becomes a variable expense for each store in the chain. The rent expense is often a semivariable expense, which occurs when the tenant is charged a fixed amount per week, month, or year in addition to a percentage of sales over and above a certain point. For example, the agreement may specify a rental of $600 per week plus 1½ percent of sales in excess of $40,000 per week. In this case, the occupancy expense can be divided into fixed and variable components for purposes of budgeting and volume-cost analysis, or it can be considered as entirely fixed if a conservative break-even point is desired. If the store building is owned by the operator, a rental charge should be assessed on the basis of the rent that could be obtained from a tenant or what it would cost to rent a similar building for use as a food store. In this case, the rent may be considered as a fixed expense.

Assume that you are preparing an estimated quarterly profit and loss statement for Big Bag Supermarket, Inc. (see Table 4-1). In preparing this detailed budget, estimate sales, gross margin, and direct, controllable operating expenses for each major department in Big Bag Supermarket. The allocation of the direct expenses of wages and laundry and supplies, which are controllable at the department level, enables management to establish an objective and evaluate the contribution to overhead (indirect operating expenses) and profit from each department. The contribution to overhead and profit is the difference between gross margin and direct, controllable expenses and can be expressed in dollars or as a percentage of sales in each department and for the entire supermarket operation. Contribution to overhead and profit indicates the amount that remains after the cost of merchandise sold and controllable expenses have been deducted from sales. This amount is available to apply to overhead expenses and net profit.

All other expenses, except cost of goods sold, are listed as indirect

TABLE 4-1   Pro Forma Operating Statement First Quarter, Big Bag Supermarket, Inc.[a]

	Total		Grocery		Meat		Produce	
	$	%	$	%	$	%	$	%
Sales	520,000	100.0	348,400	67.0	130,000	25.0	41,600	8.0
Cost of goods sold	421,200	81.0	288,080	82.7	104,000	80.0	29,120	70.0
Gross Margin	98,800	19.0	60,320	17.3	26,000	20.0	12,480	30.0
Controllable Expenses								
Wages (incl. benefits)	44,200	8.5	26,832	7.7	13,000	10.0	4,368	10.5
Laundry & supplies	5,200	1.0	2,090	0.6	2,486	1.9	624	1.5
Total	49,400	9.5	28,922	8.3	15,486	11.9	4,992	12.0
Contribution to Profit	49,400	9.5	31,398	9.0	10,514	8.1	7,488	18.0
Operating Expenses								
Rent	7,800	1.5						
Salaries [b]	5,200	1.0						
Depreciation [b]	5,200	1.0						
Advertising & promotion [b]	13,000	2.5						
Utilities [b]	5,200	1.0						
Repairs & maintenance [b]	1,040	.2						
Accounting & legal [b]	1,040	.2						
Taxes & insurance [b]	5,200	1.0						
Miscellaneous [b]	520	.1						
Total	44,200	8.5						
Total Expenses	93,600	18.0						
Net Operating Profit	5,200	1.0						

[a] The figures and expense classifications are for illustrative purposes and are not intended to be typical.
[b] Fixed expense.

operating expenses. Even if the indirect expenses could be allocated to departments with ease, they are not really controllable within the departments so that it would not be reasonable to include them when evaluating the contribution of each department to store profit. Therefore, indirect or overhead expenses are charged to the overall operation.

Cost of goods sold is listed after sales because gross margin is the difference between sales and cost of goods sold. Remember that net operating profit is the difference between gross margin and the total of direct and indirect operating expenses.

Once the budgeted P-L statement has been completed and all expenses classified as either fixed or variable, the break-even point can be determined. From the P-L statement, it is apparent that the variable expenses consist of cost of goods sold, wages, laundry and supplies, and rent. All other operating expenses are classified as fixed.

The break-even point is that volume of sales necessary to cover all expenses—the volume that results in no net profit or loss. The break-even point can be determined by calculating the sales volume required to balance gross margin and operating expenses. Because gross margin is the amount available to cover expenses and return a profit after the merchandise has been paid for, we can ignore the cost of goods sold. Therefore, we are concerned with determining the volume of sales at which the gross margin (19 percent of sales) is equal to fixed expenses ($36,400) and variable operating expenses (wages, 8.5 percent; laundry and supplies, 1.0 percent; rent, 1.5 percent; for a total of 11 percent of sales).

We can solve for the break-even point by calculating the percentage left from gross margin after variable operating expenses have been deducted and dividing the result into the fixed expenses.

Thus:

19% Break-even sales = Fixes expenses + Variable operating expenses
19% Break-even sales = $36,400 + 11% Break-even sales
19% Break-even sales − 11% Break-even sales = $36,400
8% Break-even sales = $36,400
$$\text{Break-even sales} = \frac{\$36,400}{.08}$$
Break-even sales = $455,000

This method also tells us that a quarterly sales volume of $455,000 is required to balance gross margin and total operating expenses in Big Bag Supermarket, Inc.

The answer can be checked as follows:

Break-even sales = $455,000
Gross margin = 19% × $455,000 = $86,450
Fixed expenses = $36,400
Variable operating expenses = 11% × $455,000 = $50,050

Total operating expenses = $\underline{\$86,450}$
Gross margin = Total operating expenses

The break-even point can also be located by means of a break-even chart, which must be accurately drawn to scale on graph paper (Figure 4-2).

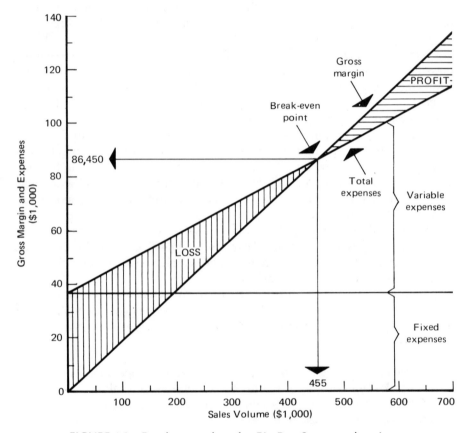

FIGURE 4-2   Break-even chart for Big Bag Supermarket, Inc.

Fixed expenses of $36,400 show as a horizontal line on the chart because they remain constant regardless of sales. Total expenses are shown as a straight line beginning at the fixed expense line at zero sales and extending to $107,900 at a sales volume of $650,000. The total expenses of $107,900 are made up of $36,400 fixed expenses and $71,500 variable expenses (11% x $650,000).

The difference or area between the fixed and total expense lines represents variable expenses. There are no variable expenses at zero sales, therefore, the total expense line begins at the fixed expense line.

The gross margin, which is 19 percent of sales, is represented by a straight line beginning at zero and ending at $123,500, which is the amount of gross margin at a sales volume of $650,000.

The break-even point is that point at which the gross margin and total expenses are equal, or, where the gross margin and total expense lines intersect. At the point of intersection, the break-even point can be read on the horizontal scale; $455,000 in this case. It should be noted that at the break-even point both gross margin and total expenses are equal at $86,450, which is read on the vertical scale.

The advantages of the break-even chart are that it provides a visual comparison of the basic factors affecting net profit and it also permits the quick determination of net profit or loss at any volume of sales. Mathematical calculations, although more accurate, only apply to a specific sales volume.

The break-even chart is helpful in gaining a clearer understanding of the relationships among fixed and variable expenses, gross margin, sales, and net profit. It shows the profit or loss at any volume of sales. Profit or loss is indicated by the area between gross margin and total expenses and can be read on the vertical scale. It is apparent that net profit increases rapidly as sales increase beyond the break-even point; and, conversely, losses mount rapidly as sales fall below the break-even point (see Figure 4-2).

The break-even point is important to food retailing firms because it defines the minimum volume of sales that must be attained in order to avoid a loss. This knowledge may be especially important when opening a new store that may not realize the complete sales potential for several months or even longer. It is important that the operator of the store know how far actual sales can drop below the budgeted volume of sales before he loses money, or, he may want to know the exact amount of loss that he will incur if sales drop below the break-even point.

In using volume-cost analysis to determine the break-even point, or for other purposes, it should be kept in mind that there are limitations. First of all, volume cost analysis is only valid within limited ranges of sales fluctuations. The cost estimates would not be accurate at sales volumes drastically above or below the budgeted sales. If sales were to increase more than, say, 20 percent above the budgeted sales, it might be necessary to add more equipment, such as checkout, and the use of labor may be less efficient due to crowded conditions. In this case, the fixed expense in dollars and the wage expense as a percentage of sales would increase. Conversely, if sales dropped far below the budgeted volume, some equipment could be removed from the store, but it may not be possible to reduce labor below a certain point in order to maintain the displays and store conditions adequately. In this case, the fixed expense in dollars would decrease, but wages would increase as a percentage of sales. However, because food store sales do not usually fluctuate drastically from one period to another, this limitation is not serious, especially for stores that are well established.

The other limitation in the use of volume-cost analysis concerns the assumptions that must be made. It must be assumed that the cost of merchandise, prices, product mix, wage rates, and the prices of other expense items, such as utilities, remain constant. It must also be assumed that the budget, upon which volume-cost analysis is based, is correct and that costs are correctly classified as either fixed or variable.

In spite of the limitations, volume-cost analysis is a useful tool in the management of retail food firms. It does require management to analyze, in a methodical manner, the likely outcome of their decisions with respect to sales, costs, margins, and profit. With experience, it is possible to estimate the budget components reasonably accurately so that the assumptions are valid for management decision-making purposes.

The Use of Break-even Analysis in Merchandising Strategy. In addition to finding the break-even point, break-even analysis is helpful in making decisions on merchandising strategy, including pricing. In order to use break-even analysis in making merchandising strategy decisions, it is first necessary to determine the changes that will take place with respect to sales, costs, and margins in the original budget. Then, the break-even calculation method can be used to predict the change in the volume-cost relationship due to the change in strategy.

For example, let's say that the management of Big Bag Supermarket is considering offering a premium to its customers that would cost the firm 1 percent of sales. Furthermore, the management wants to make certain that they realize $5,200 of net profit in the quarterly budget. The question is, what sales volume will be necessary during the quarter in order to meet the additional expense and still earn a net profit of $5,200?

First of all, we know that the premium offer will increase variable operating expenses by 1 percent of sales, making them 12 percent instead of 11 percent of sales. Second, because the management of Big Bag wishes to earn $5,200 net profit regardless of what happens to sales volume, net profit can be considered a fixed expense. Now that the changes in the operating budget have been identified, we can calculate the required sales volume, using break-even analysis.

$$\text{Gross margin} = 19\% \text{ (no changes in price)}$$
$$\text{Fixed expenses} = \$41,600 \ (\$36,400 \ + \ \$5,200)$$
$$\text{Variable operating expenses} = 12\% \text{ of sales } (11\% \ + \ 1\%)$$

Therefore:

$$19\% \text{ Break-even sales} = \$41,600 \ + \ 12\% \text{ Break-even sales}$$
$$19\% \text{ Break-even sales} \ - \ 12\% \text{ Break-even sales} = \$41,600$$
$$7\% \text{ Break-even sales} = \$41,600$$
$$\text{Break-even sales} = \frac{\$41,600}{.07}$$
$$\text{Break-even sales} = \$594,286$$

The break-even analysis shows that Big Bag sales must increase to

$594,286 during the quarter in order to offset the increase in variable expenses and return the owners $5,200 net profit. In this instance, the break-even point *includes* a net profit. Based upon the original budget, which estimated sales at $520,000, an increase of $74,286, or about $5,700 per week, would be required to successfully implement the new strategy during the quarter. Management now can make the decision concerning whether or not to implement the new strategy, knowing what will be required in the way of a sales increase to justify the strategy in terms of achieving the profit objective.

Break-even analysis can also be helpful in making price strategy decisions. A break-even chart such as that shown in Figure 4-3 allows the comparison of several price strategies with respect to the true break-even points and volume-profit relationships. The price strategies are represented by the gross-margin lines, and the break-even sales volume for each price strategy is at that point where gross margin intersects total expenses. The profit or loss possibilities in relation to sales volume are indicated by the differences between gross margin and total cost.

Figure 4-3 shows two alternative pricing strategies for Big Bag Supermarket, Inc., in addition to that included in the budget (Table 4-1). The pricing strategy upon which the budget is based calls for a 19 percent gross margin. Figure 4-3 illustrates the effects of a pricing strategy that would reduce prices so that gross margin would be 17 percent, and a strategy that would increase prices so that gross margin would be 21 percent. The alternative price strategies would presumably not affect fixed expenses and the variable-expense percentage, so the original budgeted expenses would still apply.

The chart shows that the break-even points are affected drastically when the price strategy, as indicated by gross margin, is changed from the original budgeted gross margin of 19 percent. Increasing prices to yield a gross margin of 21 percent lowers the break-even point from $455,000 to $364,000 so that a net profit can be earned at much lower sales volume. However, it is probable that sales would not be as great at a 21 percent gross margin as at a 19 percent gross margin because prices would not be as competitive. Management must estimate the reduction in sales that would occur and then determine which price strategy will yield the greatest net profit.

Conversely, lowering prices and gross margin from 19 to 17 percent raises the break-even point from $455,000 to $606,667 and would require a relatively high volume of sales before any profit is earned. Management must determine whether or not the lower prices will attract enough additional business to maintain or increase net profit compared with earnings at a 19 percent gross margin.

The advantage of the break-even chart in making price strategy decisions is that it shows visually the relationships among gross margin, total expenses, and net profit over the entire range of sales. The chart should be used only as an approximation of the break-even point or amount of profit or loss at any sales volume because it is difficult to obtain precise figures from a scale chart. Exact break-even points can be calculated mathematically

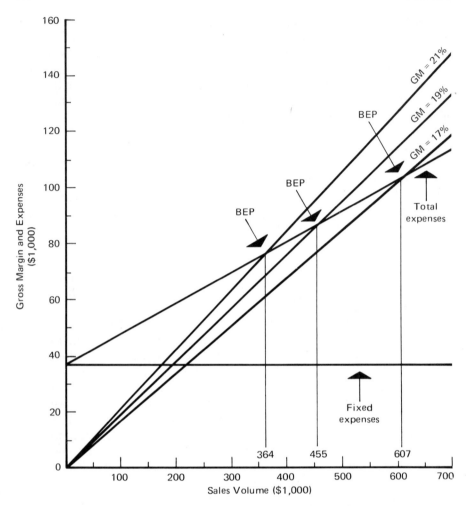

FIGURE 4-3   Price strategy break-even chart for Big Bag Supermarket, Inc.

using the break-even calculation methods described previously. Net profit or loss at any given sales volume can be calculated by subtracting fixed and variable expenses (including cost of merchandise) from sales, or subtracting fixed expenses and variable operating expenses (excluding cost of merchandise) from the amount of gross margin.

Break-even analysis can be used to determine the sales volume changes necessary to achieve a specified profit as a result of a price strategy change. Let's assume that the management of Big Bag Supermarket is considering increasing the number of price specials in hopes of attracting more customers and increasing total sales. They figure that the lower prices will reduce overall gross margin by about 1 percent of sales. They are willing to accept a reduction in net profit, at least during the coming quarter, because they feel that the increased sales will eventually lead to higher profits. However, due to various financial commitments they must earn at least $3,500 net profit during the quarter. In order to make this decision, they wish to know what volume of sales will be required to assure them of at least $3,500 net profit at the 1 percent gross-margin reduction.

The important budget components and the changes from the original budget are identified as follows:

$$\begin{aligned} \text{Gross margin} &= 18\% \text{ (down 1\% due to price specials)} \\ \text{Fixed expenses} &= \$39,900 \text{ (up \$3,500 to include net profit)} \\ \text{Variable operating expenses} &= 11\% \text{ of sales (no change)} \end{aligned}$$

Now, break-even analysis can be used.

$$\begin{aligned} 18\% \text{ Break-even sales} &= \$39,900 + 11\% \text{ Break-even sales} \\ 18\% \text{ Break-even sales} - 11\% \text{ Break-even sales} &= \$39,900 \\ 7\% \text{ Break-even sales} &= \$39,900 \\ \text{Break-even sales} &= \frac{\$39,900}{.07} \\ \text{Break-even sales} &= \$570,000 \end{aligned}$$

The management of Big Bag Supermarket now knows that sales must reach $570,000 during the coming quarter in order to realize a net profit of at least $3,500. The sales volume of $570,000 would be about a 10 percent increase over the budgeted sales of $520,000. Now the decision can be made with the knowledge of the increase in sales required to satisfy the conditions created by the contemplated strategy change.

The foregoing is just one example of the many decisions involving price and gross-margin changes that can be aided by the application of break-even analysis.

Use of Flexible Break-even Analysis in Determining the Most Profitable Price Strategy. Thus far, we have discussed the use of break-even analysis in evaluating the effects of changes from an original strategy as indicated by the operating budget. The original price strategy is indicated by the budgeted gross margin.

Break-even analysis, used with some judgment, can be useful in identifying the most profitable pricing strategy under a given set of cost conditions. Once the physical size and sales range of the food store have been established and fixed and variable costs have been estimated, break-even analysis can help to decide the most profitable overall price strategy.

The particular technique that is useful in making the basic price strategy decision is called flexible break-even analysis. This application of break-even analysis involves greater consideration of demand than does previously discussed break-even analysis, which is based upon a single estimate of demand as indicated by the volume of sales in the operating budget. In using flexible break-even analysis, potential demand at a series of price levels must be considered in the price strategy decision.

Let's assume that the management of Big Bag Supermarket used the flexible break-even method in deciding upon the price strategy that calls for a 19 percent gross margin. The procedure that they used is described as follows.

After studying the market area, they concluded that the store should be built for a sales volume of between $35,000 and $45,000 weekly, or between about $450,000 and $600,000 quarterly. Based upon this estimated range in sales, quarterly expenses were estimated at $36,400 for fixed expenses and 11 percent of sales for variable operating expenses (see Table 4-1).

Now the question was, which price strategy will yield the greatest net profit? In order to answer this question, it was necessary to estimate the volume of sales that could be achieved as a result of each price strategy. Then, the difference between total gross margin and total operating expenses would indicate the most profitable pricing strategy.

TABLE 4-2   Pricing Strategy Estimates for Big Bag Supermarket, Inc.

Pricing Strategy Gross Margin	Estimated Sales		Quarterly		
	Weekly	Quarterly	Gross Margin Dollars	Expenses[a]	Net Profit
%	$	$	$	$	$
16	50,000	650,000	104,000	107,900	− 3,900
17	47,000	611,000	103,870	103,610	260
18	44,500	578,500	104,130	100,035	4,095
19	40,000	520,000	98,800	93,600	5,200
20	35,000	455,000	91,000	86,450	4,550
21	30,000	390,000	81,900	79,300	2,600
22	23,500	305,500	67,210	70,005	− 2,795

[a] *Based upon fixed expenses of $36,400 and a variable operating expense rate of 11 percent of sales.*

Based upon the sales estimates made by the management of Big Bag, the most profitable pricing strategy is that which results in a gross margin of 19 percent (see Table 4-2). Although sales volume could be increased if prices were reduced to a level below 19 percent gross margin, the increases would not result in greater net profit because expenses would increase more than gross-margin dollars. If prices were raised so that gross margin was greater than 19 percent, the amount of net profit would be less because gross-margin dollars would decline more than expenses.

In order to visualize the relationships among price levels, sales, and expenses, and to compare break-even points and the net profit or loss for each pricing strategy, a flexible break-even chart is very helpful (see Figure 4-4).

The flexible break-even chart shows total expenses and pricing strategy

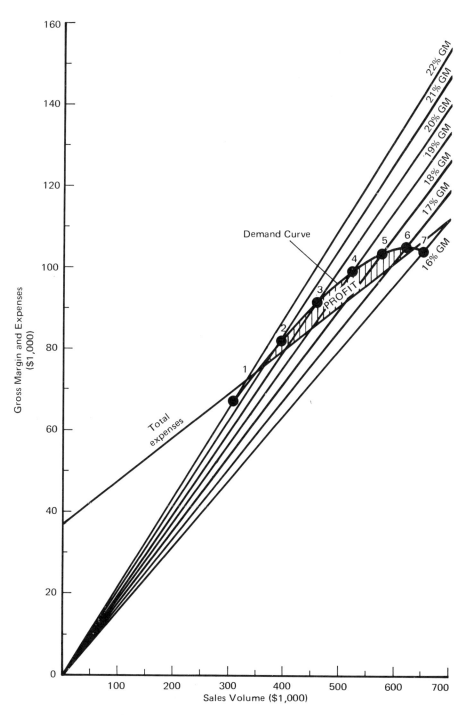

FIGURE 4-4   Flexible break-even chart for Big Bag Supermarket, Inc.

gross margins (16 percent to 22 percent) in relation to sales. Potential demand is shown for each strategy by points 1 through 7. When these points are connected, an estimated demand curve for the firm is the result.

The break-even point for each pricing strategy is the point at which the gross-margin line intersects the total expense line. The most profitable pricing strategy is indicated by the point on the potential demand curve that is the greatest vertical distance above the total expense line. Of the seven pricing strategies shown on the chart, the most profitable is based upon a gross margin of 19 percent.

Two of the pricing strategies under consideration would result in net losses. Both 22 percent and 16 percent gross margins would not result in gross-margin dollars adequate to cover total costs.

The flexible break-even approach is a useful management tool in making price strategy decisions for new stores. It requires management not only to make a complete estimate of expenses but also to evaluate the demand or sales potential in relation to alternative price strategies. If this kind of analysis indicates that the firm cannot attain their profit objective or that the profit potential is inadequate, then the original plans can be revised with respect to store size and expenses, or abandoned completely.

Flexible break-even analysis is also useful for evaluating changes in pricing strategy for existing stores. It can help management decide upon the most promising of several alternative courses of action based upon consideration of both cost and demand factors.

Zone Pricing.   Because food chains operate stores in different market areas, they frequently have more than one price policy in order to meet competition successfully and achieve the profit objective in each store as well as for the entire chain. This flexibility in pricing is achieved by grouping stores according to the consumer demand and competitive conditions within which they operate and establishing a different price policy for each group or zone. However, it is not good policy to put stores in the same trading area into different pricing zones, as the customers may shop both stores and see the different pricing systems. So, geographic considerations are also important to chain store pricing policies.

Contribution or Blend Method of Pricing to Achieve Desired Gross Margin

So far in our discussion of pricing, we have been concerned with overall store pricing policy and gross margins. However, in practice, pricing policy must include consideration of individual items, product categories, and major departments, and the contribution of each to overall store gross margin, as is shown in the breakdowns in Table 4-1.

In order to achieve the desired rate of gross margin on overall store sales, the "blend" or contribution of each product to store gross margin must be planned and controlled. Management must decide upon the gross-margin contribution from each department and then price the items and product categories so that the required departmental contribution is achieved.

First of all, pricing policy with regard to departmental gross margins needs to be established. Then, based upon the proportion of total sales from each department, the contribution method can be used to establish the overall gross margin.

In Table 4-3, the departmental product mix shows that 67 percent (or $67 out of each $100) of total sales is expected to come from the grocery department. Of the 67 percent, 49 percent will come from the sales of dry groceries and nonfoods, 7 from dairy products, 6 percent from bakery products, and 5 percent from frozen foods. In addition, 25 percent of total sales will come from the meat department, and 8 percent will be contributed by the produce department.

TABLE 4-3　Contribution to Total Sales and Gross Margin by Departments

	Percent of Total Sales	Percent Gross Margin	Contribution to Total Store Gross Margin[a]	Percent of Total Store Gross Margin
Grocery total	67.0	17.31	11.6	61.1
Dry groceries and nonfoods	49.0	16.0	7.8	41.3
Dairy products	7.0	18.0	1.3	6.6
Bakery products	6.0	21.0	1.3	6.6
Frozen food	5.0	25.0	1.2	6.6
Meat	25.0	20.0	5.0	26.3
Produce	8.0	30.0	2.4	12.6
Total	100.0	—	19.0	100.0

[a] *Rounded to nearest tenth of 1 percent.*
Source: Based on Table 4-1.

In addition to the sales mix, the price level, as indicated by the gross-margin rate, must be established for each department. In the example, the gross margins are 17.31 percent for all the grocery departments, 20 percent for meats, and 30 percent for produce. Within the grocery departments, dry groceries and nonfoods are expected to yield a gross margin of 16 percent; dairy products, 18 percent; bakery products, 21 percent; and frozen foods, 25 percent. These gross margins reflect some of the cost and demand factors discussed earlier. Produce, for example, because of high perishability, relatively high preparation costs, and the fact that it is less subject to price competition due to variation in quality among stores, is priced to return a relatively high gross margin. Meats are priced to yield a relatively high gross margin because of the perishability and high handling and preparation costs in this department. The grocery department is priced to yield a lower gross margin than either meats or produce due primarily to the highly competitive prices on dry grocery items, to the fact that there are lower handling and preparation costs, and because most dry grocery products are not subject to the perishability problems that plague the meat and produce departments. The relatively high gross margins on nonfoods help to offset the very low margins on many dry groceries, so that a 16 percent gross margin is projected for dry groceries and nonfoods combined.

The pricing of dairy products, bakery products, and frozen foods is not generally as competitive as in the case of dry groceries, so the margins are higher, especially for frozen foods.

After the sales mix and margins have been established for departments, the contribution method can be used to determine the overall rate of gross margin for total store sales. This is done by multiplying the percentage of sales times the percentage gross margin for each department and adding the results.

$$\text{Contribution to store gross margin} = \frac{\text{\% of Sales in}}{\text{category or dept.}} \times \frac{\text{\% Gross margin in}}{\text{category or dept.}} \times 100$$

$$\text{Total store gross margin} = \text{Sum of category or department contributions}$$

Example A—contribution of major departments to store gross margin:

$$\text{Contribution of total grocery department to store gross margin} = .67 \times .1731 \times 100 = 11.6$$

$$\text{Contribution of meat department to store gross margin} = .25 \times .20 \times 100 = 5.0$$

$$\text{Contribution of produce department to store gross margin} = .08 \times .30 \times 100 = 2.4$$

Example B—determination of total store gross margin by contribution method:

$$\text{Total store gross margin} = 11.6 + 5.0 + 2.4 = 19.0\%$$

Example A illustrates how the contribution of each department is calculated. In order to understand more clearly the concept of gross-margin contribution, it may help to use dollars instead of percentages. In Example A, instead of visualizing the total grocery department as 67 percent of store sales, we can think of this department as representing $67 out of every $100 of store sales. As the gross margin on sales in this department is 17.31 percent, we can determine the gross-margin dollars per $100 of store sales that is contributed by the grocery department by multiplying 17.31 percent times $67.

$$\text{Contribution of total grocery dept. sales to store gross margin} = \$67 \times .1731 = \$11.60$$

This multiplication tells us that the total grocery department contributes $11.60 in gross margin from each $100 of store sales.

The contribution method is a useful tool for planning pricing policy in order to achieve the desired rate of gross margin. It is easy to use and it indicates the relative contribution to gross margin of each department.

It is apparent that the contribution to total gross margin is influenced by both the importance of the department in the sales mix and by the percentage gross margin on sales. The grocery department categories, and especially the dry grocery and nonfoods categories, have the greatest influence upon store margin because they contribute such a high proportion of total sales. About two thirds of total food store sales are usually contributed by the grocery department.

More than 61 percent of the store gross margin is contributed by the grocery department, even though the gross margin on total grocery department sales is only 17.31 percent (see Table 4-3).

On the other hand, both the meat and produce departments contribute a higher percentage of gross-margin dollars than of store sales because of the relatively high gross-margin percentages on sales in these departments.

It is important to recognize the effect of both percentage of sales and percentage of gross margin upon store gross margin. Even small changes in the percentage gross margin in the grocery department can have a relatively large effect upon store gross margin because of the high proportion of total sales made by the grocery department. Likewise, if the proportion of total store sales from either the meat or produce department changes, the effect upon store gross margin will be relatively greater because of the high percentage gross margins in these departments compared to the grocery department.

The same principle applies within each department. Some product categories are relatively more important in their contribution to department and store gross margin because of their high gross margin percentage, sales mix importance, or both.

If the contribution method of establishing price policy results in an overall gross margin that is inadequate to realize the net-profit objective, then adjustments must be made in the blend of sales and gross margin contributions among departments. Either the sales contribution of high-margin departments must be increased or the margins must be increased in one or more departments.

Once the sales mix and gross-margin contribution from each department have been established, it is necessary to determine the pricing of each product category and item in order to achieve the gross-margin contribution required.

Here again, the contribution method can be used. The percentage of total sales contributed by each product category to the total department sales are estimated along with the product category gross margin. When both the sales and gross margin percentages are known, then the contribution method can be employed to calculate the overall departmental contribution to total gross margin.

For example, a frozen-food department gross margin of 25.2 percent is determined by adding the contributions of each product category (see Table 4-4). The difference in gross-margin contribution for each product category illustrates the influence of both sales mix and gross-margin percentage on the department's overall gross margin.

TABLE 4-4   Contribution to Sales and Gross Margin by Product Categories In Retail Frozen Food Departments

Product Category	Percentage of Dollar Sales	Percentage Gross Margin	Contribution to Dept. Gross Margin
Vegetables	23.8	26.0	6.2
Juices, ades, and drinks	14.1	25.6	3.6
Seafoods	11.2	24.6	2.8
Dinners	7.4	25.7	1.9
Pot pies	2.3	25.7	0.6
Fruits	2.1	26.9	0.6
Meat and poultry	2.1	29.4	0.6
Specialties			
Entrees	10.5	24.0	2.5
Cakes and pastries	9.2	24.4	2.2
Nationality foods	7.7	24.6	1.9
Creamers, toppings, and puddings	2.6	20.3	0.5
Other [a]	7.0	26.1	1.8
Total	100.0	—	25.2

[a] *Includes soups, dessert pies, breads, rolls, toaster and breakfast items, snacks and hors d'oeuvres, and miscellaneous items.*

Source: "15th Annual Frozen Food Age Survey," *Frozen Food Age*, August, 1970, p. 1.

In addition to planning the sales mix and gross-margin contribution of each department and product category, the same analysis is completed for each item in order to develop a pricing strategy that will achieve the overall gross-margin and net-profit objectives. The contribution method can also be used in estimating the sales and gross-margin contribution of each item in order to arrive at the product category and department sales mix and gross margin. Because there are several thousand items in the food store mix, the computer can be utilized to facilitate this task.

If the results of the item and product category contribution analysis show that the overall department contribution is inadequate, then adjustments must be made in the sales mix or gross-margin rates, or both, until the required department gross-margin contribution is achieved.

The contribution method of developing or revising price policy for items, product categories, and departments must be used in conjunction with a budget that identifies the total dollar sales, gross-margin, and net-profit objectives. Once the dollar objectives have been identified, the percentage contribution method can be used to develop or revise price policy on an item, category, and department basis.

Adjusting Prices and Margins for Shrinkage

The pricing of certain perishable merchandise must include compensation for shrinkage if the items, product categories, and departments are to make the projected contribution to gross margin. *Shrinkage,* as used in this text, refers to pilferage, loss in weight or spoilage, damage due to natural or handling causes, and markdowns or reductions in price below the original retail selling price. Whenever an item is priced on the basis of original quantity and less than the original quantity is sold due to shrinkage, the gross-margin objective for that item will not be realized. Likewise, if pricing does not reflect possible deterioration in original quality, markdowns in selling price may reduce sales and the gross-margin objective will not be achieved.

Pricing must compensate for anticipated shrinkage in order to project and control gross-margin contribution in each department. The fresh meat, delicatessen, and produce departments are the most vitally affected by shrinkage, especially spoilage and product deterioration, because of the highly perishable nature of the products.

Produce Department

The produce department requires particular care in pricing because it includes an average of 80 to 100 items, most of which are highly perishable.

There are two causes of shrinkage that are especially important in fresh produce departments—natural shrinkage, and handling and merchandising shrinkage. Natural shrinkage includes weight loss or spoilage that is due to the characteristics of the product and that can only be partially controlled through maintaining proper temperature and humidity levels. For example, fresh fruits and vegetables are living organisms and lose water during the life process. If they are sold by the pound, like potatoes, the loss of water reduces the weight during the shipping, handling, and merchandising processes, and the weight loss reduces the quantity available for sale. Also, due to the presence of microorganisms on fresh produce, some spoilage and deterioration is inevitable, and this reduces the quantity of merchandise available for sale.

There is also shrinkage due to handling and merchandising during shipping, receiving, preparation for sale, and display. Although this type of shrinkage is largely controllable, some will occur regardless of the care taken in handling and merchandising.

In addition to shrinkage losses that reduce the amount of merchandise available for sale, quality deterioration will reduce the value of some merchandise. Some merchandise will have to be sold at less than the full retail selling price because its condition is such that it is a poor value at the full price. In some cases, produce may be marked down because it is near the point of rapid deterioration and may become a complete loss unless sold quickly.

Shrinkage in the produce department affects the gross margin because it reduces the dollar sales but *not* the cost of goods sold. Therefore, the selling price must include a compensation for shrinkage in order to achieve the desired rate of gross margin for each item, category, and the entire department.

Let us study an example of how shrinkage affects gross margin and how we can compensate for this effect.

Mr. I. M. Green, the produce buyer for Big Bag Supermarket, wishes to realize a 26.5 percent gross margin on the sale of fresh bananas. Bananas are received at the store in 40-pound cartons and currently cost $4.50 per box delivered to the store. Because bananas are sold by the pound, Mr. Green calculates the cost per pound as follows:

$$\text{Cost per pound of bananas} = \frac{\text{Dollar cost per box}}{\text{Weight per box}} = \frac{\$4.50}{40 \text{ lbs.}}$$

$$= \$0.1125 \text{ or } 11.25 \cancel{c} \text{ per pound}$$

Now that the cost per pound is known, Mr. Green can calculate the selling price per pound necessary to achieve a gross margin of 26.5 percent by applying the standard pricing formula.

$$\text{Selling price} = \frac{\text{Cost}}{100\% - \% \text{ GM desired}}$$

$$= \frac{11.25\cancel{c}}{100\% - 26.5\%} = \frac{11.25\cancel{c}}{73.5\%}$$

$$= \frac{11.25}{.735} = 15.3 \text{ cents}$$

Thus, Mr. Green calculates that the selling price per pound of bananas must be 15.3 cents in order to achieve his gross margin objective on each 40 pounds. Because prices cannot include fractional cents, Mr. Green decides on a selling price of 2 pounds for 31 cents. If all 40 pounds in each box of bananas sold at this price, the total selling price per box would be $6.20 (15.5 cents per pound × 40 pounds). The gross margin would then be:

$$\text{Gross Margin} = \frac{\text{Sales} - \text{Cost of Goods}}{\text{Sales}}$$

$$= \frac{\$6.20 - \$4.50}{\$6.20}$$

$$= \frac{\$1.70}{\$6.20} \times 100$$

$$= 27.4\%$$

So the gross margin objective for bananas would actually be exceeded if *all* the bananas were sold at 2 pounds for 31 cents. However, due to natural weight loss and handling practices, each box of bananas may weigh somewhat less than 40 pounds when it arrives at the store. In addition, some spoilage may occur in the store due to handling by employees and customers, and some of the bananas may have to be marked down because of over-ripeness or poor condition. The net effect of weight loss, spoilage, and markdowns is that less than 40 pounds of bananas from each box will be available for sale, and some will be sold at less than the full retail price. Based upon past experience, Mr. Green knows that on the average out of each 40-pound box of bananas approximately 2 pounds will be lost due to natural shrinkage and spoilage and that about 4 pounds will have to be marked down to half price in order to avoid a complete loss. The total loss from weight loss, spoilage, and markdowns is equivalent to 4 pounds—2 pounds of complete loss and 4 pounds sold at half price.

Therefore, if the selling price is 2 pounds for 31 cents, each box of bananas will bring only $5.58 (15.5 cents per pound × 36 pounds) and not $6.20. The gross margin, therefore, will be:

$$\text{Gross Margin} = \frac{\text{Sales} - \text{Cost of Goods}}{\text{Sales}}$$

$$= \frac{\$5.58 - \$4.50}{\$5.58}$$

$$= \frac{\$1.08}{\$5.58} \times 100$$

$$= 19.4\%$$

Thus, due to shrinkage, a price of 2 pounds for 31 cents will result in a gross margin of only 19.4 percent on each box of bananas, considerably less than the objective of 26.5 percent. So it is apparent that an adjustment must be made in the selling price in order to compensate for shrinkage if the gross margin objective is to be reached.

The adjustment in selling price can be made if the amount of shrinkage can be estimated. Based upon experience, the buyers and merchandisers of perishable products can estimate, within reasonably accurate limits, the amount of shrinkage that can be anticipated for each perishable product.

We can illustrate the procedure for adjusting prices for shrinkage by using the bananas example. Because Mr. Green knows that the equivalent of 4 pounds of bananas will be lost from each box, he can calculate the cost per pound on the basis of 36 rather than 40 pounds. Therefore:

$$\text{Cost per pound} = \frac{\text{Dollar Cost per box}}{\text{Weight per box}} = \frac{\$4.50}{36 \text{ pounds}}$$

$$= \$0.125 \text{ or } 12.5\text{¢ per pound}$$

In other words, shrinkage increases the cost of merchandise because less than the original quantity is available for sale. So instead of pricing bananas on the basis of 40 pounds per box, Mr. Green prices them on the basis of 36 pounds, which is the amount that will be sold at the full retail price. Now that the adjusted cost is known, the retail selling price can be determined by using the standard pricing formula.

$$\text{Selling price} = \frac{\text{Cost}}{100\% - \% \text{ GM desired}}$$

$$= \frac{12.5\text{¢}}{100\% - 26.5\%}$$

$$= \frac{12.5\text{¢}}{73.5\%}$$

$$= \frac{12.5}{.735}$$

$$= 17.0 \text{ cents}$$

Now, Mr. Green knows that if he sells bananas at 17 cents per pound, he should realize a gross margin of 26.5 percent even though there will be a net loss of 4 pounds per box. We can determine the gross margin that will be realized at a selling price of 17 cents per pound, based upon a selling price per box of $6.12 (17 cents per pound × 36 pounds).

$$\text{Gross Margin} = \frac{\text{Sales} - \text{Cost of Goods}}{\text{Sales}}$$

$$= \frac{\$6.12 - \$4.50}{\$6.12}$$

$$= \frac{\$1.62}{\$6.12} \times 100$$

$$= 26.5\%$$

Therefore, the adjustment in selling price will result in the gross margin objective of 26.5 percent on banana sales if the estimate of shrinkage is correct. If shrinkage exceeds the estimate, then the pricing adjustment will result in a gross margin that is lower than the objective. Conversely, if shrinkage is less than the estimate, then the gross margin will exceed the objective. A pricing adjustment based upon an informed judgment of shrinkage is more likely to achieve the gross-margin objective than no adjustment at all.

There is another method of adjusting prices for shrinkage of perishable commodities that some may find easier to apply than the method just described. This optional method also requires an estimate of the shrinkage losses, only in terms of percentage of salable weight or retail sales instead of original weight or original retail value. For example, the percentage of shrinkage is determined by dividing the salable weight of 36 pounds into the shrinkage loss of 4 pounds. The shrinkage will be 11.1 percent of the salable quantity. The shrinkage percentage can also be based upon the dollar markdown. The original retail value of the bananas was $6.20 a box, but the actual sales would be $5.58 due to shrinkage. The markdown of 62 cents divided by the actual sales of $5.58 also gives us the shrinkage percentage of 11.1.

Once the percentage loss is estimated, the following formula can be used to determine the selling price necessary to compensate for shrinkage:

$$\text{Initial gross-margin \%} = \frac{\begin{array}{c}\text{\% gross margin} \\ \text{desired}\end{array} + \begin{array}{c}\text{\% shrinkage} \\ \text{and markdowns}\end{array}}{100\% + \text{\% shrinkage and markdowns}}$$

The initial gross margin represents the gross-margin percentage that must be used in pricing in order to achieve the gross margin desired, which is the gross-margin objective.

Using the banana-pricing example, we can illustrate the application of the formula.

$$\text{Initial gross-margin \%} = \frac{\begin{array}{c}\text{\% gross margin} \\ \text{desired}\end{array} + \begin{array}{c}\text{\% shrinkage} \\ \text{and markdowns}\end{array}}{100\% + \text{\% shrinkage and markdowns}}$$

$$= \frac{26.5\% + 11.1\%}{100\% + 11.1\%}$$

$$= \frac{37.6\%}{111.1\%} = \frac{.376}{1.111} \times 100$$

$$= 33.8\%$$

Therefore, in order to realize the gross-margin objective of 26.5 percent on banana sales, Mr. Green must price the *original* quantity, 40 pounds, on the basis of a 33.8 percent gross margin. The shrinkage rate of 11.1 percent is based upon a loss of 4 pounds from each 40-pound box.

Mr. Green can now price bananas on the basis of an initial gross margin of 33.8 percent and a cost of 11.25 cents per pound.

$$\text{Selling price} = \frac{\text{Cost}}{100\% - \text{\% gross margin desired}}$$

$$= \frac{11.25¢}{100\% - 33.8\%}$$

$$= \frac{11.25¢}{66.2\%}$$

$$= \frac{11.25}{.662}$$

$$= 16.9 \text{ or } 17 \text{ cents}$$

Either of the two methods described can be used to adjust retail prices in order to compensate for expected losses due to shrinkage. The first method involves pricing on the basis of the cost of salable merchandise only, and the second method is based upon pricing to achieve a higher margin for the original quantity, which will result in the desired rate of margin despite shrinkage.

The methods of price adjustment described above can be used for pricing any products for which shrinkage is involved. In the event that the products are priced by unit instead of by weight, as in the case of head lettuce (priced by the head) or citrus fruit (priced by the dozen), pricing can be on the basis of cost per salable unit or on the basis of the initial gross margin necessary to compensate for the estimated percentage shrinkage.

There is a basic equation for determining the effect of shrinkage upon gross margin:

Realized gross margin %	=	Initial gross margin %	−	Reduction % × (100% − Initial gross-margin %)

The reduction percentage represents shrinkage as a percentage of actual sales or salable weight.[1]

Using the banana-pricing example, we can determine the effect of shrinkage upon the gross margin realized from the sales of bananas that are priced to yield an initial gross margin of 33.8 percent.

$$
\begin{aligned}
\text{Realized gross margin \%} &= .338 - .111 (1.0 - .338) \\
&= .338 - .111 (.662) \\
&= .338 - .0735 \\
&= .2645 \\
&= 26.45\%
\end{aligned}
$$

The above example illustrates that the realized or actual gross margin

[1]John W. Wingate and Elmer O. Schaller, *Techniques of Retail Merchandising* (Englewood Cliffs, N.J.: Prentice-Hall, Inc., 1956), pp. 135-38.

from the sales of bananas that are priced to return an initial gross margin of 33.8 percent is 26.5 percent due to shrinkage reductions of 11.1 percent.

Meat Department

The retail meat department presents a unique pricing problem. In addition to shrinkage from weight loss, spoilage, and occasional markdowns, pricing must compensate for the loss associated with the preparation of retail cuts from carcasses or carcass portions. Fresh beef, pork, and lamb are merchandised as retail cuts such as steaks, roasts, cutlets, chops, and so on. These retail cuts are usually prepared in the store from larger portions such as whole carcasses, sides, quarters, or primal cuts. In the preparation process, considerable waste results from cutting and trimming. Also, the value of the retail cuts prepared from a particular portion, such as the round of beef or the pork loin, varies according to consumer demand. Top and bottom round steaks or roasts, for example, can be sold at a higher price per pound than rump steaks or roasts, cube steaks, or hamburger prepared from trimmings. Likewise, center cut pork chops and loin end pork roasts can be sold at a higher price per pound than rib end chops and rib end roasts. Thus, pricing in order to achieve the gross-margin objective from the sale of fresh meat must reflect preparation losses and other shrinkage as well as the relative yield of and consumer demand for the various retail cuts from each portion of beef, pork, lamb, and poultry.

The pricing of fresh meats that involve in-store preparation should be based upon cutting tests that indicate the cutting loss and yield by type of retail cut (see Table 4-5). The yield of the various retail cuts from beef rounds and other wholesale portions is dependent upon cutting methods, and yields (standards) should be based upon several cutting tests so that the results are reasonably typical of the carcasses or portions received. If the grade of meat purchased changes, then a new series of cutting tests should be conducted. Yield standards should be developed for all fresh meat items that are not sold in the same form in which they are purchased.

To conduct a cutting test, a wholesale meat portion, such as a pork loin or beef round, is cut into retail cuts, and each cut as well as the trimmings and waste is weighed. The yield of each wholesale portion is expressed in terms of the percentage of total weight made up by each retail cut, trimmings and waste. Retail prices are then based upon the yields, gross-margin objectives, competition, and consumer demand.

The Contribution Method. For example, Mr. Izzy Jowl, the meat buyer-merchandiser for Big Bag Supermarkets, must decide upon the selling prices for the retail cuts from pork loins during the coming week. He knows that he must pay 73 cents per pound for loins that average 14 pounds, or a total of $10.22 per loin. Based upon the pork merchandising methods and cutting techniques used by Big Bag, the pork loins will be sold as

rib end roasts, loin end roasts and center cut pork chops. Cutting tests
have determined the standard yield from each loin (see Table 4-6).

TABLE 4-5   Example of Yield Table for
Beef Rounds Based Upon Cutting Tests

Cut or Item	Percentage of Total Weight of Round
Ground beef	3.0
Lean ground	16.0
Cube steaks	7.7
Round steak	16.0
Top round	9.0
Bottom round	5.5
Eye of round	1.5
Heel of round	5.6
Rump roast	14.0
Waste [a]	21.7
Total	100.0

[a] *Bone, fat, and other unsalable trimmings.*

Source: SMI Meat System for Computer Operations (Chicago: Super
Market Institute, 1967).

TABLE 4-6   Example of Pork Loin Yield

Retail Cut	% of Total Weight	Pounds
Rib end roast	17.9	2.5
Loin end roast	32.1	4.5
Center cut chops	39.3	5.5
Waste	10.7	1.5
Total	100.0	14.0

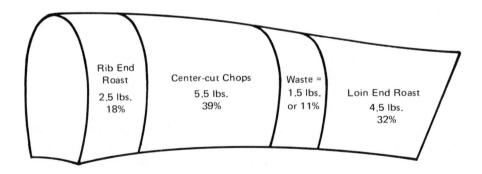

FIGURE 4-5   Alternate to Table 4-6—example of pork loin yield.

Mr. Jowl wishes to realize a 20 percent gross margin on the retail sales of pork loins. By using the initial gross-margin method, he can determine the selling price per pound necessary to achieve the gross-margin objective in view of the fact that there will be a cutting loss of one and one-half pounds per loin, which is equivalent to 12 percent of the salable amount of 12.5 pounds. However, he cannot price each retail cut the same because of consumer demand, so another method must be used to arrive at retail selling prices.

A variation of the contribution method can be used to arrive at the selling price of each retail cut necessary to realize an overall gross margin of 20 percent on each pork loin.

TABLE 4-7 Contribution Method for Determining Selling Prices of Pork Loin Cuts

Retail cut	Salable Weight	Selling Price per pound	Contribution to Sales
Rib end roast	2.5 lbs.	$ 0.79	$ 1.98
Loin end roast	4.5	1.19	5.36
Center cut chops	5.5	.99	5.44
Total	12.5	—	$12.78

Because Mr. Jowl wishes to realize a 20 percent gross margin for the entire pork loin, he must receive a total of $12.78 from all the retail cuts in the loin.

$$\frac{\text{Retail value or}}{\text{total selling price}} = \frac{\text{Cost}}{100\% - \% \text{ Gross margin desired}}$$

$$= \frac{\$10.22 \ (14 \text{ lbs.} \times 73\text{¢ per lb.})}{1.0 - .20}$$

$$= \frac{\$10.22}{.80}$$

$$= \$12.78$$

Now, Mr. Jowl must arrive at a pricing strategy that will result in selling each retail cut while realizing $12.78 (a 20 percent gross margin) on each loin. First of all, he wishes to offer a special price on center cut chops and decides to sell them at 99 cents per pound, which should be appealing in view of competition and the popularity of the item among consumers. Therefore, assuming no shrinkage other than the initial trim loss, he can expect to receive $5.44 from the sale of the center cut chops in each loin (see Table 4-7). Because loin end roasts are very desirable, he feels that he can provide a good value to the customer by offering them at $1.19 per pound. This will result in the receipt of $5.36 per loin from the sale of loin end roasts (see Table 4-7). Because he must receive a total of $12.78 for the loin, he can now determine the price necessary for the rib end roast. The center cut chops will bring $5.44 and the loin end roast (or roasts), $5.36—a total of $10.80. Therefore, he must receive $1.98 for the rib end roast ($12.78 − $10.80). The rib end roast weighs 2.5 pounds, so he must price it at 79 cents per pound ($1.98 ÷ 2.5 lbs.). Mr. Jowl decides that 79 cents is a competitive price for rib end roasts, so the pricing strategy for the loin cuts is completed. Although this example is simplified, and some trial and error is likely to be required, the method illustrated here can be used to make pricing decisions for fresh meat based upon percentage margin objectives, yield standards, and consumer demand considerations.

The Cents-per-Pound Method. Some food retailers prefer to base the selling prices of fresh meats upon a cents-per-pound markup rather than a percentage gross-margin objective. The basic reason for this practice is that prices will be more competitive and at the same time result in an adequate contribution to overhead and profit when the cost of meat to the retailer is rising.

For example, let us assume that the cost of the pork loins in the previous example increased from 73 cents to 83 cents per pound. If the pricing strategy called for a 20 percent gross margin, the amount received for each pork loin would have to equal $14.52.

$$\text{Retail value or total selling price} = \frac{\text{Cost}}{100\% - \% \text{ Gross margin desired}}$$

$$= \frac{\$11.62 \ (14 \text{ lbs.} \times 83¢ \text{ per lb.})}{1.00 - .20}$$

$$= \frac{\$11.62}{.80}$$

$$= \$14.52$$

The retail prices of pork loin cuts would have to be increased using the contribution method in order to realize a 20 percent gross margin on sales. In this example, the gross-margin dollars realized on each pork loin would be $2.90 (20 percent × $14.52). This would represent an increase in gross margin of 34 cents per pork loin because the gross margin was $2.56 per loin when the cost was 73 cents per pound, and the retail value was $12.78 (20 percent × $12.78). The average price per pound would be $1.16 ($14.52 ÷ 12.5 lbs.).

However, some retailers believe that pricing should be based upon a dollar gross margin rather than a percentage gross-margin objective because selling costs are not affected when the cost of merchandise changes. There-fore, assuming that selling costs remain the same, the original gross-margin dollar amount of $2.56 from the sale of pork loins should still be adequate to achieve the contribution to overhead of the meat department and net profit of the retail store. Because there are 12.5 salable pounds in each pork loin, the markup in cents per pound necessary to achieve $2.56 in gross margin is 20.5 cents ($2.56 ÷ 12.5 lbs.). The cost per salable pound is 93 cents ($11.62 ÷ 12.5 lbs.). Thus, the average price per pound that must be received for the pork loin is $1.14, 93 cents plus 20.5 cents, and the total amount that must be received is $14.25 ($1.14 × 12.5 lbs.).

The average difference in selling price per pound is only two cents between the percentage gross margin and cents-per-pound method of pricing based upon the example. However, depending upon the competitive situa-tion, extent of the product cost increase, and the volume of sales, even a small difference in selling price could be important, and the cents-per-pound pricing method can be advantageous when product costs are increasing or when the pricing objective is to realize a fixed amount of gross margin dollars.

PRICING STRATEGIES IN NONCONVENTIONAL FOOD STORES

Discount Pricing

In the early 1960s, a competitive strategy referred to as food discounting appeared on the scene. Basically, food discounting was a return to greater emphasis on price as a competitive strategy and some reduction in operating costs. A brief history of competition in food retailing is helpful in understand-ing the development and nature of food discounting.

The development of the supermarket in the early 1930s was a retailing revolution because it changed completely existing methods—small, clerk-service stores were replaced by large, self-service stores. The large, self-service stores were crude and simple and were able to offer food at lower prices because of lower expenses due to greater operating efficiency and the elimination of such services as credit and delivery. Price was the primary appeal to the consumer and, due largely to the depressed economic conditions of the times, the consumer response was immediate.

The crude and simple early supermarket, which lacked frills or services of any kind, gradually evolved into a more glamorous structure with the addition of customer services. These developments were in response to increased competition among supermarkets as the need for supermarket facilities began to be fulfilled after World War II. In addition, times were prosperous, and consumers were willing and able to pay for added frills and services.

As a result of rapid supermarket construction and consumer prosperity, more and more nonprice competition began to be employed by supermarkets in order to build or maintain sales. Advertising and promotion activities increased in an attempt to attract customers. Trading stamps became a popular promotional device beginning in the early 1950s and were offered in more than three fourths of all the supermarkets in the United States in 1962.[2] Various types of games and premiums were used in an attempt to increase sales volume in the face of more intense competition.

Increased nonprice competition in the form of fancier stores, customer services, and advertising and promotion were largely responsible for steadily increasing costs in food retailing during the 1950s and early 1960s. From 1954 to 1963, total operating expenses for members of the Super Market Institute, a large trade association, rose from 14.72 to 17.94 percent, or an increase of 21.9 percent.[3] A large part of the increase was traceable to increasing costs, as a percentage of sales, for advertising and promotion, store labor, and store occupancy. Trading stamps were responsible for the largest share of the increase in advertising and promotion expense. Increasing wage rates and greater fringe benefits were the primary reasons for the increase in store labor expense. Higher construction and real estate costs and the building of larger and more elaborate stores caused an increase in store occupancy expense.[4]

As a result of gradually increasing costs, retail gross margins also increased during the ten-year period, 1954 to 1963. Gross margin on sales increased from 17.4 percent in 1954 to 19.8 percent in 1963 for members of the Super Market Institute.[5]

More intensive competition among supermarkets, accompanied by higher costs and gross margins, led to a renewal of price competition in the form of food discounting on an experimental basis by companies that were looking for ways to improve profits, or at least to maintain profits in the tough competitive environment.

The early experimental food discounters began as food departments within general merchandise discount houses.[6] These food departments were often operated by existing food-retailing companies under a lease arrangement with the general-discount-house operator. In some cases, the food department was owned and operated by the general-discount firm.

The success of the early discount food departments led to both the

---

[2]*Organization and Competition in Food Retailing,* Technical Study No. 7, National Commission on Food Marketing, Washington, D.C., June 1966, p. 263.

[3]*Organization and Competition in Food Retailing,* p. 235.

[4]*Organization and Competition in Food Retailing,* p. 267-68.

[5]*Organization and Competition in Food Retailing,* p. 224.

[6]A *discount house* is defined as "a departmentalized retail establishment with either, or a combination of, owned and leased departments, selling to either a restricted clientele or to all buyers; which through its operations, merchandising, or other devices implies that it offers its wares at lower prices than will be found in conventional stores." Martin Leiman, *Food Retailing by Discount Houses,* Marketing Research Report No. 785, Economic Research Service, U.S. Department of Agriculture, Washington, D.C., February 1967, p. 22.

growth of free standing discount supermarkets, which were built adjacent to discount houses, and to the conversion of conventional supermarkets into discount supermarkets.

Thus, there are three types of establishments that follow the discount pricing policy:

1. A food department that is a component part of a discount house.
2. A free standing supermarket located adjacent to a discount house, which through advertising, or proximity to the discount house, implies that it offers its wares at discount.
3. A free standing, conventional appearing food store, not adjacent to a discount house, that through advertising, merchandising, or promotional activity claims or implies that it offers its wares at discount.[7]

A study of 37 food chains, 48 independent retailers, and 42 discount food retailers in ten standard metropolitan statistical areas indicated that discount houses had significantly higher average weekly sales and were open fewer hours during the week than conventional food stores.[8] The discounters' gross margins on selling prices were significantly lower than those of the conventional food stores, as were labor and other costs. The discounters had both a higher customer count and a higher average sale per customer, yet they offered their customers a smaller variety of merchandise. An examination of prices for 30 identical items showed that the discounters' prices were significantly lower. The discounters had larger stores both in terms of total store and selling area and also had larger parking lots. Thus, the study showed that there were many significant differences between discount food retailers and conventional food stores.

It is apparent that the true food discount operation does offer lower prices than the conventional food retailer. The effect of lower prices and gross margins was partly offset by operating efficiencies that reduced labor cost. The curtailment of store hours by early discounters as well as the fewer customer services that were available were two reasons why some discounters were able to reduce labor costs. Also, relatively few food discounters offered trading stamps, which cost the retailer between 2 and 2½ percent of sales. The reductions in expenses in addition to higher sales volumes presumably enabled the early food discounter to earn reasonably satisfactory profits despite lower prices and gross margins.

The success of the food discounters depends on the attractiveness of the price appeal to consumers, and it appears that a broad segment of the consumer food market remains very price conscious. Although price was the initial appeal of the depression-born supermarket, other appeals such as services, convenience, and quality have become more important in comprising value to the customer. However, it appears that some of the "extras,"

---

[7]*Food Retailing by Discount Houses*, p. 1.

[8]*Food Retailing by Discount Houses*, pp. 2-15.

such as trading stamps, that add to cost have lost their appeal and that price has reemerged as a more important appeal to a substantial part of the consumer food market. The increased importance of price as an appeal probably differs from that of the original supermarket because of the sweeping changes that have occurred in the socioeconomic status of the population. Since World War II, consumers have become generally more affluent, better informed, and more discriminating. Consumers have indicated their desire for more services of many kinds by the types of food purchased and the successful growth of retail food firms, which offer attractive stores and other extras. Along with the increasing economic and social status of the consumer, many more alternatives are competing for the consumers' dollar than ever before. The demands upon consumer income for recreation, housing, household furnishings, education, and other needs and desires probably encourages consumers to save on their food store purchases in order to have more money available for these other goods and services. Also, in a period of rising prices, such as we have experienced in the United States, consumers are more conscious of food price increases because of the importance of food in the family budget and the high frequency of food purchases. Therefore, consumers are more sensitive to food prices and are likely to respond favorably to lower prices during periods of price inflation. It is apparent that a goodly proportion of consumers will forgo some of the frills, such as trading stamps and carry-out service, in order to have more money available for other needs and desires.

It is also apparent that discounting does not represent a revolution in distribution but is merely an adaptation of the conventional supermarket. The discount food store is not unlike a supermarket in terms of physical arrangement, organization, and merchandising techniques. It does encompass some competitive advantages because of pricing and promotional policy as well as operating methods. However, these differences could be and have been adopted by many conventional supermarkets. "Food discounting is actually a marketing strategy. ... The food discounter has no inherent operating advantages over the conventional supermarket. The real challenge of the food discounter is that he may be fulfilling customer wants not being met by competing conventional supermarkets; that is, a desire for lower food prices."[9]

In a study of more than 125 chain and independent stores, it was found that prices, gross margins, and expenses were lower in discount food stores than in conventional supermarkets. It was also concluded that the elimination of trading stamps was the greatest source of expense reduction for the discount food store.[10]

In recent years, food discounters have become more difficult to distinguish from conventional supermarkets. Discount food stores have extended

---

[9]Robert J. Minichiello, "The Real Challenge of Food Discounters," *Journal of Marketing*, April 1967, p. 42.

[10]"The Real Challenge of Food Discounters," p. 38.

hours of operation and expanded product selection and services in response to consumer demand, and conventional supermarkets have adopted some of the cost-cutting and price-cutting techniques that were pioneered by the discount stores. Many conventional supermarkets have dropped trading stamps since the advent of food discounting, as indicated by the fact that the percentage of supermarkets offering stamps dropped from a high of 78 percent in 1961 and 1962 to only 20 percent in 1972, according to a Super Market Institute member survey.[11] Those stores dropping stamps have either reduced prices or shifted to other types of promotion, such as premiums. Both discounters and conventional stores are devoting increased attention to cost-cutting techniques to offset rising labor costs.

There are various degrees and methods of food discounting. Some firms that claim discount prices only reduce selected items in order to give the appearance of overall discounting. Some discount retailers reduce prices across the board on many items, although others restrict price reductions mostly to the grocery department.

The trend toward discounting and attempts to create a discount image reflects the importance of price in providing value to the retail food store customer. However, there are many other reasons why consumers patronize a specific store, which may be no less important than price, depending on the nature of consumer demand in the particular market area. The appeal of the discount strategy also depends upon the extent of savings available to the consumer in discount stores compared with conventional stores in the trading area.

Warehouse Markets

A more recent development in food retailing strategy is the warehouse or pineboard store. This type of retail food merchandising originated in the Midwest and West in the early 1960s, and although it has not grown appreciably, there are a few companies that operate successful warehouse markets.

The warehouse market is an application of the wholesale cash-and-carry operation to food retailing. A cash-and-carry outlet is a self-service wholesale store that sells grocery products to small retailers and institutions in full-case or less than full-case quantities. The cash-and-carry outlet serves accounts that are too small to be served efficiently from the large wholesale warehouse that usually does not sell less than half cases and sets a minimum order quantity for delivery. Due to the relatively small quantities purchased by these buyers, they may not be able to buy or get delivery from the large grocery warehouse without paying prohibitive service and delivery charges. However, by assuming the responsibility for selecting, loading, and delivering the merchandise displayed in half-case and full-case lots in the cash-

---

[11]*The Super Market Industry Speaks, 1972* (Chicago: Super Market Institute, Inc., 1972), p. 12.

and-carry outlet, the small retailer or institutional buyers can buy at wholesale prices.

The warehouse store is basically a wholesale cash-and-carry outlet for consumers. The facility is extremely austere; bare floors and exposed ceilings give it a warehouse or pineboard appearance. Construction cost is only a fraction of that of the conventional supermarket.

The size of the warehouse store is comparable to that of the conventional supermarket; however, all the floor space is used for displaying and selling merchandise in the warehouse store. There is no storage or preparation area.

Most warehouse stores offer a nearly complete selection of dry grocery products, some nonfoods, and a limited line of produce, dairy, frozen food, and cured meats. The emphasis is placed upon grocery warehouse merchandise, which includes dry groceries and nonfoods. Nationally advertised brands predominate in the selection of grocery merchandise. Perishables, which require refrigerated equipment and special handling, are limited in selection.

In some stores, customers shop with flatbed hand trucks that can accommodate more merchandise than the conventional shopping cart. Quantities purchased range from a single unit to one or more cases of an item. The store may even require the customer to price his own purchase with a grease pencil if the unit of purchase is less than a whole case. The price per unit and per case is marked on the outside of each case. The honor system is in effect when customers mark the prices on their purchases.

There are no customer services such as bagging or carry-out service. In fact, in many warehouse markets there are no shopping bags available, and customers must bring their own boxes or containers to carry their groceries home. Advertising is by word of mouth, with only an occasional mailer sent to the customers. There is often a membership fee, or a monthly fee of about two dollars.

The average sale per customer is much higher in the warehouse store than in the conventional supermarket because customers buy in larger quantities, although less frequently. The warehouse market, because of much lower construction and operating costs, can operate profitably at lower prices and gross margins than either the discount food store or the conventional supermarket. Most warehouse markets reportedly realize an overall gross margin of from 9 to 11 percent of sales, which is considerably below the gross margin achieved by either the discount or conventional food store. However, the product mix is quite different in the warehouse market, which has a much higher proportion of sales contributed by dry groceries than either the discount or conventional store, and the gross margin on dry groceries is normally less than that on perishables.

In spite of the differences in product mix, the warehouse food store can apparently offer savings to customers on the items that they carry. In view of the limited selection of items and the lack of customer services, the warehouse store appeals to consumers who are highly price conscious. It is likely that the consumers who patronize warehouse markets stock up on dry groceries in the warehouse store and purchase most of their perishables in conventional or discount stores.

The development of the warehouse store represents another attempt on the part of food retailers to implement a merchandising strategy, including pricing, that appeals to a particular segment of the consumer market. This particular strategy appears to have a much more limited appeal than discounting, but it has proven its place in the retail merchandising of food products.[12]

In assessing the profit potential of a discount strategy, the food retailer should consider the needs and attitudes of the consumers whom he serves. He should determine the appeal of lower prices compared with other strategies available to him. He should also make certain that cost reductions and sales increases will be adequate to offset lower gross margins so that the profit earned will be as great or greater than the profit resulting from another strategy. Flexible break-even analysis can be helpful in evaluating the profitability of discount pricing. Typical operating-statement projections list the same net-profit opportunities for all types of retail operations. In other words, conventional, discount, and warehouse markets have the potential to realize the same net profit. Much depends, of course, on how successful they are in carrying out their merchandising and operating functions (see Table 4-8).

TABLE 4-8 A Comparison of Possible Operating Statements of Various Types of Food Retailers

Item	Supermarkets	Discounters	Warehouse Markets
Gross Margins			
Grocery	18.0%	13.0%	9.0%
Meat	25.0	25.0	25.0
Produce	30.0	30.0	28.0
Total	21.5	15.0	10.0
Expenses			
Labor	8.0	6.5	4.0
Rent	1.6	1.0	.7
Other	9.9	5.5	3.3
Total	19.5	13.0	8.0
Net Profit before taxes	2.0	2.0	2.0

Convenience Stores

Still another merchandising strategy that has gained in consumer acceptance in recent years is the convenience store. Convenience stores began in the warm climate of the Southern states as open-front markets located on

---

[12]The information concerning warehouse markets is based upon a survey conducted by *Chain Store Age* magazine and reported in *Chain Store Age*, January 1967, pp. 32-34.

heavily traveled highways. They were small, compared to the supermarket, and catered to the consumers' fill-in needs between trips to the supermarket. The open-front stores were open long hours, seven days a week, and concentrated upon staple and convenience items such as milk, bread, eggs, cigarettes, ice cream, soft drinks, candy, picnic supplies, a limited selection of other dry grocery items, and some perishables.

For reasons of public health, shopping comfort, and quality control, the open-front stores became closed front, but continued to operate in much the same manner. The convenience-store concept spread to other parts of the country, and it has been estimated that the Southern region accounts for 55 percent of the total convenience stores today as compared with 83 percent in 1962.

The modern convenience store represents a unique type of food merchandising strategy. It is based upon a desire for convenience on the part of the consumers, in terms of location, shopping time, and hours of operation. Therefore, the convenience store is an attempt to fulfill certain consumer needs that are not met by the conventional supermarket or discount store.

The convenience store is usually located closer to the customer than is the conventional, discount, or warehouse store. The location provides an opportunity to purchase needed items with less travel time, which is especially important when time is at a premium. The convenience store, due to its small size and low average sale, also makes it possible to shop in less time and avoid long waits at the checkout, which is especially appealing when only a few items are required. Last, the convenience store makes it possible for the consumer to purchase items when supermarkets are often closed: nights, Sundays, and holidays. The convenience store, in effect, extends the shopping hours for the customer.

It is apparent that the convenience store supplements the supermarket by satisfying certain needs that cannot be met by the supermarket. Both types of stores serve the same customers, but in different ways.

John P. Thompson, Chairman of the Southland Corporation, Dallas, Texas, the largest operation of convenience stores in the United States, described the average convenience store as follows:[13]

Size	2400 square feet
Parking space	10-15 cars
Average sale	$0.80-$1.25 per customer
Employees	3-3½
Weekly sales	$3,000-3,500 (up to $8,000 in some metropolitan area stores)
Number of items	2,500-3,000
Gross margin	22-28%

---

[13]"The Convenience Food Store Industry—Past, Present and Future," paper presented before the 7th International Congress of Food Distribution, Madrid, Spain, July 1-4, 1969.

The modern convenience store is therefore smaller, has a lower average sale, fewer employees, a smaller selection of merchandise, and operates on higher prices and gross margins than supermarkets. Also, the convenience store is usually located close to suburban housing and is open at least 16 hours a day, seven days a week, and some are open 24 hours a day.

The convenience-store staff of three to three and one-half employees usually consists of a manager, at least one full-time employee, and part-time help.

Advertising and promotion is limited to occasional newspaper, radio, and direct-mail efforts. Emphasis is placed upon convenience and service with some price specials and coupons that entitle the customer to price reductions on certain items. Stamps or games are rarely used.

The convenience store represents a marketing strategy that has been aptly described as follows:

> The convenience store concept implements a marketing strategy which identifies and successfully caters to a specific market segment commonly referred to as the "pick-up" or "part-time" shopper. Today's affluent consumer desires and can afford to pay higher prices for convenience while shopping. This factor has caused the "pick-up" shopper market to expand, and largely explains the success of the convenience store concept. While convenience stores are not competing directly with supermarkets for the bulk of the consumer budget, they are competing vigorously and effectively for any supplemental food purchases that might be made. The "bantams" are not replacing supermarkets ... they are merely supplementing them.[14]

Thus, the modern convenience store is a unique food retailing organization in terms of merchandising strategy. It is not a modern version of the old "mom and pop" store or the specialty store. However, many old-line dairy stores have been converted to convenience stores through extension of product line and longer hours of operation. This is particularly true in the Northeast and Midwest, where dairy stores are similar to convenience stores in size and location and can be converted into full-fledged convenience stores fairly easily.[15]

The success of the convenience store is indicated by the fact that the number of convenience stores increased from 500 to 11,620 in the period 1957-1969. Convenience store sales made up only 0.2 percent of total U.S. grocery store sales in 1957 and accounted for 2.6 percent in 1969.[16]

Many existing supermarket and wholesale supply firms have recognized the potential of the convenience store by developing separate divisions that operate convenience stores, usually under a different name than that used for the supermarkets. There are also several corporations that operate

---

[14]LCDR Steven H. Evans SC, USN, and LCDR Francis L. Filipiak, SC, USN, "The Convenience Store as a Marketing Strategy," unpublished paper, Food Markting Program, Michigan State University, East Lansing, Michigan, March 1969.

[15]"The Convenience Store as a Marketing Strategy."

[16]*Progressive Grocer,* April 1970, pp. 82-83.

convenience-store chains. Some of the chain convenience stores are corporately owned and operated; others are franchised. It is estimated that there will be 25,000 convenience stores in operation by 1975 and that at least two thirds of these will be franchise operations.[17]

SUMMARY

Pricing is a vital part of the merchandising process because it affects sales, gross margin, and net profit. The objective for pricing for most retail food firms is a net return that is adequate to earn a satisfactory return on investment in the long run. This is known as target-return pricing.

In the short run, the pricing objective may be in terms of achieving a certain share of the sales in the market area in which the firm operates or it may be simply a matter of maintaining the status quo.

The establishment of a price strategy or policy by each firm requires decisions as to what level of prices will be charged as indicated by the gross margin on sales. Flexible break-even analysis is a useful tool for determining the price policy, which will most likely be formulated to achieve the profit objective, because it can be helpful in determining the most profitable price level once the level of expenses associated with the facilities and services has been estimated. This analysis requires an estimate of expenses and demand (sales) at each alternative price level (gross margin). The price level that results in the greatest positive difference between gross margin and total expenses indicates the most profitable pricing policy or strategy. The most successful pricing and merchandising strategy depends upon an analysis of consumer demand and the determination of that combination of products, services, and prices that best fulfills consumer demand in a given market area.

In developing overall pricing strategy, the contribution to gross margin technique can be used to blend price levels for departments, product categories, and individual items in order to derive the overall gross-margin objective. The velocity of sales and percentage gross margin determine the contribution of items, product categories, and departments to the overall store gross margin.

Break-even analysis is a useful tool in estimating the effects of changes in expenses or gross margin on the sales volume required to achieve the desired profit. It is also useful in determining the sales volume necessary to cover all expenses, a figure that is especially important when opening a new store, which may not achieve the potential sales volume for some time.

Variable-markup pricing is the method most commonly used in pricing individual food and related products. This method is based upon the application of varying rates of markup to items, categories, and departments depend-

---

    [17]"Bantam Franchise Boom," *Chain Store Age Western Supermarket Managers Edition,* July 1969, pp. 19-20.

ing upon both cost and demand factors. Cost factors include labor, equipment, processing, shrinkage and space requirements. Demand factors include sales velocity, competition, and consumer psychology.

In view of the multitude of items and the difficulty in identifying the true selling costs associated with individual items, variable-markup pricing is probably the most effective pricing method available. It may afford the food retailer the best chance of achieving the profit objective because it requires the consideration of both cost and demand factors.

The pricing of perishables requires adjustment for shrinkage. In addition, the pricing of fresh meat requires a determination of the yield of the various cuts and the loss due to bones and trimming in order that prices enable the realization of the gross-margin objective.

Discounting and warehouse markets represent two pricing and merchandising strategies that have gained consumer acceptance in recent years. Both strategies are based primarily on the appeal of prices lower than those offered by conventional supermarkets.

Another strategy that has resulted in success is the convenience store, which emphasizes service and convenience at a higher price level than the conventional supermarkets.

5

Advertising and Promotions

INTRODUCTION

Developing successful promotions is one of the most important elements in the merchandising activity of any food retailing firm. Although the purpose and goal of a successful promotion is often stated to be an increase in sales and profits, there is a long-run goal that is even more important. A promotion should be designed not only to increase sales for the duration of the promotional period but also to develop long-run customer loyalty. It should be looked upon as a means of building loyalty among present customers and as an introduction of the store's services and products to new customers. To achieve this goal, the merchandiser must emphasize three important elements in the promotion: *price, value,* and *service.*

Price is important from a merchandising standpoint because it attracts new customers and caters to those customers who make decisions regarding what to buy and where to buy it on price considerations alone. But to be effective in the long run, price must be combined with value.

Value is that element which relates price with the benefit received. For example, a firm may feature chuck steaks at a price 20 cents below the regular retail, but sell only the less-desirable cuts at this lower price, or they may fail to trim the steaks with the normal care that they exercise when the cut is not on sale. In cases such as these, the price may be lower, but it represents no additional, real value to the customer. If there is no additional or special value in the items included in the promotion, there is no lasting benefit from the promotion in terms of new, satisfied customers who will come back the following week. Value is the ingredient that builds a growing business.

Service also contributes to growing customer satisfaction and provides special appeal to a certain clientele that is not motivated by price alone. It is sometimes difficult to include service and low price equally in a promotion without destroying the effectiveness of one or the other. Promotions often tend to develop the image of either low price or good service and therefore appeal on one basis only. Very few firms have been successful by emphasizing service alone. However, although price plays the dominant role in promotional activities, service is a key factor in developing customer loyalty. Little customer loyalty can be expected when promotions are based on price alone. Consumers who are motivated by low prices alone will be loyal only to the lowest price, and they will shift to the stores that they feel offer the lowest prices at any given time. So, something more than low prices or good value is needed to build up a steady clientele, and that something is service.

Typical services that have been effective in developing a strong consumer franchise include: special attention to the meat and produce departments (as well as to other perishables departments); courteous employees; carry-out service; check cashing; delicatessen and seafood departments; and such features as community bulletin boards, community meeting rooms, and so on. Any of these can be highlighted in a promotion along with the price specials.

For maximum effectiveness, a promotion must combine the elements of price, value, and service. In this way only can a promotion introduce new customers to the store's products and services and develop a long-range sense of customer loyalty. Good promotions are essential in attracting customers on a week-to-week basis in view of the high proportion of customers who "shop around."

In the following sections, we will examine how promotions are prepared by looking at types of promotions, the coordination of promotional activities, the steps required to set up the promotion, and special promotional activities.

PLANNING A PROMOTION

One of the first considerations in planning a promotion is timing. Certain seasons of the year and national holidays dictate the type of promotion that is appropriate. However, there are other factors to consider, such as paydays, transient trade, and local shopping habits, and there are also some traditional promotional themes that have been used in the past.

Grand Opening Sale

The grand opening sale is a traditional promotion that is usually held the first week or the first two weeks that the store is open. However, in some cases firms may postpone this promotion until new store employees can be trained and the day-to-day store operation is somewhat normal. This is often the case with smaller chains or independent supermarkets to which a reservoir of trained employees is not available. In order that a store hold its grand opening sale the day the store opens, well-trained, experienced employees are needed. It is a difficult job just to open a new store with inexperienced employees. A store that tries to conduct a grand opening sale with new employees will find that the confusion of the new store plus the inexperience of the employees will result in unsatisfied customers, and this is a disastrous way to start a business. If there are not sufficient experienced employees for a smooth-running operation when the store first opens, this promotion should be postponed until the employees have received proper training.

Sometimes, the supermarket may be the first store to open in a new shopping center. In this case, the firm may prefer to delay the grand opening sale until the rest of the center is open, or they may repeat the grand opening promotion when the other stores hold theirs.

Anniversary Sale

An anniversary sale may celebrate the anniversary of a particular store or a special date in the history of the firm, such as "50 years of serving the Capital City area." This type of sale is most effective in small towns or local communities where the anniversary date has a special significance and where store employees are well known. Another type of sale that is effective in small towns is one that celebrates a town anniversary or event.

Seasonal and Holiday Sales

All retailing firms plan special promotions around seasons of the year and the major national holidays. Effective seasonal promotions include harvest, spring, cook-out, and back-to-school sales. These seasons dictate the theme of the promotion; for example, a back-to-school promotion would probably feature items for box lunches from the food departments and items such as loose-leaf fillers and pencils from the nonfood departments. It might also include price specials on sandwich and lunch bags.

New Year's, Washington's Birthday, Memorial Day, Fourth of July, Labor Day, Thanksgiving, and Christmas are the holidays that are marked by special promotions. Religious holidays, such as Easter and Passover, are also often given special promotional attention. For these promotions, traditional and special foods should be featured in weekly ads and special in-store displays. They should be planned far enough in advance of the holiday so that consumers can stock up at their convenience. There are, however, other timing considerations besides holidays and seasons of the year that are important to planning a successful promotion.

Pay Weeks

In many areas, sales fluctuate widely from week to week depending on the pay schedules of local business, industry, and government, including social security. Most businesses today pay their employees every two weeks or twice each month. There are usually many more sales during pay weeks than during nonpay weeks. If this sort of sales fluctuation is prevalent in your community, when should you plan a special promotion? During the nonpay week, in an attempt to smooth out the highs and lows of the sales cycle? Or should the promotion be scheduled for the pay weeks, when the customers have the most money to spend?

Most merchandisers agree that the best choice is the pay week. They cite these reasons:

1. Customers are doing their heavy shopping and will tend to shop the entire store and not just pick out specials.
2. Because more people are doing their heavy shopping, the pay week provides the best opportunity to obtain *new* customers.
3. With more consumer money being spent, the potential for a sales increase is greater.
4. It is easier to justify the cost of a large promotion (additional advertising, markdown costs, and so on) if a large sales increase can be obtained.

How long should the promotion last? The answer to this question depends on a number of factors, many of which may be peculiar to the individual firm or the individual store. Most merchandisers agree that the ideal promotion should be planned for not more than one week. Although some promotions are designed for a two-week period, there is usually a noticeable decline in the sales impact during the second week. This is a very natural occurrence. Most households shop for food at least once a week, and if the food advertisement serves as a shopping guide, it is unlikely that most customers would be impressed by the same special the second week, having stocked up on it the week before.

To maximize the impact of a promotion, the firm may schedule the promotion for less than a week, for example, Wednesday through Saturday. However, with the tendency toward longer store hours and seven-day openings, promotions have begun to tend toward week-long events.

COORDINATION OF PROMOTIONAL ACTIVITIES

Successful promotions usually include all the departments within the store. Therefore, planning should involve all the department heads, whether these are managers of departments in the store or merchandising managers at headquarters with overall responsibility for a specific department in all stores in a chain.

This type of coordination is important to maximize the benefits of tie-in promotions. If the meat merchandiser, for example, were to feature a steak sale as part of the promotional activity, the produce department would want to include items in the promotion that would tie in with the steak sale. Mushrooms would be a natural produce feature to go along with the steaks. Other such tie-in items might include cabbage and corned beef. The grocery department might feature mint jelly when the meat department featured lamb, or the bakery department might feature sandwich rolls when the meat department featured ground beef. All such tie-in promotions are not necessarily meat-department oriented. The dairy department might special butter or a particular brand of butter with a sweet-corn feature in the produce department, or cottage cheese could be promoted with canned peaches or canned pears, and so on.

Once the planning for the promotion has been completed through the coordinated efforts of the department heads at the company headquarters, careful follow-up and execution of the promotional plan is necessary at the store. This requires a coordinated effort by the department managers at the store. They must decide where and how to display and promote these tie-in items and the other promoted items. They often receive merchandising help and display suggestions from the headquarters merchandising staff. In some cases, certain displays are required and are so designated by headquarters directives for each department within the store. It is important that each department know what other departments are featuring for a given promotion and how the other departments plan to present and display their specials in order that the promotion achieve its full effectiveness for the store.

SETTING UP A PROMOTION

There are five basic steps to setting up a promotion. These apply for special-event promotions, such as Thanksgiving and New Year's, as well as a firm's regular weekly promotion. These steps are:

1. Develop the theme
2. Select the items
3. Establish the promotional prices
4. Decide on advertising methods

Develop the Theme

We have already discussed the various types of promotions that are commonly used by food retailers. In this section, we will examine how these themes are developed and the effectiveness of various promotional themes. Promotions that center their attention on holidays utilize that specific holiday theme. In a recent study by the Food Trade Marketing Council of *Family Circle* magazine, retailers were asked to rank the promotions that they felt were most successful, as well as those they felt were least successful for their company. In this study of 229 firms, dollar-day sales received the highest number of votes. Second was a promotion that utilized multiple-unit sales. In view of the controversy between single-unit pricing and multiple-unit pricing, it is interesting to note that these firms rated their most successful promotional activity as that which resulted from a pricing structure (both dollar-day sales and multiple-unit sales) that employs a form of multiple pricing. These two categories accounted for more than 50 percent of all "most successful" responses. The dollar-day sales received 34 percent of most successful responses, and the multiple-unit sale received 20 percent of the most successful ratings.[1] Seasonal themes ranked third but received only 16 percent of all most successful responses from those companies surveyed.

Although some firms preferred promotions such as celebration sales and special weeks, these were generally considered by most companies as being very weak promotional themes. In fact, stock-up sales, celebration sales, seasonal themes, and special-week promotions (such as National Dairy Month, National Baby Week) were ranked as the least-successful promotions by these 229 firms. Half the companies responding said that the stock-up sales and celebration sales were the poorest types of promotions. Twenty percent of the respondents felt that seasonal themes were the weakest type, and 14 percent said that special weeks provided the least promotional impact.

From the responses of these firms, we can conclude that price is an important factor in developing a promotional theme. These retailers have indicated that their most successful promotions emphasize price and their least-successful promotions are those that are general in nature.

The following are some specific comments from these retailers that reflect their reasons for citing general-theme promotions as the least successful.

Celebration Sales[2]

"Too general in nature—has least amount of meaning to consumers."

". . . it does not seem to have any real 'Money Saving' value to customers."

"Does not have the impact or attraction to the customer. Whereas Multiple Dollar Sales create more desire on the part of the customer to buy."

"Nearly all competitors have same thing—does not build up preference for our store."

Seasonal Themes[3]

"They do not provide enough originality to reflect a store image."

"When tied in with a Dollar Sale or a good low price Stock-up Sale they are very successful."

---

[1]John J. Sheehan, *Marketing Practices and Preferences in the Food Industry* (New York: Family Circle Magazine), p. 28.

[2]*Marketing Practices and Preferences in the Food Industry,* p. 32.

[3]*Marketing Practices and Preferences in the Food Industry,* p. 33.

"Does not have any valid reason to entice customers to buy more products."

"Does not prescribe definite course of action."

"Possibly because it is least related to price."

Special Weeks[4]

"Often other advertising scheduled in support of 'Special Weeks' fails to materialize (TV spots, newspaper tie-ins, etc.)."

"Usually not as closely related to individual stores as we would like—a canned effect."

"Usually several stores have this theme at the same date, therefore no advantage for pulling traffic or extra sales."

"Public has been overbombarded with special week advertising."

In developing a promotional theme, it is important to remember that no one theme will be successful for all firms. All the promotonal themes we have discussed in this chapter are presently being used by food companies with varying degrees of success. A promotional theme that works well for one company may not be successful for another. The *Family Circle* study does indicate, however, that themes that emphasize price are more successful than other themes for most retailers.

Select the Items

The second step in developing a promotion is the selection of individual items that will be included in the promotion. Many merchandisers feel that this is the most important step in the entire promotion plan. They claim that a promotion is made up of individual items, and how well these individual items create a total impression on the customer determines the success of the promotion.

There are five primary criteria that should be used in selecting an item for a promotion:

1. Sales potential
2. Price impact
3. Customer value
4. Profit potential
5. Advertising allowances

Sales Potential

Most merchandisers agree that an item with good sales potential is more effective in a promotion than a slow-moving item. It is certainly true in some cases that slow-moving items, when promoted properly, become fast moving

---

[4]*Marketing Practices and Preferences in the Food Industry,* p. 33.

items with good sales volume. However, there are many items with limited sales potential, such as gourmet foods, that will never respond to promotional pricing or advertising, and these should not be included in a special promotion.

Sales potential stems from a strong consumer demand. The consumer demand may have been developed over the years to a point where a particular item has a strong customer appeal on a full-time basis. Sometimes, customer demand is generated by a specific effort by the manufacturer of the product. This may be in the form of a specific advertising campaign, couponing of the product, or door-to-door sampling. The demand for some products varies greatly from one season of the year to another. For example, the demand for pumpkin derivatives and cranberry sauce increases greatly during the Thanksgiving and Christmas seasons. The inclusion of these items in a promotion at the right time of the year helps to make the promotion successful. It is always a safer bet to select an item for promotion that has proven sales potential than one that does not.

Price Impact

It was indicated earlier that price is an all-important element in a good promotion. For a product to have price impact, the price must be known to the customer, and the customer must be able to recognize the feature price as a savings from the regular shelf price. If the customer does not recognize this difference, the price impact is lost.

The question that becomes important, considering the statements just made about price impact, is how many of the 8,000-plus items in today's food store can the customer accurately identify with the correct price? (See Chapter 3 for the details of the study done on this subject.) The important results of a study made to answer this question is that very few consumers can identify actual prices of items, but many can come within five percent either way of the correct price. Even though consumers could not give the correct price for even the most frequently advertised items, they did known the approximate price, and they knew prices for private-label items as well as they knew those for national brands.

It is important from a merchandising standpoint to use those items in a promotion for which customers have some price awareness, or they will not be able to recognize the promotional price as a savings. This awareness of the savings is the price impact.

Customer Value

A mistake often made in pricing individual items for a promotion is to assume that a lower price automatically represents a value to the consumer. This is not always the case. In order that a product be of value to a consumer, the consumer must have a current need and desire for the product. Timeliness is an important ingredient in determining the extent of customer demand for an item. For example, in colder climates a reduction in the price of charcoal during the winter months would not represent a value to most customers. Customers recognize a product as having value only when they feel they are getting more value for their money than normal prices would provide. This concept of "normal price" is important in projecting a value to the consumer. When this normal price is exceeded, as when the market conditions force prices above normal levels, the concept of value is lost. This is important from a merchandising standpoint. It means that it is difficult to convey the impression of value on those products for which prices are above "normal." Even when the price is reduced from current levels, if the promotional price is above what customers visualize as the normal promotional price, the item will not carry the message of value to the customer. This means that commodities in good supply and at low price levels and for which there is a strong current demand will be the most effective promotional items and will convey the impression of value to the consumers.

In order that an individual item be effective in a promotion, it should be presented and sold in the store in the same physical form that is available to customers during nonpromotional weeks. It goes without saying that Heinz Ketchup is the same product at all times, regardless of its price. This is not always true, however, of fresh produce and meat. A wide variation in grade and quality often make it difficult for consumers to recognize value in the products they buy from these departments.

With the increased emphasis on consumerism, merchandisers should be careful to assure that promotional items are of the same grade and quality as those normally offered in their store. If cantaloupes are to be featured in a special promotion, they should be the same size and quality as those normally sold by the store, and the same principle applies for other items. Offering lower quality merchandise for a lower price is not offering additional or special value to the consumer, and this defeats one of the main purposes of a promotion—that of building repeat business from new customers.

Store managers must also emphasize the importance of the customer-value concept to employees. Too often, store employees take the attitude that they are doing the customer a favor by selling a product at a special price. The classic example of this attitude is the butcher who says, "Lady, at these prices I can't afford to trim the steaks any better." If store employees have this attitude, the chances of any promotion building new business are extremely remote. Even if new customers are attracted to a store by low prices and clever advertising, low-value promotions or poor employee attitude will bring an end to their patronage. It is also extremely important that managers order sufficient quantities of the advertised product to meet anticipated consumer demand. This is also a form of customer value that is important in developing customer loyalty. Items that are included in promotion must offer real value to the consumer, and the employees must reflect a belief in that value.

Profit Potential

Although perhaps much less important than the other factors already mentioned, the profit potential must be considered when selecting an item for promotion. If the item is to achieve price impact and customer value, it is unlikely that it can also provide a satisfactory gross margin for the retailer. Most items featured in a promotion return a much smaller gross margin (or sometimes no gross margin) because the merchandiser tries to emphasize the low price and value. This is especially true with leader items, which usually return little or no gross margin or may even represent a gross loss to the retailer. However, it is sometimes possible for a retailer to increase low gross margins by using advertising and promotional allowances, which are available to him from food manufacturers.

Advertising and Promotional Allowances

In Chapter 2, we discussed how advertising and promotional allowances work. We said that manufacturers make these available to retailers in order to increase the sale of the manufacturers' products. Promotional allowances in particular are designed to encourage retailers to feature an item in a promotion. The majority of nationally branded items that appear in a retailer's promotion are selected because of the special advertising and promotional allowances offered by the manufacturer. Promotional allowances make it possible for retailers to achieve price impact, customer value, and usually a profit for themselves. Therefore, retailers look to these allowances when selecting items for their promotions. In a study conducted by the management consulting firm McKinsey and Company, it was brought out that retailers who made the most extensive use of manufacturer-promoted items in weekly ads earned almost seven times as much income as the retailer that made only limited use of them.[5] This study noted that there are roughly 50 to 100 manufacturer promotions having a duration of 4 to 6 weeks available to retailers at any one time. Most retailers do not come close to using all of them.

Establish the Promotional Prices

Pricing for the day-to-day operations of the food store has been discussed in Chapters 3 and 4. We will now look at how promotional prices are established.

The Concept of Mix

As with everyday pricing, the concept of mix in promotional pricing is important. Just as no single markup is used to establish the price on the 8,000 items in a supermarket, so no single markup is used on promotional items. Items that are included in a promotion do, however, generally fall into one of three categories.

---

[5]McKinsey and Company, *McKinsey-Lever Promotion Study* (New York: Lever Brothers, 1965), pp. 13-24.

1. The main or primary feature item (or items) is usually sold at or below cost. If the main feature item does not carry any markup, it is a loss leader. A loss leader is used to attract customers to the store. It is not uncommon to have one or more loss leaders featured in a promotion for each department in the store, so that customers are attracted to each department.

2. The second category includes subfeatures that are priced at a low retail but carry some gross margin. These subfeatures are designed to attract customers by the low prices and implied customer value but at some gross margin for the store.

3. The third category of items included in a promotion are those that carry a good gross margin and represent a good profit potential to the retailer. These items are usually priced below regular retail but provide a profit opportunity to the retailer because they are backed by promotional allowances from the manufacturer or are available to the retailer at a lower than usual cost. These profit-potential items are often seasonal or tie in with the main feature. By associating these profit-producing items with the main feature, the customer is encouraged to purchase the item on the basis of convenience or as part of the total meal and not simply on the basis of price.

Although all promotional items do not fall neatly into these three categories, they do represent three general areas that describe the overall concepts behind promotional pricing.

Single-unit Pricing versus Multiple-unit Pricing

It is important to understand the purpose of single-unit pricing and multiple-unit pricing as used for promotional pricing. Single-unit pricing is designed to emphasize low price without encouraging the customer to purchase in quantity. This is not to say that it may not accomplish both price impression and sales volume, but its purpose is to emphasize a single low price. Multiple-unit pricing is designed exclusively to generate sales. It may give the impression of low price, but its purpose is to create sales volume.

When the retailer is attempting to convey the impression of a low unit price, single-unit pricing should be used with the leader in the promotion and with many of the feature items that carry a low gross margin. It is not wise to use multiple-unit pricing on the main feature that is being sold at cost or below cost. A retailer does not usually need to encourage customers to stock up on these items. Multiple-unit pricing should be used on items in the promotion that carry a reasonably good gross margin. In these cases, the retailer wants to encourage the customer to buy more than one item.

As we discussed in Chapter 3, multiple-unit pricing is not usually effective when the multiple exceeds a dollar. In general terms, higher-priced multiples are less effective than lower-priced multiples. For example, six for $1.59 is less effective in promotional pricing than three for 79 cents, even though the value to the consumer remains essentially the same.

Decide on Advertising Methods

Once the theme for a promotion has been developed, the items selected, and the prices established, the next step is to select the advertising media to carry the message to the consumers. The advertising media available to food retailers fall into three categories: printed matter, radio, and television.

In 1970, 70 cents out of every advertising dollar were spent on printed matter (see Table 5-1). This represents a slight decrease from 1969, when 72.7 cents out of every dollar went to printed advertising. Although food retailers are allocating more money for radio and television advertising than ever before, it still represents only a small percentage of the total. Twenty percent of total advertising expenditures went for radio and television advertising combined in 1970. This does represent a substantial increase over the previous year, however, when only 15.7 percent was channeled into radio and television advertising.

TABLE 5-1   Percentage Share of Advertising Expenditures by Retail Food Chains

Year	Print		Broadcast		Miscellaneous		Total
	News.	Mags.	Radio	TV	Outdoor	All Other	
1970	67.2%	2.8%	12.0%	8.0%	1.5%	8.5%	100.00%
1969	70.7	2.0	10.7	5.0	2.0	10.1	100.00
Percentage Change	−5.0%	+40.0%	+12.1%	+60.0%	−25.0%	−15.8%	

Source: "Budgeting Today's Ad Dollar," *Chain Store Age Supermarkets Executive Edition*, April 1970, p.30.

There are four important factors that influence the decision regarding what type of media to use in a promotional campaign. These are: (1) type of promotion; (2) market area to be covered; (3) concentration of stores within that area; and (4) availability and effectiveness of various types of media within that specific area. Retailers often use two or more types of media to present promotions to the public in order to get full coverage and effectiveness from the campaign.

Printed Matter

In the broad category of printed matter, there are three specific areas with which we are interested: newspapers, circulars, and special mailers. Each of these advertising media is presented on the printed page, and each may carry the same message. However, the usefulness, readership, and distribution of each is very different.

Newspapers.   Newspapers are the advertising media most commonly used by food retailers, accounting for 67 percent of their total advertising budgets (see Table 5-1). Newspapers have been effectively used for all types of promotions. In large metropolitan areas where one or two newspapers predominate, retailers can obtain effective coverage, at a low per person cost, through newspaper ads. As the concentration of food stores within an area covered by a newspaper increases, the cost of advertising per store declines. In other words, it becomes much more economical for a large chain in a metropolitan area to advertise in a newspaper than for a smaller chain or an independent. By spreading the costs over many stores, the total cost per store and relative to sales of using newspaper advertising is reduced. Besides the economy of newspaper advertising, it has the advantage of reaching many people. There is usually someone in every household who reads a newspaper, and most food shoppers look in newspapers for retail food specials. Also, the retail firm itself does not have to distribute this type of advertising—they have only to submit the copy to the newspaper, and the distribution is then out of their hands.

There are, of course, many areas throughout the country where good newspaper advertising is not available. Many communities are caught between two large cities, and therefore no one newspaper predominates. In this case, it becomes difficult to reach all households through any one newsaper advertisement, and it is often too costly to advertise in all the major newspapers or even in more than one newspaper. So, the lack of control over distribution becomes a problem. Another disadvantage of newspaper advertising is its widespread use by other food retailers. With so many food ads appearing in newspapers, the impact of any particular promotion is greatly reduced. Consumers are not as aware of any one ad and the promotions it offers when they have to sort through five or six major food ads in a single issue of a newspaper. In many cases, the entire ad may be overlooked because the reader's attention is drawn to another ad or to some other portion of the paper. Newspaper advertising is limited to the area covered by the circulation of the newspaper, and even then there is no guarantee that any one ad will be read.

Although newspaper advertising still accounts for two thirds (67.2 percent in 1970) of all advertising expenditures by supermarkets, this amount has been decreasing (down from 85 percent in 1960) as retailers devote more and more money to other media.

Circulars. The distribution of circulars, unlike newspapers, is controlled by the retailer, and therefore there is a greater chance that this advertising will reach the households that are potential customers. Because they can be aimed at a specific audience, circulars are often used to advertise a promotion for a single store within a chain or by independents. Circulars are more likely to be used in areas in which a firm does not have a heavy concentration of stores. The audience for the advertising can be pinpointed more readily with circulars than with newspaper advertising in a large, densely populated area. Circulars also have the advantage over newspapers of greater advertising impact because the firm's ad is not surrounded by ads for other firms. Like newspapers, circulars are suitable for any type of promotion.

However, circulars are usually reserved for major promotions because of the advertising impact they afford and also because the preparation and distribution costs far exceed those for newspaper advertising. Although it may not be economically feasible to distribute circulars to all households in a metropolitan area, they can still be a powerful advertising medium if selectively distributed to areas immediately surrounding each store. Distribution may be accomplished by using selective mailing lists, postal routes, or hand delivery.

Special Mailers.   Special mailers are used primarily for company-wide promotions that are designed to last for several weeks, as opposed to the selective promotion of a single store that is accomplished by using circulars. Because special mailers are usually tied to a company-wide promotion, all stores within the chain or cooperative advertising group must participate.

The special mailer is used in conjunction with a promotional program that is designed to build customer traffic for a period of 8 to 15 weeks, and hopefully permanent customers will be the long-term result. The special mailer typically carries a special coupon that permits the customer to obtain a premium or cash discount on a weekly basis for the duration of the promotion. For example, it might contain ten coupons, each good for one free dish a week. In addition to offering the free dish, other ads in the mailer might encourage the customer to purchase a complete set of dishes and various grocery items.

The primary advantage of the special mailer is its promotional impact. Because it is more elaborately prepared than a newspaper ad or a circular, it commands more attention and therefore creates more customer awareness of any given promotion. Another advantage of the special mailer is that it gives the customer a reason to come back and shop week after week by providing special-discount or free-merchandise coupons. This hopefully creates new shopping habits for new customers—having been introduced to the store by the promotion, they will shop there after the promotion is over.

The primary disadvantage of the special mailer is its cost. Because special mailers are usually more elaborate than newspaper and circular advertisements, their preparation cost is higher. Also, the cost of distributing special mailers is higher than newspapers and often higher than circulars. Another disadvantage is that mailers tend to lose impact after the first few weeks. The interest in this type of promotion varies greatly, but in all cases there is a decrease in customer interest in the latter weeks. A further disadvantage is that this type of promotion places the food retailer in a very inflexibile position. Once the special mailer containing the coupons is distributed, the retailer is committed to continue the promotion for the number of weeks indicated in the predetermined promotional plan. Should market conditions change during this period, the retailer is not in a position to adjust to this change by changing prices.

Radio

Radio is a commonly used media for food retailing promotional activity, accounting for about 12 percent of total advertising expenditures. Its primary use is to highlight features or special promotions. Radio can effectively be used for any type of promotion and has the advantage of reaching a broad area. Radio becomes more effective and less costly per store when there is a concentration of stores in the listening area. Radio is therefore a more effective tool for large chains in metropolitan areas than for smaller retailing firms or independents.

When used with a specific promotion, radio advertising finds its effectiveness in increasing customer awareness of a promotion rather than in giving specific details or carrying a specific selling message. Its value is primarily that of an "attention getter."

A distinct disadvantage of radio advertising is the limited message that can be effectively conveyed to the customer. This is important not only from a cost standpoint but also from an individual comprehension standpoint. The listener is not likely to remember a long or involved message. Therefore, to be effective radio advertising must be brief. Also, radio advertising is effective only when persons have their radios on and are listening attentively.

It is estimated that nearly 90 percent of all supermarket shoppers drive to their favorite store. In this case, radio advertising could be an important factor in forming last-minute shopping decisions.

Television

Television advertising by food retailers has begun to come into its own in recent years. Eight percent of the supermarket's advertising dollars are now spent on television ads, and this amount is growing every year.

Television, like radio, has its greatest effectiveness in developing customer awareness of specific promotional activity. As with radio advertising, the message must necessarily be concise, but the nature of television gives this medium an advantage over radio. The combination of sound and visual action afforded by television creates a greater impact on customers than either printed media or radio. The visual dimension also allows for more information in a given time period than can be expressed by sound alone. The availability of color television in more homes has increased the effectiveness of this type of advertising because products look real and can be very appealing. The sight and sound combination also creates a longer lasting impression than does sound (radio) or sight (printed matter) alone.

Although the traditional use of television has been to highlight specific products, many companies are now making use of television to carry institutional messages. Institutional advertising stresses the firm, the services it offers, and the overall quality of its merchandise or overall price range rather than stressing a specific product or promotion. One of the pioneers of highly creative television advertising was Almac in Providence, Rhode

Island. Its television ad program was credited with moving the chain to the number one market position in Providence. Almac, like the increasing number of major Eastern food chains that are using creative institutional advertising, enlisted the help of an advertising agency to create the television ad campaign. These food chains found that creative, often humorous television ads did more for sales than their earlier television campaigns that stressed promotions or customer testimonials. The long-run benefits of this type of advertising may prove much more valuable than the short-run sales increase that comes from highlighting a product and a price. Institutional advertising, when done creatively, creates much customer goodwill. Although the long-run benefits produced by institutional advertising are more difficult to measure than short-run sales increases, television advertising of this type should not be overlooked as an opportunity to gain new customers.

A disadvantage of television advertising is that its audience is limited to those who are watching television at the time the advertisement is presented. Cost is the biggest disadvantage to television advertising, however. The costs for even a 30-second ad during prime time (when most people watch television) can be prohibitive, and color ads might be completely untouchable for the smaller retailing firms. The high costs stem from high preparation costs and from the very high fees charged by broadcasting companies for the air time.

Waste in Advertising

The question of what types of media to use and how much to spend on each is a difficult question for most food chain executives. An article in the *Harvard Business Review* pointed out that *poor allocation* of advertising money was one of the four main causes of waste in retail advertising.[6]

Poor allocation is the use of the same amount of advertising week after week. By not reducing the amount of advertising on "off weeks" (nonpay weeks or weeks directly following periods of high food expenditures, such as holidays) or by not increasing advertising for special promotions, the most effective use is not made of advertising dollars. Waste also occurs when retailers improperly allocate advertising money to the various media. For example, too much could be put into newspapers and not enough into television in a highly competitive metropolitan area in which other food retailers rely heavily on television advertising.

Waste also occurs when indiscriminate pricing practices are followed in weekly ads. A primary example of indiscriminate pricing is the type of sales-oriented pricing described in Chapter 3 that takes place when one retailer lowers his prices and the other retailers in the area try to duplicate or undercut these prices. This intense competition usually results in excessive losses. Generally, very little long-term benefit is gained from these promo-

---

[6]John O. Whitney, "Better Results from Advertising," *Harvard Business Review,* May-June 1970, p. 111.

tional "price wars," and the short-term benefit is often not worth the cost.

A third type of waste occurs when retailers use advertising only for its short-run benefit—as a sales tool—and do not follow through with good product, convenience, and business values to create repeat business. Certainly, sales are the ultimate goal of advertising, and the effect of advertising—at least in the short run—is measured by sales. However, the long-term objective of advertising should be to create a favorable image in the customer's mind about the store or company. An institutional message that deals with the quality of the meats or the courtesy of the employees is valuable for its long-run benefit—for the image that it builds in the customer's mind over a period of time. Retailers who fail to incorporate a long-run objective into their ads are not taking full advantage of advertising's potential.

A fourth area of waste that occurs in advertising deals with its limited use in building better employee relations and loyalty. Ads that stress well-trimmed meats or high-quality ground beef have a very positive effect on employee pride and workmanship. Meat cutters take pride in the fact that their department is featured in the ad as having exceptionally well-trimmed meat. They tend to try a little harder to produce *the best* and they are proud that their company's publicity proclaims their efforts. Although retail advertising is aimed primarily at the consumer, there are many benefits that can be derived by keeping the employee in mind. Advertising should not be limited to selling "price" to customers. Employees read, listen to, and watch the ads, too, and their attitudes are shaped by what they see and hear in the company's advertising message.

Summary

Most major promotions by food companies today are introduced by a combination of printed advertising, radio advertising, and television advertising. The extent to which each of these is used depends a great deal on the type of promotion, the area to be covered, concentration of stores within that area, and the availability and effectiveness of the various types of media within that area. Newspapers, radio, and television are all mass media—they are directed to the public as a whole. Circulars and special mailers are selective advertising media—they are distributed to a predetermined audience in a specific area. Retailing firms that have a high concentration of stores in a metropolitan area are best served by some form of mass media. Because their stores serve all sections of the city, all radio listeners, television watchers, or newspaper readers are potential customers. Also, firms with a high concentration of stores can use mass media more economically than can smaller firms because their cost per store is lower. However, just as mass media favor the larger firms or those with a denser concentration of stores, the selective advertising methods (circulars and special mailers) tend to favor the smaller firms. Mass media is the shotgun approach; circulars and special mailers are the rifle approach. Considered carefully, each medium or a combination of media can be useful and highly effective for all types and sizes of food retailing firms.

SPECIAL PROMOTIONAL ACTIVITY

In addition to regular promotional activity, special promotions are used by food retailers. The area of special promotions includes three categories: trading stamps, games, and continuity promotions.

When trading stamps are used as a promotional activity, they are used by the retailer on a continuous basis. That is, the retailer issues trading stamps on all purchases and is not likely to switch back and forth from a policy of issuing stamps to a policy of not issuing stamps. On the other hand, games and continuity promotions are not continuous in nature but are used selectively by food retailers. Some retailers use as many as four or five special promotions over a twelve-month period. Other retailers may promote only one or two games or continuity promotions over the course of a year.

All three categories of special promotions are important forms of non-price competition. Historically, nonprice competition has been equally as important as price competition among food retailers. This can be seen and measured most dramatically with the retailer use of trading stamps. Because trading stamps stand apart from all other types of promotional activity, it becomes easy to pinpoint their cost, use, and effect on retail sales.

Trading Stamps

History of Trading Stamps

Trading stamps were not innovated by food retailers. The first trading-stamp company was organized by Thomas Sperry in 1896. Sperry was the first to sell a stamp program to a variety of retail businessmen. His company, Sperry & Hutchinson, was sold to a group of New England retailers who then dispensed stamps to their customers as a cash discount on small purchases. Sperry & Hutchinson, commonly identified today as the S & H Green Stamp Company, set the pattern for our modern trading-stamp redemption. They supplied the stamps to the retailers and premium catalogs and stamp books for their customers. They also established the ratio of issuing one stamp for each ten-cent purchase at retail, a policy that is followed today by all major stamp companies.[7]

Although trading stamps have been in use for nearly 100 years, their use was very limited until the 1950s. Prior to this time, most retail competition was based on price. Nonprice competition in the form of extra service did, of course, exist (such as delivery and credit), but service is more difficult to pinpoint than a specific item such as stamps. From 1900 to 1930, less than 10 percent of total retail trade found it advantageous to issue trading stamps. Trading-stamp use during World War I, the Depression, and World War II dropped substantially. During World War I, it is estimated that retailers giv-

---

[7]Dan Padberg, *Economics of Food Retailing* (Ithaca, N.Y.: Cornell Home Study Program), p. 142.

ing trading stamps accounted for only about 2 percent of retail trade.[8] During the Depression, few retailers were financially able to afford the luxury of such nonprice competition as trading stamps. During World War II, when food products and other merchandise were in extremely short supply and rationing was in effect, the added inducement of trading stamps to increase customer purchases was unnecessary and useless.

Use of trading stamps by food retailers began to grow in the 1950s. Their greatest growth occurred at the end of the supermarket building boom—between 1954 and 1960. World War II had restricted new construction and, of course, new supermarket development. Following World War II, the supermarket building boom began. During the immediate postwar period of 1945 to 1952, there was no great need for supermarkets to use trading stamps. However, as many communities became saturated with supermarkets in the late 1950s, sales became more difficult to obtain so that nonprice competition—in the form of trading stamps—became a predominate merchandising tool.

In 1952, there were approximately 16,540 supermarkets in the United States. By 1954, this number had mushroomed to 21,440, and by 1960, to 33,000—twice as many as were in existence in 1952. In 1952, $57 million worth of trading stamps were purchased by retailers. By 1954, this had increased to $122 million, and by 1960 it had grown to $540 million. In other words, during this eight-year period when supermarkets more than doubled in number, the amount of trading stamps purchased grew almost ten times greater (see Table 5-2).

TABLE 5-2   The Growth in Supermarkets and Trading Stamps

Year	Number of Supermarkets [a]	Trading Stamps Purchased [b] (millions of dollars)
1952	16,540	57
1953	18,940	87
1954	21,440	122
1955	24,700	192
1956	27,100	375
1957	28,800	380
1958	29,900	395
1960	33,300	540

[a] *Source: Facts in Grocery Distribution (New York: Progressive Grocer, annual survey).*
[b] *Source: Sperry & Hutchinson Company, unpublished report on trading stamps.*

By 1962, trading stamps had reached their peak, and it is estimated that about three fourths of all supermarkets were issuing stamps. This type of nonprice competition leveled off in popularity during the late 1960s and early 1970s. The use of trading stamps has declined continually since 1962,

---

[8]*Economics of Food Retailing*, p. 142.

and only about 20 percent of all supermarkets were issuing stamps in 1972.

How a Trading Stamp Promotion Works

A number of food chains actually own their own stamp companies or have a controlling interest in a stamp company. For example, the Kroger Company organized Top Value Enterprises; the Grand Union Company organized and operates Shop & Save Trading Company (Triple S Blue Stamps); and Food Fair organized the Merchants Green Stamp Company. In most cases, however, food chains that are trading-stamp users obtain their stamps from private stamp companies.

Step One—Retailer Obtains a Trading-stamp Franchise. It has long been the policy of the major trading-stamp companies to issue their trading stamps to only one major account in each trading area. (A major account is selected by its sales volume and is usually a supermarket company or a department store.) This is known as an exclusive franchising agreement because it permits only one type of firm in each area to carry the stamp. It would be possible, however, for a supermarket company and a department store to both issue the same trading stamp if they were not competitors. Exclusive franchising agreements for key accounts give the retailer the exclusive rights to use the stamp in his trading area. One of the main reasons for food retailers to use stamps is to build customer loyalty. When a particular trading stamp is available only at one food store (or chain of stores) in a given area, customers who start saving that stamp must shop that store in order to continue saving those stamps.

In addition to franchising major accounts, stamp companies develop associate accounts to support the major account in the community. Associate accounts usually include gas stations, dry cleaners, drug stores, and other smaller businesses. There is no restriction among associate accounts regarding competitors issuing the stamps.

Over the years, certain stamp companies have developed better consumer followings than others. Those with the best consumer franchises are the ones that have historically been most sought after by retailers. The value of this consumer following to retailers is best illustrated by the situation that occurred in the late 1960s when many food chains were dropping trading stamps in favor of direct price competition and other types of promotional activity. During this period, those trading stamp companies that were considered to have the best consumer following were not only the last to be dropped by retailers switching to discounting but they were also the ones that were often picked up by another competitor in the same trading area. In 1965, Stop & Shop in Boston relinquished their franchise with Top Value Stamps when they embarked on a "mini-price" program (a promotional program that emphasized price rather than nonprice competition). One of their competitors, Star Markets, immediately picked up the Top Value Stamp franchise and dropped their company-owned Star Gold stamps. This action was inspired by the fact that Top Value was considered to have a better consumer following in the New England area than Star Gold stamps, and also because Star Markets felt that they could convert some of the stamp-saving customers from Stop & Shop to their stores by making Top Value Stamps available at Star Markets.

In the early 1950s, those companies that were first in their trading area with a stamp franchise realized the greatest increase in sales from this type of nonprice competition. Food retailers that joined the trading-stamp bandwagon late in the 1950s found themselves in a "me too" position. Although trading stamps were still being widely used and were widely accepted by consumers, the initial impact had worn off and therefore they had less merchandising value as a form of nonprice competition.

Between 1953 and 1955, the average sales gain in supermarkets giving stamps far exceeded the sales gain in the nonstamp supermarkets (see Table 5-3). After 1955, the sales gain in supermarkets giving stamps was equal to and in some years actually below the average sales gain for supermarkets not giving stamps. Therefore, in retrospect it can be seen that even though many food companies were still adding trading stamps as a means of nonprice competition in the late 1950s, the importance of trading stamps was declining. Had these companies channeled their promotional efforts in directions other than trading stamps, they would probably have been more successful in terms of increased sales. As with other types of promotional activity, the greatest benefits from trading stamps were received by the innovators.

TABLE 5-3   Effect of Trading Stamps on Supermarket Sales

	Average Sales Gain	
	Supermarkets Giving Stamps	Supermarkets not Giving Stamps
1954 vs. 1953	18%	12%
1955 vs. 1954	25	12
1956 vs. 1955	13	14
1957 vs. 1956	14	14
1958 vs. 1957	10	12
1959 vs. 1958	9	10
1960 vs. 1959	8	10

Source: *Facts in Grocery Distribution* (New York: Progressive Grocer, 1959, 1960, and 1961). Table prepared by the Federal Trade Commission.

Step Two—Retailer Buys Trading Stamps.   Retailers purchase trading stamps from the major stamp companies in books of 5,000 stamps. The price to the retailer depends on the retailer's volume and on the individual pricing policy of the stamp company. The price range for a book of 5,000 stamps is from $8.75 to $15.00. This generally means that the larger accounts (or the major accounts in each trading area, such as a supermarket chain or a department store) pay approximately $10.00 for a book of stamps. At this price, the cost of trading stamps to the retailer amounts to approximately 1½ to 2 percent of sales because the stamps are not issued for all purchases. This would be an added expense to the retailer if sales volume did not increase sufficiently to offset the cost of the stamps, unless stamps were substituted for other methods of promotion. To figure the sales increase necessary to cover the cost of trading stamps, it is helpful to use break-even analysis. If the sales increase exceeds the break-even point, it is not necessary to increase retail prices. However, in reviewing food prices within various companies that issued stamps in the early 1950s, the National Commission on Food Marketing concluded that there was a slight increase in the retail prices of stores issuing trading stamps. This information came from a study conducted by the United States Department of Agriculture in 1958 titled "Trading Stamps and Their Impact on Food Prices." The study concluded that stores that added stamps in 1956 and 1957 had increased their prices by .7 percent above the level charged before stamps in 1953 to 1955. In the same 21 cities where this study was conducted, nonstamp stores increased prices by only .1 percent. Therefore, the net difference in price increase of stamp stores versus nonstamp stores was .6 percent. However, from a realistic standpoint the consumer was still better off shopping stores that issued trading stamps because they could effect a net savings of approximately 1.4 percent, the difference between the value of the stamps (about 2 percent of purchases) and the increase in prices (.6 percent).

Step Three—Retailer Issues Stamps.   After the retailer obtains a stamp franchise and arranges to buy the trading stamps, the next step is to establish a policy to issue trading stamps. Since Sperry & Hutchinson began issuing stamps in 1896, retailers have given one stamp for each ten-cent purchase. There are, however, many exceptions as to the type of merchandise for which stamps can be issued. In some states, it is against the law to issue trading stamps on fair-traded items. The courts have interpreted this type of promotional activity as a discount below the fair-traded price. In many states, it is illegal to issue trading stamps on items such as milk, tobacco, and alcoholic beverages.

Bonus stamps are often issued to customers with the purchase of specific merchandise. Coupons in the store's weekly newspaper ad provide the primary vehicle for issuing bonus stamps. Typical applications of bonus stamps would be a special coupon designating 100 free stamps with a ten-dollar grocery purchase, or 50 free stamps with the purchase of three pounds or more of ground beef. What is the cost and impact of bonus-stamp coupons? Remember, we indicated that the cost of stamps to the typical food retailer was ten dollars for a book of 5,000 stamps. This is equal to a cost of two dollars per thousand. At this price, 100 stamps cost the retailer 20 cents. The value of using bonus-stamp coupons must be weighed against the value of reducing a product by the cost of the stamps to be issued. In other words, the retailer must determine the impact of a bonus-stamp coupon worth 50 free stamps on the purchase of an item, for example three pounds or more of ground beef, versus the impact of reducing the price of the item by 10 cents (the cost of 50 stamps). In many cases, the stamp alternative provides the greatest impact in terms of increased sales. When the cost alternatives are the same, the retailer simply decides whether stamps or price will produce the best results, and then he selects that alternative.

Merchandisers have found that in most cases the cost of price reductions to sell a given quantity of merchandise is greater than the cost involved in using bonus-stamp coupons in situations where trading stamps are well accepted by consumers.

Therefore, one of the primary advantages of the bonus-stamp coupon on specific items is that it produces a greater effect in terms of increased sales at a lower cost than a corresponding effort using price alone.

Step Four—Stamp Redemption. In most cases, the responsibility for redeeming trading stamps lies with the stamp company. Typically, the trading-stamp company establishes redemption stores where customers can exchange accumulated stamps for merchandise. Although stamp companies provide catalogs and stamp-saving books, retailers make these available to their customers when they shop their stores. The supply of these materials is built into the cost of the trading stamps, and they are considered a service of the stamp company.

The redemption process provides several opportunities for the stamp companies to earn a profit. First, all the stamps purchased by retailers are not redeemed by customers. However, most studies indicate that the redemption rate is very high. The Sperry & Hutchinson Company has estimated that 97 percent of their stamps are redeemed at some time. Whatever the unredeemed quantity may be, this represents a profit margin for the stamp companies because they have sold stamps without the burden of redeeming them.

A second profit opportunity for the stamp company lies with their redemption value of merchandise. Stamp companies redeem stamps for merchandise based on the retail value of the merchandise, but they obtain the premiums at a wholesale price. In some cases, the actual redemption value in terms of stamps required far exceeds the normal retail price of the item. In one study, it was found that a General Electric Steam Iron that retailed for $14.89 in a metropolitan department store required seven and one-half S & H Green Stamp books. According to Sperry & Hutchinson, the books are valued at $3.00—which represents a price of $22.50 for the steam iron. This type of overpricing also provides a profit opportunity for the stamp company.

A third area of profit opportunity deals with the time value of money. Retailers purchase stamps and the stamp company has the use of this money until the customer cashes in the trading stamps that have been accumulated. This is normally a matter of several months, which enables the stamp company to use or invest the retailer's money during this period of time.

Games

Although games have been used as a promotional device for many years, the height of their use occurred during the 1950s along with the extensive use of trading stamps. During this particular period, nonprice competition was at its height, and games, like stamps, were an important form of nonprice competition.

A supermarket game is a promotional activity that can be played by any person coming into the retail store. It is important to note that games are not restricted to paying customers. In other words, it is not necessary to make a purchase to play a supermarket game. The purpose of the game is to build store traffic. As one merchandiser put it, "nothing has ever done as much to build store traffic as supermarket games for the cost involved." Games are designed to create excitement for the shopper and to keep the shopper coming back to the same store for a period of several weeks. This must all be done at a reasonable price to the retailer.

The cost of games averages between 0.4 percent and 0.75 percent of total store sales. This is far less than the 1½ to 2 percent of sales that it costs retailers to issue trading stamps. The typical supermarket game lasts about 13 weeks. This length of time is designed to re-establish the shopping habits of the new customer that the game attracts to the store. Some games may be longer or shorter in duration, but they must be long enough to attract new customers back to the store for several weeks.

Types of Games

Games can be generally classified into four categories: (1) collector games; (2) probability games; (3) television games; and (4) punch cards.

Collector Games. The collector game has historically been the most popular and has perhaps been considered the most successful of all types of retail games. The collector game usually requires some type of card on which the customer collects various game pieces (see Figure 5-1). One of the advantages of the collection game is that the customer has the collector card in his possession as a reminder as well as an incentive to continue to play the game. Generally, the shopper receives a game piece on each store visit (see Figure 5-2). Because no purchase is required, anyone coming into the store may receive a game piece upon request.

One type of collector game is the matching game. The shopper receives a game piece and by matching this with a like game piece or the other half of the same piece receives a prize. Very often, matching games do not require a collector card but they do require that the shopper save the various pieces to find a match.

The second type of collection game is bingo. Various forms of bingo have been used, and these do require a collector card on which the shopper places the various game pieces (see Figure 5-3).

Other types of collection games might be names of states, or names of presidents, that would be collected over a period of time to fill any given

FIGURE 5-1   Crossword collector game, as used by Jewel food stores. Courtesy of Herron-Kienzle, Inc., and Jewel, Inc.

FIGURE 5-2 Game piece used with crossword collector game, as used by Jewel food stores. Courtesy of Herron-Kienzle, Inc., and Jewel, Inc.

collection card. The game rules usually state that when some or all of the card is filled the shopper will receive a prize.

One of the drawbacks to the collection game is that it takes several weeks for anyone to win. This has a dampening effect on the promotional value of the game. In other words, when a retailer introduces the game and encourages his customers and shoppers to play he does so by implying that they will win. However, during the first few weeks it is impossible for shoppers to collect enough game pieces to fill the collector card or to qualify as a winner. To offset this disadvantage and create more interest early in the collector game promotion, many games include a feature known as "instant winners."

The instant-winner feature is built into certain game pieces in such a manner that shoppers receiving the game piece will know immediately if they have won. This is often accomplished by having the game piece concealed when it is given to the customer. Concealment may be a tear-off strip, an ink spot that must be rubbed off, or the game piece may simply be packaged in a small envelope. Concealing the instant-winner feature in this manner prevents the shopper from knowing its value until it is revealed.

Another feature that is often built into the collector game is known as the "everybody wins" feature. When games are used in retail stores, many customers become ardent game players. They play the game week after week expecting to win. If they do not win, they become very discouraged and disenchanted with the entire concept of game playing. In an attempt to satisfy these true game players, some collector games, as well as other types of games, provide a prize for everyone—even if it is a very small prize. The everyone-wins feature need not add to the overall cost of the game, but it does require that the prizes be broken down into smaller units.

FIGURE 5-3   Bingo collector game and game piece. Courtesy of Herron-Kienzle, Inc., and Super Valu Stores, Inc.

When there are only a few winners, the prizes have greater individual value. However, the total amount to be distributed in prizes could be the same if there are few or many prizes being distributed.

Many game and merchandising people feel that the everyone-wins feature dilutes the promotion by reducing the value of the top prizes and thereby lessens the impact of the total game. They feel that playing a game when there are prospects of winning $10,000 creates more excitement than a game that awards a small amount and for which the top prize is only $2,000 or $3,000.

Collector games may or may not be used in conjunction with the instant-winner feature or the everybody-wins feature. Also, the game may include one of these features without the other.

Probability Games.   Unlike the collector game, the probability game provides the shopper with the opportunity to play and win each time he enters the store. With the probability game, there are no game pieces to be saved from week to week. A new game piece is provided the customers on each shopping trip. Here again, no purchase is required.

An example of a probability game is one for which the shopper receives a card with nine spots. Under each spot is a number. If the customer can uncover three of these spots and reveal consecutive numbers, he wins. Because the numbers on the cards are placed at random, the customer never knows in advance which numbers are under the spots. The law of probability determines how frequently customers will select the numbers in their correct sequence. This can be predicted in advance and prizes allocated on the predicted frequency of winning.

The appeal to customers of this type of game is that they have a chance of winning every time they enter the store. They do not have to wait until they collect a certain number of pieces or until they match certain pieces.

Probability games have never been very popular with supermarket operators. The principal disadvantage of this type of game is that the customer does not take home a game piece that acts as a reminder to return to the store and play the game again. Lacking the ever-present reminder of a take-home game piece, the customer does not maintain the incentive to return to the store. Also, if the customer does not win the first few times the game is played, much of the excitement and enthusiasm for the game is lost. Another disadvantage of the probability game is that the game must be played under the supervision of authorized store personnel. In other words, the customer cannot take the game home and try to win but must go through the game process in the store. This can cause delays if the game is played at the checkstand or requires additional people to supervise the game if it is played at a courtesy counter or some other central point within the store.

Television Games.   The most famous of all television games is one called "Let's go to the races." Retailers using this game provide cards or game pieces to persons entering their store during a given week. The game cards indicate winners of horse races. The cards have no value when that are issued to shoppers, and shoppers can collect a card each time they enter the store (no purchase necessary). One evening a week is designated as race night, and films of actual races are shown on television.

The names of the horses in the race correspond to the names on the game pieces. At the conclusion of the race, shoppers who hold cards bearing the name of a winning horse can go back to the store and collect their prize. The interesting feature of this game is that the game pieces have no value until the race is shown on television.

An advantage of this type of game is that winners must return to the store to collect their prize. The more winners, the more shoppers returning to collect. This adds to the traffic-building effect of the game.

Punch Cards. A fourth type of game, which must be categorized apart from others, is the punch card. This game is unique because it does require a purchase by the customer. A typical punch card is designed with blank spaces to be punched by the checker at the store each time a purchase is made. In the center of the punch card is a spot covered by ink that can be removed with a moist cloth. Under this spot is a dollar figure, from $1 to $500.

Customers who play this game are not permitted to remove this spot until the entire card has been punched. When all spaces on the card have been punched, only an authorized store representative can remove the ink spot and reveal the dollar amount to the customer. At this point, the customer is guaranteed to be a winner. Although this type of game includes the everybody-wins feature, it is different in that it does require a purchase by customers. Because customers are guaranteed a substantial prize at the conclusion of the game, the cost to the retailer for the punch card game is higher than other types of games. The cost of running a punch card game averages from 1.3 percent of sales to 1.75 percent of sales as compared with other games, which cost between 0.4 percent of sales and 0.75 percent of sales.

Many retailers who have used this game feel the additional cost is worthwhile because customers tend to play the game longer than other types of games. Because there is a guaranteed dollar prize at the conclusion of the game, there is a greater incentive for the customers to complete the entire punch card.

Advantages and Disadvantages of Games

We have already discussed some of the advantages and disadvantages of specific games. Here we will look at the overall advantages and disadvantages of using games as a special promotion.

Certainly, from a retailer's standpoint a major advantage of using games as a special promotion is the additional traffic it brings into the store. Games are proven traffic builders.

Second, games are easy to administer. Compared with other types of promotions, including trading stamps and continuity promotions (which will be discussed in the next section), it is easy for retailers to get in and out of games. There is no long-run commitment to a game. It begins on a certain date and lasts for a predetermined number of weeks. Unlike stamps, for which a retailer commits himself to a long-run promotional program, games are designed for short-run impact with lasting effects.

A third feature of games is their attraction to customers and the excitement they add to food store shopping.

A fourth and very important advantage is the economy of using games. The cost of games is less than for most other types of promotions, and can be carefully controlled and predetermined.

There are, of course, a number of disadvantages to using games, which explains in part why they are not more widely used today. First and foremost is customer attitudes toward games. The present consumerism movement has instilled in shoppers the belief that games add significantly to the cost of retailing—consequently, to the cost of groceries. When customers feel that they are paying for games, the promotional impact is lost.

A second disadvantage is also the result of customer dissatisfaction. In many cases, regular customers do not win when games are used. These customers tend to feel that they were better off without the game if there is some added expense. People that do not win games are always doubters who eventually become discouraged and stop participating in the game. This type of adverse feeling translated into word-of-mouth advertising can have detrimental effects on game promotions.

A third disadvantage stems from government regulations concerning games. The FTC (Federal Trade Commission) has set down specific rules that make games more difficult for the retailer to handle. Although by and large these rules protect both the retailer and the customer from disreputable game companies and misleading games, they do make it more difficult for the retailer to administer the game.

Summary

Supermarket games, like stamps, tend to be cyclical in nature. When the emphasis is on price competition, they are used less frequently than when retailers are emphasizing nonprice forms of competition. As a special promotion, games can be used with stamps or as a separate promotional activity.

The frequency with which games are used is restricted by the FTC ruling on this subject, which restricts the number of games that a retailer may use during any one year.

Although there are advantages and disadvantages to using games as a promotional device, they have a proven track record as an effective means of building store traffic, at least for short periods of time.

Continuity Promotions

A continuity promotion is one that runs continuously for a specified period of time. Continuity promotions tend to be approximately the same length as games—10 to 15 weeks.

A premium is utilized in a continuity promotion that is made up of individual parts (a series of items) that can be collected as a set. This type of premium might include a set of dishes, a set of stainless steel flatware, a set of encyclopedias, or a set of other related books such as cook books. During the 10 to 15 weeks that the promotion is run, customers are able to obtain one or more pieces of the set each week.

Purpose

There are two types of continuity promotions—the traffic-building continuity promotion and the profit-building continuity promotion. Although the purpose of each is self-evident, it is important to understand the merchandising principles behind each type of promotion.

First, let's look at the traffic-building continuity promotion. Its purpose, like that of most games, is to attract new customers to the store. Its purpose can best be related to that of games. With this type of promotion, the retailer is interested in attracting new customers and in keeping them coming back to his store for a sufficient period of time so that they develop new shopping habits.

The principle behind this promotion is to attract customers to the store by offering a free premium or a premium at a very low price. If the continuity promotion is utilizing dishes, the customer might receive a free dish every week for the duration of the promotion. The same might be true of flatware or encyclopedias.

An alternative to this method is commonly used with encyclopedias or book continuity promotions. The first edition of the book is offered to the customer free, and each successive edition is available at a very low price.

This type of promotion is not designed to earn money for the retailer. The cost will be approximately the same as games, about .5 percent of sales, or it could be a break-even situation. The variation in cost depends on the pricing of the premiums that are offered to customers. The traffic-building continuity promotion may be run with stamps but would not be used in conjunction with a game. A game and a traffic-building continuity promotion have the same purpose, and it would be a duplication of costs to have them running concurrently.

The profit-building continuity promotion is not designed to attract new customers but to sell this same type of special premium to present customers. Dishes, flatware, or encyclopedias are used just as with the traffic-building continuity promotion; however, they are made available to present customers at a fair retail price, but at a price that gives the retailer a profit.

The profit-building continuity promotion may be run in conjunction with a game promotion as well as with stamps. The purpose of this promotion does not conflict with the purpose of the game.

It is conceivable that a retailer might utilize a game promotion, a profit-building continuity promotion, and trading stamps all at the same time. The purpose of the game would be to increase store traffic by attracting new customers. Trading stamps would be used to help keep them as permanent customers when the game had expired. The merchandising principle here is that once a family starts saving stamps they will develop a desire to continue, and of course that particular trading stamp would only be available at the supermarket in the immediate trading area. In addition to the game and stamps, a profit-building continuity promotion would take advantage of the increased store traffic by offering a set of premiums that would represent a value to the customer as well as a profit to the retailer. In this case, the profit-building continuity promotion would help offset the cost of the game.

Summary

Continuity promotion success depends in large part on the attractiveness of the premium offered. They are often introduced in a trading area by a special mailer. The special mailer was described earlier in this chapter, and it was indicated that it was especially useful in introducing company-wide promotions that were designed to run for several weeks. The special mailer would include coupons that would allow the customer to obtain the special premium at a discount price or free each week for the duration of the promotion.

This type of promotion, however, does place the retailer in a somewhat inflexible position. In other words, once the promotion is introduced, the retailer must carry it through to conclusion. If it is a 13-week promotion, the retailer has no alternative to this predetermined program during that 13-week period.

As with other types of long-run special promotions, the continuity promotion tends to lose its impact in later weeks. The greatest impact is usually realized during the first week of the promotion. Interest and customer response tends to decrease in subsequent weeks. To help offset this decline in interest, retailers who introduce the promotion with a special mailer usually reinforce it in their weekly advertising.

6

Display

All merchandise sold in a retail store is displayed in some manner. The self-service food store displays dry grocery products on conventional shelving; perishable products, in refrigerated or freezer cabinets; and general merchandise (or nonfoods), on pegboard displays or grocery shelving.

In addition to these built-in features, special displays are constructed to feature sale items, seasonal, or other merchandise in various sections of the stores' selling area. We will first discuss these special displays and then present the principles of shelf display and the gouping of commodities within the regular shelf space.

PURPOSE OF SPECIAL DISPLAYS

Few retailers today would underestimate the value and sales potential of special in-store displays. One Northeast regional chain estimates that 20 percent of their dry grocery sales each week come from special displays. Displays can certainly be an effective in-store merchandise tool to maximize sales, and this is the primary goal of a special display. But as most good merchandisers are aware, there are other purposes for special displays. Special displays should also be designed to accomplish these important secondary goals:

1. Give a low-price impression
2. Give impression of high sales volume
3. Affect store traffic
4. Meet sales demands
5. Store excess merchandise
6. Increase gross margin

Every display should be designed to accomplish one or more of these goals. A display should not be built until the builder knows exactly what is to be accomplished by the display. The location of the display, the type of display, the product to be displayed, and the price of the item will all have an important bearing on how effectively the display accomplishes its purpose.

Low-price Impression

Many retailers build all their displays with the assumption that they are creating a low-price impression, but customers do not develop a low-price impression from all merchandise displays. In many cases, the regular retail prices of the displayed merchandise are unknown to the customer, as when a new product is displayed, and no reliable comparison can be drawn. In other cases, an item may be displayed at regular retail as a suggested tie-in or related selling item. Here again, no favorable price impression would be left with the customer. Retailers are most successful in creating a low-price impression with special displays that feature advertised items because these are usually items that consumers normally buy at higher prices.

By displaying the same items that appear in the weekly newspaper ad, the retailer establishes a point of mental recall in the store that reinforces the newspaper ad. Assuming that the newspaper ad carries a low-price impact, the in-store display will reinforce this impact by presenting a visual reminder to the customer when he shops in the store.

To be effective in creating a low-price impact, displays must be clearly price marked. The use of additional signs and price information is helpful. The sign should carry the currently advertised price. It also might point out the regular retail price and the savings that this represents to the customer.

In addition to a special price sign on the display of the advertised feature, attention must be given to the pricing of the items in the display. There are a number of approaches used, the most common of which are:

1. Price marking each item with the special advertised price.
2. Leaving the items marked with the regular retail and providing the checkers with a list of special, advertised prices.
3. Leaving the special display items unmarked and providing the checkers with a list of special advertised prices.
4. Crossing out or marking over the regular retail and putting the advertised price on the items near this crossed-off price so that the customer can compare prices and compute the savings.

Although any one of these methods may be made to work in a given company under certain situations, it is probably best to mark each item with the advertised price only. If price comparison is desirable, this can be conveyed to the customer by signs attached to the display. This is a foolproof method of assuring that the customer actually receives the merchandise for the correct price and helps build customer confidence in the checkout operation and the store. The other methods leave open the possibility that the checker will ring up the wrong price and thereby reduce customer confidence in checker accuracy and in the store's pricing accuracy and ethics.

High Sales Volume Impression

Displays that are built to create the impression of high sales volume must be massive and prominent. They require a large quantity of merchandise—the customer should get the feeling that the retailer has made a special quantity purchase of the particular item being featured with the expectation of selling a large volume of the product to customers. Customers are likely to respond favorably to massive displays because they conclude that special quantity purchase items must be a good value.

Naturally, it is necessary that the retailer select appropriate items and appropriate prices for the items. It is not desirable to build massive displays of loss-leader items. Remember that the retailer uses a loss leader to increase store traffic and build new customers. Although a retailer is responsible to provide all customers with a sufficient quantity of advertised specials (including loss-leader items), he does not want to encourage customers to purchase more of a loss-leader item than they intended to purchase before coming to the store. A massive display should encourage customers to purchase additional quantities of the item on display. Therefore, it is desirable to encourage customers to purchase additional quantities of an item with a reasonable gross margin, as opposed to encouraging their purchase of additional items that are being sold at no gross margin or in some cases at a direct loss to the store. However, the price of items in a massive display must still represent a value to the consumer—that is, be lower than regular retail.

Retailers who use massive displays as part of their regular merchandising activity find that customers respond favorably to them. Although many retailers use the massive display approach week in and week out as part of their merchandising program, most retailers use massive displays on a rather selective basis for special purchases, seasonal items, or special promotions. Whichever approach is used by the retailer, it must be kept in mind that the purpose of the massive display is to create the impression of high sales volume and to encourage the customer to purchase additional quantities of the item on display.

Affect Store Traffic

The location and positioning of special displays in a retail store can have a direct effect on the traffic flow within the store. There are three ways that displays can be used to affect the flow of traffic.

1. **Direct the traffic flow**—by spacing displays throughout the store, the customer is led from one display to another.

2. Draw customer traffic into dead areas—displays can be used to attract customers into sections of the store where they might not normally shop in their regular tour of the store.

3. Slow the traffic flow—displays can be used to slow down traffic flow in the selling area by extending a display out into the aisle, or by building displays in the center of the aisle, which is an attempt to draw the customer's attention to the product by having him go around the display.

The desired effect on traffic flow will dictate the position for the display to be used. For example, in the first two cases, displays are used to attract customers—effective displays will lead the customer to specific areas. In the third case, the display is brought to the customer—it is placed in such a position that the customer cannot avoid seeing it. By understanding these three approaches, it becomes evident that a different type of display and product is required to attract customers than to stop them in the aisle.

In order to lead customers from one display to another or to draw them into dead areas of the store, the display and the product must have a specific attraction to the customer. This attraction might be: (1) a product with a low feature price; (2) a leader; (3) a seasonal item that is in high demand; or (4) a new item that has been highly advertised and promoted by the manufacturer. (An ideal item is one for which a manufacturer has distributed coupons and therefore has helped the retailer presell the item). In all these cases, there is some specific attraction for the customer that will help direct or draw store traffic to the display. From a retailer's standpoint, it is advantageous to use low-profit items for this purpose. By locating a display of an advertised leader item in a relatively dead area in the store, customers could be attracted to this area, where they could be exposed to high-margin impulse items such as nonfoods, candy, or snack items.

Displays that are used in an aisle or to attract attention by extending prominently into an aisle should contain high-margin impulse items. In these situations, the display is being brought to the customer whose attention is drawn to it because the display is so prominent. The high-margin impulse item has no drawing power by itself but holds a real opportunity for the retailer to improve his gross margin through special display. In summary, it could be said that if the product does not draw the customer to the display—take the display to the customer.

Meet Sales Demand

Special displays are often thought of as a means of selling more of a given item. However, in some cases displays must be built simply to keep pace with the consumer demand for a given product. Demand is often generated by the store's own weekly advertising or advertising by a manufacturer of a specific product. In either case, the quantity demanded may be more than the normal shelf space for a given item can accommodate. When sales cannot be met by the amount of merchandise on the shelf, special displays are required.

Special displays to supply high customer demand are used:

1. To back up advertised specials.
2. To back up regular weekly demand for high-volume, bulky items.
3. For seasonal items.
4. For new items or items receiving special promotional assistance from manufacturers.

Displays to Back Up Advertised Specials

Keeping in mind that one of the main purposes of advertising is to bring people into a store, the reinforcement value of a display to support an item being advertised tends to strengthen the overall advertising message.

It is a desirable merchandising practice to have prominent displays in the store of those items being featured in the store's weekly advertising. This should be true in every department of the store. If steaks are being featured in the meat department, one of the most prominent displays in the meat counter should be steaks. If cucumbers are featured in the produce department, a large display of cucumbers will tell the customer that this really is the special feature of the store's produce department.

In most cases, these displays are needed to meet the consumer demand generated by the ad. However, their presence is also desirable from a merchandising standpoint to reinforce the store's advertising program. Not only should the store resemble the picture created by its advertising department but employees should be cognizant of advertised features and their special prices. They should be prepared to answer questions about the advertising and know where special advertised features are displayed within the store.

High-volume, Bulky Items

Displays are also important to back up regular customer demand for high-volume, bulky items. Because of the physical characteristics of certain products sold in today's supermarkets, regular shelf space or shelf stock is often insufficient to meet customer demand during peak selling periods. These items, such as large bags of dog food and liquid bleach, take up so much shelf space that it is often impossible for a store to stock a sufficient supply to meet peak selling demands on its regular grocery shelving. To meet this problem, many stores build special displays in an area close to the regular department where the item would normally be found or near the front of the store to make it easier for the customer to carry the item to the car. If large, bulky items were not close to the checkout counter, the customer would have to carry the item around while shopping, which might discourage sales of the large item or of other items if the shopping cart were too full to accommodate many additional items once the bulky item was in it.

Seasonal-item Displays

Special displays may also be necessary for certain seasonal items with heavy sales demand. Some merchandise sells at a faster rate during certain seasons of the year and therefore may require a special display to avoid out of stocks. During the summer months, the demand for charcoal and other picnic supplies may increase to such an extent that regular shelf supplies are inadequate to meet consumer demand. Many food stores also find it helpful to build special displays for other seasonal items, such as canning supplies at the end of the summer, cranberry sauce and stuffing around Thanksgiving and Christmas, ice-melting chemicals in the winter, and grass seed and lawn food in the spring.

New-item Displays

It is often necessary to build displays for new items because of the heavy promotional effort by the manufacturer. This promotional effort may include radio, television, and printed advertising; couponing; the distribution of small samples of the product to consumers; or any combination of these approaches. When a large number of customers come to a store seeking the new item, it is a good idea to have it available on a special display for several reasons:

1. Shelf stock may be inadequate to hold the quantity required.
2. Customers may not be familiar with the new product location on the regular grocery shelving, and a special display helps them find the item.
3. A display will act as a reminder to those customers who have seen the new product advertised, but may have forgotten to include the item on their shopping list.
4. It adds interest and excitement to the merchandising activities of the store because it helps to provide the customer with something different.

Store Excess Merchandise

One of the functions of a special display is to act as a reservoir for the surplus merchandise that the store has ordered. Retail stores today are continually expanding the selling area of the store at the expense of back-room storage space. This has come about and been made possible by the more efficient ordering systems discussed in Chapter 2. In the past, it was often necessary that a store place an order for grocery merchandise a week in advance. This meant a great deal of speculation by the retailer as to what quantities might be sold in the intervening time. This speculation often led to errors and a need for extra reserve stock to compensate for out of stocks at the warehouse and fluctuations in sales at the store.

Today, orders are placed several times a week and received from modern food-distribution centers within hours from the time the order was prepared. This faster turn-around time has eliminated much speculation in the ordering function at the retail store and allowed retailers to reduce the amount of back-room space previously required for reserve stock.

With less storage area today, retailers must consider how to handle large orders or shipments of special merchandise. One alternative commonly used is to place the merchandise immediately on the selling floor on a special display. This procedure is used for: (1) Seasonal or holiday merchandise, such as halloween candy, watermelons, or canned pumpkin. (2) Special buys, which are occasionally offered by manufacturers in the form of special buying allowances to encourage retailers to increase their regular orders. Special buys might include a reduced purchase price, a premium pack, or some type of special pack such as an extra four ounces of the product in a larger package at the same retail price. When a large order of this type of merchandise arrives at the store, it is often placed immediately on the selling floor rather than being stored in the back room of the store. (3) Ordering errors that a retailer made in the preparation of his grocery order. Rather than return the merchandise to the warehouse, the retailer may decide to build a display and dispose of the merchandise over the next few weeks. Very often, new sales opportunities are created from this type of problem situation. Imaginative and creative retailers who can make the most of an over-stocked situation often find an opportunity for additional sales and profits.

Generally, a display that is used to store excess merchandise remains in place longer than normal special displays. The retailer is combining two functions in this type of display: the storage function and the selling function. If the merchandise is not sold during the first or second week it is on display, the retailer usually has no recourse but to leave the display intact. If storage was a problem when the merchandise arrived at the store, it probably will still be a problem one or two weeks later. To provide a change of pace for regular customers, retailers often move this type of display or combine it with other merchandise after one or two weeks.

Increase Gross Margin

Certainly one of the most important reasons that retailers build displays is to increase gross margin. It is extremely important in an overall in-store merchandising program to include high-profit displays along with or in addition to displays of advertised features or leaders. In some cases, high-margin displays do little more than offset the low gross margins earned on advertised feature displays or leader displays. However, even in this capacity high-margin displays are important.

It was stated that the primary purpose of a display is to increase or maximize sales consistent with the net-profit objective. Let's review how this is accomplished. In self-service stores, displays take the place of the sales clerk. Displays are suggestive selling tools. They call the customer's attention to specific items and they should encourage the customer to purchase the item. How do displays act as suggestive selling tools?

1. Displays are used to introduce a new product. They suggest to the customer, "Try me, I'm new."

2. Displays suggest related items for meal planning. These are called tie-in displays, and suggest to the customer items that can be served together.

3. Displays add variety and excitement for the shopper. Grocery shopping becomes a dull routine for many people. There are many ways to make a food store a pleasant place in which to shop. One way is to provide interesting and useful special displays. When displays challenge the imagination of the shopper by suggesting new items or items for menu planning, the dull routine becomes an interesting shopping experience. This, too, is suggestive selling.

4. Displays suggest holiday and seasonal items. Many new opportunities present themselves for suggestive selling during special holidays and as seasons of the year change. This also provides the retailer an opportunity to give the store a face lifting by altering in-store displays and decorations.

So, displays can increase customer demand and therefore gross margin through suggestive selling.

Displays, however, can and do accomplish much more than increase sales. These secondary goals have also been described in this section. Remember, know the purpose of the display before you build it; or to put it another way, build a display with a purpose in mind.

TYPES OF DISPLAYS

In this section, we will look at types of displays in two ways: the most common methods of building displays and methods of presenting merchandise in special displays. We will discuss the three most common methods of building displays:

1. The cut-case display
2. The jumbled or dump display
3. The formal display

We will then discuss the three most common methods of presenting merchandise:

1. Single-product displays
2. Multi-product displays
3. Tie-in displays

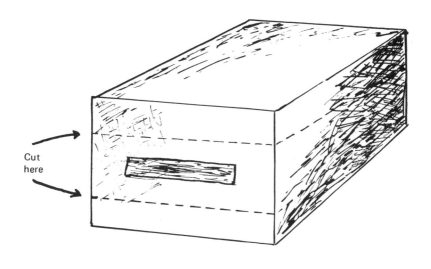

Cut here

Separate the top and bottom

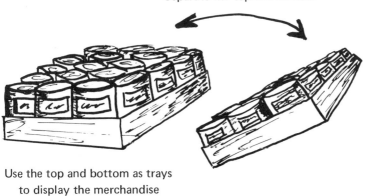

Use the top and bottom as trays to display the merchandise

Throw away the middle section of the case

FIGURE 6-1   How to prepare a cut-case display.

The Cut-case Display

The cut-case display, or tray pack, has increased in popularity during the past few years primarily because of the lower labor cost associated with building this display. The cut-case display is constructed by cutting the case of merchandise one to two inches from the bottom and top and then using the bottom and top of the case as a tray to hold the contents (see Figure 6-1). These trays of merchandise can then be easily price marked and handled as a single unit. The trays are easily stacked and present a neat, attractive display (see Figure 6-2). The advantages of this type of display are that it is easy to construct, it is low cost in terms of man-hours required, and it is easy to move if necessary. The trays on which the merchandise is displayed are strong and durable enough to store the merchandise if it has to be returned to the storage area. The fact that the entire contents of the tray can be handled as a single unit is a time- and labor-saving feature.

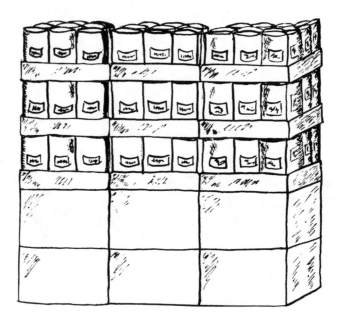

FIGURE 6-2   Cut-case display.

One of the disadvantages of this type of display is that the empty cardboard trays must be periodically removed to keep the display neat and attractive. As merchandise is sold from the display, the empty tray remains and tends to clutter up the display. Also, some retailers feel that the trays obscure part of the merchandise and therefore do not present an attractive display. However, the wide acceptance and use of the cut-case display tends to indicate that most retailers feel that the advantages far outweigh the disadvantages.

The Jumbled Display

The jumbled (or dump) display is popular with many retailers for certain items. To build a jumbled display, merchandise is price marked and then dumped on to a table or into a basket or a shopping cart (see Figure 6-3).

FIGURE 6-3 Jumbled display.

The advantages of a jumbled display are that it is a low-cost, easy-to-build display that requires little or no maintenance. It is easy for customers to shop and especially desirable for certain items that customers might normally sort through before selecting an item to purchase, such as grapefruit on a produce table, children's tennis shoes in the nonfoods department, colored bars of bath soap in the grocery department, and for certain fast moving items such as frozen orange juice concentrate.

A disadvantage of the jumbled display is that it is difficult for the retailer to store the merchandise when it is removed from the display (unless master containers are saved, the display piece is a basket or container, or the remaining merchandise can be accommodated on the grocery shelving). Also, the jumbled display is best for those products that will not easily bruise or break—the products must withstand the handling that they will receive in this type of display.

The Formal Display

The formal display requires that each item of merchandise be stacked by hand. It represents a very attractive picture to the customer and can be built in various shapes and sizes (see Figure 6-4). Formal displays are used much less in food stores today than they once were due to the high labor costs involved in building them. The advantages of this type of display lie primarily in its attractiveness. Many display builders have perfected their art to such a point that they can create a formal display that is a thing of beauty. This type of display needs very little maintenance and can fit into any available area.

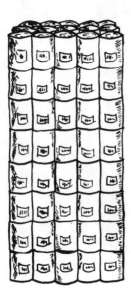 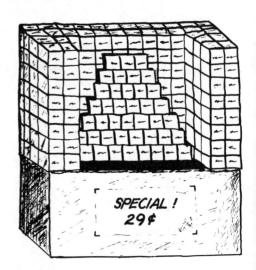

FIGURE 6-4   Formal displays.

A disadvantage of the formal display is that it almost looks too pretty to disturb. Many customers are reluctant to touch or remove items from a display that has been so carefully constructed. Studies indicate that customers are more receptive to displays that look "shopped." The jumbled display is a case in point. Another disadvantage of the formal display is the labor cost involved. Because each item must be hand stacked, it takes much longer to prepare this display than either the cut-case display or the jumbled display. A further drawback to the formal display is the problem of dismantling the display and disposing of the excess stock. This is the same type of problem that presents itself with the jumbled display.

Single-product and Multi-product Displays

Basically, there are three methods of presenting merchandise in a display: (1) the single-product display; (2) the multi-product display; and (3) the tie-in display. When a display is composed of only one item, it is known as a single-product display. When two or more items are incorporated into one display, it is a multi-product display. When the items in the display are related in terms of how they are prepared or served, the display is called a tie-in display or related-items display. In order to decide how merchandise should be grouped in displays, it is again important to analyze the purpose of the display. Generally speaking, a single product is presented in a display under the following conditions.

1. When the item is large or bulky—paper products are often featured in a single-product display because they are bulky and require a large display to meet consumer demand.

2. To create the impression of high sales volume.

3. To store the excess products—sometimes a product is seasonal in nature and may be delivered to the store in one shipment early in the season. To eliminate the need for holding the merchandise in the back room, a large, single-product display may be employed.

Multi-product displays are used under the following conditions:

1. To display advertised feature items together.

2. To include a high-profit item with the advertised feature.

3. To present several small items—it is difficult to build massive displays of a single item such as bar soap, canned tuna, or sliced cheese, but these items could be combined with other items in a multi-product display to give a full and attractive appearance.

4. To combine several single-product displays that have become depleted. A retailer is confronted with an inventory problem when a large, 50-case single-product display sells down to 15 cases. At this point, the massiveness of the display is lost and a decision must be made regarding what to do with the remaining merchandise. It can be moved to the storage area and used to replenish shelf stock, or the entire 15 cases can be moved to another location and combined with other merchandise in a multi-product display. Many retailers prefer this latter solution because it eliminates large back-room inventories and the necessity to handle the merchandise several times.

Tie-in Displays

A tie-in display is a multi-product display in which the merchandise is related by its final consumer use. An example of a tie-in display in the grocery department might be instant coffee and a nondairy cream. Other examples of related-item displays might be canned soup and crackers, canned tuna and mayonnaise, or peanut butter and jelly. Other related-item displays involve items from different departments. There are many combinations that have been proven successful by retailers. Tie-in displays are of course an excellent reinforcement for a tie-in promotion.

ECONOMICS OF DISPLAYS

In the final analysis, displays must be measured by their overall contribution to the profit of the store. The profitability or value of a group of displays can be measured in the same manner that the profitability of a store is measured. Many of the same guidelines can be employed. It is possible to set up a partial operating statement for displays that includes some of the same elements that are on a store operating statement. This includes gross margin less the direct expenses of building the displays. Gross margins are made up of the sales mix generated by the various displays in the store and the percentage gross margin for each product. This mix is just as important for displays as it is for merchandise sold from the shelves. Some displays contain advertised feature items that carry no gross margin or a very low gross margin. Others contain high-margin impulse items that are designed to offset the low gross from the advertised features. In order that displays in a store be truly successful, a balanced gross margin must be obtained from the various displays; that is, adequate to cover the direct expenses of building the displays and maintaining them and to make some contribution to general overhead expenses and store net profit.

Although gross margin is usually indicated by a percentage figure, the dollar gross margin is even more important. Building high-profit displays may look good on paper percentage-wise, but unless the merchandise is actually sold in sufficient quantities to return the dollars necessary to pay operating expenses, the display has no value. Therefore, the gross-margin dollar figure is extremely important.

Sometimes, store managers in their over-zealous effort to increase gross margins include too many high-margin items in the display mix. This often adversely affects sales. Of course, the opposite can also occur. In an effort to build up sales, managers may concentrate on low-margin advertised features in the choice display locations—sales may soar, but gross margins will be seriously reduced. Therefore, a combination of low-margin and high-margin items are necessary to maximize dollar sales and gross-margin return.

Just as important as maximizing gross margins and total sales from displays is the minimizing of the costs associated with building displays. Here again, there is a similarity in the effectiveness of displays and the success of total store operation. In building displays, just as in running a successful store, it is necessary to control expenses, especially the labor, which is the major expense in building special displays.

When expenses exceed gross margin, there is a loss. When the cost of building a display exceeds the gross-margin dollars that the display returns, the value of the display is lost. For some displays of low gross-margin items, the cost will inevitably be greater than the gross-margin dollars returned. However, on high-margin item displays this should not be true, and the overall cost factor for all displays should be less than the gross-margin dollars that the displays return.

The cost of building displays varies by the type of display. In ranking the displays in terms of preparation costs, the dump or jumbled display is the least expensive, cut-case displays are more expensive, and the formal display is the most expensive type of display to build. In measuring costs of moving displays, the cut-case display is least expensive, the jumbled display is more expensive, and the formal display is the most expensive.

SHELF DISPLAY

Very few areas of food retailing have received as much attention over the years as methods of displaying products on grocery shelves. Since Clarence Saunders opened his first self-service store in 1916, retailers have been experimenting, testing, and analyzing the effect of various grocery-shelving layouts.

Shelf Allocation

The decision as to how much shelf space to give to each grocery item is commonly referred to as shelf allocation. Space is allocated for grocery products on the basis of *facings*. One facing allows that only one can, box, or package of an item to be exposed along the front edge of the grocery shelving. Three facings means that there are three items displayed along the length of the shelf. There may be additional cans of the same item stacked on top of these three facings, but the shelf allocation is measured in linear feet of shelf space and not in height (see Figure 6-5).

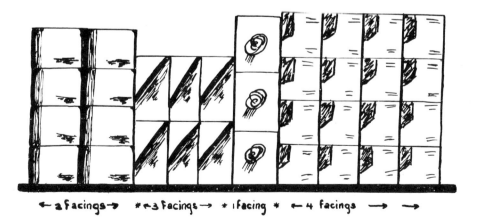

FIGURE 6-5   Shelf allocation—facings.

Space for grocery products is allocated both as a means of meeting consumer demand and as a means of influencing consumer demand.

Meet Consumer Demand

When space is allocated to meet consumer demand, it means that space is provided for products in direct proportion to their sales velocity. This is often likened to the "bath tub" approach. When you open the drain in the bath tub, the water goes down evenly throughout the entire tub until it is completely drained. If the merchandise on the shelves of a food store were allocated in direct proportion to consumer demand, the level of merchandise should be depleted just like the water draining out of the bath tub. In other words, the space for each item would be allocated based on the anticipated consumer demand, and as long as the demand stayed constant the products would be purchased from the shelves at a rate proportionate to their quantity. Products with high consumer demand would be given more shelf space than products with low consumer demand. However, they would be allocated proportionately so that the level of the fast moving items would stay equal to the level of the slow-moving items on the shelf.

There are, of course, a number of physical constraints that make it impossible for this theory to work in practice. For example, certain items (such as beer, soft drinks, fresh milk, liquid bleach, and some paper products) have such a high rate of turnover and are so bulky that it is not practical to allocate shelf space in proportion to their weekly movement. Whereas most items can be given sufficient shelf space to accommodate their weekly movement, these fast moving items require replenishment several times each week.

At the other extreme are slow-moving items that sell in quantities of less than a case per week. It is impractical to stock only a few units of any particular item or in less than case lots. Therefore, with slow-moving items the tendency is to overstock for the convenience of placing an entire case of merchandise on the shelf at a time (as previously described under the SLIM system—see Chapter 2).

Influence Consumer Demand

Although shelf space for most products is allocated according to previous movement, it also may be allocated in an attempt to influence consumer demand. Studies indicate that there is a direct relationship between the number of facings for a product on a shelf and the sales of that item. As shelf space increases, so do sales. In a study conducted in Houston, Texas, it was found that by varying the amount of shelf space devoted to private-label and national-brand tea products, sales of these products could also be varied. In the stores included in this study, private-label tea accounted for 27 percent of total tea sales from 40 percent of the shelf space. When private-label

The following items were stocked originally at waist-level in both test stores. During the two-week test period, they were shifted to eye-level position in one store and to a floor-level position in the other store.

	Items	Unit Sales		Percent Change	Number of Unit Change
		Waist Level	Eye Level		
Waist level to eye level	Lard, 1 Lb. Carton	12	14	+ 17%	+ 2
	Sunshine Pickled Peaches	17	20	+ 18%	+ 3
	Jif Peanut Butter, 12 oz.	19	48	+152%	+29
	Welch's Grapeade, tumbler	11	14	+ 27%	+ 3
	ALL ITEMS	59	96	+ 63%	+37
		Waist Level	Floor Level		
Waist level to floor level	Lard, 1 Lb. Carton	12	8	−33%	− 4
	Sunshine Pickled Peaches	29	12	−58%	−17
	Jif Peanut Butter, 12 oz.	15	10	−33%	− 5
	Welch's Grapeade, tumbler	18	14	−22%	− 4
	ALL ITEMS	74	44	−40%	−30

The following items were stocked originally at floor-level position in two stores. During the two-week test period, these items were shifted to waist-level position in one store and to eye-level position in the other.

		Floor Level	Waist Level		
Floor level to waist level	Pinto Beans, Red Gate, 4 lb.	9	16	+ 76%	+ 7
	Karo White Syrup, Quart	4	21	+425%	+17
	White House Applesauce, 20 oz.	3	18	+500%	+15
	Raisins, Sunmaid, 1 pound	168	192	+ 14%	+24
	ALL ITEMS	184	247	+ 34%	+63
		Floor Level	Eye Level		
Floor level to eye level	Pinto Beans, Red Gate, 4 lb.	8	16	+100%	+ 8
	Karo White Syrup, Quart	6	13	+117%	+ 7
	White House Applesauce, 20 oz.	3	9	+200%	+ 6
	Raisins, Sunmaid, 1 pound	66	110	+ 67%	+44
	ALL ITEMS	83	148	+ 78%	+65

The following items were stocked originally at eye-level in two test stores. For a two-week period, they were shifted from this eye-level position to waist-level in one store and to floor-level in the other store.

		Eye Level	Floor Level		
Eye level to floor level	C/S Peas, Small Sweet, #303	41	9	−78%	−32
	Puss & Boots Cat Food, 15 oz.	43	38	−12%	− 5
	Minute Rice, 5 oz.	31	17	−45%	−14
	Ocean Spray, 300 Size	114	91	−20%	−23
	ALL ITEMS	229	155	−32%	−74
		Eye Level	Waist Level		
Eye level to waist level	C/S Peas, Small Sweet, #303	30	20	−33%	−10
	Puss & Boots Cat Food, 15 oz.	48	40	−17%	− 8
	Minute Rice, 5 oz.	36	30	−17%	− 6
	Ocean Spray, 300 Size	129	104	−19%	−25
	ALL ITEMS	243	194	−20%	−49

FIGURE 6-6 Effect of shelf position on sales. Source: *The Colonial Study* (New York: Progressive Grocer, 1963), p. C127.

tea was given an additional 10 percent of shelf space, sales increased to 38 percent of total tea sales.[1]

Knowing that customer demand can be influenced in this manner, retailers have attempted to expand facings on higher profit items in order to favorably affect their sales. However, as additional facings are added for the same product, the law of diminishing return applies, and sales tend to increase at a decreasing rate. Products that lack customer appeal and that have little customer demand to begin with do not benefit from increased shelf space. In the Houston study, a local brand of tea that had a very low sales volume was given extra shelf space—no additional sales were recorded.[2] Poor products cannot be saved by giving them more facings.

A second shelf allocation technique that is used to influence consumer demand is the altering of the vertical shelf position of a product. Items that are stocked closest to eye level have a sales advantage over products located at waist level or floor level. According to the study conducted by Progressive Grocer, "The point which offered the least resistance to normal physical movement—the eye level shelf position—proved to be a vital product paradise for maximum sales."[3] In this study, items that were normally displayed at eye level were moved to waist level for one week and then moved to floor level for the second week. Each time a product was moved from its favored eye-level position, there was a decrease in sales (see Figure 6-6). On the other hand, as items were moved from floor level or waist level to eye level, sales increased. For example, 20-ounce jars of applesauce increased in sales by 500 percent when they were moved from waist level to eye level. One-pound boxes of raisins increased 67 percent in sales when moved from floor level to eye level. Sales drops were just as dramatic when products were moved from eye level to lower levels. Cranberry sauce dropped 20 percent in sales when moved from eye level to floor level. Canned peas dropped 33 percent in sales when moved from eye level to waist level. National brands lost sales just as readily a private-label products. A well-known brand of quick-fix rice lost sales when moved to a lower shelf position; so did a nationally advertised brand of grape jelly. The eye-level position is extremely valuable in terms of sales velocity.

Retailers who desire to improve the mix of higher margin items may find that they can maximize their sales potential by displaying these products at or near eye level.

A third means of allocating shelf space to influence consumer demand has to do with the grouping of related items on the grocery shelving. In

---

[1]Charles W. Hubbard, "The 'Shelving' of Increased Sales," *Journal of Retailing,* Vol. 45, No. 4 (Winter 1969-1970), pp. 81-82.

[2]"The 'Shelving' of Increased Sales," p. 83.

[3]*The Colonial Study* (New York: Progressive Grocer, 1963), pp. 126-27.

the *Dillon Study* conducted by Progressive Grocer, two specific methods of grouping products were cited as having made more productive use of shelf space:

1. All like items displayed together for faster item location within the several hundred different product groups (see Figure 6-7).
2. Clearly defined blocks of merchandise define types of products and make them easier for customers to locate (see Figure 6-8).

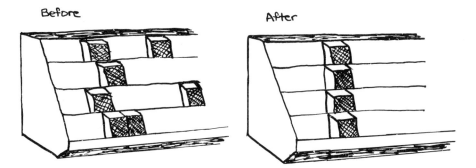

FIGURE 6-7   Better grouping of products.

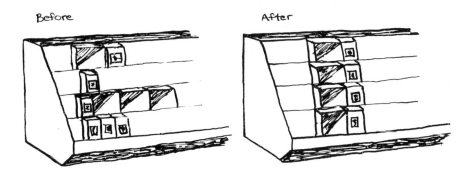

FIGURE 6-8   Clearly defined blocks of merchandise.

Both of these grouping methods use what is commonly referred to as the ribbon display. Ribboning is a technique by which similar merchandise is displayed vertically in one portion of the grocery shelving. Displaying or grouping like products in this manner (see Figures 6-7 and 6-8) provides the customer with easy access to a large block of similar items. This also facilitates price comparisons, and many retailers feel that it also improves the appearance of the shelf display. Allocating vertical sections of space in grocery shelving is still a widely accepted practice among successful food retailing companies.[4]

Shelf Allocation Methods

Gross Margin Tells Only Half the Story

We have discussed how space allocation can be used to influence consumer demand. This is accomplished by expanding the facings of certain products or by relocating them on easier-to-reach shelves. Attention is usually drawn to those products that carry the highest gross margins in an attempt to improve the overall profitability of the store or department.

Recent studies indicate that gross margins do not provide enough information on which to base valid decisions regarding the profitability of specific items. Although gross margin clearly indicates the difference between the actual cost of a product and its retail selling price, it does not take into account the costs required to bring the product to the shelf, to prepare it for display, or the cost of the display space.

When it is possible to attribute all the costs of handling, receiving, pricing, displaying, and overhead directly to each specific product, it becomes possible to measure the net profit of the item—and not just gross margin.

Direct Product Profit. Net profit is difficult to determine for individual items because of the many common costs that are impractical to allocate to individual items. The food industry has chosen to use *direct product profit* to describe the profit contribution of individual items. The direct-product-profit concept takes into account the cost of handling the product along with other direct costs and subtracts these from the gross-margin contribution.

The major factor in computing direct product profit is the variable handling costs. The handling-cost formula is illustrated in Figure 6-9. Included in this formula are all the significant cost elements that can be directly assigned to an item as it is handled through the physical distribution network from the warehouse receiving dock to the store checkout counter.

Approximately 50 percent of all operating costs are included in the handling costs. Not included are fixed costs, such as supervisory expenses, in-store space expense, and corporate headquarter expenses. The cost of handling the merchandise through the system is related to the physical characteristics of the product and the methods used in handling it. These characteristics are the foot cube of the case, number of units per case, dollar value of the case, unit case cost, and handling methods. The major considerations in assigning cost to the physical characteristics are summarized in Figure 6-10.

---

[4]*The Dillon Study* (New York: Progressive Grocer, July 1960), p. 34.

HANDLING COST FORMULA
PRODUCT DISTRIBUTION NETWORK

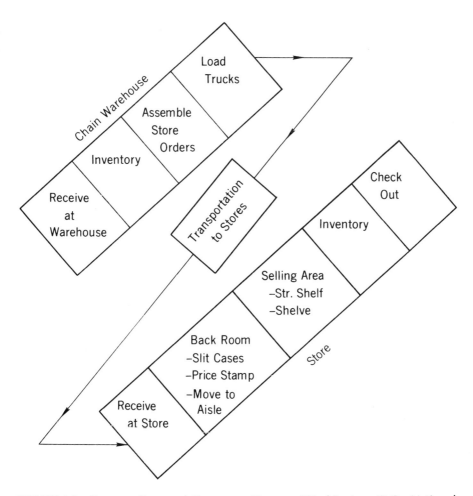

FIGURE 6-9   Source: Case and Company, *Cosmos* (Washington, D.C.: National Association of Food Chains, October 1968), p. 26.

In addition to the cost of physically moving the merchandise through the distribution system, the cost of carrying inventory is also taken into consideration. The formula for calculating the inventory carrying charge per case is:

$$\text{Inventory carrying charge} = \frac{\text{Value of the case}}{\text{Annual turnover}} \times \text{Annual cost of capital}$$

PRODUCT CHARACTERISTICS USED IN ASSIGNING COSTS

The basis for assigning cost is the physical characteristics of individual products and product packaging—units per case, case cubage, case value and handling methods utilized.

Costs which vary with the number of units in the case:

- ▶ Price stamping
- ▶ Shelving (also varies with package size)
- ▶ Cash register ringing
- ▶ Bagging

Costs which are the same for each case handled:

- ▶ Stacking individual cases
- ▶ Checking off incoming cases on the invoice
- ▶ Slitting cases

Costs which vary with the cubage of each case:

- ▶ Moving palletized loads
- ▶ Delivering merchandise to stores

Costs which vary with the value of the case:

- ▶ Inventory carrying charges
- ▶ Trading stamps

Costs which vary with the methods used:

- ▶ Receiving (palletized, direct delivered, etc.)
- ▶ Moving merchandise (tow line or fork lift truck)
- ▶ Back room organization
- ▶ Shelves

FIGURE 6-10   Source: Case and Company, *COSMOS* (Washington, D.C.: National Association of Food Chains, October 1968), p. 27.

Each food chain or wholesaler will need to insert its own unique cost factors into this formula in order to calculate the total handling and carrying charges for each product. The handling-cost factors developed by each company will consider present facilities, merchandise, handling methods, and wage rates. Changes in any of these factors will in turn affect the total handling and carrying charges for the items involved.

The total cost to be charged against the gross margin of each product must include an occupancy cost in addition to handling and carrying costs. The occupancy cost can best be described as the rent that each product pays for the space it occupies on the grocery shelving. The rent is determined by each company's overhead. For an entire food chain, it is a generally accepted practice to accept one figure that represents the total overhead for the company operation.[5]

Application of the Direct-Product-Profit Concept. The importance of any concept or statistic, whether it be gross margin or direct product profit, is how practical it is. Let us examine here how the direct-product-profit concept can be applied to specific situations.

One of the revealing findings when the direct-product-profit concept was first applied to actual retail store situations was that wide differences in profitability existed among individual products. These wide differences were not apparent when measured by gross-margin contribution because the gross margins were comparable. However, when the direct costs of handling and displaying the product were taken into account the product differences became apparent. Within a typical product subcategory, the direct-product-profit contribution among seven items varied from a minus $2.70 per week to a positive contribution of $3.35 per week (see Figure 6-11). Although the average gross margins of these items were nearly identical, the handling and display space costs varied considerably and clearly indicated which products were making the greatest direct-product-profit contribution to the department.

With this type of specific knowledge about profits, the retailer is now in a position to take positive action to reduce the loss indicated by product G in Figure 6-11. Although products E and F also will need some review, you can see that if the retailer could put product G on the profit side of the line it would make a significant contribution to the total profitability of the entire department. At the present time, the loss from product G ($2.70) completely wipes out the profit contributed by product B ($2.24) and product D ($.45), which means that products B and D contribute nothing to the total profitability of the store simply because of the loss that is being incurred by product G.

Let's single out product G and see what courses of action are open to the retailer. The following is a list of considerations or actions that the retailer might take:

1. Increase or decrease retail price.
2. Increase or decrease the number of facings allotted to the product.
3. Relocate the item on the shelves.
4. Substitute a new product being offered on the market.

---

[5]Case and Company, *COSMOS* (Washington, D.C.: National Association of Food Chains, October 1968), Appendix A, pp. 25-28.

Among these four considerations, there are a number of alternatives or combinations of alternatives that would have a specific effect on the direct product profit of product *G*.

Although we do not know the specific nature of the problem with

DIRECT PRODUCT PROFITABILITY VARIES WIDELY
WITHIN A TYPICAL PRODUCT SUB-CATEGORY

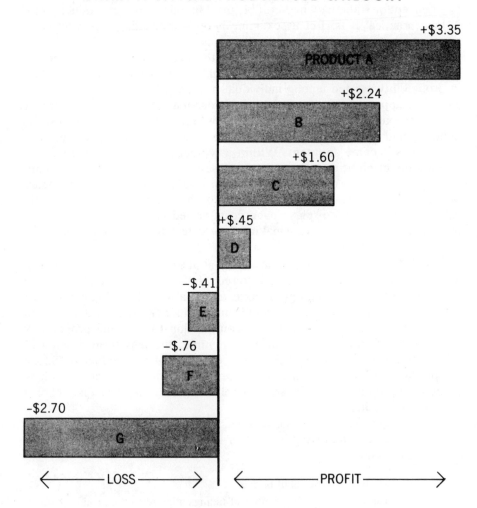

DIRECT PRODUCT PROFIT PER ITEM PER WEEK

FIGURE 6-7   Source: Case and Company, *COSMOS* (Washington, D.C.: National Association of Food Chains, October 1968), p. 17.

product *G,* we can speculate how a number of these alternatives would affect the direct product profit. Perhaps an increase in price or a reduced number of facings would improve the direct product profit of *G*. Moving the product to a different shelf location might also help. The specific action to be taken would necessarily depend on the product itself, including such factors as its price sensitivity, consumer demand, and so on. However, knowing its profit contribution on a direct-product-profit basis enables the retailer to pinpoint this problem item and take specific action.

Space Yield Studies

Supreme Markets. A wide-scale application of the direct-product-profit concept was made at Supreme Markets (now Purity Supreme), a regional New England chain, by *Chain Store Age* in 1965. The purpose of the study was to determine the yield, measured by direct product profits, of various product categories within the grocery department. By studying product movement and applying the direct-product-profit principles, Supreme Markets was able to analyze the direct-product-profit contribution for each item within these specific categories.

The following formula was used to provide information: Assume that this is cost information for product X. The handling cost from its receipt at the warehouse until the time the individual item was placed on the shelf amounted to 42 cents per case. Product X sold two cases per week, which resulted in a total handling cost of 84 cents. This product was given four facings, which resulted in a 12-inch linear exposure to the customer. The shelves were 18 inches deep. The total exposed space used was one and one-half square feet. This figure multiplied times the occupancy cost of 10 cents per square foot resulted in a total occupancy cost of 15 cents. Retail sales for item X amounted to $6.00 per case times two cases, or $12.00. The gross-margin dollars at 20 percent gross margin equaled $2.40. At this point, it is important to point out that many other products in this same category also returned a 20 percent gross margin. This, however, does not indicate that all products with a 20 percent gross margin will return the same direct product profit to the store. In this specific case with product X, handling costs of 84 cents and occupancy costs of 15 cents (84 cents + 15 cents = 99 cents) had to be subtracted from gross-margin dollars in order to derive the total direct-product-profit yield, $1.41 ($2.40 - $.99). In order to equate the direct product profit of this item to other items in the store that may take up more or less shelf space, the direct product profit is converted to a yield per square foot of exposure. Therefore, the $1.41 net profit yield is divided by one and one-half square feet to give the direct product profit per square foot per week: $1.41 ÷ 1½ = $.94.[6]

---

[6]Ray Kaplan and John P. DeLuca, "Space Yield Findings on Canned Meats," *Chain Store Age Supermarket Managers Edition,* March 1965, p. 97.

Based on this type of information from individual products within specific categories, Supreme Markets was able to reallocate shelf space and substantially improve their total shelf displays. Based on these space yield findings, Paul Cifrino, then president of Supreme Markets, indicated that they were able to accomplish the following:

1. Give profitable product categories more display space.
2. Locate these desirable categories in a more favorable position within the store.
3. Reduce the variety (number of items) in low-yield lines.
4. Add to the variety in high-yield lines.

Category by category, the result of these improvements made it possible for Supreme Markets to improve their total store profits.

COSMOS. Since the Supreme Market study was completed in 1965, other attempts have been made to apply the concept of direct product profit to shelf and space allocation within the retail store. One of the most elaborate and sophisticated approaches to this application is known as COSMOS— Computer Optimization and Simulation Modeling for Operating Supermarkets.

The theory behind COSMOS is simply to take the direct-product-profit information and apply it to the day-to-day operation of a food store. As the name implies, COSMOS is a computer optimizing and simulating program that monitors the profitability, space allocation, and turnover of each product within the store. It is based on the principle that profit improvements are available from the wide range of direct product profits. We have just discussed this range and considered how profit could be improved within certain product groups by improving the direct product profit of individual items. The advantage of COSMOS over other methods is that it calculates and compares various direct product profits through a computer program. This allows COSMOS to deal with every item in the store and to consider many more variables than it would be possible to cope with in any other manner.

After reviewing these variables inherent in each product, COSMOS will recommend changes based upon the volume, profit, and sensitivity to space change characteristics of each product. These changes are summarized in computerized "Recommended Action Reports," which suggest improvements in the following key merchandising areas in the store:

1. Space assigned (facings) to each product item within a product commodity group.
2. The location of each product item within its commodity group.
3. Identification of product items for price adjustments—increases or decreases.
4. Suggested substitutions of new product offerings for low-yield products.

Although COSMOS is a problem solver, the appropriate manager must make the final decision regarding the implementation of the recommendation.

These recommended action reports are designed to serve as action guides only. The merchandising and in-store personnel who will gain the most benefit from their implementation must review the recommendations and insure that they are practical and in accordance with market and competitive conditions.

The application of these computerized programmed recommendations is mainly designed to affect big profit makers and big profit losers within each commodity group. If a product item is very profitable, the action recommended may be to increase the number of shelf facings and to assign this product to the best shelf position in the section. On the other hand, highly unprofitable items may be recommended for deletion, price revision (often price increases), or substantially reduced space.

Whenever a drastic change is recommended for an item, the COSMOS system will also recommend an alternative action. Therefore, if the first action cannot be initiated because of competitive market conditions, customer relations, or management policies, the second alternative will provide a possible course of action that will improve the profit situation. Using the information from Figure 6-11, the following recommended action report might result:

Product Item	Direct Product Profits per Week	Action Recommended	
		First Choice	Second Choice
A	+$3.35	Add 4 facings	Improve Position
B	+ 2.24	Add 2 facings	
C	+ 1.60	No change	
D	+ .45	No change	
E	− .41	No change	
F	− .76	Reduce 2 facings	
G	− 2.70	Increase price	Reduce 4 facings

Source: Case and Company, *COSMOS* (Washington, D.C.: National Association of Food Chains, October 1968), p. 10.

You will note that COSMOS has given a second choice on recommended action for the big profit maker and the big profit loser in this subcommodity group. Product **A** is a big profit maker, contributing $3.35 of direct product profits each week, and product **G** is the big profit loser, showing a loss of $2.70 of direct product profits per week. These are the two most sensitive areas, and so specific action is most important in these two areas.

Profit Improvements from the System. Can a computerized shelf allocation and shelf display program actually improve the profitability of a store? Case and Company, the firm responsible for the installation and development of COSMOS, says yes. Their initial results from test stores, as tabulated in October 1968, indicated that the average supermarket could improve their dollar profit by $3,800 per year when COSMOS was applied. The following is a summary of the results of the four product groups tested:

1. Weekly direct product profits were increased by 16.8 percent in the two test stores (as compared with two control stores)

2. Increasing the number of facings assigned to highly profitable items resulted in increased sales in 19 product subgroups, no increase in sales in 3 subgroups, and a decline in sales in 3 other subgroups. Profits, however, were improved by 27.5 percent.

3. Decreasing the number of facings assigned to highly unprofitable items resulted in decreased sales in nine product subgroups, no change in one, and increased sales in six subgroups. Profits were improved by 7.7 percent (by decreasing facings) with no change in stockouts.

4. When price increases made during the test period are included in the analysis, profits were increased by an additional 37.6 percent above the profit increase from space allocation changes alone.[7]

Summary

The allocation of space to individual items in the grocery department of a modern food store will have a direct effect on the store's profitability. Improvements in profitability can be made by simply matching shelf space to consumer demand.

When additional information about products is known, such as direct product profit, major profit improvements are possible. This is illustrated by the application of the direct-product-profit concept to shelf displays in the Supreme Market study.

Computer analysis of shelf allocation, pricing, and turnover provide the retailer with a sophisticated approach to maximizing profits. COSMOS makes this computer application possible. It takes much of the guesswork out of space allocation decisions, but it leaves the final decision up to the manager—the person who will have to see that the recommendation is carried out, and who will benefit from its correct application.

How to Reset Shelves

When it is necessary to reallocate shelf space to increase direct product profit or to meet the requirements of SLIM or other inventory control systems, a proper procedure facilitates the task. In planning for the reset, the manager should consider (or discuss with his district manager) such factors as the use of shelf break-ins, dummies, or shelf readjustments. Also, prior to the reset the manager should analyze the size of the shelving and the number of available shelves to be sure they are right for the size of the products that will be displayed.

Once the proper shelving is obtained, the manager and his reset crew (employees from the grocery department and, in a chain, sometimes an assis-

---

COSMOS, p. 13.

tant from headquarters) start on their six steps to resetting the gondola.[8]

1. *Preparation.* The first step in preparing to reset the grocery shelves is to check the order book to be sure that all authorized items are displayed. (In a chain, discuss any additions or deletions with the district manager.) Start with one section of one side of an aisle. This is a good time to price check all items in this section. If you have an out-of-stock situation at the time of the reset, substitute similar size items for those out of stock.

2. *When to start.* Select a time that will least inconvenience your customers. Saturday afternoons or Monday mornings are good starting times. Stores open on Sunday will find Monday a better starting time than the weekend.

3. *Change alignment.* Start with the top shelf. Place one item per facing from the shelf on the floor. Line up each item against the base of the gondola, making sure first and last items line up accurately with the length of the gondola. Follow the same procedure with the other shelves, placing the items from each shelf six inches in front of the items already on the floor.

4. *Establish facings.* Using the floor as a simulated gondola, move items on the floor to the row in which they will appear when replaced in the gondola. In other words, you may want to move some items from the top shelf (the back row on the floor) to the bottom shelf (the front row). Change facings as required for direct product profit, SLIM, or your inventory control requirements. Be sure to include the grocery manager and the clerk responsible for stocking the aisle when resetting. These people will be responsible for maintaining the reset and should be included in the planning and reset process. Their commitment to the program will be greater if they have some part in this process.

5. *Change shelf merchandise.* When realignment of the items on the floor is complete, have clerks remove all the merchandise from the shelves and put it in carriages, cartons, or on portable gondolas. Be sure that dented cans or damaged containers are removed. Also, check for out-of-date merchandise, correct prices as necessary, and thoroughly wash the shelving. Where necessary, dust and wash merchandise. Place rows from the floor in their respective positions on the shelves. When the merchandise is moved from the floor to the shelf, you will have one row of merchandise containing the exact number of facings desired for the reset. At this point, you should make whatever minor changes required to give correct spacing for the shelf. It is better to have extra space at the time of the reset to allow for new items or to expand fast movers if necessary. If you have extra space, give the fast movers the extra room.

6. *Wrap up.* Restack the merchandise on the shelves in accordance with your reset plan. Be sure that all merchandise is rotated and that new

---

[8]Adapted from "Inventory Management, Part V," *Chain Store Age Supermarkets Managers Edition,* February 1964, pp. 96-97. This procedure can also be useful in allocating shelf space in new stores.

merchandise is placed on the shelves first. After price moldings have been cleaned, replace price tickets or tags if these are used in your store. Be sure that the aisle is completely cleaned up after the reset. Dispose of damaged merchandise by returning it to the vendor, reducing it in price, or donating it to a charitable organization.

7

Store Layout

INTRODUCTION

Store layout and product location became a critical part of food merchandising strategy as a result of the development and refinement of the self-service method of selling.

Prior to self-service, the physical layout of food stores and the location of products was geared to the requirements of clerk service, that is, the major consideration was the ease of locating and obtaining the products requested by the customer. Customer shopping was done mostly on the basis of a list, either written or mental, that the customer recited to a store clerk who obtained the merchandise from shelf storage. The clerk was an important factor in selling because he could influence consumer purchases through the power of suggestion. Merchandise was stored in family groups, such as canned fruits and vegetables, primarily in order to facilitate selection by the clerk. Perishables such as fresh meat and produce were also prepared, when necessary, and obtained for the customer by a clerk. So, the arrangement of departments, display fixtures within departments, and products was based primarily upon the needs of store personnel in providing service to the customer.

The introduction of self-service merchandising in the supermarket changed the entire concept of store layout and product location in food merchandising. It also brought about an important change in the way consumers made food-buying decisions. The consumer began to rely on the wide choice of merchandise presented to him in the self-service displays rather than on the suggestions of a clerk.

Upon entering the average [self-service] Super, the shopper was confronted with an unprecedented expanse of colorful merchandise, abundant and dramatically mass-displayed. She took her cart or basket at the entrance, which made it easy for her to shop from display to display, from department to department.

Her freedom and leisure of choice raised the average food purchase in the Super Market of that day to between $1.50 and $2.00 per customer, as compared with 60 cents in the [service] chain and 35 cents in the corner grocery.

As for the operator, it was soon demonstrated to him that when left to herself, the average housewife sold herself far more than the best clerk behind the counter did in his palmiest days.[1]

With self-service, the displays themselves serve as a shopping list or reminder to the consumer. As the customer walks through the self-service food store, he is reminded of his product needs by what he sees on display, and makes his specific choice based upon the selection of items available.

The importance of in-store displays and their locations is brought out in a series of studies concerning consumer food store buying habits conducted by the DuPont Company. These studies indicate that most shoppers carry no shopping list and make most buying decisions on the basis of what they see in the store. The 1965 DuPont study of supermarket shopping habits in the United States showed that only 37.4 percent of supermarket shoppers carried a written shopping list.[2]

TABLE 7-1   Nature of Consumer Purchase Decisions in Supermarkets, 1949, 1954, and 1965

| Nature of Purchase Decision | Year | | |
	1949	1954	1965
	(% of purchases)		
Specifically planned	33.4	29.2	31.1
Generally planned	26.7	21.0	17.2
Purchased as a substitute	1.5	1.8	1.8
Purchased without any previous plan	38.4	48.0	49.9
Total	100.0	100.0	100.0
Decisions made in the store [a]	66.6	70.8	68.9

[a] *Includes all purchases other than those "specifically planned."*
Source: *The 6th and 7th DuPont Buying Habits Studies,* 1964, 1965.

The importance of in-store buying decisions is illustrated in Table 7-1, which shows that less than a third of consumer purchase decisions in supermarkets are specifically planned prior to entering the store. A purchase is considered specifically planned when the consumer intends to buy a specific brand or item upon entering the store and then follows through on that intention.

Of the two-thirds of all purchasing decisions that are made in the store, some purchases are planned generally, such as a loaf of bread or some

---

[1]M. M. Zimmerman, *The Super Market–A Revolution in Distribution* (New York: McGraw-Hill Book Company, Inc., 1955), p. 52.

[2]*The 7th DuPont Consumer Buying Habits Study,* E. I. DuPont De Nemours and Company, Wilmington, Delaware, 1965.

meat, but the specific item or brand decision is made at the point of sale most of the time. Some purchases are made as substitutes in place of a specifically or generally planned item because of the unavailability of the planned item, the price, or other reasons. Nearly half the purchases made by supermarket shoppers in 1965 were completely unplanned, based upon shopper interviews as they entered the store compared with actual purchases. The completely unplanned purchases are sometimes called "impulse" buying because it appears that this type of purchase is made spontaneously, that is, without any prior intention. The proportion of impulse sales has steadily increased since the advent of self-service.

In the early days of self-service,

> ... a Super Market operator went into business in an abandoned garage or factory building. Then it was simply a matter of bringing the merchandise into an open area, loading it on platforms or shelves conveniently within the reach of the customers. Displays were improvised with cartons and crates, planks on wooden horses, discarded tables, and cast-off display stands from other retailing establishments. Very little thought was given to the placement of these various departments, to lighting, or to the shopping atmosphere.[3]

As self-service merchandising matured into the supermarket, it required a much more sophisticated approach to store layout, one that was based upon the shopping habits and needs of customers. Self-service meant that the physical presentation of merchandise in the store assumed a new and essential role. The products became salesmen as the personal contact between the clerk and the customer was removed for grocery items, and, ultimately, for most perishable merchandise. The power of suggestion was, in effect, transferred from the clerk to the merchandise display. The type, size, location, and method of display now had an important effect upon the sale of food in retail stores.

The nature of consumer demand in making self-service supermarket buying decisions places great importance upon the way in which merchandising strategy is developed and carried out at the point of sale, especially with respect to store layout and product location.

THE BASICS OF STORE LAYOUT

Store layout has been defined as "the arrangement of selling and nonselling departments, aisles, fixtures, displays, and equipment in the proper relationship to each other and to the fixed elements of the building structure."[4] Effective store layout requires that merchandise and service areas be classified into related groups or departments. The general type of arrangement,

---

[3]*The Super Market,* p. 180.
[4]William R. Davidson and Alton F. Doody, *Retailing Management,* 3rd ed. (New York: The Ronald Press Company, 1966), p. 163.

amount of space allocated to each department, department location, and strategic arrangement of merchandise within departmental groupings constitute the layout decisions that must be made.

The overall objective of food store layout is to *maximize sales and profit consistent with customer convenience.* It is important to realize that satisfactory profits can only be maintained through continued customer satisfaction and repeat sales, so store layout and product-location decisions must be made with value to the customer as the primary consideration if maximum sales and profit are to be realized over time.

There are several basic considerations in planning the store layout for the selling and service areas—the parts of the store to which customers have direct access—to achieve maximum sales, profit, and value to the consumer.

Exposure

The cardinal rule for self-service food store layout is to expose as much of the product line as possible to each customer because *the rate of exposure is directly related to the rate of sale of merchandise.* This is true regardless of whether the product is a staple like salt or an impulse item like anchovies. Customers must see or be aware of the choices available to them before sales can take place in self-service merchandising.

Ideally, a store would be designed in such a manner that customers would pass by all items in the store during their normal shopping tour. Under this ideal situation, there would be maximum and equal exposure to all products on the shelves, and sales would reach an optimal level. However, it is not practical in the conventional store to channel customers down every aisle and past every product. Most customers are not interested in viewing each department and would consider such a layout an imposition on their shopping convenience. Therefore, the store planner must strive for maximum exposure through a subtle means of guiding the shopper through each department in the store.

There are three ways by which shopping patterns and the rate of exposure can be influenced in store layout and product location.

First of all, the *location of departments* influences the exposure of products to customers through its effect on the flow of customer traffic. The sales mix and gross margin contribution can be affected through department location.

Second, the *arrangement of selling fixtures within departments* affects the rate of exposure of customers to the products displayed in the department through influencing customer traffic flow.

Third, the *location of product categories and items* in the display fixtures affects both exposure and sales through influencing customer traffic.

Convenience

Customer convenience, along with exposure, is a major consideration in planning store layout and product location. If exposure were the only basis for making layout decisions and customers were forced to travel down every aisle in the store, many would become discouraged because of the shopping inconvenience and shift their patronage to other stores. If this happened often enough, exposure might be more than offset by a reduction in customers so that sales and profits would suffer. Therefore, planning store layout and product location according to the principle of maximum exposure must be done within the context of customer convenience values.

Customer in-store shopping convenience has three aspects that are important to store layout and product location:

1. Time
2. Ease of movement
3. Ease in locating merchandise

Although it might be desirable from an immediate sales and profit point of view to require the customer to be exposed to every display in the store, the shopping time required would be likely to cause a serious inconvenience to the consumer. Both layout and product location should be planned so that the consumer can complete her shopping, either for a few items or her weekly needs, in a reasonable amount of time.

In order to facilitate consumer shopping, store layout should be designed to prevent congestion and confusion that might require additional time on the part of the consumer as well as interfere with the consumer's access to displays of merchandise, and, consequently, reduce sales and profit.

In addition to considerations of shopping time and ease of movement, the ease with which customers can locate merchandise should be considered. Store layout and product location should be based upon consumer shopping habits, particularly with respect to the grouping of items within departments. In general, consumers tend to buy products in family groups or categories, so that merchandise should be displayed in that manner. Frequent relocation of merchandise may also create confusion among shoppers who are accustomed to finding frequently purchased items in the same location.

Costs

In addition to merchandising consideration, there are some cost or operational considerations that relate to store layout and product location. Because building space represents a major expense in food retailing, it is important that space be used as productively as possible. This requires that as much of the selling area of the store as possible be devoted to the display of merchandise. Space that does not serve a useful function represents an unnecessary cost. Therefore, store layout should avoid the inefficient use of floor space without creating congestion, confusion, or obstructed access to merchandise for the consumer.

Another cost or operational consideration is that of the stocking and restocking of merchandise. Merchandise that is processed in work areas and restocked frequently, such as fresh meat and produce, is usually displayed adjacent to the work area along the perimeter of the store. This location expedites the stocking procedure, which is important from a cost and physical effort standpoint, and is also important for quality control in the case of highly perishable merchandise. Locating fresh meat, produce, dairy products, and frozen foods near the point of storage reduces the time that the product remains out of low-temperature storage. Some perishable merchandise, especially dairy products, is displayed in fixtures that are stocked from the storage area in the rear of the display case. In these instances, the display must be located on the perimeter of the store. Fresh meats are usually stocked from the rear of the self-service display cases from a narrow aisle between the display cases and back-room work area. This procedure requires a perimeter location for the meat department.

Another advantage of locating high-turnover perishables departments near the point of storage is that interference with customer traffic is reduced. Clerks do not have to move products through the display area in order to achieve necessary, frequent restocking of high-turnover merchandise if the merchandise is stored adjacent to the display.

In summary, there are three basic considerations that should be involved in making store layout and product-location decisions. First of all, maximum exposure of products to customers is the guiding principle. Exposure can be affected by the location of departments, the arrangement of selling fixtures, and the location of products. The rule of maximum exposure, however, must be applied in view of two other considerations: customer convenience and operating costs. The store layout and location of products should enable the consumer to locate his needs easily, move about the store with little or no congestion and confusion, and complete his shopping within a reasonable period of time. The other consideration relates to costs of operations. The store layout and product location should result in an efficient use of space in order to keep operating expenses at a reasonable level. Also, quality control and restocking requirements of each department and product category ought to be considered so that labor cost and interference with customer traffic can be minimized while quality is maintained at the highest possible level.

TRAFFIC FLOW STUDIES

The supermarket shopper is perhaps the most studied individual alive. The choice of stores and preferences for products have been the subjects of numerous research studies by food processors and distributors as well as other private and public agencies with an interest in food distribution.

Over the last 10 to 15 years, a considerable body of knowledge has been assembled concerning consumer shopping behavior in retail food stores. The research technique utilized to obtain and analyze the information, referred to as customer traffic research or customer shopping pattern research, was pioneered by the United States Department of Agriculture. Customer traffic research has provided much valuable information concerning the relationship of store layout and product location to customer shopping behavior. As a result of customer traffic research, guidelines are available that are useful in planning store layouts, in locating products, and in planning other merchandising practices in order to maximize sales and profit.

Sample Size and Selection

Customer traffic research is a type of demand study that indicates what consumers actually do when shopping in retail stores. It requires the systematic observation and recording of the shopping behavior of a sample of the customers patronizing a food store over a period of one or two weeks.

The minimum sample size recommended for observation per store is 3 to 5 percent of one week's customer count, or a total of between 200 and 300 observations.[5] This number of observations is sufficient to give a representative picture of the shopping behavior of all the customers shopping the store.

The observations should be collected in the same proportion as the number of shoppers that patronize the store for representative hours of the day. In other words, if 2 percent of the weekly customer count is experienced from 9:00 A.M. to 12:00 noon on Mondays, then 2 percent of the total observations should be made during that time. This procedure is important if the shopping pattern information is to be truly representative of shopping behavior during the entire week. If there is little or no interest in customer shopping behavior during the early part of the week when a relatively small proportion of the weekly business is done, then all the observations can be made during the last three or four days of the week.

The selection of customers to be observed can be made by using any sound sampling technique; however, time may be saved by taking the very first customer entering the store after the enumerator is ready to begin.[6] From then on, the enumerator can take the next customer to enter the store after completing each observation, until the required number of observations is reached. This procedure can be followed regardless if there are one or two enumerators. It is recommended that not more than two enumerators be in the selling area at any one time, to avoid customer consciousness of being observed.

---

[5]*Customer In-Store Shopping Behavior and Store Layout,* Department of Agriculture; presentation to the National American Wholesale Grocers Association's Store Planning Seminar, Memphis, Tennessee, May 27, 1963.

[6]Hugh N. Smith, *Uniform Methods for the Collection and Presentation of Basic Customer Shopping Pattern Data,* Market Development Research Division, Agricultural Marketing Service, United States Department of Agriculture, Washington, D.C., February 1960.

Information Required

First of all, general information should be recorded for each store being studied in order to make more meaningful evaluations of the customer observations and so that the observations from similar stores can be combined or compared. The general information that should be recorded for each store is indicated in Figure 7-1.

1. Project leader_____ Address_____
2. Dates of observations: From_____To_____
3. Number of patterns used in analysis_____
4. Which days of week were included in study?
    M_____Tues._____W_____Thurs._____F_____ Sat._____Sun._____
5. Store information
    a) Name_____ No._____Address_____

    b) Corporate group_____   Co-op or voluntary
                                                   group_____

        Independent_____
    c) Year opened _____   Year last remodeled_____
    d) Square feet of   No. of checkouts_____
        selling area_____
    e) Average sales: Annual_____ Weekly_____
    f) Customer count during study: Total _____
                    Mon._____   Thurs. _____
                    Tues._____ Fri._____
                    Wed._____   Sat._____
                        Sun._____
    g) Approximate distance of closest one or two competitors and type of
        stores_____

    h) Type of location (downtown; shopping center; suburban free-standing;
        rural; etc.)_____

    i) Type and amount of parking_____

    j) Type of trade (income, predominate nationalities, occupation, etc.)

    k) Special features with respect to physical characteristics, services or
        products_____

    l) Store layout (attach a diagram of the store which indicates location and
        arrangement of departments, fixtures, product categories, service areas
        and entrances and exits)

FIGURE 7-1   Standard information sheet for stores included in customer traffic studies.

Second and most important is the information to be recorded from observing the customers. Basically, the observations should describe the customers and indicate where they went and what they did.

The observations should be recorded on a store layout sheet, and a separate sheet should be used for each customer in the sample (see Figure 7-2). The use of a layout sheet facilitates recording observations quickly and accurately. The layout sheet should be detailed to show the major departments, product categories, and important physical features.

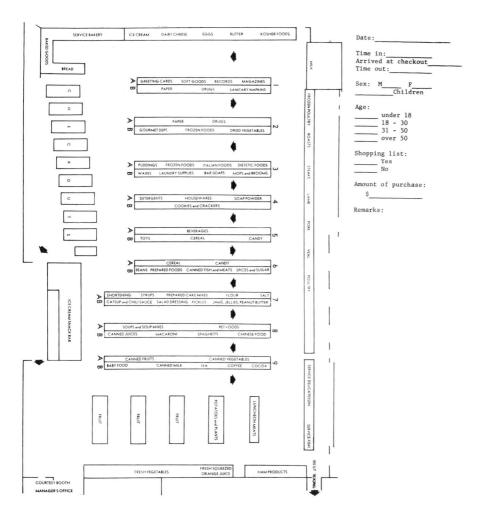

FIGURE 7-2 Example of information collection sheet for shopper in a retail food store traffic study. Courtesy of Food Marts, Inc., Holyoke, Massachusetts.

The specific information that should be recorded, which is illustrated in Figure 7-2, is listed as follows:

1. *Date*—The day of the week, month, and year that the pattern was taken. This information can be abbreviated so that Monday, October 1, 1973, would be entered on the form as M 10/1/73.

2. *Time in and out*—The time of day that the customer entered the store and the time the customer completed the shopping should be entered. Shopping is considered to be completed when the checkout transaction is completed.

It may be useful to determine the amount of time that customers must spend in the checkout process, including waiting time. This information is helpful in evaluating checkout service. If this information is desired, it is necessary to indicate also the time that the customer reaches the checkout after the final purchase.

3. *Sex and number in shopping party*—The sex of the shopper can be indicated by checking *M* or *F* on the form. If a man and woman shop together, this fact can be indicated by checking both *M* and *F* on the information sheet. In this instance, it is assumed that only one household is represented. It may be desirable to know the number of shoppers who were accompanied by children during the shopping trip. If this is the case, the number of children should be indicated in the appropriate space.

4. *Approximate age*—It is useful to analyze shopping habits by age of the consumers. Therefore, some indication of age is necessary. It is recommended that the enumerators estimate the age of the shopper according to the following age categories:

Under 18
18-30
31-50
over 50

Additional age categories are probably not useful enough to offset the loss of accuracy that will likely result.

If two people shop together, the age of the individual who makes most of the buying decisions should be indicated.

5. *Shopping list*—If the customer refers to a shopping list or other type of reminder at any time during the shopping trip, they should be credited with using a list. This information is useful in assessing whether purchasing decisions are made entirely at the point of sale or whether some decisions were made prior to entering the store.

6. *Amount of purchase*—The amount spent by customers is important information because it can be related to the amount of time spent in the store as well as to the traffic patterns followed by customers. The amount spent by each customer can be read from the cash register and marked on the data sheet. If possible, the amount of the purchases should exclude

state sales taxes, and the amount of the tax on the total order should be listed separately.

7. *Remarks*—Often the enumerator will notice situations during observations of customers that, although not part of the study, will contribute to the analysis. For example, customer confusion, unusual congestion due to bottlenecks caused by layout or employee activity, employee handling of customer requests, accident hazards, and so on are situations that are important in evaluating merchandising effectiveness in the store. These situations should be noted briefly by the enumerators in this section on the information sheet.

Each enumerator should identify himself by placing his initials on the information form. If there is ever a question about any of the entries on the form, the enumerator can be consulted.

The most important information to be recorded is the actual behavior of the customers during the shopping trip with respect to where they went and what they did. This information is the real purpose of the study and defines the shopping or traffic pattern.

In order to record where they went, a continuous line, with arrows showing the direction of travel, should be drawn to describe the path taken by the customer with a shopping cart. If the customer does not use a shopping cart or parks the cart and shops some distance from it at any time, a broken line with arrows should be used to indicate the shopping path. Because customers who do not use shopping carts are probably in the store for only one or two items, it is most useful to confine the study to shoppers who use shopping carts.

In addition to a description of the path followed by the customers, which shows where they went, it is important to record what they did in terms of examining and purchasing merchandise. This can be done by marking an X on the layout sheet whenever a selection is made by the customer. The X should indicate the product category from which the selection was made. If the product categories are listed on the layout sheets, an X can be marked in the appropriate category. Otherwise, the name of the product or category will have to be written beside the mark. An X should be marked for each item selected, even when more than one item is purchased from the same product category.

There may be instances when it is desirable to know the exact items purchased by customers. In this case, it is necessary that the enumerator write the name of the item alongside the X. Identifying the exact items selected requires closer observation of the customers and entails a greater risk of being "discovered" by the customers. Because customers may alter their shopping behavior if they are aware that they are being observed, the enumerators should be discreet while following customers. If it becomes apparent that a customer is aware of being observed before he reaches the checkout area, then that customer should be dropped from the sample, and the enumerator should discontinue recording his activities.

Tabulation of Information

After all the observations have been made, it is necessary to tabulate the information collected so that the merchandising effectiveness of the store layout and product location can be evaluated in relation to the characteristics of the store's customers.

Description of Customers

The customers should be classified according to approximate age, sex, number in shopping party, and the proportion who used a shopping list.

Shopping Behavior

For each product category, aisle, or display fixture, determine the proportion of customers that purchased one or more items, the proportion that passed but did not purchase, and the proportion that did not pass. These tabulations can be presented in various ways depending upon the intended use. Figure 7-3 illustrates a simple exposure chart that shows the proportion of total customers that shopped each aisle. Additional tabulations and charts can be prepared to show purchase rates, the proportion of customers passing certain points or displays, the effectiveness of one-way aisles, and so on.

Byproduct Information

Other tabulations can be made that are helpful in understanding customer shopping habits and in evaluating merchandising effectiveness in each department as well as in the entire store. These include average shopping time, average and distribution of customer purchases in terms of dollars and number of items, proportion of customers shopping the entire store, average checkout time, and the proportion of customers that shop each department completely. Some of the tabulations may be cross-tabulations that involve more than one piece of information. For example, it may be helpful to know the relationship between age of the customer and the amount purchased, in which case the average purchase is tabulated by age group.

Use of Information

The information obtained in customer traffic flow studies can be invaluable in evaluating and improving the merchandising effectiveness of store layout and product location. It provides a better understanding of how customers react to the physical features and the arrangement of merchandise in the store.

Flow studies are helpful in pinpointing strengths and weaknesses indicated by rates of exposure and sales in the aisles and for individual product categories and displays. Obstructions or bottlenecks that restrict the flow of traffic, and, consequently, exposure and sales, can be identified. The results of customer flow studies can be used to modify or change layout

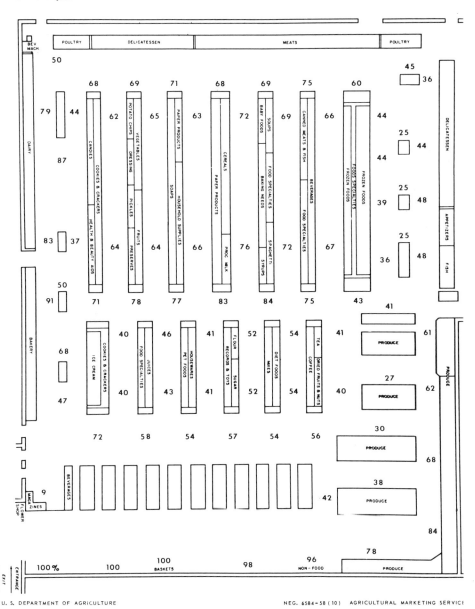

FIGURE 7-3 Percentage of customers passing selected locations in a retail food store. Source: Agricultural Marketing Service, U.S. Department of Agriculture.

and product location in existing stores as well as to provide a basis for new store planning in order to achieve maximum exposure consistent with customer convenience. Perhaps the best way to illustrate the usefulness of the results of customer flow studies is to list the major findings of the studies.

PRINCIPLES OF STORE LAYOUT

Since 1955, many customer traffic studies have been conducted by industry, government, and university researchers. The most extensive of these was a study of 3,200 customers in 13 supermarkets in the Boston metropolitan area conducted by the United States Department of Agriculture in 1957. The findings of this study and others have had an observable influence on food store layout and product location.

Based upon the USDA study of New England supermarket shoppers and more recent studies conducted by university extension specialists in several states, a general set of conclusions has been developed concerning store layout and product location in retail food stores. These conclusions seem to be just as relevant to food store layout today as when the first studies were made.

Locating for Maximum Exposure

Sales vary directly with customer exposure to products. As stated earlier in this chapter, the primary goal of good store layout is to expose as many products to customers as possible, or to look at this in another way, to expose as many customers to the products in the store as possible. Studies show that the greater the rate of exposure, the greater the sales. The highest traffic areas in supermarkets today are the outside or periphery aisles. The rates of exposure in these aisles are the highest, and therefore the rate of sale in these aisles are the highest. The rates of exposure in the interior aisles vary according to the type of location and the products included in the aisles.

1. *Locate the high-profit departments around the periphery of the store.* Because the greatest traffic flow is found around the outside aisle of the store, it is a good merchandising practice to locate the high-profit departments and high-profit items in this aisle. Because the perishables departments generally contribute relatively high gross margins and contributions to overhead and profit, it is desirable from a merchandising standpoint to locate them in the mainstream of traffic flow—in the periphery aisles.

The location of departments in the store arrangement is a very important decision because the rate of customer exposure and, consequently, the departmental sales and store product mix are affected. The perimeter of the store is especially important with respect to departmental locations because of the relatively high proportion of customers shopping the perimeter area.

The best documented cases of the effect of location upon departmental exposure and sales are studies of the produce department. Several studies, including a USDA study, have indicated that the rates of exposure and sales in the produce department are generally from 1 to 1½ percent higher as a percentage of store sales when the department is located first in the shopping pattern than when it is located in the last aisle or in an intermediate position in the back of the store.[7]

TABLE 7-2 Produce as a Percentage of Annual Sales in Seven Pairs of Stores With Produce First and Produce Last in the Shopping Patterns, in a Midwestern Chain

| | Produce Percentage of Store Sales | |
Pair	Produce First	Produce Last
A	8.8	8.3
B	10.7	9.2
C	11.4	9.6
D	11.4	9.6
E	10.0	9.2
F [a]	8.9	8.7
G [a]	9.0	7.6
Average	10.0	8.9

[a] *Based upon six-month sales data.*

Source: *Display Location and Customer Service in Retail Produce Departments,* Marketing Research Report No. 501, U.S. Department of Agriculture, Washington, D.C., October 1961, p. 7.

Table 7-2 shows that produce sales as a percentage of total store sales averaged more than 1 percent higher in stores where produce was located first in the shopping pattern, that is, in the first department that the shopper entered, which would be the right- or left-hand side perimeter aisle in a conventional store arrangement. Each pair of stores in the study was similar with respect to type of location and total sales volume.

Similar studies have not been made for other departments in conventional store layouts, but it is only reasonable to expect that there is some relationship between location, exposure, and sales for each department in the store because of the inherent advantages of certain locations. The first aisle that the customer enters in a conventional store layout has the highest rate of exposure, and therefore will probably result in a higher proportion of store sales for whatever department or product categories are located there.

However, some departments and product categories will respond more to this favored location than others. Produce sales show a relatively high response to the first-aisle location because of the impulse nature of most produce purchases. Customer shopping exposure and purchase rate in the meat department do not seem to be as responsive to location as in the produce department, apparently because meat purchases have less of an impulse nature. In other words, customers are more likely to seek out the meat department regardless of where it is located, so that the meat department

[7]*Display Location and Customer Service in Retail Produce Departments,* Marketing Research Report No. 501, Agricultural Marketing Service, Transportation and Facilities Research Division, U.S. Department of Agriculture, Washington, D.C., p. 8.

exposure and sales rate are not as responsive to the first-aisle location.

The same is probably true of the dairy and bakery departments, both of which include items with a very high drawing power and are, therefore, more likely to be sought out by the consumer. Frozen foods, on the other hand, are purchased more on an impulse basis than meats, dairy products, and bakery goods, so that putting the frozen-food department in a preferred location is likely to result in noticeable gains in exposure and sales.

The purchase of many nonfoods, such as housewares, health and beauty aids, toys, and records, is also of a highly impulse nature, so that these product categories can also be expected to respond well to a first-aisle location.

2. *Advantages and disadvantages of continuous gondolas.* A question that is often debated by merchandising experts is whether to have long continuous gondolas running the length of the store or to interject cross-over aisles at some point in the gondola to permit the customer to move to the next aisle. There are advantages and disadvantages to both methods, and this is one reason why both types of layouts are found in supermarkets today.

The advantages of the continuous aisle is that it provides greater control of traffic flow than the cross-over aisle layout. By ''forcing'' the customers to shop the entire aisle, the store is assured greater exposure to the products in that aisle.

A disadvantage of the continuous gondola layout is the shopping inconvenience that it may place on the customer. In many cases, a customer may be forced to walk the entire length of an aisle without purchasing any products in that aisle or purchasing only one or two items. However, the customer must continue the full length of the aisle in order to reach the next aisle in the shopping pattern or must double back, which can result in more time and inconvenience.

3. *Advantages and disadvantages of cross-over aisles.* The cross-over aisle is exactly what its name implies—it provides the customer with an opportunity to move between aisles without having to walk the full length of the aisle. Customers who are familiar with the store will utilize cross-over aisles as they move from purchase to purchase. However, customers unfamiliar with the store may find that they miss items because they do not follow a uniform shopping pattern under this type of store layout.

Another advantage to the cross-over aisle layout is that it provides additional display ends for the store. These end displays provide merchandising opportunities to promote and sell high-margin impulse items as well as seasonal items and new items. The opportunity for these additional displays often is the deciding factor in many supermarket layout decisions.

A disadvantage of the cross-over aisle is that it breaks up the uniform flow of customer traffic and creates certain ''dead areas'' in the store shopping pattern. Because customers are not required to travel the entire length of the aisle, they will often miss certain sections of the store and therefore

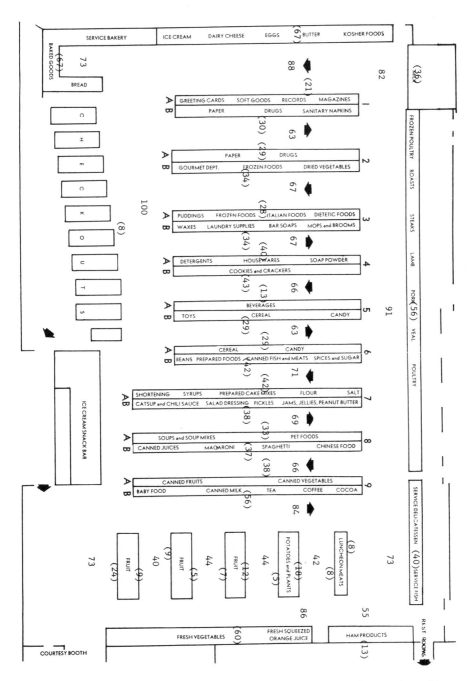

FIGURE 7-4 Percentage of shoppers passing and purchasing from selected locations in a retail food store. Numbers in ( ) indicate % purchasing from each side of gondola or department. Other numbers indicate % passing through aisle or department. Courtesy of Food Marts, Inc., Holyoke, Massachusetts.

not be exposed to the products that are displayed in these areas. This reduced exposure can result in lost sales.

As shown in Figures 7-3 and 7-4, the rates of exposure and sales are generally highest when continuous rather than divided gondolas are used in the grocery department. The use of divided gondolas creates cross aisles that tend to result in an uneven and less-complete customer traffic pattern within the grocery department.

The same general conclusion can be made for other departments, based upon customer traffic studies. The most definitive research concerning the relationship between department arrangement and exposure and sales is that conducted by the U.S. Department of Agriculture on produce-department arrangement.[8]

The USDA studies identified customer traffic patterns associated with five different produce-department display fixture arrangements in common use. Because produce departments are usually located in a perimeter aisle on either side or in the rear of the store, considerable flexibility exists in the arrangement of selling fixtures.

The arrangements, traffic patterns, and purchase rates for the five types of produce-department arrangements are illustrated in Figures 7-5 through 7-9.[9]

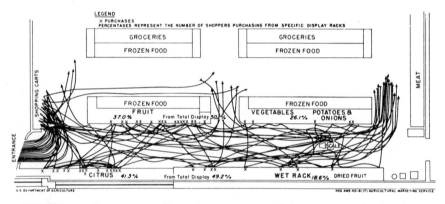

FIGURE 7-5   Customer traffic and percentages of shoppers purchasing from various displays in store A, a straight-line produce department with a split gondola and no secondary aisle. Source: *Display Location and Customer Service in Retail Produce Departments,* Marketing Research Report No. 501, U.S. Department of Agriculture, Agricultural Marketing Service, Washington, D.C., October 1961, p. 10.

---

[8]The illustrations and data in the remainder of this section are taken mostly from *Display Location and Customer Service in Retail Produce Departments,* Marketing Research Report No. 501, U.S. Department of Agriculture, Agricultural Marketing Service, Transportation and Facilities Research Division, Washington, D.C., October 1961, pp. 9-13.

[9]The lines in the customer traffic flow diagrams represent the paths of about 25 customers selected randomly from the total sample. The diagrams are reasonably typical of the shopping patterns of all customers.

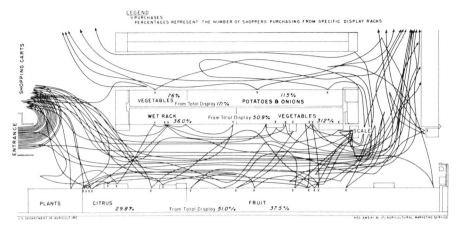

FIGURE 7-6   Customer traffic and percentages of shoppers purchasing from various displays in store B, a straight-line produce department with a secondary aisle. Source: *Display Location and Customer Service in Retail Produce Departments*, p. 10.

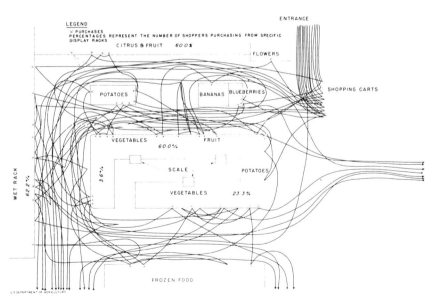

FIGURE 7-7   Customer traffic and percentages of shoppers purchasing from various displays in store C, a corner L-shaped produce department with a secondary aisle. Source: *Display Location and Customer Service in Retail Produce Departments*, p. 11.

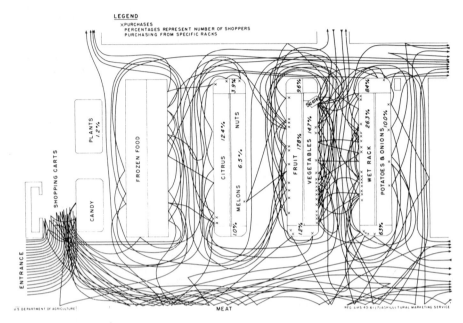

FIGURE 7-8   Customer traffic and percentage of shoppers purchasing from various displays in store D, a gondola-type produce department. Source: *Display Location and Customer Service in Retail Produce Departments*, p. 12.

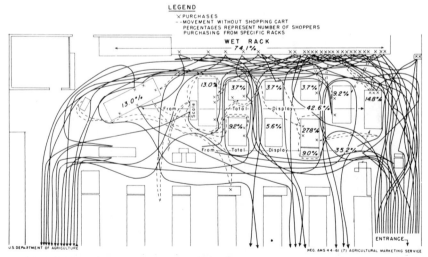

FIGURE 7-9   Customer traffic and percentages of shoppers purchasing from various displays in store E, a produce department with individual tables opposite the refrigerated wall counter. Source: *Display Location and Customer Service in Retail Produce Departments*, p. 12.

256

Stores A and B represent two types of straight-line departments (Figures 7-5 and 7-6). Store A has an "escape" opening in the center of the gondola on the customer's left. Store B has a display of onions and potatoes down one side of secondary aisle. Both straight-line layouts result in "bounce" patterns—the customer shops the counters on each side of the aisle alternately as she passes through the aisle. The bounce pattern is associated with a high rate of exposure and sale. The rates of exposure and sale in secondary aisles as shown in Store B are usually much lower than in the main aisle. Once customers pass through the main aisle of the department, they are apparently interested in moving on to other departments and are reluctant to shop the secondary aisle. This same pattern has been observed in frozen-food departments that are arranged with one main aisle and a secondary aisle. The rates of exposure and sale in the secondary aisle are usually much lower than in the main aisle. This is true regardless of whether the frozen-food department is located in a perimeter aisle or in the interior of the grocery department.

Store C is similar to stores A and B, except that the long aisle is turned 90° to make an L-shaped aisle (Figure 7-7). The bounce pattern is apparent in the major aisle, but the rate of purchase declines as the customer moves into the secondary aisle opposite the frozen-food department.

Store D represents a less-well-defined department, with several aisles surrounding the gondola-type produce display fixtures (Figure 7-8). The bounce pattern of shopping is found only in the two center aisles, primarily between the wet rack and the vegetable counter.

Store E is similar to store A, except that instead of a long gondola opposite the refrigerated wall display, numerous small tables are used with many aisles and passageways that customers can enter (Figure 7-9). Very little bounce shopping is evident, and the exposure and sales rates are extremely low in many of the short aisles.

TABLE 7-3 Customer Traffic in Five Differently Arranged Produce Departments

Store and Type of Arrangement	Percentage of Customers Shopping Produce Dept.	Percentage of Produce Shoppers Who Shopped Entire Dept
A—Straight-line with split gondola	87.9	76.9
B—Straight-line with secondary aisle	90.2	25.2
C—Corner L-shaped with secondary aisle	—	21.1
D—Three gondolas	81.2	7.5
E—Wall counter and individual tables	78.3	5.6

Source: *Display Location and Customer Service in Retail Produce Departments,* Marketing Research Report No. 501, U.S. Department of Agriculture, Washington, D.C., October 1961, p.11.

The results of the customer traffic studies in the five produce departments are summarized in Table 7-3. It is apparent that the straight-line arrangements not only attracted a higher proportion of total shoppers, but resulted in more complete shopping of the department by those shoppers who entered the produce department. The straight-line department with the split gondola was far more effective than the straight-line department with a secondary aisle in achieving a high rate of complete shopping. The extremely low traffic in the secondary aisle in store B was responsible for this difference. The corner L-shaped department was nearly as effective as the straight-line department with a secondary aisle in terms of complete customer shopping. The department with three gondolas and the department with the wall counter and individual tables were both quite ineffective in achieving complete customer shopping.

The long, narrow produce departments with continuous produce displays on both sides of a single aisle generally result in higher rates of exposure, complete shopping, and purchases than other types of layouts. In most instances, this type of layout results in a more efficient use of floor space as well. The ratio of display space to aisle space is higher in straight-line departments, and the cross aisles and displays that generate very little customer traffic are eliminated.

In order to test the advantages of long, narrow produce departments with continuous produce displays, the USDA studied five stores in which the produce departments were converted to the straight-line layout with a single aisle. The produce departments in these stores previously had a series of multiple tables in a large, open area adjacent to a wall produce display similar to the layout in store E. The results of the study showed that, on the average, produce sales increased from 7.9 percent to 9.3 percent of total store sales in five stores after the conversion.

End Displays

End displays are considered to be prime selling locations by many merchandisers; however, customer traffic studies indicate that a relatively low proportion of customers purchase from end displays and that the rate of purchase varies widely among end displays depending upon the type of merchandise displayed. Figure 7-10 shows the rates of purchase from grocery end displays as determined from a traffic flow study in a food store. The rates of purchase range from a low of 1 percent to a high of 7 percent of the shoppers.

The Department of Agriculture found that the proportion of total purchases made from end displays was only slightly higher in stores with split grocery gondolas than in stores with continuous grocery gondolas (see Table 7-4). Therefore, it is doubtful whether the additional end displays in the split-gondola layout are effective, especially in view of the lower rates of customer exposure in the grocery aisles of the split-gondola arrangement.

When end displays were used for staple items that were sale priced and

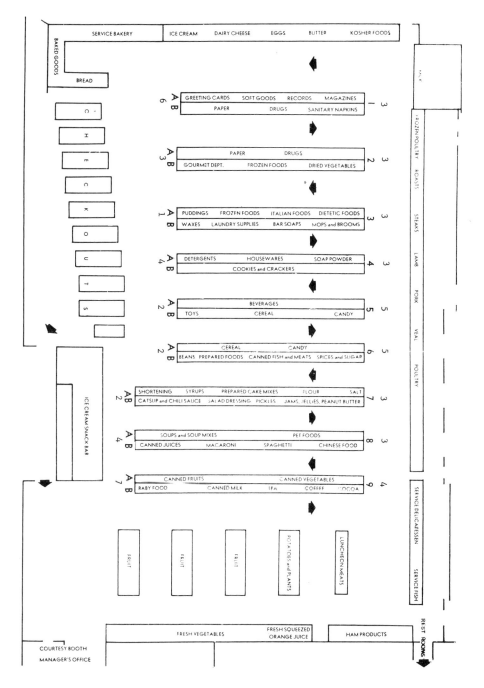

FIGURE 7-10 Rates of purchase from grocery end displays in a retail food store. Courtesy of Food Marts, Inc., Holyoke, Massachusetts.

advertised, there was a noticeable decrease in customer traffic in the grocery aisles. Apparently, many shoppers of the specials found it unnecessary to enter some of the aisles because of the availability of needed items on the end displays.[10]

TABLE 7-4   Percentage of Total Purchases From End Displays[a]

Type of Layout in Grocery Department	Number of End Displays	Percentage of Total Purchases From End Displays
Split gondolas	18	2.9
Continuous gondolas	10	2.7

[a] In three stores with split gondolas and eleven stores with continuous grocery gondolas.
Source: Presented by Lewis F. Norwood, Federal Extension Service, United States Department of Agriculture, at Purdue University, March 20, 1961.

The ends of grocery gondolas are exposed naturally to a high percentage of customer traffic (from 70 to 90 percent). Items that will increase impulse sales most are probably the most appropriate for featuring on end displays. Traffic builders, such as advertised specials, can then be placed within the gondola sections to improve the overall distribution of customer flow in the aisles of the grocery department in order to maximize product exposure.[11]

Some retailers like to display some price specials prominently on end displays in order to project a low-price image. In these instances, it is advantageous to display a relatively high-margin, related impulse item along with the price special.

Traffic studies indicate that customers tend to pass most end displays rather hurriedly on their way from one aisle to another. Therefore, end displays should be planned so that they will attract the customer's attention in order to achieve maximum effectiveness.

Locating by Drawing Power

The proportion of customers purchasing one or more items varies widely among product categories, reflecting differences in both number of customers demanding them and frequency of purchase.

Table 7-5 indicates the leading commodity groups in terms of "drawing power," that is, the commodity groups from which one or more items are purchased by a high proportion of the customers. Drawing power should not be confused with turnover or dollar sales, which involve quantity purchased as well as the number of customers purchasing. Drawing power only indicates the proportion of customers purchasing one or more items from each commodity group and not the quantity or value of purchases.

---

[10]*Customers' Shopping Patterns in Retail Food Stores,* U.S. Department of Agriculture, Agricultural Marketing Service, Market Development Research Division, Washington, D.C., August 1960, p. 9.

[11]*Customers' Shopping Patterns in Retail Food Stores,* p. 10.

Drawing power is important because it is directly related to customer traffic; the greater the drawing power of an item or commodity group, the greater the flow of traffic past the display of the item or group. Therefore, products with a high drawing power will attract a relatively high proportion of the customers into the aisles or areas where they are displayed. The strategic location of products with a high drawing power can contribute to greater exposure and sales of all products.

The strategic location of frequently purchased items and commodity

TABLE 7-5   Proportion of Customer's Making Purchases From Selected Food Commodity Groups in Six Food Stores

Commodity Group	Proportion of Customers Purchasing	
	Mean (Average)	Confidence Range [a]
Small variation among stores		
Bread, rolls, and pastry	66%	54-78%
Milk	37	26-48
Cookies and crackers	36	26-46
Canned vegetables	32	22-42
Cereal	38	21-35
Beer and soda	23	19-27
Canned fruit	22	17-27
Dressings and spreads	21	13-28
Flour and flour mixes	21	16-26
Ice cream	19	14-24
Soup	19	14-24
Sugar	18	13-23
Frozen juices	17	10-24
Preserves and peanut butter	15	12-18
Baby food	9	6-12
Onions	7	4-10
Processed milk	7	4-10
Medium variation among stores		
Coffee, tea, and cocoa	26	12-40
Potatoes	18	8-28
Canned juice	17	9-25
Pet foods	12	7-17
Gelatins and puddings	10	6-14
Shortening	8	4-12
Frozen prepared dinners	8	4-12
Large variation among stores		
Eggs	27	12-42
Spaghetti, rice, dried beans and peas	22	10-34
Chips and pretzels	21	6-36
Bananas	17	7-27
Frozen vegetables	17	7-27
Citrus fruits	15	1-29
Canned tomatoes and sauce	12	0-27
Frozen fish	8	1-15

[a] This range indicates the interval between which the mean (average) proportion of customers purchasing would be expected to occur in two-thirds of the observations.

Source: *Shopping Behavior of Customers in Modified and Conventional Layouts of Retail Food Stores,* Marketing Economics Division, Economic Research Service, U.S. Department of Agriculture, Washington, D.C., 1964, p. 27.

groups complements good store layouts and compensates for inefficient layouts, to a degree, by encouraging more uniform and complete shopping of a store. Customer traffic in gondola aisles can be increased further by locating price-featured items near the center of the gondola.[12]

In order to promote more complete customer shopping of the grocery department, it is best to distribute the displays of product categories so that each aisle contains at least two categories with relatively high drawing power. Each gondola should contain at least one such category so that customers will be encouraged to shop both sides of each aisle. In addition to the food commodity groups with high drawing power shown in Table 7-5, there are nonfood commodity groups that are purchased by a high proportion of customers—soaps and detergents and paper products.

The drawing power of some food commodity groups varies considerably among stores, as shown in Table 7-5. This variation reflects differences in tastes and preferences among consumers as well as the nature and extent of competition in each market area. These factors should be considered by the food retailer when assessing the drawing power of commodity groups.

Island Displays

In many retail food stores, it is a common practice to build or locate special island displays in the center of the aisles, especially in the wide aisles in the produce and meat departments. Island displays are also used in other departments, including the grocery department.

The island displays usually consist of small tables, piles of boxes or crates decorated with paper, or promotional display pieces furnished by food manufacturers. The island displays are frequently used to display feature items in anticipation of greater sales because of the prominent position.

Traffic flow studies indicate that island displays often cause congestion because they obstruct the free flow of traffic and, consequently, reduce exposure and sales in the aisle, especially during peak traffic periods. The narrower the aisle, the greater the congestion created by the island displays.

Figure 7-11 illustrates the traffic patterns in a produce department with and without island displays in the main aisle. The effect of the island displays is to create two aisles, which tends to divert the customer traffic flow into only one of the aisles, thereby reducing the exposure and sales in the other aisle. Produce sales decreased in the store shown in Figure 7-11 when island displays were used even though the islands increased the counter display area by 13.4 percent. Congestion was undoubtedly a major factor, as sales on Tuesday, a light day, were 5.0 percent higher without islands, and on Friday, a heavy day, were 19.6 percent higher. As shown in Figure 7-11, the removal of the islands resulted in heavier shopping on both sides of the main aisle.

---

[12]*Shopping Behavior of Customers in Modified and Conventional Layouts of Retail Food Stores*, p. 26.

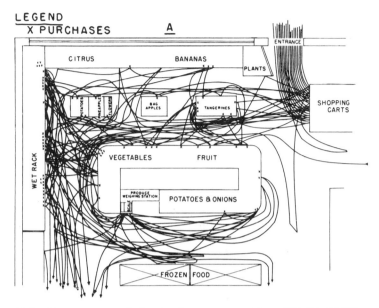

U.S. Department of Agriculture   Neg. AMS 50-61(7)

With islands.

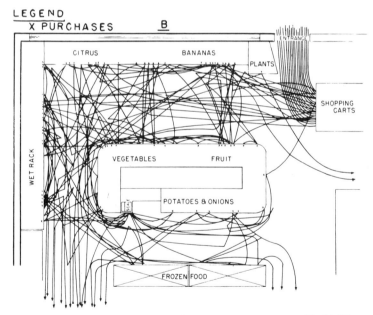

U.S. Department of Agriculture   Neg. AMS 51-61(7)

Without islands.

FIGURE 7-11   Customer traffic patterns in the produce department with and without island displays. Source: *Display Location and Customer Service in Retail Produce Departments,* p. 21.

Observations of shopping patterns in the meat department and other departments also indicate that island displays often lead to congestion and the tendency for customers to avoid the congestion and possible delays by simply moving away from the island display without inspecting or purchasing the merchandise displayed.

It is clear that island displays should be used with consideration of the aisle width and effect upon traffic flow, or overall reductions in exposure and sales may result.

TYPES OF STORE LAYOUTS

Conventional and Common Variations

Since the development and growth of the supermarket in the 1930s, the basic shape and layout of the selling area utilized by most operators have undergone little, if any changes. The conventional supermarket selling area layout has remained essentially a square or rectangular area with the selling fixtures arranged parallel or perpendicular to the walls and each other (see Figures 7-3 and 7-4). This arrangement is referred to as a gridiron pattern.

The gridiron pattern is desirable from a cost standpoint because it utilizes floor space efficiently by providing the greatest amount of display space relative to aisle space. In a free-flow pattern, where the fixtures are arranged in a random or nonstandardized pattern, the amount of display space relative to aisle space is less. The free-flow pattern is most frequently seen in department stores or specialty stores devoted to nonfood merchandise.

In addition to the advantage of more efficient space utilization, the gridiron pattern is more effective in controlling customer traffic, and, consequently, in achieving greater exposure and sales. The gridiron pattern is more appropriate for the display of convenience goods—relatively low-value items that are purchased frequently and with little time spent in inspecting and comparing. It is for these three reasons—more efficient space utilization, control of customer traffic, and the convenience nature of the merchandise—that the gridiron pattern has been predominant in supermarket layout.

The gridiron pattern, in spite of its advantages, is a highly standardized and monotonous layout, and it is difficult for a retailer to create or contribute to a distinctive store personality or image with it.

In an attempt to achieve individuality, some innovative food retailers have departed from the basic square or rectangular shape of the selling area, and others have modified the gridiron pattern within a rectangular area.

Figure 7-12 illustrates food store layouts that depart from the conventional both in terms of shape and arrangement. Figure 7-13 illustrates layouts that are based upon modification of the gridiron pattern within square and rectangular areas.

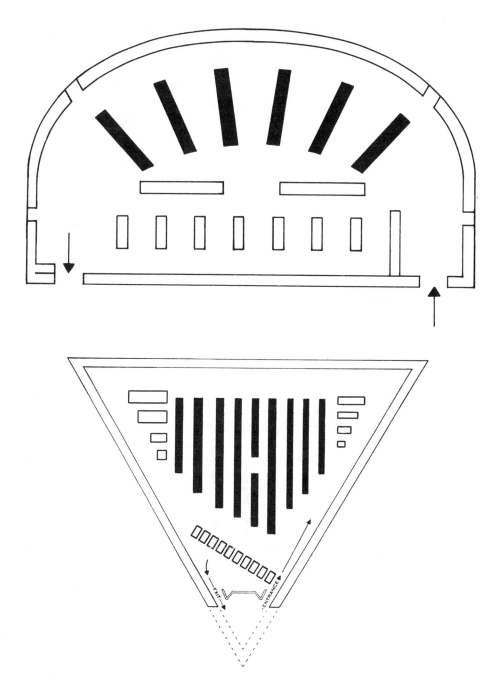

FIGURE 7-12 Examples of food store layouts that depart from conventional shape and arrangement. Bottom layout courtesy of Star Market Co. (Div. of Jewel Co. Inc.), Cambridge, Mass.

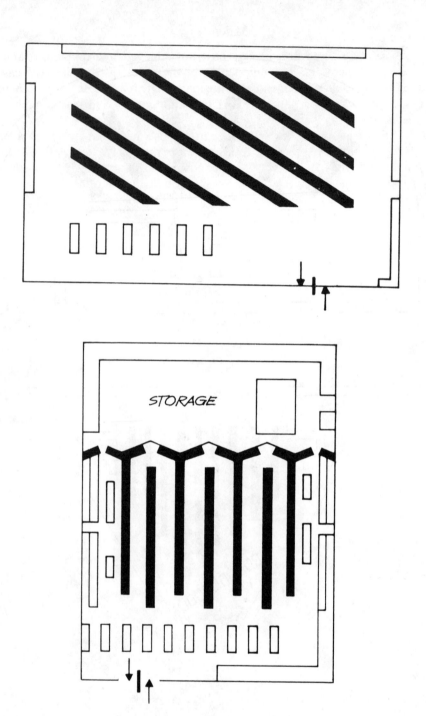

FIGURE 7-13 Examples of food store layouts that are modifications of gridiron pattern. Bottom layout courtesy of Big Discount Wonder Markets, Worcester, Mass.

The odd-shaped store designs have not achieved much popularity among food store operators. The uniqueness of these designs has, in most cases, apparently resulted in benefits that are inadequate to offset the disadvantages associated with them, such as loss of traffic control and less-efficient use of space.

Modifications of the gridiron pattern also have not achieved a high degree of popularity among food store operators. Customer traffic flow studies have indicated that rates of exposure in the grocery aisles are lower for the diagonal arrangement than for the conventional gridiron arrangement of grocery departments. In addition, the use of space is less efficient in the diagonal layout than in the conventional gridiron design. There have been several other variations of the gridiron design, including the second design shown in Figure 7-13. This design has been used in four of the Big Discount Wonder Markets in Worcester, Massachusetts. According to the president, David Gould, the layout has resulted in a more complete customer shopping pattern, but it requires more space than the conventional layout. He does not recommend the layout for stores with an annual sales volume of less than four million dollars.

The Loewy Concept

In 1960, a report entitled *Super Markets of the Sixties* was completed by the Raymond Loewy Corporation for the Super Market Institute. This report has had and still has an important influence on food store layout.[13]

The Loewy Report was based upon a study and projection of consumer attitudes and needs and contained recommendations as to how food stores could do a better job of meeting consumer needs and expectations through merchandising, especially through new concepts in store layout and design.

The study concluded that consumers associate fresh foods with the supermarket and that store design should project a strong food image and appetite appeal combined under the same roof with convenience and merchandising excitement added by general merchandise (nonfoods). Thus, Loewy recommended that departmentalizing needed to be more effective in projecting a strong food image, which is the primary appeal of the super-market, and in capitalizing on the potential of nonfood sales in supermarkets.

The importance of more effective departmentalizing was stated as follows:

> Developing self contained, logical and well-defined departments within the supermarket is vital to creating maximum impact for merchandise, maximum convenience for customers and establishing a sound basis for future expansion of individual departments.[14]

---

[13]The Raymond Loewy Corporation, *Super Markets of the Sixties* (Chicago: Super Market Institute, 1960), Volumes 1 and 2.

[14]*Super Markets of the Sixties,* Volume 1, p. 25.

The Loewy Report placed major emphasis upon layout of the perishables departments, especially meat and produce. It concluded that meat was the key perishables department because of the importance of meat as the central item in menu planning and that food-store layout should create a butcher-shop atmosphere in order to project a powerful image. The report states that "the objective of good meat department layout is to surround the customer with meat, so that what she sees all around her is a functional display of meat appealing to her basic requirements as a housewife and at the same time offering considerable appetite and end-use appeal."[15]

Produce was also singled out for greater emphasis because of its profit potential and the need to stem the decline in fresh produce consumption. "Garden Fresh" was indicated as the image that should be projected by produce-department layout and merchandising practices.

Delicatessen, dairy, and bakery goods were the other perishables departments considered to be critical in strengthening the food image in supermarkets.

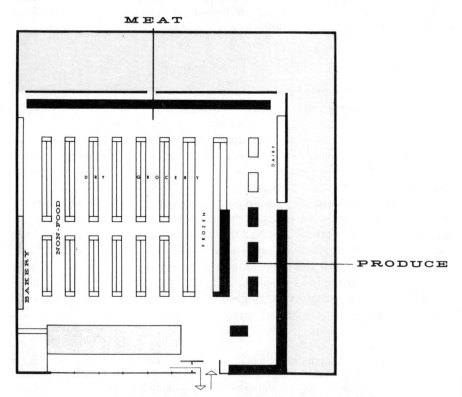

FIGURE 7-14   Typical supermarket layout (13,400 square feet of selling area). Source: The Raymond Loewy Corporation, *Super Markets of the Sixties* (Chicago: Super Market Institute, Inc., 1960), Vol. 2, Present Floor Plan.

---

[15]*Super Markets of the Sixties,* Volume 1, p. 50.

The Loewy Report contained several plans for modifying, in evolutionary fashion, typical store layouts in order to achieve greater merchandising effectiveness. The proposed modifications ranged from minor changes in conventional layouts to drastic departures from the typical arrangement. The plans varied with respect to square feet of floor space and location and arrangement of departments.

The typical supermarket layout of 1960 (see Figure 7-14) is not basically different from most of the supermarkets of today, although modifications recommended in the Loewy Report have had an influence on the layout of many new and remodeled markets. The typical layout was criticized in the Loewy study because it represented a distribution center more than a retail store, had monotonous fixtures, nonfoods were scattered, and perishables received no emphasis.

As the first step in the Loewy plans for modifying the typical store layout, cross aisles in the grocery department and produce tables are eliminated and the checkout area is reduced slightly in order to make a home for general merchandise, which is given a wall background and a departmental setting (see Figure 7-15). This plan includes nearly twice as many linear feet of display area for nonfoods with little change in the linear feet devoted to food.

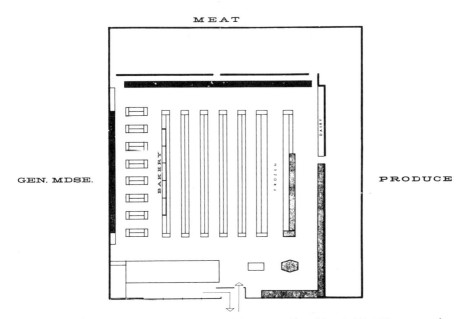

FIGURE 7-15 Loewy store layout modification, Plan No. 1 (13,400 square feet of selling area). Source: The Raymond Loewy Corporation, *Super Markets of the Sixties* (Chicago: Super Market Institute, Inc., 1960), Vol. 2.

An intermediate step in the evolutionary Loewy modification of the typical supermarket layout includes 3,500 more square feet of selling area than the typical plan, and much of the increase is devoted to general merchandise (see Figure 7-16). A delicatessen or delicacy department has been added, and it along with bakery goods has been incorporated into an island concept to strengthen the food image. The meat department incorporates a U-shaped projection of display cases from the rear wall in order to break up the monotonous, straight line of the typical meat department. The produce department has also been rearranged in order to create a more forceful impact. Dry groceries have been de-emphasized by locating grocery fixtures in less-prominent positions in the layout. General merchandise is displayed in a separate area and utilizes several promotional islands and many cross aisles.

In the plan that the Loewy designers regard as the nearest to achieving all their principles, the size of the selling area is nearly the same as in the intermediate plan, but several changes have been made in the layout (see Figure 7-17).

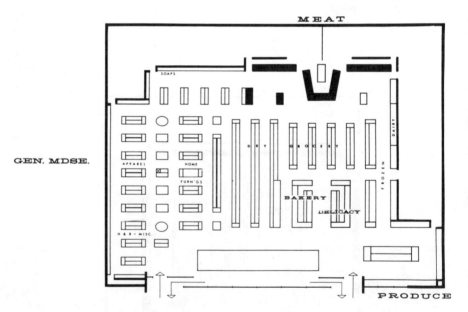

FIGURE 7-16   Loewy store layout modification, Plan No. 4 (16,900 square feet of selling area). Source: The Raymond Loewy Corporation, *Super Markets of the Sixties* (Chicago: Super Market Institute, Inc., 1960), Vol. 2.

The perishables departments are tied together in a prominent position in the front of the store, and dry groceries are entirely in the rear. The delicatessen and bakery islands, which employ low gondolas, result in an open center so that there is visibility into all departments. The meat depart-

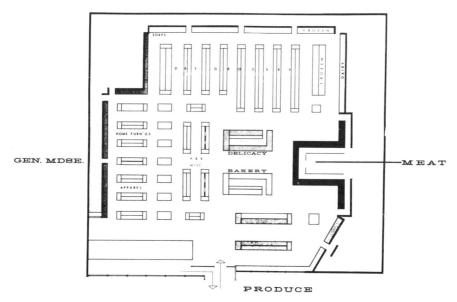

FIGURE 7-17 Loewy store layout modification, Plan No. 9 (16,800 square feet of selling area). Source: The Raymond Loewy Corporation, *Super Markets of the Sixties* (Chicato: Super Market Institute, Inc., 1960), Vol. 2.

ment incorporates the U-shaped arrangement extending from the side wall, and produce, which is located adjacent to meat, is designed with two aisles in a modified corner arrangement.

The layout is intended to project a strong food image through imaginative and dramatic arrangement of the perishables departments while also creating a strong general merchandise impact. The dominance of the dry grocery department has been eliminated.

Although the aisles are parallel or run at right angles to each other in this layout, the monotony of the gridiron arrangement in the typical store has been offset by the unique features of the meat department, the delicatessen and bakery islands, and the use of many islands and cross aisles in the general merchandise department.

Although the Loewy layout concepts are very appealing from an aesthetic point of view, the important question concerns their effectiveness from a merchandising standpoint. Does the layout that employs the Loewy concepts result in greater exposure and sales in foods and general merchandise than more conventionally arranged stores?

Customer traffic flow studies indicate that the extreme Loewy modifications (Figure 7-17) result in lower rates of exposure and sale than those in conventional stores. One study of modified store layouts was conducted by the USDA in cooperation with university extension specialists in three states. In each of the states, a pair of stores operated by a chain were studied in order to compare customer shopping behavior in conventional and modified layouts. One store in each pair was conventional with respect to layout, and the other store had a modified layout based upon the Loewy concepts. The stores in each pair were as nearly alike as possible with respect to factors other than layout that might affect shopping behavior; for example, size and location of store and socioeconomic characteristics of customers.

Customer traffic flow studies in each of the six stores showed that rates of exposure and sale in the departments as well as complete coverage of the store were usually less in the modified than in the conventional layouts.

The percentage of customers entering the food departments in the conventionally arranged stores compared with the modified layout stores did not differ greatly except for frozen foods (see Table 7-6). The proportion of customers entering the nonfoods section was much higher in the conventional than in the modified-layout stores, however. The percentage of customers purchasing was greater in the conventional stores than in the modified stores in the nonfood section and in each food department except produce.

TABLE 7-6   Percentage of Customers Entering and Making Purchases in Specified Departments in Six Food Stores by Type of Layout

Department	Modified Layout		Conventional Layout	
	Entering	*Purchasing*	*Entering*	*Purchasing*
Grocery	98%	92%	99%	95%
Meat	92	66	91	70
Produce	85	78´	88	76
Dairy	83	63	85	73
Frozen foods	87	37	76	52
Nonfoods	79	30	95	41

Source: *Shopping Behavior of Customers in Modified and Conventional Layouts of Retail Food Stores*, p. 24.

A greater proportion of the customers entered the frozen-food department in modified stores than in conventional stores, yet the percentage of customers purchasing frozen foods in modified stores was well below that in the conventional layout. Two factors appeared to be responsible for the disproportionate number of customers entering the department and purchasing frozen foods in the two types of stores. The frozen-food cases in modified layout stores were short, which is not conducive to impulse purchasing because they can be spot shopped easily from the cross-aisles without traveling the entire length. In addition, customers entering these aisles were counted as entering the frozen-food department, whereas some of them may have entered merely because the aisles were a convenient path to something else.[16]

---

[16]*Shopping Behavior of Customers in Modified and Conventional Layouts of Retail Food Stores*, p. 24.

Relationships were established between actual distances traveled by customers and total distances that customers could have traveled through selling areas of departments in both types of store layouts.

Coverage of the conventional stores was greater in each department (see Table 7-7). Customers of conventional stores covered 52 percent of the distance through the total selling area; in modified-layout stores, shoppers covered only 32 percent. The difference in coverage was greater in the nonfoods department than in the food departments.

TABLE 7-7   Proportion of Selling Area Covered by Customers in Six Food Stores, by Type of Layout

| Department | Proportion of Selling Area Covered | |
	Modified Layout	Conventional Layout
Grocery	48%	56%
Meat	62	69
Produce	46	52
Dairy	70	73
Frozen foods	47	62
All food departments	48	58
Nonfoods	12	30 [a]
Total store	32	52

[a] *One conventional layout store did not have a separate nonfoods department.*

Source: *Shopping Behavior of Customers in Modified and Conventional Layouts of Retail Food Stores,* p. 23.

The modification of conventional store layouts according to all the Loewy principles appears to result in reductions in exposure and purchase rates and less-complete shopping of the total selling area. There are two major factors that probably reduce the merchandising effectiveness of the modified layouts.

First of all, the use of short gondolas, island displays, and many cross aisles results in much less control of customer traffic flow than the conventional store layout with its long, continuous gondolas and few cross aisles. The modified layout encourages a freer, less orderly flow of traffic and, consequently, customers tend to shop less of the total selling area than in more conventional stores.

Second, the complete separation of nonfoods from the grocery and other food departments results in a much lower rate of exposure and sale in the nonfoods department. Nonfoods apparently require the exposure created by the food departments. This may be due to an inadequate selection or quality of general merchandise in food stores compared to other types of retail establishments, or to the customer's preference to buy most general merchandise on separate shopping trips, or to a combination of the two. In any case, the sales of nonfoods are greater when the display of nonfoods is integrated with grocery and other food departments than when nonfoods are segregated into a department or section apart from the food departments.

From a merchandising standpoint, it does not appear that some of the

Loewy recommendations for modification of conventional store layouts are generally effective. The segregation of nonfoods and the free-flow traffic pattern created by island displays and many cross aisles reduces the merchandising effectiveness. These recommendations have not been adopted to an appreciable extent by the retail food industry in planning store layout.

However, considerable application has been made of the Loewy concepts of emphasizing and individualizing the perishables departments in order to strengthen the food image. For example, the meat-department layout featuring the projection of the display cases from the back or side wall can be found in many stores. Also, many firms have incorporated unique features into the design of perishables departments, such as canopies and unusual decor along with names such as the "Deli-Hut," in order to provide a distinctive atmosphere or image. These unique features have been undoubtedly prompted by the Loewy study.

In addition to the layout changes recommended in the Loewy study, there were several recommendations concerning equipment and merchandising methods to bolster the impact of perishables departments. These recommendations included the design and use of display fixtures, packaging, consumer education, display methods, and advertising and promotion, and they have had an important influence on food store design and merchandising.

LOCATION AND ARRANGEMENT OF DEPARTMENTS

One of the most difficult and important decisions that must be made by the food retailer is the location of departments in the overall store layout. As indicated previously, the location of departments affects the rate of exposure and sales in the departments as well as in the entire store.

Department location considerations have been described as follows:

> Departments within a supermarket are located for strategic, logistical and tactical reasons. The overall strategy in planning department location is to deploy departments throughout the store in a manner which exposes shoppers to the maximum number of items. For logistical reasons perishable departments have traditionally been located on the perimeter of the store, but there are indications that thinking in this area may be changing. For tactical reasons low demand product categories are placed close to high demand categories in the grocery department.[17]

The first location in the perimeter as the customer shops the store is the highest exposure area in the entire store in conventional layouts. As a general rule, the department or product group located in the first aisle will achieve a higher rate of exposure and sale than in any other location

---

[17]Randall E. Webber, *Interior Store Layout—An Objective Analysis,* Food Marketing Paper No. 6, Food Marketing Program, Michigan State University, March 1968, p. 8.

in the store. However, the first-aisle location can only accommodate a limited number of departments or product groups, so the retailer must decide what he wishes to feature in this preferred location. Likewise, he must decide upon the location or placement of each department based upon the traffic flow pattern, the characteristics and requirements of each department, and the overall objective of maximum exposure and sales consistent with customer convenience.

Inasmuch as both customer preferences and the merchandising effectiveness of retailers vary, there is no single strategy of department location that can be considered as ideal in all situations. However, there are certain characteristics and merchandising requirements associated with individual departments as well as knowledge of customer shopping habits that can serve as guides to each retailer in making layout planning decisions with respect to departmental location.

Perishables Departments

One important consideration in locating departments should be the preferences of consumers. Presumably, the store that is arranged according to consumer preferences will achieve greater sales than the store that is not arranged according to consumer preference.

Because the dry grocery department lends itself to a mid-store location due to the amount of display space required and a generally less-frequent restocking cycle, the primary departmental location decisions that must be made concern the location of the perishables departments in the perimeter of the store. Depending upon the size of the store and departmental space requirements, one or more of the perishables departments may have to be located in mid-store aisles within the dry grocery department.

A study made in Cleveland, Ohio, surveyed consumer preferences for the location of perishables departments (see Table 7-8).

TABLE 7-8   Consumer Preferences for the Location of Perishables Departments in Retail Food Stores, Cleveland, Ohio

| Department | Percent of Consumers Preferring Each Location | | | | Total |
	First Aisle	Mid Store	Rear Store	Last Aisle	
Meat	36	—	59	5	100
Produce	35	3	11	51	100
Dairy	46	4	10	40	100
Frozen food	23	11	5	61	100
Bakery	44	8	3	45	100

Source: *Consumer Dynamics in the Super Market,* (New York: Progressive Grocer, 1966), p. 84.

The study shows that a rear-store location was preferred by a majority of consumers for the meat department, although more than one third of the customers interviewed preferred a first-aisle location.

Slightly more than half the consumers interviewed in the Cleveland study preferred a last-aisle location for the produce department, but more than one-third showed a preference for a first-aisle location.

The dairy department was preferred in a first-aisle location by 46 percent of the customers; 40 percent indicated a preference for a last-aisle location.

A strong preference was indicated for a last-aisle location for frozen foods (61 percent), but only 23 percent preferred a first-aisle location, and 11 percent indicated a preference for a mid-store location.

Consumers were about evenly divided with respect to their preferences for the location of the bakery department; 44 percent preferred a first-aisle location, and 45 percent indicated a last-aisle preference.

In view of consumer preferences as shown by one study and the retailer's objective of maximum sales and profit, where should each of the perishables departments be located? In order to answer this question, the overall merchandising requirements and objectives in relation to expressed consumer preferences and actual shopping behavior with respect to each perishables department should be considered.

Meat Department

The meat department is perhaps the most important department in the retail food store. It normally accounts for about 25 percent of total store sales and is the most important single product group in terms of consumer expenditures for food. In addition, meat quality and selection is usually mentioned as one of the most important reasons for the selection of a favorite food store by consumers. Meat departments are most commonly located in the rear of self-service food stores because this location will pull shoppers through the rest of the store. Also, meat storage and processing areas are often located in the rear of the store, so a rear-store display area facilitates stocking.

Some retail operators prefer a first-aisle location for the meat department because of the impact that a well-run meat department can have upon consumers.

Another reason for placing the meat department in the first aisle is the feeling of some operators that because meat is the main item in meal planning, consumers wish to purchase meat first and then base the remainder of their purchases around the meat items selected. Although meat is the central item in most meals, it is doubtful that consumers have a strong desire to purchase meat first as indicated by the fact that relatively few customers will purchase meat first in stores where the meat department is located in the rear of the store. Several traffic flow studies showed that only about 1 out of 20 shoppers proceeded to the meat department first when a rear-store location was selected for meat.

Meat departments are infrequently located in the last aisle as most retailers apparently feel that meats should be located either in a first-aisle or rear-store location so that the consumer is afforded the opportunity of making her meat purchase relatively early in her shopping trip. The Consumer

Dynamics study of Cleveland food shoppers tends to confirm the undersirability of a last-aisle meat location; only 5 percent of the customers indicated a preference for a last-aisle meat department.

The delicatessen section, whether service or self-service, is usually located adjacent to the meat display cases and is generally considered part of the meat department. The same general considerations that apply to the location of the meat department also apply to the location of the delicatessen section.

Produce Department

The produce department, like meat, is a key department in attracting customers to the store. Although produce accounts for only about 8 percent of store sales, it ranks high in the reasons mentioned by consumers for selecting a favorite food store. Both meat and produce departments contain many highly perishable items, and the manner in which they are handled, prepared, and merchandised directly affects the quality, appeal, and value to the customer.

The produce department is often considered the showcase of the supermarket because of the natural beauty of the products. Produce is colorful and naturally attractive and has more merchandising appeal than perhaps any other group of products sold in the food store.

Another important characteristic of the produce department is the relatively high gross margin on produce sales. Gross margins in the produce department are higher than those in any other department. Even though operating expenses are also relatively high, the produce department has a high potential contribution to overhead and profit.

Because of its visual merchandising appeal, its importance in attracting customers, and the high profit potential, produce is commonly located first in the shopping pattern. Produce sales as a percentage of total store sales are higher when produce is located first in the shopping pattern than when it is located last in the store (see Table 7-2). Thus, many retail operators believe that the first-aisle produce location not only promotes the overall store image but also increases store profit because of increased sales in this high-margin and profit-contributing department.

On the other hand, because of its highly perishable nature and the possibility of damage to soft items like bananas, peaches, and so on, many retailers prefer to position the produce department in the last aisle. A last-aisle location enables consumers to place their produce purchases on top of other purchases, especially canned goods, so that the possibility of damage to the tender produce items is lessened. Consumers in the Consumer Dynamics study in Cleveland showed a preference for the produce-last location, which indicates that consumers are concerned about possible damage to the product.

The best location for the produce department is complicated by the apparent contradiction in consumer preference and acceptance. Although consumers indicate a preference for a produce-last location, produce sales are higher in relation to total store sales when produce is located in the first aisle. The decision as to where to locate the produce department should be made after carefully weighing the advantages and disadvantages of each alternative with respect to customer preference, the merchandising impact of the particular produce operation, and, ultimately, the estimated overall sales and profit results.

Dairy Department

The dairy department was preferred in the first aisle by 46 percent of the Cleveland consumers, and 40 percent preferred a last-aisle location. The lack of a clear-cut preference would tend to indicate that the dairy department can be located either first or last without any serious objections on the part of consumers. There does not seem to be a predominant preference on the part of retailers for the location of dairy departments, which tends to confirm the indifference of consumers with respect to a first- or last-aisle location.

Dairy departments are usually located on the perimeter of the store for easy restocking, especially if rear-feed dairy cases are utilized. Dairy departments are often located in a rear corner of the store so that part of the department is in the rear of the store and part in either the first or last aisle. One of the reasons for the rear-corner location is that milk has very high drawing power, and customers will be exposed to many other products on their way to the dairy department to buy milk. This is particularly important in the case of the shopper who may come to the store for only a few items—one of those items is likely to be milk.

Frozen-food Department

The frozen-food department represents one of the fastest growing product groups in the retail food store and one of the most profitable. The University of Massachusetts-Elm Farm study was one of the first attempts to identify the net profit contribution of retail frozen-food departments. This study indicated that frozen foods yield a relatively high net profit per dollar of sales, depending upon the turnover rate.[18] The McKinsey-Birds Eye study confirmed the relatively high net-profit contribution of the frozen food department.[19]

The frozen-food department is characterized by a rapidly expanding selection of convenience-type foods, which have gained steadily in popularity among consumers. The importance of frozen foods to total store sales increased rapidly in the years following World War II but slowed down after reaching about 5 percent of total sales. Nevertheless, the constant

---

[18]*Expense and Profit Analysis of Eight Retail Frozen Food Departments,* Food Distribution Program, University of Massachusetts, Amherst, Massachusetts, November 15, 1962.

[19]*McKinsey-Birds Eye Study,* the Economics of Frozen Foods, General Foods Corporation, March 1964.

addition and acceptance of new, convenience-type items and the high profitability of frozen foods make this department increasingly important.

Frozen foods are very perishable and will deteriorate rapidly if held at temperatures above 0° F. for even brief periods of time. For this reason alone, a last-aisle location is advisable for the frozen food department.

The Consumer Dynamics study showed a strong consumer preference for a last-aisle location for the frozen-food department: 61 percent of the consumers interviewed preferred the last aisle. This strong consumer preference suggests that customers are aware of the perishability of frozen foods and, therefore, wish to purchase them last in order to minimize the exposure to high temperatures. Customer traffic flow studies show that many consumers, as many as one-third in one study, will wait until the end of their shopping trip to purchase frozen foods when a first-aisle location is selected for frozen foods. This is a further indication of the concern of consumers for the constant low-temperature protection of frozen food.

A mid-store location is frequently used for the frozen-food department. In view of consumers' concern for quality protection, it seems advisable to locate the frozen-food department near the end of the shopping pattern, preferably in the last mid-store aisle, if the last perimeter aisle is not to be used for this department.

Another consideration in locating the frozen-food department is the impulse nature of most frozen-food purchases and their high-profit potential. A mid-store location is usually not as conducive to stimulating sales in frozen foods as is the last perimeter aisle.

Although ice cream and frozen specialties are usually considered as dairy products, the same considerations apply in determining the best location for these products as apply in the case of frozen foods. Like frozen foods, ice cream and frozen specialties require low-temperature protection and should be located near the end of the shopping pattern so that exposure to high temperatures is minimized. Also, like frozen foods, ice cream and frozen specialties respond well to a high-traffic location in a perimeter aisle.

Bakery Goods

The location of bakery goods is also subject to differences of opinion among retailers. Some believe that an outstanding bakery department can add glamour and excitement to the store and locate it in the first aisle for immediate customer impact. Others feel that bakery goods should be last in order to prevent bread, cake, and other soft baked goods from being crushed by other merchandise. Still others place bakery goods in a mid-store location.

In the Consumer Dynamics study, consumers were about evenly divided with respect to their preferences for the location of baked goods—45 percent preferred a last-aisle location and 44 percent indicated a first-aisle preference.

The type of bakery goods section is an important consideration in determining the best location. If there is an on-premise bakery, or if clerk service is provided, a perimeter-aisle location is usually required. If the bakery merchandise is prepared prior to delivery to the store and is sold entirely on a self-service basis, then there is greater flexibility in the location. Another consideration is the fact that bread is one of the top drawing items in the entire store. This means that the bakery department, like the dairy department, will attract a high proportion of shoppers no matter where it is located.

There is no single, ideal plan for the location of departments in the retail food store. These decisions must be made on the basis of operational and merchandising requirements and characteristics of each department, the merchandising strategy with respect to the major appeal or image that the operator wishes to project and, last but not least, the preferences and shopping habits of the consumers that are to be served. In assessing these factors, the overall objective of maximum exposure and sales consistent with customer convenience should be the foremost consideration.

Width of Aisles

One important aspect of store layout is the width of aisles. Aisles should be wide enough to prevent congestion and permit a smooth flow of customer traffic during peak shopping periods. On the other hand, aisles that are wider than necessary represent a wasteful and costly use of floor space.

The appropriate width of aisles in a conventional layout depends upon the traffic anticipated and the area of the store. Aisles throughout the middle of the store, which is primarily the dry grocery area, should usually be from six to seven feet wide in order to provide shopping ease on both sides of the aisle. Aisles less than six feet wide tend to cause confusion, and aisles wider than seven feet result in the customer shopping only one side of the aisle.[20]

Some retailers use aisle widths of from five and one-half to six and one-half feet in the grocery department and attempt to encourage one-way traffic through the use of directional arrows and signs. Customer flow studies have shown that attempts to encourage one-way traffic have not been highly successful. In some stores, the flow of traffic in the wrong direction and in both directions exceeded the flow of traffic in the direction indicated by the one-way signs in some of the aisles.

The perimeter aisles are usually nine to ten feet wide and sometimes as much as twelve feet wide in front of the meat display cases. The extra width in the perimeter aisles is necessary to permit customers to shop the perishables unobstructed by the relatively high rate of traffic.

The aisle in front of the checkout stands must necessarily be wider than in other areas of the store in order to allow for a smooth flow of traffic from one aisle to the next without interfering with customers waiting to be checked out. This aisle ranges in width from 10 to 16 feet.[21]

---

[20]*Interior Store Layout–An Objective Analysis*, p. 23.
[21]*Interior Store Layout-An Objective Analysis*, p. 23.

Location of Products

Within departments, the goal of locating commodity groups and individual items is to expose as many customers as possible to as many products as possible. This goal must be consistent with customer convenience or a loss of customers and a reduction in sales and profit may be encountered.

Traffic flow studies have shown that the rate of exposure and sales is influenced by the location of products as well as by the layout and arrangement of physical facilities. As shown previously, drawing power varies widely among product categories so that some categories are more effective than others in creating customer traffic (see Table 7-5). It is important to identify the power categories in each department in order to plan for effective product location.

Power categories are those that are purchased frequently by a high proportion of consumers. Customer traffic flow studies are one method that can be used to obtain this information. In lieu of traffic studies, sales or velocity reports can be used to indicate the power categories and items in each department. It should be recognized, however, that dollar or unit sales figures may not give a true indication of the power of a category or item. Sales figures are influenced by both the number of customers purchasing and the amount purchased, whereas the power of a category or item is really determined by the proportion of customers who purchase it during each shopping trip.

Power categories and items should be distributed throughout each department in order to create as much traffic as possible in all areas of the store. This strategy is consistent with customer convenience as congestion during peak periods can be reduced by separating power categories and items.

Figure 7-18 illustrates the distribution of power categories in a single-deck frozen-food display case. In this illustration, the three categories with the greatest drawing power have been dispersed along the entire length of the display cases in order to encourage complete shopping of the department. High-margin impulse categories are displayed between the power categories for greater exposure and sale.

Figure 7-19 illustrates the location of the three major power categories along with the three secondary power categories in a frozen-food department composed of display cases on both sides of an aisle. In this situation, it is necessary to locate the power categories on both sides of the aisle in order to encourage complete shopping of the department. The location of power categories on both sides of aisles is important to creating a "bounce pattern" of shopping whereby consumers alternately shop both sides of the aisle, or "bounce" from one side to the other.

In addition to the strategic location of product categories according to drawing power, consideration must be given to the power of individual items. Although it is advisable to display product categories together for consumer convenience in making buying decisions, it is still possible to

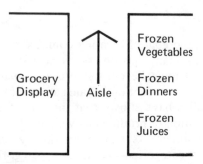

FIGURE 7-18   Location of primary power categories in a frozen-food department located on one side of an aisle.

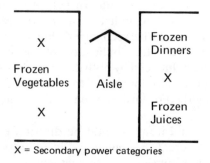

X = Secondary power categories

FIGURE 7-19   Location of primary and secondary power categories in a
frozen-food department located on both sides of an aisle.

separate the major power items within categories in order to encourage
more complete shopping.

Figure 7-20 shows the effect of strategic placement of power items
upon the customer shopping pattern in a retail produce department. The
original arrangement of items resulted in a concentration of purchases in
certain portions of the display area because the power items were not strategi-
cally located. Considerable congestion also resulted from this arrangement.

Rearrangement of the power items including lettuce, tomatoes, apples,
oranges, and bananas resulted in a more even dispersion of sales throughout
the department. The distribution of power items on both sides of the aisle
resulted in a bounce pattern of shopping that increased the exposure and
sales of the impulse items located next to power items.

The location of product categories and items has an important effect
upon the traffic flow and rates of exposure and sales in retail food stores.
Careful consideration should be given to the relative drawing power of each
category and item in order that merchandise location will contribute to more
complete shopping of the entire store, and, consequently, increased sales
and profit consistent with customer convenience.

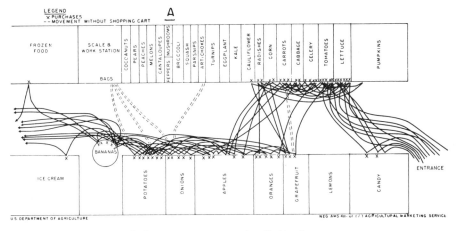

Before rearrangement of displays.

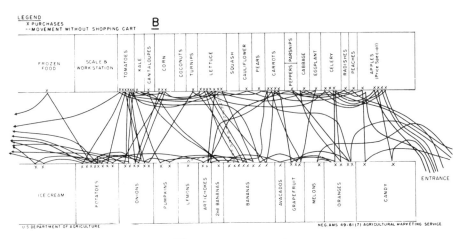

After rearrangement.

FIGURE 7-20 Customer traffic patterns and purchases in a retail produce department before and after rearrangement of product location. Source: *Display Location and Customer Service in Retail Produce Departments*, p. 18.

8

Profit Planning and Control

SETTING FINANCIAL OBJECTIVES

Achieving the profit objective of the retail food firm requires careful planning and follow-through on a day-to-day basis. The stakes are much too high to leave the earning of profit entirely to chance. Careful planning, along with the effective execution of the plan, including identification of problems and remedial action when necessary, will be much more likely to result in the achievement of the profit objective than merely hoping for the best.

Planning and control should include sales, gross margin, and expenses for each major department and the entire store. Planning involves the estimation of the volume of sales, amount of gross margin, and level of expenses that will result in the net-profit objective. This process of planning is also referred to as budgeting and includes *financial* objectives. These objectives define the end results that are desired in terms of net profit and the basic elements of net profit—sales, gross margin, and expenses.

There is also another type of objective that is important to the achievement of financial objectives and should be included in the planning and control process. This type of objective defines the value to the customer that the firm attempts to provide through the merchandising program. These objectives are the key variables that have an important influence upon customer value and satisfaction and, consequently, sales, gross margin, and net profit. The key variables that need definition include customer services, quality, selection, display methods, housekeeping, customer relations, and any other component of customer value that can be influenced in the day-to-day operation of the store and that can affect financial objectives. This other type of objective will be referred to as a *merchandising* objective.

There are several requirements for preparing good objectives. First of all, good objectives should be *measurable or observable*. The more specific or measurable the objective, the less the confusion or misunderstanding about results expected. Financial objectives can be stated in very specific terms, such as dollars or percentage of sales. Merchandising objectives, however, often deal with results that cannot be expressed in measurable terms because they concern such subjective factors as quality, cleanliness, and customer service. In these instances, objectives should be stated in observable rather than measurable terms so that it can be observed whether the desired results are being achieved.

A second requirement of a good objective is that it should be *attainable,* that is, there should be a reasonably good chance of reaching the objective with the resources available. Setting an objective that is unrealistic because of limitations imposed by the available labor, equipment, competitive conditions, or other internal or external conditions can lead to frustration and poor morale among managers and employees. For example, setting a gross-margin objective that is practically unattainable because of pricing and product mix may lead to many undesirable effects. Likewise, a checkout level of service objective that cannot possibly be provided because of limitations in the amount of labor that can be afforded will not serve a useful purpose and may quite likely do more harm than good. Thus, it is important that both financial and merchandising objectives be realistic. This does not mean that they should not be challenging and require a great deal of effort and imagination in order to reach them, but only that they should be reasonably possible to achieve under existing conditions.

Good objectives should also be *results oriented.* This means that the objectives should only specify the results expected and not the procedures to be employed. Although procedures are important, the purpose of good financial and merchandising objectives is to define the results or *what* is expected and not the method or procedures that indicate *how* the results are to be attained.

If *timing* is an important consideration, it should be indicated in stating that objective. For example, in setting sales and gross-margin objectives, it should be specified as to when the objectives are to be reached, that is, whether they are weekly, quarterly, or for some other period of time. The same reasoning applies to merchandising objectives. For example, if it is important that product availability or the construction of a particular display be accomplished by a certain time of the day or week, then the time should be specified in stating the objective.

It is important that all objectives be *stated in writing* and that the written objectives be provided to all who share in the responsibility for achieving them. By writing objectives there is much less chance for confusion, misunderstanding, and differences in interpretation than if they are passed along by word of mouth. It is extremely important that everyone in the retail food firm has a clear understanding of what is expected, and written objectives contribute to a common understanding by all concerned.

Finally, objectives should be stated *positively.* Rather than negative statements that indicate incorrect or undesirable results, objectives should be written so that they describe desirable results. Positive objectives help lead to positive thinking and concentration on what is right.

Control involves the comparison of planned financial and merchandising objectives with actual results, the identification of descrepancies, and the action taken to correct them. Control also includes any measures to improve the chances of achieving the desired objectives.

Long-term and Short-term Planning

There is a need for both long- and short-term planning of financial objectives. Long-term planning includes plans that extend beyond one year; short-term planning includes plans that include one year or less.

Long-term plans point the way to earning an adequate return on investment, which involves a long-term commitment. So, in order to realize a projected return on a long-term investment, profits must be adequate over the entire term of the investment (see Chapter 1). Long-term plans for sales, gross margin, expenses, and net profit should be prepared for from three to five years in the future, and even these are tentative because of the changes that may affect and alter future plans. The longer the time period, the greater the uncertainties and, consequently, the greater the inaccuracies. Therefore, long-term plans should be established only as tentative objectives that may have to be modified as conditions change.

Short-term planning is the most useful in the management of retail food stores because it deals with the more immediate concern of meeting current net profit objectives. One year is the basic short-term planning period and, even during a year, many changes can take place that may affect the achievement of sales, gross margin, expense, and net-profit objectives. Planning periods must be much shorter than one year in order to identify and correct problems before they can have a serious effect upon net profit and to execute a dynamic merchandising program that will help to achieve the planned objectives.

In addition to the annual plan or budget, planning should be done on a quarterly as well as on a weekly basis.

Table 8-1 shows a suggested timetable for the development of plans, both on a total store and departmental basis. A complete annual plan should be developed for the store including sales, gross margin, all expenses (controllable and overhead) and net profit. This annual budget serves as the basic planning tool and indicates the objectives that the firm hopes to achieve by the end of the year. The shorter-term plans are based upon the annual budget, and actual results are evaluated on the basis of the progress toward the achievement of the objectives in the annual budget. The annual plan should also include sales, gross margin, and controllable expense objectives for at least each major department. The grocery, meat, and produce departments are those generally regarded as the major departments. Objectives may also be established for other departmental breakdowns such as frozen foods, bakery, dairy products, or the delicatessen depending upon whether or not sales, gross margin, and controllable expense data are available, and how important the additional breakdowns are regarded by the management of the firm in the planning and controlling process.

TABLE 8-1   Suggested Timing for Sales, Gross Margin, Expense, and Profit
Planning, by Department

Time Period	Total Store	Major Departments
	Item	
Annually	Sales, gross margin, controllable and overhead expenses, net profit	Sales, gross margin, controllable expenses
Quarterly or four-week periods	Sales, gross margin, controllable expenses (overhead expenses)[a]	Sales, gross margin, controllable expenses
Weekly	Sales, controllable expenses	Sales, gross margin,[b] controllable expenses

[a] *Optional*

[b] *Only for meat, produce, and other departments when weekly physical inventories are taken.*

Only controllable expenses, those that are assignable and can be affected substantially within the department, are included in the departmental plans. Overhead expenses are either not assignable to individual departments or cannot be controlled to any appreciable extent by department managers.

The use of either a quarterly or four-week planning period depends upon the accounting system in use by the firm. Some prepare statements of results once every 13 weeks; others utilize 13 four-week reporting periods. The shorter periods may be an advantage inasmuch as they permit more frequent evaluation of progress toward the annual plan.

The quarterly or four-week plans for overall store results need not include overhead expenses unless there is a reason to believe that one or more of them may exceed the annual objective. Overhead expenses are mostly fixed and will vary little from the annual plan unless an error was made in the original planning. There are some overhead expenses, such as utilities, that are not completely fixed and it may be desired to include them in quarterly or four-week budgets in order to monitor them. For example, overhead expenses may change during the year due to increased power requirements, changes in power rates, or insurance premiums, so that interim plans are useful in identifying the cause of such changes. However, overhead expenses are not controllable during the year to any appreciable extent, and it is not really useful to include them in quarterly, four-week, or weekly plans for the store and individual departments.

Weekly plans are very short-term objectives that are extremely important in the dynamic retail food business. Merchandising strategy is carried out on a day-to-day, week-to-week basis in food retailing because of the rapidly changing competitive conditions. As a result, weekly plans are important in developing a merchandising strategy that will contribute to the achievement of longer term objectives. The weekly merchandising plan should include sales and controllable expense objectives for each major department and the entire store. Because accurate gross margins depend upon physical inventories, weekly gross-margin objectives are usually established only for the meat and produce departments. Gross-margin objectives for the grocery department, as well as for the entire store, are normally planned on a quarterly basis.

Although the short-term planning and control of expenses is important to the achievement of net-profit objectives, merchandising deals primarily with the planning and control of sales and gross margin on a weekly basis. The planning and control of sales and gross margin is the primary responsibility of the *director of merchandising* or whoever is assigned the merchandising function. The planning and control of expenses is most commonly the responsibility of the *director of operations* or whoever is assigned the cost-control function. The two functions must be coordinated in order that the overall net-profit objective can be achieved. For example, the director of merchandising must understand the necessity to keep labor costs within limits and, therefore, must not plan a merchandising strategy that requires a labor cost that is so high that the profit objective cannot be reached.

So it should be apparent that the merchandiser must consider controllable expenses when planning and executing the weekly sales and gross margin plan. Because the primary responsibility of the merchandiser is the planning and control of sales and gross margin, this chapter will deal mainly with that responsibility on a short-term, weekly basis. However, it is important to remember that one of the primary uses of the weekly sales plan is the scheduling of labor, the largest single controllable expense. Weekly labor must usually be scheduled in advance, and an accurate sales plan is necessary to schedule an adequate labor force yet maintain the labor expense at a reasonable level.

Planning Sales Objectives

External and Internal Factors

In making a weekly sales plan it is important to make an evaluation of all the conditions that are likely to have an effect upon store sales during the week. Because the weekly sales estimate is made in advance, that is, during the previous week, not all the conditions that affect sales will be known. However, some effects are known in advance, and others can be anticipated so that an attempt should be made to evaluate all the factors likely to influence sales during the week for which the estimate is being made.

There are two types of conditions or factors that can influence weekly store sales: those that are *external,* or beyond the control of the individual retail food firm; and those that are *internal,* or can be influenced or controlled by the firm.

External Factors.   The external factors include competition, economic conditions, weather, and seasonal and trend movements.

Competition.   The actions of competitors with respect to merchandising strategy can be expected to have an effect upon weekly sales of a retail food store. The effect of competitors' actions will depend upon the number of competitors in the trading area and the nature of their strategy. The intensity of advertising, number of price specials, extent of the price cuts, the items utilized for price specials, and the number and type of special promotions used by competitors will all have some effect upon customer traffic and sales during any particular week. This effect is usually difficult to determine in advance unless one or more of the competitors is carrying on a continuous type of campaign that is predictable from week to week, or unless prior knowledge is gained of an action planned by a competitor. In any case, the exact effect of competitors' actions upon weekly sales is difficult to estimate, but a sales record with notations of competitors' merchandising strategy, especially unusual activities, can be helpful in establishing a pattern of competitors' strategy as well as an indication of the probable effect upon sales.

In addition to the actions of existing competitors in the trading area, the entrance of new competitors will also affect sales. A new store opening can have a drastic effect upon sales, especially during the first few weeks that the new store is in operation. The permanent effect of new competition depends upon the appeal of the new store to consumers compared with the appeal of existing stores.

Economic Conditions.   Because expenditures for food are related to consumer income, economic conditions that affect consumer income can be expected to have an effect upon store sales.

Employment conditions often affect weekly store sales. The level of employment is important, and sudden changes in the employment situation in the area, such as large layoffs or a strike, will likely affect sales from week to week. In some areas, employment is highly seasonal, for example, a vacation resort area, so that sales will change greatly at the beginning and the end of the season.

Still another condition that influences weekly food store sales is the timing of pay periods by local employers, or the issuance of social security and welfare checks by government agencies. The weeks during which checks are issued are usually associated with increases in store sales.

Weather.   Customer shopping behavior is influenced by weather, and extreme weather conditions are likely to result in reductions in sales. The period of time during which sales will be affected depends upon the duration and severity of the weather conditions. Snowstorms, heavy rainstorms, or high winds may only result in postponement of food shopping for a day or two at most, but prolonged bad weather may result in sales declines that last for a week or more. In these situations, sales are likely to increase substantially during the week after the bad weather. When severe weather occurs during a weekend, an increase in sales during the following week can be anticipated.

Seasonal Effects.   One of the most important external factors that normally influences weekly food store sales is that of seasonal effects. Seasonal effects include the effects of changes in food buying patterns during the course of a year and the effects of holiday food buying.

There is a predictable pattern of sales during the year that tends to change during certain seasons. Food store sales are usually highest during the September to December period and lowest during July and August. The peaks and valleys in sales are related to the school year, the vacation and travel season, the weather pattern, and holidays. The beginning of the school year in September is normally accompanied by increasing food store sales that peak at the Christmas holiday season and then decline to a low in August. The changes are not constant, and there are week to week increases and decreases due to holidays, other external conditions, and internal factors.

Once the seasonal pattern is known, the weekly sales estimates should reflect the effects of seasonal factors.

Trend.   Trend is a gradual change in sales over a relatively long period of time, at least one year. Increasing population, greater food expenditures, higher food prices, or greater acceptance of the store by consumers in the area may result in a gradually increasing volume of sales. Conversely, opposite changes might result in a declining volume of sales over time. In either event, continuous comparisons of the current sales volume with sales during comparable periods of the year before will help to identify the existence of a sales trend. Once a trend is identified, weekly sales estimates can be adjusted to reflect the probable effect.

Internal Factors.   There are internal factors that affect weekly sales, which include those conditions that influence weekly sales and that can be controlled by the firm. The internal factors, basically, are those conditions that affect value to the customer, and consequently store sales and profit. The merchandising strategy and the effectiveness with which the strategy is carried out have an important effect upon both long-term and short-term sales. Methods for assessing and controlling week-to-week merchandising strategy will be discussed later in this chapter.

Weekly Sales Log

The estimation of weekly sales is the first, and perhaps most important step, in sales and profit planning and control. The level of sales determines the amount of merchandise required, affects the amount of labor needed,

Period — From ———
To ———

Week Ending	Total		Grocery		Meat		Produce		Notations of Events and Conditions Affecting Sales
	Est.	Actual	Est.	Actual	Est.	Actual	Est.	Actual	
	$	$	$	$	$	$	$	$	
Jan. 2									
9									
16									
23									
30									
Feb. 6									
13									
20									
27									
Mar. 6									
13									
20									
27									
Apr. 3									
10									

FIGURE 8-1 Example of weekly sales log including estimated and actual sales, by department, with notations.

and along with gross-margin percentage establishes the amount of gross margin realized. Thus, all other planning depends upon the estimation of a weekly sales volume.

In making a reasonably accurate estimate of weekly food store sales, a record or history of past sales is very important. This history, along with an evaluation of the factors that affect sales on a week-to-week basis, provides the basis for an estimate of weekly sales. A record or log of weekly sales, by department, along with the estimates, should be maintained in order to serve as a basis for future weekly sales estimates and to indicate the degree of accuracy of past estimates. An example of a sales log is shown in Figure 8-1. This log provides for a weekly record of actual sales, by department, as well as estimated sales. Some retailers combine sales data with records of gross margin, labor expense and other pertinent information. The particular method of maintaining sales records is not really important as long as a complete record is available for planning purposes.

The sales log shown in Figure 8-1 also includes space for notations of the external and internal conditions and events that are expected to influence sales. These notations along with the sales record provide an indication of the effects of important conditions and events that can be considered in making current sales plans.

Weekly Sales Chart

In addition to a weekly sales log, a weekly sales chart is a valuable aid in making the sales plan. The sales chart simply shows graphically what is in the sales log so that it is possible to identify, visually, the weekly sales pattern and the effects of both external and internal conditions. As shown in Figure 8-2, the sales chart should include not only a record of weekly sales for an entire year but also notations of conditions or events that may have influenced weekly sales. The sales chart provides a pictorial record that can be referred to quickly and easily when making the weekly sales plan. The current year's as well as the previous year's sales charts should be used in the planning process.

Figure 8-2 shows a seasonal sales pattern and indicates the effects of holidays and the actions of competitors as well as internal competitive strategy events expected to influence the weekly sales pattern.

Departmental sales, as well as total store sales, should be included in the weekly sales chart (or on separate charts) in order to indicate differences in the sales patterns among departments and between departments and total sales. Departmental sales tend to follow the same general pattern as total store sales so that the sales mix (the percentage of total store sales accounted for by each department) is reasonably consistent from week to week. However, there are occasional differences in the sales mix because of competitors' actions, seasonal effects, or other conditions that have different effects upon the major departments during some weeks. For example, produce department sales may decline as a percentage of store sales during

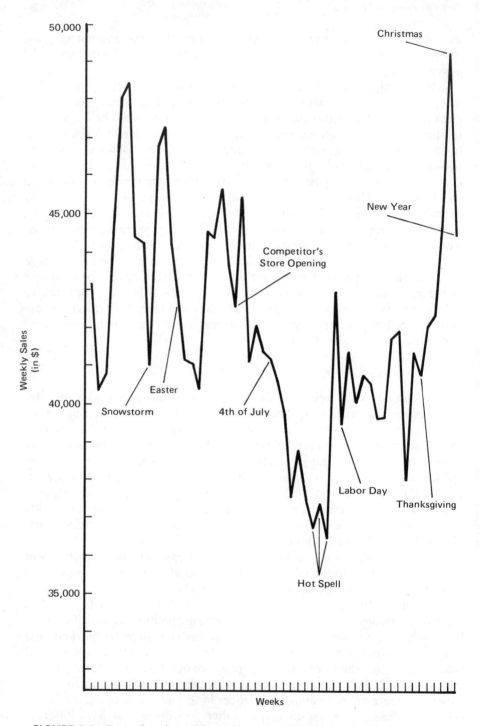

FIGURE 8-2 Example of weekly total store sales chart with notations of important events, and conditions that influence sales, for one year.

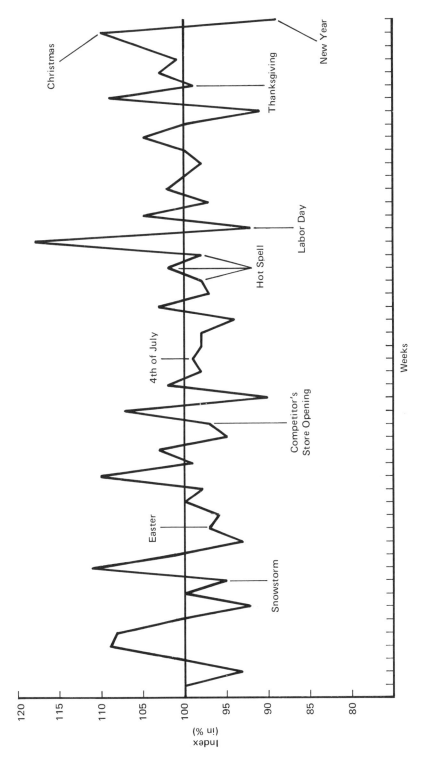

FIGURE 8-3   Index of weekly store sales, with notations, for one year (previous week = 100)

the season when locally grown fruits and vegetables are marketed at roadside stands. Likewise, meat department sales may decline as a percentage of total sales during weeks when one or more competitors utilize deep price cuts on popular meat items. Also, unusual conditions such as a shortage of beef accompanied by abnormally high prices may affect the percentage of sales in the meat department during certain weeks. The same effect may apply to other departments depending upon the items involved. For these reasons, it is important to maintain adequate records so that when unusual circumstances can be predicted or anticipated, their probable effect upon the weekly sales of individual departments can be taken into account when the overall store sales plan is developed.

Weekly Sales Index Chart

As an aid in formulating the weekly sales plan, the sales index chart is useful. The sales index chart is based upon the sales log and shows the percentage change in dollar sales from week to week, along with notations of external and internal conditions that are expected to affect weekly sales (see Figure 8-3).

The sales index expresses dollar sales during each week as a percentage of dollar sales during the previous week so that it is possible to estimate the percentage increase or decrease in sales due to specific conditions or events. This information is helpful in making current and future sales plans. For example, in making the sales plan for a holiday week one can refer to the sales index for the previous year or two and determine the percentage change that occurred in sales during the same holiday week. Past results may not indicate precisely what will happen during the current year, but they provide a factual basis for making a reasonably accurate estimate. Because some holidays occur on different days each year, and holiday weeks also vary from year to year, it is important to make notations on the sales charts in order to identify and interpret correctly the effect of past holidays upon weekly sales and to apply this knowledge to the current calendar. In addition to identifying the effects of holidays, it is helpful to know the effects of other events and conditions in terms of percentage changes in sales from week to week. For example, if a new competitor is opening during the week for which a sales plan is being made, a sales index chart might prove an indication of what to expect, based upon the effect of past new store openings, upon sales during the week of the opening and thereafter.

Basically then, the usual method for making weekly sales forecasts is to use the previous week's sales as a base that is adjusted for known or anticipated external and internal factors that are expected to influence sales. Although judgment must be used in making weekly forecasts, the degree of accuracy is likely to be much greater if the judgment is based upon the best information available. A complete record of weekly sales with notations of pertinent conditions and events provides factual information that is invaluable in making sales plans. Whether the records are utilized in a sophisticated computer program or simply as points of reference in preparing sales plans manually, the margin of error is likely to be much less than if records are not maintained and used.

Product Category and Item Sales Plans

In order to prepare merchandise orders and project gross margin on a weekly basis, departmental sales plans should be broken down into product category and item sales estimates. Here again, adequate records should be maintained in order to estimate the departmental product mix from week to week.

Some of the same factors that affect total weekly sales also influence the product mix within departments. Competitors' actions and seasonal changes in consumption are the external factors that are most likely to influence product mix within departments. If one or more competitors offer a weekly price special on an item, the sales of that item may account for a smaller percentage of departmental sales than usual.

Seasonal effects also influence product mix. For example, the sales of frozen lemonade will decline in the fall and winter seasons in most parts of the country so that it will account for a higher proportion of frozen-food sales during the summer season than during other seasons of the year.

In the meat department, luncheon meats and barbecue items are in greater demand during the summer vacation months so that they account for a higher proportion of meat sales during that period.

Fresh fruits and vegetables are seasonal because of the production cycle so that their availability and quality varies during the year. Thus, the product mix in the produce department varies according to the seasonal nature of fruit and vegetable production.

Holidays influence the sales of some commodities. For example, the sales of cranberry sauce, fresh cranberries, and turkeys at Thanksgiving; fruitcake, nuts, and dried fruit at Christmas; and ham at Easter.

In addition to seasonal effects, the merchandising strategy of the firm will affect the product mix within each department. Price specials and promotions influence the sales of individual items, and consequently the weekly product mix within departments.

In order to provide a basis for estimating the weekly sales of items and commodity groups within departments, a record of sales should be maintained. This record can be a byproduct of the departmental inventory control and ordering system that should be maintained in each department in order to facilitate the ordering of merchandise during each week based upon expected sales and the level of inventory.

As in the case of total store and departmental sales logs, the item inventory control and order forms should include notations of external and internal factors that may influence sales during each week. These notations should include unusual weather conditions, the selling price of each item, price specials and promotions, quality variations, and other factors that may have had an effect upon the sales of individual items or the department as a whole. These records will be invaluable in estimating the sales of individual items during any given week so that a factual basis exists for ordering products as well as projecting gross margin for each department.

Planning Gross-Margin Objectives

As pointed out previously, gross margin is critical in the retail food business because it determines the amount available from each dollar of sales to cover all operating expenses and the net-profit objective. The control of gross margin from week to week is necessary because of the effects of price specials, changes in product mix, and shrinkage. Projections of weekly gross margins, by departments, are necessary in order to adjust pricing to reflect competitive conditions and other factors that may affect gross margin from week to week. Without weekly projections, the gross margin may not be adequate to make the contribution required to meet the annual gross-margin objective. In this event, the annual net-profit objective would not be achieved. Thus, weekly planning of gross margin is essential to the systematic progress towards the annual net-profit objective.

The weekly gross-margin objective is planned in conjunction with the sales plan because pricing strategy has an important effect upon sales. In the short-term, week-to-week planning process, dollar gross margin is critical because even the variable operating expenses are relatively fixed; therefore, gross margin must be adequate to cover all operating expenses if a contribution toward the overhead expenses and net profit is to be realized. Therefore, on a weekly basis, the gross-margin *percentage* objective must be planned in conjunction with the *dollar* sales objective in order that the gross-margin dollars are adequate to cover variable or controllable operating expenses and make some contribution toward fixed overhead expenses and net profit.

Markdown Analysis of Price Specials

One of the most important aspects of planning weekly gross margin is the selection of price specials and their effect upon gross margin. The purpose of price specials is to maintain or increase customer traffic and total store sales from week to week. However, price specials can have a devastating effect upon both percentage and dollar gross margins unless they are planned very carefully. The effect of price specials upon gross margin depends upon the importance of the items specialed in the sales mix and the extent of the price cuts. The greater the importance of the items on special with respect to department and store sales, the greater the effect upon gross margin. Likewise, the more severe the price cuts compared with normal selling prices, the greater the effect upon gross margin.

Table 8-2 illustrates the effects of product mix and the extent of the price cut upon the gross margin in a retail food store department.

Example A shows the effect of two price specials, for items A and B, upon the overall departmental gross margin using the contribution method.

TABLE 8-2 Effect of Price Specials Upon Gross Margin
in a Retail Food-store Department

Item	% of Dept. Sales	Normal Gross Margin %	Special Gross Margin %
Example A			
A	10	25	10
B	5	25	10
All other	85	30	30
Total	100	XX	XX
Example B			
A	10	25	0
B	5	25	0
All other	85	30	30
Total	100	XX	XX

Item	Normal Contrib. to Gross Margin	Special Contrib. to Gross Margin	Diff. Between Normal and Special Contrib. to Gross Margin
Example A			
A	2.50	1.0	-1.50
B	1.25	0.5	-0.75
All other	25.5	25.5	—
Total	29.25	27.0	-2.25
Example B			
A	2.50	0	-2.50
B	1.25	0	-1.25
All other	25.5	25.5	—
Total	29.25	25.5	-3.75

The contribution to gross margin based upon a normal gross margin of 25 percent is calculated for both items A and B. Item A is twice as important in the sales mix of the department because it contributes twice as much to the departmental gross margin as item B. If the prices of both items are reduced so that the gross margin is only 10 percent on the sales of each, the contribution to departmental gross margin by both items is reduced, but the reduction is twice as great for item A because it accounts for 10 percent of sales compared with item B's 5 percent contribution.

In *Example B,* the gross-margin contributions of items A and B are compared based upon normal gross margins of 25 percent and special pricing

Store_____Department_____Week Ending_____

| Item Description | Selling Price | | Projected Sales | Cost | | Retail Extension | | Projected Gross Margin | | Normal Gross Margin* | | Markdown | |
	Regular (1)	Special (2)	(3)	Unit (4)	Total (5)	Unit (6)	Total (7)	% (8)	$ (9)	% (10)	$ (11)	GM $ (12)	Sales (13)
Bananas, 40# box	17¢ lb.	12¢ lb.	70 bx.	$4.00	$280.00	4.80	$336.00	16.7	56.00	41.2	126.00	70.00	140.00
Pascal celery, 1½ doz. crate	35¢ buch.	25¢ buch.	15 crts.	4.50	67.50	4.50	67.50	0.0	0.00	28.6	18.00	18.00	27.00
Seedless grapes, 28# lug	39¢ lb.	29¢ lb.	12 lugs	6.50	78.00	8.12	97.44	20.0	19.44	40.5	30.94	11.50	33.60
Total					$425.50	--	$500.94	15.1	75.44	39.3	174.94	99.50	200.60

Note: No adjustments have been made for product shrinkage. Selling prices must include an adjustment for shrinkage if the projected sales and gross-margin figures are to be achieved. Pricing methods to compensate for product shrinkage are described in Chapter 4.
* Based upon normal sales of 45 boxes of bananas, 10 crates of pascal celery, and 7 lugs of seedless grapes.

FIGURE 8-4   Markdown analysis worksheet for planning weekly department price specials and their effect on gross margin.

at cost. The specials, at cost prices, result in no gross margin for either item and a reduction in contribution to departmental gross margin equivalent to the total contribution at the normal selling price and gross-margin percentage.

Thus, the effect of price specials upon departmental and store gross margin is directly proportional to the severity of the price cuts and the importance of the specialed items in the sales mix.

Markdown analysis is a method for planning the effect of price specials upon gross margin in order that the effect can be controlled. The markdown analysis is made in conjunction with the sales plan because the price specials are expected to have some effect upon sales.

Figure 8-4 illustrates a markdown analysis worksheet for planning price specials in a produce department. In this example, three weekly price specials are planned: bananas, pascal celery, and seedless grapes. As shown in Figure 8-4, bananas are to be priced at 12 cents per pound compared with a regular price of 17 cents; pascal celery is to be offered at 25 cents a bunch compared with the normal price of 35 cents, and seedless grapes are to be sold at 29 cents a pound instead of the regular price of 39 cents.

The first step in estimating the effect of the planned price specials is to estimate the sales. Records that indicate sales increases when these items were offered as price specials at a previous time are very helpful in making the sales estimates.

Once the sales estimates are made, the total cost, total retail value, and gross-margin dollars and percentage are calculated for each special and for all specials combined. In the example, the special on bananas is expected to yield a gross margin of $56 or 16.7 percent. Pascal celery will be sold at cost so that no gross margin will be realized. Seedless grapes are expected to return $19.44 in gross margin for a percentage of 20 percent. The combined sales of the three items on special are estimated at about $501 with a gross margin of $75.44 or 15.1 percent.

The next step in the planning process is to determine the gross margin that would normally be realized from the sale of the items on special so that the loss or markdown in gross margin can be calculated. The normal gross-margin dollars and percentages are calculated for each item and for the three items combined. The total cost and total retail value (extension) of the specials, based upon normal sales, are not shown in Figure 8-4, but they are calculated in the same manner as shown for the specials. The method shown in Figure 8-4 is to multiply the sales in wholesale units times the cost per unit (Col. 3 x Col. 4) and retail value per unit (Col. 3 x Col. 6). The gross-margin dollars are then determined by subtracting the total cost from the total retail value (Col. 7 − Col. 5), and the gross-margin percentage is the result of dividing the gross margin dollars by the total retail value (Col. 9 ÷ Col. 7).

The normal gross margins in dollars and percentages for the three specials are included in Figure 8-4 (Cols. 10 and 11) along with the gross-margin dollar markdown, or the difference between the normal gross margin and that estimated for the specials (Col. 11 − Col. 9). The estimated gross-margin loss or markdown is greatest for bananas because of the importance of banana sales, both normally and at the special price. The price special is expected to reduce the gross-margin percentage from 41.2 percent to 16.7 percent and the gross-margin dollars from $126 to $56, a reduction of $70. The effect of the price special for pascal celery is not as great as for bananas even though celery will be sold at cost and will not make any contribution to gross margin. The reason for this is that celery is not nearly as important as bananas with respect to either percentage gross margin or the sales mix, so that the normal gross-margin contribution of celery is much less than that of bananas. Seedless grapes are normally somewhat more important in the sales mix and carry a higher gross-margin percentage than pascal celery, but the special price cut is not as severe as that for celery, so that the gross-margin markdown is not as great for seedless grapes as for celery.

The overall gross-margin percentage of the three items on special is normally 39.3 percent, and the contribution to gross-margin dollars is normally about $174.94. Thus, the gross-margin markdown is estimated at $99.50 based upon the normal gross margin of $174.94 and the estimated gross margin of $75.44 when the items are specialed.

Markdowns due to specials are also sometimes expressed in sales dollars and percentages. The loss or markdown in sales dollars is calculated by multiplying the estimated sales in units (either wholesale or retail) times the markdown per unit from the normal selling price. In the example, the normal selling price of bananas is 17 cents per pound, or $6.80 per 40-pound box, compared with 12 cents per pound, or $4.80 per box on special. Thus, the markdown per box is $2.00, and the total markdown is determined by multiplying the estimated sales, 70 boxes, times the markdown per box, $2.00. The total markdown for bananas is $140.00, and this is shown in column 13 on the worksheet. The retail sales markdowns are calculated for pascal celery and seedless grapes in the same way, and the total estimated retail markdown due to the three price specials is $200.60. The dollar markdowns are usually expressed as a percentage of sales, which then serves as a guide in controlling the extent of markdowns due to specials. For example, if weekly sales in the produce department are estimated at $3,250, then total markdowns due to specials will be 6.2 percent of sales ($200.60 ÷ $3,250). The percentage markdown figure indicates the extent of price specials and the likely effect upon gross margin, but it is not especially useful in projecting gross margin. The markdown percentage may be used as a guide in limiting the number of price specials. For example, the merchandiser may plan price specials so that the retail markdowns do not exceed a certain percentage because markdowns in excess of that percentage may be too difficult to offset through the merchandising program, and the overall gross-margin objective will not be achieved.

The most significant figures in the gross-margin plan are the markdowns in gross-margin percentage and dollars due to the price specials. From the markdown analysis worksheet, it is determined that the projected gross-margin percentage on the sales of the price specials is 15.1 (Col. 8) compared with a normal gross margin of 39.3 percent (Col. 10). The importance of this reduction in percentage gross margin is the effect that it will have on dollar gross margin, which is the most critical short-term objective. The reduction in department gross-margin dollars, based upon the anticipated sales of specials, will amount to $99.50. Unless this loss in gross-margin dollars can be offset through the merchandising plan, the contribution to profit will be reduced because most expenses are fixed from week to week.

Compensating for Price Specials

The next step in developing the weekly gross margin plan is to plan a strategy for compensating for the effect of price specials. This can be done in several ways; by promoting the sales of high-margin items, by increasing the gross margin on some items, by increasing total sales, or through some combination of the above.

Part of the merchandising plan involves the use of promotional items as a means of compensating, in part, for the effect of price specials. Promotional items are those items that are a good value to the customer and that yield a relatively high gross margin. Promotional items may be those that normally carry a high gross margin or those that yield a higher than usual gross margin because of a decline in cost or promotional allowances from manufacturers. In either case, it is advantageous to promote the sales of these items in order to compensate for the effects of price specials.

The promotion of high-margin items is accomplished through advertising, merchandising emphasis, or both. Promotional items are often included in advertising along with price specials, especially if an advertising allowance is available from the manufacturers. The promotional items are sometimes referred to as "secondary" or "feature" items in advertising, and price specials are referred to as "lead" items (see Chapters 3 and 5).

Increasing total sales will also help to offset the effects of price specials upon gross margin in individual departments and the store. The lower gross-margin percentage due to price specials can be offset if total dollar sales increase enough to compensate for the reduction in gross-margin percentage. In other words, the total gross-margin dollar objective can be reached even though the gross-margin percentage is reduced because of price specials, if sales can be increased adequately.

The most practical method for achieving the budgeted gross-margin dollar and contribution to profit objectives is through some combination of the above, that is, through the use of promotional items to influence the product mix and achieving some increase in sales because of the price specials and overall merchandising plan.

Figure 8-5 illustrates a procedure for planning departmental gross margin by estimating the effect of price specials and alternative methods of compensating for this effect.

Store_____ Dept._____ Week Ending_____

Item	Projected Sales	Sales Mix		Gross Margin			Contrib. to Gross Margin		
		Normal	Projected	Normal	Projected		Normal	Projected	
					(1)	(2)		(1)	(2)
Price specials*	$ 501	13.7%	15.4%	39.3%	15.1%	15.1%	5.4%	2.3%	2.3%
Promotional items	328	8.3	10.1	30.0	40.0	40.0	2.5	4.0	4.0
All other	2421	78.0	74.5	31.5	31.5	35.2	24.6	23.5	26.2
Total or Average	$3250	100.0%	100.0%	— —	— —	— —	32.5%	29.8%	32.5%

*Based upon markdown analysis in Figure 8-4.

FIGURE 8-5   Worksheet for estimating the effects of specials and promotional items on sales mix and gross margin.

The first step is to determine the effect of the price specials upon the sales mix, that is, the proportion of department sales made up by the specials normally and during the week when the items will be offered at a special price. In Figure 8-5, it is shown that the three items on special normally account for 13.7 percent of sales compared with an estimated 15.4 percent of sales during the coming week, assuming that the total dollar sales in the produce department are $3,250 both normally and during the coming week.

The sales of the items being offered as price specials are estimated at a higher proportion of department sales than normally, even though the selling prices are lower than usual, because of the increased quantities that are expected to be sold at the special prices. The net effect of the higher proportion of total sales and lower gross-margin percentage is a much lower contribution to department gross margin on the part of the items on special. The normal contribution of the planned specials to department gross margin is 5.4 percent compared with 2.3 percent at the special prices.

The promotional items are planned in the same way as the price specials, that is, the sales and gross-margin percentages and dollars are calculated based upon both normal and promotional sales, so that the net increase in contribution to gross margin can be determined.

In the example shown in Figure 8-5, promotional items are expected to account for 10.1 percent of sales during the coming week, as compared with 8.3 percent of sales normally, with an estimated gross margin on sales of 40.0 percent compared with 30.0 percent during normal weeks. Due to the increased gross margin and importance in the sales mix, the promotional items are expected to contribute 4.0 percent to the department gross margin compared with the normal contribution of 2.5 percent.

If the prices on the remaining items in the department are to remain the same as normally, then the gross margin for these items will still be 31.5 percent, but the contribution to the department gross margin will be less because of the change in the sales mix. Because the price specials and promotional items are expected to account for a higher proportion of produce department sales, the remainder of the items will account for a smaller proportion of total departmental sales. Thus, instead of accounting for 78.0 percent of sales, the remainder of the product line in the produce department (all items except price specials and promotional items) will make up only 74.5 percent of total sales. If prices on these items are not increased, then their contribution to department gross margin will be 23.5 percent instead of the normal 24.6 percent.

The overall department gross margin, under normal conditions is 32.5 percent. The department gross margin as a result of the price specials and promotional items will be only 29.8 percent, however, if total sales are $3,250.

The net result of the planned specials and promotional items then, assuming the same dollar volume of sales, is a department gross margin of 29.8 percent. The increased contribution of the promotional items will partly offset the reduced contribution of the price specials but will not be adequate to fully compensate for their effect. The contribution of items other than special or promotional items will be reduced slightly because of the smaller proportion of sales due to some substitution of specials and promotional items for other items.

Therefore, if no increase in sales is realized, the net effect of the specials and promotional items will be a reduction in gross-margin percentage from 32.5 percent to 29.8 percent of sales, or from $1056.25 to $968.50 in gross-margin dollars, a net reduction of $87.75. Therefore, the merchandising plan must be adjusted if the normal weekly gross margin in the department is to be achieved.

One possible way to achieve the desired rate and amount of gross margin is to increase the sales of high-gross-margin items. In order to determine the extent to which the gross margin would have to be increased on items other than specials and promotional items, it is first necessary to determine the contribution to total gross margin required. Because the normal gross-margin percentage in the department is 32.5 percent, and the contribution of specials and promotional items is 6.3 (2.3 + 4.0) percent, the contribution required from all other items is 26.2 percent (32.5 − 6.3). Thus, all other items must yield a gross-margin percentage that is adequate to make a contribution of 26.2 to the department gross margin. Because all other items are expected to account for 74.5 percent of sales, the required rate of gross margin is calculated by dividing 74.5 into 26.2. The result is 35.2 percent, the gross margin that must be realized on the sales of items other than specials and promotional items in order to achieve an overall gross margin of 32.5 percent in the produce department (see Col. 2 under Contribution to Gross Margin, Figure 8-5). This can be accomplished by increasing the proportion of sales made up by high-margin items through effective merchandising.

Increasing total department sales is another way to compensate for the reduction in gross-margin dollars due to price specials. Because the normal or budgeted gross margin will be $1056.25 at a department gross-margin percentage of 32.5 and total weekly sales of $3250, the sales necessary to achieve the budgeted gross margin of $1056.25 at a gross-margin percentage of 29.8 can be determined as follows:

$$\underset{\text{(Gross margin \%)}}{29.8\%} \times \underset{\text{(Sales volume)}}{X} = \underset{\text{(Gross margin \$ required)}}{\$1056.25}$$

$$X = \frac{\$1056.25}{.298} = \$3544$$

Therefore, in order to realize a gross margin of $1056.25 at a gross margin percentage of 29.8, weekly produce sales will have to reach $3544, or $294 over and above the original estimate of $3250. This amounts to an increase of slightly more than 9 percent of the original estimate.

Store_____ Week Ending_____

Department	Projected Sales		Actual Sales		Gross Margin		Contrib. to Gross Margin	
	$	%	$	%	Projected	Actual	Projected	Actual
Grocery	27,219	67.0			18.8		12.6	
Meat	10,156	25.0			20.0		5.0	
Produce	3,250	8.0			30.0		2.4	
Total	40,625	100.0			XX		20.0	

FIGURE 8-6 Example of summary worksheet for estimating and recording weekly store gross margin including the effects of specials and promtional items, by major departments.

An increase in sales of this magnitude may be very difficult to achieve, especially in view of the fact that the original estimate includes consideration of the effects of specials and promotional items. However, a carefully planned and executed merchandising program in the department may result in some increase in sales over the original estimate so that part of the reduction in gross-margin dollars due to specials may be offset.

Thus, in planning the weekly gross margin for each major department, the effect of price specials must be offset by promotional items, a higher margin contribution from the remainder of the product line, increased sales, or, more practically, some combination of these methods, if the gross-margin dollar objective is to be achieved. If the departmental gross-margin percentage cannot be "blended" to achieve the desired gross-margin dollar contribution then either the other departments will have to compensate for the reduction, or the budgeted contribution to store overhead and net profit will not be attained for the week.

Because the achievement of the overall weekly store sales and gross-margin objective is the ultimate aim, it is important that the planning process be coordinated. The purpose of price specials and promotional items is to maintain and hopefully increase customer traffic in *all* departments, so that the merchandising plan in terms of both sales and gross margin should be an integrated, coordinated effort to reach the overall sales and gross-margin objective.

A summary worksheet for projecting the overall store sales, gross-margin percentage, and contribution by major department helps to monitor the results (see Figure 8-6). The plan should provide for the budgeted gross-margin dollars and, consequently, the budgeted contribution to store overhead and net profit. In order to develop both sales and gross-margin projections for each department, the sales, percentage gross margin, and gross-margin contributions for each item and product category needs to be estimated. This task is expedited through the use of the computer.

It is also useful to maintain a record of actual results along with projections for reference in evaluating the degree of accuracy in developing the projections and for reference in making future plans.

The importance of weekly sales and gross-margin projections cannot be overemphasized. Without carefully considered projections based upon an evaluation of external and internal factors, the chances of achieving the long-term net-profit objective is much more likely to be jeopardized. Even though the future cannot be predicted with certainty, the chances of achieving desired results are improved through careful planning.

Equally as important as planning sales and gross-margin objectives are plans for how the objectives are to be achieved in terms of specific merchandising activities. These plans should specify methods of display, the design and use of advertising and promotional materials, and other activities necessary to carry out the plan successfully. In the final analysis, the success of the firm depends upon the ability to provide consistently good value to the customer.

SETTING MERCHANDISING OBJECTIVES

The second type of objective that needs to be defined is the merchandising objective. Whereas financial objectives indicate what results are expected in terms of sales, gross margin, expenses, and net profit, merchandising objectives specify the values to the customer provided through merchandising that lead to the achievement of financial objectives. In other words, merchandising objectives describe the results or conditions that must be attained in the store in order to provide the desired set of attributes or value to the customer on a day-to-day basis.

The merchandising objectives should define or describe the results or conditions that are considered acceptable in a well-run department and store and that can be controlled or at least influenced at the store level. For example, the type of display equipment is not a merchandising attribute that can be controlled at store level on a day-to-day basis. However, the use of display equipment in presenting merchandise to the customer with respect to display method, cleanliness, the use of point-of-sale promotional materials, and so on, can be controlled in the day-to-day operation of the store, and appropriate objectives should be prepared. Likewise, the original quality of perishable products delivered to the store cannot be changed, but the manner in which they are handled, stored, and displayed can affect the preservation of the original quality on a day-to-day basis.

Importance of Merchandising Objectives

The importance of merchandising objectives is indicated by studies that have shown that the failure to define expected results is directly related to problems in the management of retail food stores. First of all, if expected results are not defined clearly, there is no common language for communication among employees, department managers, store managers, and supervisors or merchandising specialists, and different interpretations of what constitutes acceptable store conditions may lead to poor employee-management relationships, lower value to the customer, and failure to reach the financial objectives.

The absence of merchandising objectives is also a handicap to employee training. One of the major causes of employee dissatisfaction and high turnover is the failure to provide employees with a clear understanding of what is expected of them. Without an objective definition of expected results, a consistent and fair evaluation of employee performance is much more difficult, and greater employee dissatisfaction and turnover is more likely to result.

Merchandising objectives focus attention on results that are important and enable all concerned to determine quickly whether or not a problem exists so that immediate action can be taken to identify the cause and correct it. If objectives are well written, it should be possible for anyone in the organization to determine whether or not the conditions in the store are acceptable.

Thus, merchandising objectives provide the basis for effective training and supervision in the retail food store that directs the efforts of everyone concerned toward providing maximum value to the customer.

Preparing Merchandising Objectives

Merchandising objectives should be established according to the criteria discussed at the beginning of the chapter. One of the greatest problems in preparing merchandising objectives is the subjective nature of many merchandising factors, such as what constitutes quality and customer service, so that objectives cannot be stated in measurable terms. In these instances, the desired results must be described in observable terms, and judgment is required in order to determine whether or not the objective is being achieved. Merchandising objectives should not be an attempt to eliminate judgment, but rather to place judgment within a consistent framework so that judgments, when necessary, are based upon consistent criteria.

There are some objectives that cannot be stated in exact, measurable terms but that are acceptable within a particular range of measurement. In these cases, the range of acceptability should be indicated.

In preparing merchandising objectives, vague, indefinite terms such as *adequate, proper,* and *satsifactory* should be avoided. It goes without saying that results should be adequate, proper, and satisfactory, but it is meaningless to use such words, unless they are defined in terms that are more specific. One of the primary purposes of merchandising objectives is to avoid the vagueness of terms such as *adequate selection, proper display,* and *satisfactory service.*

The foregoing points can best be illustrated by examples of merchandising objectives. The first question is: what aspects of in-store merchandising require statements of objectives? Table 8-3 illustrates the major elements of merchandising that contribute to customer value and that are controllable at store level and examples of specific points that should be defined in the statements of objectives. The examples are merely illustrative and are not intended to be all-inclusive or appropriate for every food store.

Product Quality or Condition

Some guidelines should be established for judging the quality or condition of perishable merchandise in the food store, especially meats and produce, because of their importance in providing value to the customer.

"Trim on all beef steaks and roasts is a minimum of ¼ inch and a maximum of ½ inch of finish around entire cut."

The quality objectives should stress whatever is considered most important and should require store personnel to look at perishable products through the eyes of the customer. In the example above, the objective is intended

TABLE 8-3   Guidelines for Preparation of Merchandising Objectives Based Upon Value to the Customer

Controllable Merchandising Elements	Specific Points Requiring Definition
Product quality or condition	Uniformity; general appearance
Product quality control	Rotation; temperature; level of display; turnover
Assortment of merchandise	Items available; quantity on display
Packaging and unitization	Sizes available; materials used
Display methods	Space allocation; product location; merchandise grouping
Price identification	Position of tags, signs, and price marks; accuracy; price changes
Promotional materials	Advertised items; general use
Customer service and convenience	Courtesy; requests and complaints; condition of shopping area; checkout
Housekeeping	Equipment; floors; parking area
Employee appearance	Wearing apparel; personal hygiene

to bring about uniformity in the trimming of beef cuts. Objectives could also be written to stress freshness, color, or other quality characteristics. The desired quality characteristics vary among products within departments, but rather than prepare objectives for each item it is more practical and effective to group items into categories whenever necessary.

Product Quality Control

Though the evaluation of quality is often subjective, it is possible to prepare rather specific quality-control objectives that are measurable or observable. The achievement of quality-control objectives gives some assurance that products are being handled and displayed so that the original quality is being preserved to the highest possible degree, which means that the customer is more likely to receive a good value and that spoilage will be minimized. Quality-control objectives should indicate what conditions will exist when product handling and display are conducive to maintaining quality at the highest possible level.

"All products are rotated on a first-in first-out basis except when condition warrants otherwise."

Rotation is an important step in quality control and the objective is to sell first that merchandise that has been on hand for the longest time, except in instances when the product received most recently should be sold first because of condition. For example, a shipment of fresh tomatoes received today may be riper than those that were received two days ago so that the riper ones should be sold first. In order to observe with certainty whether the rotation objective is being met, the use of a code or date is required in order to indicate when the product was packed, received, displayed, or processed in the store. There is a trend toward the use of actual dates rather than code markings to indicate the age of products. In the case of highly perishable products such as baked goods and hamburger, an expiration date is commonly used that indicates when the product should no longer be sold. The use of actual dates is referred to as "open dating" and has the advantage of being easily understood by both customers and employees who have the responsibility for rotation. If codes are used, they must be explained to all personnel, and this is complicated by the different systems in use by manufacturers as well as among departments in the store.

"The temperatures in the meat display cases are between 32°-35° F."

Objectives that specify display temperatures are measurable, as shown by the meat display-case-temperature objective above. It is necessary to have an accurate thermometer attached to the display case or a portable thermometer that can be used to check temperatures periodically. It may be desirable to indicate a range of acceptability for display-case temperatures because some fluctuation is bound to occur, and slight fluctuations are not critical in the maintenance of quality. In some instances, a maximum temperature may be stated in the objective when it is important not to exceed a certain temperature. For example, it is best to keep frozen foods at 0° F or below.

The display of products in refrigerated cases can affect the temperature and flow of air that in turn can affect product quality. For example, by overloading or otherwise interfering with the efficient functioning of the equipment, the quality-control capability may be reduced. For example, "All merchandise is below or behind the load line in refrigerated cases," is an objective that relates to the correct way to display products in refrigerated cases.

The rate of turnover of highly perishable items is important in providing the customer with the best possible quality. Merchandising objectives that specify conditions necessary to realize a high rate of turnover are important. For example:

"All fresh hamburger is ground on the same day that it is displayed for sale."

Here again a date or code on the package label provides the means for observing whether the objective has been met.

The level of display may influence the quality of highly perishable items like soft fruit, and merchandising objectives, as illustrated by the following example, serve to describe display conditions that protect quality.

"Highly perishable items like grapes, ripe tomatoes, peaches, cut squash, and soft pears and plums are not stacked over 2 or 3 high."

Assortment of Merchandise

One of the most important components of value to the customer is the availability of a complete assortment of products. Merchandising objectives should indicate what constitutes a complete selection in terms of *what* should be available, *when* it should be available, and in *what quantity* it should be available to the customer.

Most food retailers would wish to make certain items available to all their customers in order to provide a reasonably complete selection of merchandise. The overall assortment will depend upon the size of the store, the items available, consumer tastes and preferences, the policy of the retailer, and the type of organization. Some chain or affiliated multi-unit organizations provide a basic selection of items in every store but give the store manager and department managers authority to determine the remainder of the assortment based upon consumer demand in their market area. Others provide lists of items, each of which is authorized for a particular group of stores. The stores are usually grouped according to size, sales volume, and location; and the authority of store managers and department managers to select from the authorized list varies according to the policy of the firm.

"All items on the 'must list' are available to the customer at all times."

is an example of an objective that specifies that the store must make a certain assortment of items, designated as the "must list," available to all customers. Other objectives could be prepared to provide guidelines for product selection judgments on the part of store and department managers.

An important aspect of product assortment that is frequently overlooked is that of timing, or when a particular selection is to be available. This is especially important in the meat and delicatessen, produce, bakery, and dairy departments where there is a high rate of turnover, and merchandising objectives call for daily turnover for the most highly perishable items. This means that some items must be displayed and when necessary prepared fresh each morning. Hamburger, fresh fish, bread, milk and cream, prepared delicatessen items like ham salad, green leafy items like lettuce, and soft fruits like fresh strawberries, are examples of highly perishable items that should be ordered, prepared, and displayed for daily turnover whenever possible. The need for daily preparation and setup of highly perishable items creates a problem in that there is often not enough time in which to make a complete selection of merchandise available to the customer before the store opens for business. This problem is particularly serious in stores in which the entire fresh meat, delicatessen, and produce displays are taken down each night or on Saturday nights in stores that are closed on Sundays. With the labor that is available, it is practically impossible to have a complete selection of all merchandise on display by the time the store opens each morning, unless the opening time is delayed until late morning or noontime. Even then, a complete selection may not be available depending upon the amount of labor, number of products in the line, and the stock condition with respect to the amount of replenishment required. The result of this situation is that early-morning and especially early-week customers are not likely to have a complete selection to choose from, which may lead to customer dissatisfaction and a loss of business if the problem is serious enough. Early-week and early-morning customers are not usually concerned with buying their weekly needs but are more interested in obtaining a few items needed until the next regular shopping trip. Therefore, it is important for the retailer to provide a minimum quantity of the most frequently purchased items for the early-bird shopper who probably doesn't expect a completely stocked store, but who does expect to find a reasonably complete selection of the items most important in the family diet. The following is an example of a merchandising objective that defines store opening conditions in terms of the merchandise available in a meat or produce department.

"A minimum display (one layer) of at least the ten fastest selling items is available when the store opens and a complete selection is available by 1:00 p.m."

This objective is based upon timing and priority, two important concepts in providing good value to the customer through merchandise assortment. It is based upon the concept that completeness of assortment, as soon as possible, is more important than the amount of each item available. In other words, it is more important to offer the consumer a reasonably complete selection of items in limited quantity than larger quantities of a smaller selection of items.

Merchandising objectives are also useful in defining display quantities based upon quality control and merchandising appeal. The quantity on display should be adequate to prevent out-of-stocks, but in the case of perishable products not excessive so that product damage and deterioration can be minimized. For example, merchandising objectives can provide guidelines for minimum acceptable quantities of all products as well as maximum display levels for perishable commodities. The maximum display levels for perishable products may be tied to the expected volume of sales. It is not necessary to maintain display quantities at the same level during the early part of the week as during the latter part of the week, when sales are greater. The following illustrate display quantity objectives, the first being a specific definition, the second providing a guideline for judgment.

"The level of display of fresh fruits and vegetables is not more than two high during Monday and Tuesday."

"The quantity on display is adequate for the anticipated volume of business."

Packaging and Unitization

The type, size, and color of trays and the type, size, and weight of film should be indicated by merchandising objectives whenever necessary to achieve uniformity, merchandising impact, quality control, or economy in the use of such materials. For example, the following objective pertains to the type of tray used for prepackaged, fresh meat.

"Transparent plastic trays are used for all packaged beef and pork items."

If it is considered important to provide a wide range of package sizes in order to accommodate the customer who may wish to purchase a very small quantity, as well as those who wish larger quantities, then a guideline objective like the following example is appropriate for items packaged in the store.

"The range of package sizes available satisfies the needs of the customer who wishes to purchase a small quantity and the customer who wishes to purchase a large quantity."

Display Methods

Merchandising objectives should be used to spell out requirements that are considered important in displaying products in the store. These requirements may include the method of display, product location, merchandise grouping, number of facings, or other display considerations.

For example, if it is considered essential to display certain items in refrigerated display cases, the items to be included should be specified. If it is considered important that formal displays be used under certain conditions and jumble displays be used at other times, appropriate merchandising objectives should be developed to indicate when each type of display should be used.

Examples of merchandising objectives that define display methods are illustrated by the following:

"There are at least two facings of every item on display in the grocery department."

"All items in the same product category are grouped together on display."

Price Identification

Price identification objectives may include a description of the way in which prices are posted and marked on packages and requirements for accomplishing price changes. For instance, the following objective defines marking requirements in terms of the items included and the accuracy and readability of the price marks.

"Each product package or unit, except those displayed in bulk, has an accurate and legible price mark."

The determination of accuracy depends upon the availability of an up-to-date price list whereas the legibility of the price mark is a matter of judgment.

Merchandising objectives can also describe the position of price marks on the packages and the use of shelf tags if these are considered important. If the posting of unit prices is required by law or provided voluntarily as a value to the customer, the items included as well as the method of posting the unit prices should be described by merchandising objectives.

Price changes, if not made promptly, may cause consumer dissatisfaction or may be costly to the store. Completing price changes on time is usually considered a high-priority task; so, the requirement should be defined as illustrated by the following objective statement.

"All weekend special prices are marked and posted by the time the store opens on Thursday morning."

Similar objectives may be desired to describe the timing of price changes for all items in the store, even those not on special.

Promotional Materials

Promotional materials such as signs, shelf-talkers, and special display pieces can contribute to more effective merchandising. If there is a particular way in which promotional materials are to be used, the requirements or guidelines can be indicated in merchandising objectives. For example, the following objective states a requirement for the use of promotional materials in conjunction with the display of advertised items.

"All advertised items are identified at the point-of-sale by the posting of 'special cards' provided to the store."

Customer Service and Convenience

The extent of services as well as the manner in which they are provided to customers constitutes one of the most important components of value to the customer. Merchandising objectives can be very helpful in identifying what is expected from all employees in their relationship with customers, and, even though most of the objectives must be observable, they serve to acquaint everyone on the store team with what is considered as acceptable behavior and as a framework for evaluating performance.

Courtesy is basic to maintaining good customer relations, but acceptable relations with customers need to be defined in more specific terms. For example, the following objectives indicate the behavior expected from any store employee when handling customer requests or complaints.

"Customers requesting information on the location of products are conducted personally to the appropriate aisle or display."

"Customers with complaints are conducted personally to the appropriate department manager or store manager."

Additional objectives may spell out expected behavior in resolving customer complaints.

Customer shopping convenience is an important value, and objectives help describe store conditions that contribute to greater convenience. For example:

"Cartons and other containers are removed from the selling area as soon as they are emptied."

"There are no unattended stock carts or other pieces of equipment in the display area."

The checkout operation is probably the most important customer service function in the retail store, and the level of service as well as the treatment of the customer at the checkout are critical to providing customer value through service and convenience. The following objectives are examples of how the expected level of service and employee conduct at the checkout can be defined. Both require judgment but provide points of reference that serve to direct the efforts of all employees toward building an acceptable level of customer service and customer relations.

"Additional checkouts are opened if more than two customers with large orders or four customers with small orders are in line at each operating checkout."

"Each customer is extended a friendly greeting at the beginning of the checkout transaction and receives a 'thank you' at the completion of the transaction."

Housekeeping

Cleanliness and neatness are important aspects of customer value but are difficult if not impossible to express in measurable or observable terms. Cleanliness is a matter of degree and cannot be described in words. Neatness and orderliness can be described to some extent, but, with few exceptions, must also be limited to rather general statements.

However, objectives like the following examples that specify cleaning requirements at least help to insure that a regular cleaning schedule is followed so that the chances of maintaining an acceptable level of cleanliness in and around the store are improved.

"The parking lot is policed daily and all debris and shopping carts removed."

"Refrigerated display cases are washed thoroughly at least once each week."

"The sales area floor is swept daily and scrubbed at least twice each week."

Other cleaning objectives should be developed, especially where a lack of sanitation may lead to a dangerous growth of microorganisms, such as in the meat department or in the delicatessen where ready-to-eat foods are prepared. Local and state health regulations may require certain sanitation procedures, in which case objectives should be developed that describe conditions that will exist when the regulations are being met. Irrespective of rules and regulations, however, the consumer has a right to expect a high degree of cleanliness in an establishment that handles and sells food, and objectives should focus attention on the conditions necessary to maintain a clean and orderly selling environment as well as healthful foods.

Employee Appearance

Customers also have a right to expect store employees to be clean and neat, and employees should know what is expected of them in terms of wearing apparel and personal hygiene. Here again, judgment is often involved, but statements of objectives can indicate what is considered most important as shown in the following examples.

"All male employees are wearing clean white shirts and ties."

"All female employees in the meat and delicatessen departments are wearing hairnets."

Summary

Merchandising objectives should be measurable or observable and capable of achievement and can be developed for each controllable element of customer value. Objectives should concentrate on what is expected and not the procedures that are to be followed. Each firm must develop its own set of objectives based upon its particular competitive strategy and the customer values it wishes to provide.

A complete set of merchandising objectives provides a common language for more effective communications among employees and all levels of management. The objectives also provide the basis for training and evaluating employee performance.

CONTROLLING RESULTS

Once financial and merchandising objectives have been established, it is important to follow a procedure for checking upon progress because one of the basic purposes of planning is to furnish a basis for controlling

RETAIL FOOD STORE FINANCIAL ANALYSIS

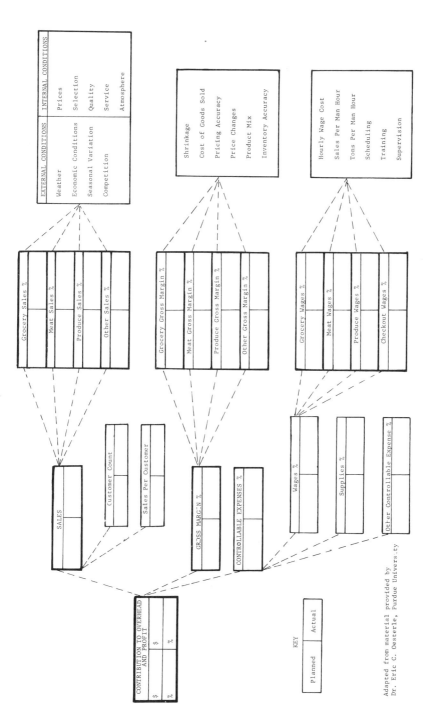

FIGURE 8-7 Retail food store financial analysis.

Adapted from material provided by
Dr. Eric C. Oesterle, Purdue University.

results. Control involves the comparison of plans with interim or short-term results so that problems can be identified and corrective action taken before they affect long-term results seriously.

Analyzing Financial Objectives

Progress toward both short-term and annual financial objectives should be evaluated at the end of each planning period, which is weekly for many of the objectives, and every four weeks or quarterly for others.

A form is useful for making weekly or other short-term analyses of financial objectives (see Figure 8-7). The analysis form should provide for a comparison of planned objectives with actual results and, through a systematic analysis, be designed to help pinpoint the cause or causes of failure to reach the planned objectives. For purposes of the following discussion, assume that the short-term financial analysis is made on a four-week basis.

Contribution to Overhead and Profit

The starting point of the analysis is contribution to overhead and profit in dollars, which is the difference between gross margin and controllable expenses. Because overhead expenses are essentially fixed and not easily allocable to departments, the important short-term objective is the achievement of an adequate contribution to overhead and profit based upon gross margin and controllable expense objectives that, over a period of one year, will cover overhead expenses and the net-profit objective.

If the four-week or other short-term contribution to overhead and profit objective is achieved, or exceeded, then there is little or no reason for concern. However, if the contribution to overhead and profit objective is not reached, then it is necessary to identify the reasons for the lack of achievement. Even if the overall contribution to overhead and profit objective is reached, the analytical procedure illustrated in Figure 8-7 should be followed in order to evaluate the plans and performance in each department with respect to sales, gross margin, and controllable expenses, the basic elements of net profit.

Sales Analysis.   Assuming that the four-week contribution to overhead expenses and net profit has not been achieved, the next step is to analyze total dollar sales and the sales mix. If total dollar sales have fallen short of the objective, it is helpful to know whether the decline in sales is due mostly to fewer customers or lower sales per customer. Therefore, the number of customer transactions from the cash registers as well as dollar sales per customer (total dollar sales ÷ number of customer transactions) should be included in the financial analysis. If the number of customers was less than anticipated, it would indicate that (1) competitors have been able to attract potential customers because of price specials or other promotional activities; (2) the merchandising program during the past weeks has not been effective in providing good value to the customer; (3) external conditions have resulted in fewer customers in the trading area; or (4) some combination of these factors has occurred. On the other hand, if the reduction in sales has been due mostly to lower sales per customer, it would indicate a weakness in one or more departments so that customers are buying less of their needs in your store and more in competitors' stores. Perhaps customers are buying specials in your store and more of their regular needs in other stores, or it may be that customers are simply spending less in food stores. In any event, it is useful to know whether the problem is mostly a result of a loss of customers or lower sales per customer in order to plan a strategy for reaching sales objectives in subsequent weeks.

The next step is to analyze the sales objectives and results by individual departments to determine whether the failure to reach the planned sales was a general problem or was attributable to only one or two departments. This can be accomplished by analyzing the dollar sales in each department or the sales mix or percentage distribution of total sales by department.

The factor or factors associated with low sales volume, whether it be general or confined to one or two departments, need to be identified. It is important to know whether the problem is related to conditions external to the store, which are mostly uncontrollable, or to in-store merchandising, which is controllable. It is helpful to know whether there was a general decline in food store sales in the area during the period, for if this was the case, it tends to confirm that the cause was due to external conditions. Vendors of direct store delivery products are usually aware of general sales patterns as well as individual store sales and should be consulted for their judgment as to whether sales were generally lower in the trading area or if one or more competitors were able to increase their market share. If competitive activity was responsible for the problem, the exact nature of the competitors' actions and their effects should be assessed so that adjustments can be made to offset the effects in subsequent weeks.

The low sales volume problem may also have been associated with in-store merchandising in that value to the customer was inadequate to realize the customer acceptance necessary to achieve the sales objective. The problem may have been due to prices, assortment, quality, service, or some combination of these merchandising factors in one or more departments. The definition and evaluation of merchandising objectives is an effective way to control value to the customer and to identify in-store merchandising problems that may reduce value to the customer.

Gross-margin Analysis. After the sales analysis has been completed, the actual overall and departmental gross margins should be compared with the projections. Physical inventories are necessary in order to obtain accurate gross-margin figures. It is important to evaluate gross margins on a short-term basis because of the serious effects that reductions in gross margin can have upon contribution to overhead and net profit, and because of the fluctuation that can occur from period to period due mainly to shrinkage.

Shrinkage Measurement and Control.   Because shrinkage is a major cause of dollar loss, low gross margin, and net profit reductions, it is important to establish an accurate measurement of shrinkage. Measurement is necessary in order to develop short-term, preferably weekly, controls that indicate when shrinkage is excessive so that the cause can be identified and eliminated or at least reduced before the losses become even more serious (see Chapter 4 for the definition of shrinkage and the methods of pricing to adjust for shrinkage).

The causes of shrinkage include everything that has the effect of reducing the retail value of merchandise available for sale. Spoilage, weight loss, internal and external pilferage, damage, price-marking errors, cash transaction or bookkeeping errors, and markdowns from the original retail selling price due to product deterioration, price specials, or price changes to meet competition are all sources of shrinkage.

Shrinkage can be measured or estimated for each department for which sales are itemized. This usually includes at least the grocery, meat, and produce departments. Actual physical inventories are necessary to measure shrinkage accurately, just as they are necessary to derive accurate gross margins. In the meat and produce departments, physical inventories should be taken weekly or every other week because of the high degree of product perishability and the need for very close control of inventory spoilage and markdowns.

Measuring Shrinkage in the Perishable Departments.   The procedure for measuring weekly shrinkage in produce, meat, or other departments where inventory and sales data are available on a weekly basis is shown in Figure 8-8.

Retail value of beginning inventory	$ 500
Retail value of shipments to store	+3850
	4350
Retail value of ending inventory	- 350
Retail value of merchandise available for sale	4000
Retail markdowns from regular prices	- 200 (5% of retail value)
Retail value of merchandise available for sale less markdowns	3800
Actual sales	- 3560
Shrinkage other than markdowns	$ 240 (6% of retail value)
Total shrinkage excluding markdowns	6% of original retail value
Shrinkage allowance standard exclusive of markdowns	-5% of original retail value
Controllable shrinkage	1% of original retail value

Note: These figures are hypothetical and do not represent typical or average results.

FIGURE 8-8   Procedure for measuring weekly shrinkage in a retail produce department.

1. The retail value, at regular retail prices, is determined for beginning inventory, which is the merchandise on hand at the beginning of the week. The retail value of merchandise shipped to the store during the week is calculated at regular retail prices. The sum of the retail value of the beginning inventory ($500) and the extended retail value of shipments to the store ($3,850) is $4,350.

2. The retail value of the inventory on hand at the end of the week ($350) is then deducted from the sum of the retail value of beginning inventory and shipments to the store ($4,350). The result is $4,000, which represents the total retail value, at regular selling prices, of the merchandise available for sale during the week.

3. The retail markdowns are then determined. Markdowns include reductions in the retail value due to price specials or unplanned competitive price reductions as well as reductions in price because of quality deterioration. The extended retail value of shipments to the store should be adjusted to compensate for merchandise that is unacceptable upon delivery to the store because of damage or poor quality and is returned to the warehouse or supplier.

In order to determine the amount of markdowns, the quantity of each item sold at less than the regular retail price must be recorded or estimated. The department manager is usually responsible for providing this information, and his accuracy in furnishing it determines the accuracy of the markdown figures. In the example in Figure 8-8, the weekly markdowns were $200 or 5 percent of the total retail value of $4,000. This means that markdowns in price resulted in a reduction in retail value of $200, or that $200 more would have been received if all merchandise had been sold at regular retail prices. Because markdown losses are mostly not controllable at the department level, they are calculated separately. Knowing the extent of markdowns is also important in planning and evaluating price strategy and gross-margin objectives as shown earlier.

4. The total retail value is then adjusted for markdown losses, and the result, $3,800, indicates what actual sales should be if no shrinkage other than markdowns has occurred.

5. By subtracting actual sales, $3,560, from the adjusted retail value, $3,800, the amount of shrinkage other than that due to markdowns is determined to be $240, or 6 percent of the original retail value of the merchandise available for sale.

The total dollar shrinkage from all causes is $440 ($200 + $240), which is 11 percent of retail value and 12.4 percent of actual sales. At least 5 percent of the total shrinkage is mostly uncontrollable at the department level because it is due to price reductions and not to mishandling. Of the remaining 6 percent, some is controllable, and some is not. Natural weight loss and preparation loss are unavoidable to some extent, and some spoilage of highly perishable merchandise is inevitable, the actual amount depending partly upon the condition of the merchandise when received at the store. On the other hand, the manner in which products are handled, stored, prepared for sale, and displayed does affect the amount of shrinkage. Therefore, in order to estimate the extent of controllable shrinkage, it is necessary to establish some standards or benchmarks against which to compare actual shrinkage. Based upon studies and records of shrinkage, it is possible to establish shrinkage standards or objectives based upon estimates of what uncontrollable shrinkage should be. These objectives must take the season of the year into account as well as other factors that may affect the amount of uncontrollable shrinkage. The shrinkage standard shown in Figure 8-8 is based upon uncontrollable shrinkage losses exclusive of markdowns. The difference between the standard and actual shrinkage exclusive of markdowns is an estimate or approximate measure of controllable shrinkage (1 percent in the example).

Some chains prefer to adjust the extended retail value of merchandise shipped to the store. A shrinkage allowance based upon an estimate of uncontrollable shrinkage is used as a basis for the adjustment. In this case, controllable shrinkage is the difference between the retail value of the merchandise available for sale less markdowns and actual sales. The controllable shrinkage figure is useful in evaluating shrinkage control in individual departments and in identifying excessive shrinkage situations that require corrective action. Pilferage is considered part of controllable shrinkage because there is no way to separate it from shrinkage due to handling, and it can be controlled to a certain extent.

Measuring Shrinkage in the Grocery Department. The grocery department and sub-departments pose a special problem in measuring shrinkage because of the intervals between physical inventories, the number of items involved, and the numerous sources of losses from shrinkage. Physical inventories are taken less frequently in the grocery department than in the meat and produce departments because of the magnitude of the task. The meat and produce departments can be inventoried relatively quickly and easily at the end of each week because there are relatively few items involved and inventory levels are normally low due to the high turnover of perishable merchandise. The grocery department, on the other hand, contains a large number of items, and the task of taking inventory is much more time consuming and costly. Therefore, grocery department inventories are usually taken no more frequently than quarterly and often are taken semiannually or annually.

The grocery department includes most of the items offered in a retail food store and represents approximately two-thirds of total dollar sales. Although most of the items are less perishable than those carried in the meat and produce departments, they are generally more susceptible to pilferage. Shrinkage in the grocery department, whether due to pilferage or other causes, is serious because of the effect upon overall store profit, and the measurement and control of grocery department shrinkage is crucial to the attainment of financial objectives.

Figure 8-9 illustrates a detailed method for identifying and measuring most sources of shrinkage in a retail grocery department. This method requires a considerable amount of paperwork and bookkeeping, but it does provide detailed information on shrinkage. The advantages of this system are that it enables a firm to identify the importance of each source of shrinkage and, consequently, to develop specific means for controlling shrinkage more effectively. The cost of obtaining the detailed information must be compared with the potential benefits of shrinkage control in order to determine whether the system is practical for a food retailing firm.

Store No._____

Period from_____

to_____

	$	%	Company $	Avg. %
1. Beginning Inventory				
Purchases				
2. Warehouse				
3. Vendors				
4. Bakery—company				
5. Bakery—vendors				
6. Inter-store transfers				
7. Total Purchases				
Credits				
8. Warehouse returns				
9. Bakery returns and reduced				
10. In-store use				
11. Warehouse credits				
12. Claims				
13. Inter-store transfers				
14. Total Credits				
15. Total Net Purchases				
16. Total Merchandise Available				
Markdowns				
17. Price specials and other markdowns				
18. Coupon redemptions				
19. Damaged merchandise				
20. Refrigeration breakdowns				
21. Price Changes				
22. Total Markdowns				
23. Total Merchandise Accountability				
24. Gross Sales				
25. Voids and Returns				
26. Net Sales				
27. Retail Accountability				
28. Actual Ending Inventory				
29. Shrinkage or Expansion				

Courtesy of Star Market Co. (Div. of Jewel Co. Inc.), Cambridge, Mass.

FIGURE 8-9 Retail grocery shrinkage report (all figures at retail).

The first step in measuring grocery department shrinkage is to determine the retail value of the merchandise available for sale during the inventory period. The method illustrated in Figure 8-9 is based upon physical inventories every quarter (13 weeks).

The beginning inventory is the retail value of all merchandise on hand at the beginning of the period. The total purchases during the period include the retail value of all grocery merchandise delivered to the store either from the company warehouse (or major wholesale supplier), direct store vendors, company bakery, direct vendor bakeries, and interstore transfers (items 2 through 6 in Figure 8-9). Interstore transfers in this instance represents the retail value of merchandise transferred *from* other stores during the period.

Total purchases are adjusted for any credits to the store during the period including merchandise returned to the warehouse or bakery, retail reductions for bakery items, the value of merchandise used in the store, warehouse credits for unsalable or damaged merchandise, claims against suppliers or vendors for damaged or unsalable merchandise on hand and interstore transfers (items 8 through 13 in Figure 8-9). Credits account for any measurable reductions in the value of merchandise delivered to the store. If merchandise is billed to the store but is not shipped or is damaged or unsalable, then a credit must be recorded for the store.[1] If merchandise is returned to the warehouse or bakery or is reduced in price because of condition, the value of the returned merchandise or the loss in retail value of reduced items must be recorded. If certain items such as soaps, detergents, and other cleaning supplies are taken from store inventory for use in the store, then the retail value of the items should be credited to the store and included as a supply cost. If any items are transferred to other stores to relieve stock shortages, the value should be credited to the store from which the merchandise is transferred.

Total purchases (item 7) less total credits (item 14) equals total net purchases (item 15). Total merchandise available (item 16) is the sum of beginning inventory (item 1) and total net purchases (item 15) and represents the retail value of the merchandise for which the store is held accountable, or the list price value of the merchandise that was actually available for sale during the inventory period.

As you learned previously, shrinkage in the retail store is due to reductions in retail value from various sources. A comprehensive shrinkage measurement method is designed to identify and measure as many of the sources of shrinkage as possible in order to provide a basis for controlling

---

[1]Errors are sometimes made by the warehouse or supplier in filling orders so that some incorrect items are shipped to the store. If the errors are discovered when the merchandise is received, a credit can be issued to the store and the merchandise returned, or the incorrect items might be accepted by the store and an appropriate adjustment made on the invoice. In some instances, store personnel simply count the number of pieces delivered without checking to see if the correct items have been shipped. If there is a shortage in the number of pieces shipped, some companies credit the store on the basis of the average value, at cost, of a case of groceries.

shrinkage. In addition to the reductions in merchandise value associated with warehouse, wholesale supplier or direct vendor delivery, and interstore transfers, there are several sources of shrinkage that occur in the merchandising process that can be measured (items 17 through 20 in Figure 8-9).

One of the major sources of shrinkage is that of price specials and other markdowns. In order to determine the reduction in retail value due to price specials and other markdowns, it is necessary to record or estimate the number of units of specials or other markdown items that are sold at the regular price and at the special markdown price. This requires physical inventories at the time the special or markdown prices go into effect and then again when the regular retail prices are reinstated.

The redemption of store coupons by customers, merchandise that is damaged by employees or customers, and products that must be disposed of because of refrigeration equipment breakdowns are other sources of markdowns in retail value that are itemized in the grocery shrinkage report.

Changes in regular shelf prices during an inventory period can either increase or decrease the retail value of merchandise, depending upon the extent to which prices were raised or lowered and the unit sales at both the old and new prices. In order to determine accurately the net effect of price changes, it is necessary to take physical inventories of the items when the price changes go into effect and at the end of the inventory period (item 21).

After all the markdowns have been determined and adjusted for the effect of price changes, a total markdown figure will be the result (item 22). By deducting total markdowns (item 22) from total merchandise available (item 16), the total merchandise accountability (item 23) can be measured. Total merchandise accountability indicates the retail value of the merchandise for which the store is accountable from opening inventory and additions to inventory during the period after adjustments for all measurable shrinkage have been made. Total merchandise accountability should be equal to sales plus ending inventory unless there were some sources of shrinkage that were not measured.

The net sales figure (item 26) is determined by adjusting gross sales (item 24) for voids and merchandise returns (item 25).

Deducting net sales (item 26) from total merchandise accountability (item 23) indicates the retail accountability (item 27), which is the retail value of the inventory that should be on hand at the end of the period. By comparing the retail accountability with the actual ending inventory (item 28), the shrinkage or expansion (item 29) can be determined. If retail accountability is greater than the ending inventory value, then some unexplained shrinkage has occurred that could be due to pilferage, errors in ringing merchandising through the cash registers, or errors in recording inventory, purchases, or other items in the shrinkage report.

If retail accountability is less than the ending inventory, an expansion has occurred, probably due to errors in recording inventories or other items in the shrinkage report. Inventory expansions will occur much less often than shrinkages.

The shrinkage report shown in Figure 8-9 provides a complete record of all measurable sources of shrinkage. Disregarding possible errors in recording the necessary information, the inventory shrinkage figure provides a reasonably good measure of pilferage and checkout transaction under rings. In addition, a comprehensive shrinkage report identifies the importance of each source of shrinkage so that control measures can be developed and monitored to reduce shrinkage and its effect upon gross margin and net profit.

Shrinkage Control. If it is concluded that controllable shrinkage is excessive in any department, the cause or causes should be determined and corrective action taken as soon as possible.

The ordering function should be reviewed to make certain that the quantities ordered are in line with sales so that reserve inventories are not excessive. Excessive inventories result in lower turnover rates and contribute to greater product deterioration and damage.

Inventory control with respect to rotation is another merchandising activity that can lead to increases in shrinkage if it is done improperly. Rotation practices should be checked to make certain that all merchandise on display and in reserve is rotated on a first-in first-out basis as a general rule. The more perishable the product, the more important it is to follow correct rotation procedure.

Handling, preparation, storage, and *display* practices are other possible causes of a high incidence of shrinkage, especially for highly perishable merchandise. Rough handling increases damage to all types of merchandise and increases the spoilage of highly perishable products.

The preparation of perishable merchandise including fresh meat, delicatessen products, and fresh produce should be investigated as a source of controllable shrinkage. Improper or excessive cutting and trimming, the use of improper packaging materials, or excessive production of prepared items relative to sales can all result in unnecessarily high shrinkage.

Storage procedures should be checked to see that damage from improper stacking is prevented and that the correct temperature and humidity are being maintained.

Display conditions can be a source of controllable shrinkage that should be checked closely. Display levels of soft and perishable items and temperatures in refrigerated display cases should be appropriate for the control of product quality.

Merchandising objectives are important aids in defining and evaluating conditions necessary to control shrinkage of merchandise in the retail food store and, when used effectively, will help prevent excessive controllable shrinkage due to handling and merchandising practices in the store. In the event that shrinkage exceeds acceptable limits, merchandising objectives should also provide a framework for identifying the cause of the problem.

Another cause of shrinkage that may lead to unacceptable shrinkage levels is pilferage. Pilferage includes merchandise that is stolen by customers, employees, or suppliers, as well as merchandise that is consumed on the premises by customers or employees without being paid for. In either case, the result is an increase in shrinkage and the effects upon gross margin and net profit can be devastating if pilferage is not kept under control.

Effective control of pilferage requires adherence to carefully defined security procedures in the receiving and display of merchandise as well as in the checkout operation. The best protection against pilferage is prevention of the conditions that encourage it, and this involves the development and implementation of security measures on a continuing basis.

Pilferage control is a highly specialized subject that involves legal aspects, particularly in the apprehension of suspected or known pilferers, and no attempt will be made to cover the subject in this text. However, due to the serious consequences that can occur as a result of pilferage, it is extremely important that each firm develop procedures to deal with and control pilferage to minimize its effects upon shrinkage. It is advisable to consult expert sources of information on the subject because of its complexity.[2] Many firms employ security specialists whose main responsibility is the control of pilferage.

There is one other source of shrinkage that should be mentioned because it can be serious, depending upon the checkout system employed, and that is the failure to charge for merchandise in the bottom of shopping carts. This problem occurs because cashiers fail to check the bottom of the cart. It can be prevented or controlled through training and supervision or a checkout system that does not permit the customer to use the same cart to do shopping and to transport purchases from the store.

Gross-margin Allowance. Once shrinkage allowances in terms of actual sales have been estimated, it is necessary to adjust prices to compensate for shrinkage including markdowns so that the realized gross margins are adequate to meet the objectives. The methods for making these adjustments were described in Chapter 4 and earlier in this chapter.

Other Factors Affecting Gross Margin

In addition to shrinkage, there are several other factors that can affect gross margin. The cost of merchandise may increase, and if retail prices are not increased proportionately, gross margins will decline.

The accuracy in marking or posting prices can affect gross margin. Incorrect prices will either raise or lower gross margins depending upon whether the prices are marked higher or lower than the correct prices. The results are undesirable in either case because prices that are too low may reduce gross margin below the planned objective and prices that are too high may create customer dissatisfaction and lead to reduced sales in the future.

Failure to make price changes on time will affect gross margin because

---

[2]For example, see Bob Curtis, *Security Control: External Theft* and *Security Control: Internal Theft* (New York: Chain Store Publishing Corp., 1971 and 1973).

a higher proportion of sales will be made at the former price. The effect on gross margin depends upon whether the price change is upward or downward. Here again, either situation is undesirable because of the downward effect upon gross margin in the event of delays in making upward price changes, and the negative customer relations effects if there are delays in making downward price changes, especially if the prices that are advertised are not available.

The product mix with respect to the proportion of sales made up by relatively high-margin and low-margin items will affect gross margin. The higher the proportion of sales accounted for by relatively high-margin items, the higher the gross margin, and vice versa. Thus, in store merchandising can exert an important influence upon gross margin through product mix.

Errors in taking physical inventories will result in incorrect gross margins because the inventory errors will be reflected in the cost of goods sold. For instance, if the physical inventory at the end of the week in the meat department was overestimated, the gross margin would appear to be higher because the cost of goods sold would be underestimated. The error would be self-correcting during the following inventory period, however, because the incorrectly high ending inventory for the previous period will become the beginning inventory for the next period. The cost of goods sold during the next period will be overestimated and, as a result, the gross margin will appear to be lower than the true gross margin.

Expense Analysis

The final step in the four-week financial comparative analysis is to compare controllable expenses with planned objectives. The major controllable expenses are wages and supplies, although there may be other expenses that are considered controllable on a four-week basis. For example, trading stamps are sometimes considered a controllable expense because if they are not handled and dispensed with care the result may be an unnecessarily high expense. When they are included as a controllable expense in the short-term financial analysis, it is possible to determine if the trading-stamp expense is out of line with the planned expense rate. Other expenses that are controllable, at least in part, can also be included in the analysis if it is considered important to monitor them on a short-term basis.

Supply expenses can also exceed planned limits if their handling, storage, and use is not supervised carefully, especially in departments where product packaging is done. For this reason, the supply expense should be included in the short-term financial analysis.

The most important controllable expense is wages, which is the largest single operating expense in the retail food store. The wage expense should be budgeted and evaluated weekly because of its important effect upon net profit and the need to control it as closely as possible.

The wage expense should be analyzed on a departmental basis, and it is useful to separate the checkout wage expense from the remainder of grocery department wages. The checkout operation is a service function that really serves all departments and accounts for a relatively high proportion of store wages, and, because of its unique and important role, should be evaluated separately with respect to the wage expense.

If wage expenses are out of line in one or more departments, an analysis should be made to identify the problem. First of all, it should be recognized that the weekly wage expense is usually determined during the previous week because of the fact that work schedules must be made out in advance. The amount of labor scheduled for each week is based upon the sales estimate, and if the sales estimate is too high, the labor expense percentage is also likely to be higher than the plan because of the commitment that has already been made. Therefore, the labor expense is controllable only within narrow limits in the short term, especially if full-time and part-time help is guaranteed a minimum number of work hours each week.

Excessive wage expense may be associated with the average hourly wage cost. The average hourly wage cost is determined by dividing the total number of hours worked into the total weekly payroll cost for each major department. The hourly wage cost depends upon the hours worked at various rates of pay, and the amount of variation from week to week depends upon the differences in pay rates among employees. For instance, if the pay rate for part-time employees is lower than that for full-time employees, the average hourly wage cost will decrease as the proportion of total hours worked by part-time employees increases. In other words, the higher the proportion of total hours worked by employees at a relatively high hourly wage rate, the higher the average hourly wage cost, and vice-versa. For this reason alone, wages as a percentage of sales is not a good indication of the productivity of labor.

In order to avoid the problem of variations in hourly wage rates, sales per man hour can be used as an indication of productivity. Sales per man hour is calculated by dividing the total dollar sales by the number of hours worked during the week for each major department. Even sales per man hour may not measure labor productivity accurately because of changes in product mix, prices, and the nature of the functions that must be performed in the store each week. For example, changes in the product mix may influence productivity because some types of merchandise require more handling than others because of bulk or special handling requirements. Also, changes in the product mix along with price changes may change the value per unit of merchandise handled so that sales do not accurately reflect changes in the physical quantity of merchandise handled. For instance, if beef prices were to decline due to seasonally larger supplies, a fixed quantity of beef would result in lower sales that, in turn, would result in a lower sales per man hour in the meat department if the number of hours worked remained unchanged. The reduction in dollar sales per man hour in the meat department would not be a result of lower productivity, but rather would reflect a lower product value. In other words, the amount of product handled per man hour would be as great as during previous weeks, but each dollar of sales involves more product than before.

Some firms use tons per man hour as a measure of productivity in order to avoid the problem of changes in product value. However, tons per man hour does not reflect changes in product mix that affect labor requirements.

All the common measures of labor productivity have limitations that must be considered when using them to evaluate the causes of changes in labor expenses. They are useful as benchmarks for comparison so that the existence of problems can be identified.

If the labor expense exceeds the planned objectives in one or more departments, an analysis of scheduling, training, and supervision should be made. Scheduling involves having the right amount of labor available at the right time and in the right place. This involves an accurate definition of the workload in each department. Identifying the functions that must be performed in each department during each day of the week is a valuable aid in scheduling labor. Figure 8-10 shows a breakdown of functions in a retail produce department that provides for an estimate of the number of hours required during each day of the week to complete each function. The time required depends upon several factors, including departmental sales, product mix, physical facilities, merchandising objectives, amount of in-store preparation and packaging, and the skill of the labor force. The functional approach to labor scheduling does provide a systematic method for defining the weekly work load, which is basic to achieving the desired results at the lowest possible labor cost in each department and in the entire store.

Training and supervision are the keys to implementing the labor schedule effectively. Training is the means for providing the labor force with the skills and knowledge necessary to achieve desired results while supervision monitors results and takes whatever corrective steps that may be necessary to modify the schedule or improve employee performance.[3]

As an aid in setting financial objectives as well as in evaluating actual results, retail food industry averages are available from trade associations, universities, and other sources. These average figures are usually classified by size of company, geographic area, and other characteristics that may influence financial results. Most of these financial reports are published annually, although at least one, the *Super Market Institute Figure Exchange,* is available to participating members on a quarterly basis.[4]

The industry comparative data are especially useful in identifying trends in sales, gross margins, and expenses as well as important short-term charges. They should serve only as guides in setting and evaluating objectives, however, because they are averages that may reflect a wide range of operating and merchandising conditions. Each company should develop its own set

---

[3]For a comprehensive treatment of the subject, see Edward M. Harwell, *Personnel Management and Training* (New York: Chain Store Publishing Corp., 1969).

[4]A widely used annual report is *Operating Results of Food Chains* (Ithaca, N.Y.: New York State College of Agriculture, Cornell University).

Store_____

Week_____

Est. Sales_____

Function	Daily Man-Hour Estimates							
	Mon.	Tues.	Wed.	Thurs.	Fri.	Sat.	Sun.	Total
Take inventory								
Prepare order								
Receive and store								
Process and package:								
Trim or cull								
Condition								
Bag								
Wrap								
Scale and price								
Handle trash and salvage								
Re-process merchandise								
Stock displays								
Police displays								
Make price changes								
Customer service								
Police and clean:								
Backroom								
Display area								
Supervision and								
Administration								
Special*								

*Includes building special displays, putting up promotional materials and other unplanned or irregular activities.

FIGURE 8-10 Example list of functions in a retail produce department with provision for daily estimates of man-hours required.

of objectives based upon its own particular operating conditions, merchandising program, and experience.

Analyzing Merchandising Objectives

In addition to a systematic procedure for analyzing short-term financial objectives, a similar approach is needed for evaluating merchandising objectives. Merchandising objectives are directly related to the achievement of financial objectives and, therefore, should be part of the short-term control process. Merchandising objectives provide the basis for evaluating the effectiveness of the merchandising program, which is an internal factor affecting sales and gross margin. Thus, a systematic analysis and control of merchandising objectives is part of the short-term financial analysis.

Merchandising objectives define value to the customer in terms of the conditions that will exist when convenience, quality, selection, and atmosphere are considered adequate to achieve financial objectives. Once value to the customer is specified, there needs to be some means for assuring that it is maintained satisfactorily on a continuing basis.

The checklist system is an effective method for monitoring value to the customer as defined by merchandising objectives in order to identify problems and take corrective action before customer satisfaction is reduced seriously enough to prevent the achievement of financial objectives. The checklist system involves the systematic, day-to-day evaluation of store conditions based upon merchandising objectives. As in financial analysis, deviations from the objectives are analyzed in order to identify and correct the cause or causes of the deviations or exceptions.

The advantages of checklists can be illustrated by using the example of the jet airliner. Before each takeoff, the captain of the jet airliner is responsible for the completion of a checklist by the crew. The checklist requires the crew to observe and evaluate the functioning of each piece of mechanical and electronic equipment that is important to the safe performance of the plane. Each function must conform to a predetermined standard or level of performance and deviations from the standard must be corrected before takeoff is permitted. This procedure does not guarantee a perfect performance or a safe flight, but it greatly improves the chances for safe arrival at the final destination. The checklist provides a methodical procedure or discipline for insuring that each vital function is checked before the flight begins in order to provide the greatest possible chance for a successful performance. In addition to the preflight check, the vital functions of the jet are monitored constantly during the flight so that problems can be identified and corrected, if possible, in order to provide the greatest possible chance for a successful performance of the jet.

The jet airliner illustration is analogous to the retail food store in the sense that some methodical procedure or discipline is necessary to make certain that conditions provide the best possible chance for reaching the destination, which is the sales and profit objective. The use of checklists does not guarantee success, but it does require the store "crew" to check to determine whether the merchandising conditions are such that the chances for a successful arrival at the sales and profit destination are as great as possible. The checklist should include the major elements of value to the customer that are controllable in the store and should be used frequently enough to make reasonably certain that conditions are satisfactory based upon the merchandising objectives.

A complete set of merchandising objectives is extremely important in evaluating and controlling value to the customer through merchandising. Without the objectives, there is no common basis upon which to judge merchandising conditions and problem identification is made more difficult.

Figure 8-11 is an example of a retail food store checklist for the meat department. This checklist includes the merchandising conditions that are considered important in providing the desired value to the customer. The statements on the checklist are presented in question form, which requires judgments as to whether the conditions are acceptable. Some of the questions indicate the conditions that are acceptable; others depend entirely upon merchandising objectives to define acceptable conditions. If any of the conditions indicated on the list are unacceptable, the evaluator is required to list the reasons for the exceptions along with recommendations for improvement.

FOOD MART MEAT DEPARTMENT EVALUATION REPORT

STORE_____ EVALUATOR_____

DATE_____ TIME_____

	SALES AREA	YES	NO
1.	Is all merchandise fresh and appealing - no darkened cuts or torn packages?	___	___
2.	Is merchandise cut and trimmed uniformly?	___	___
3.	Are all packages tight and not bloody?	___	___
4.	Is there an adequate selection of all items for the volume of business?	___	___
5.	Does case look full - no bare spots showing?	___	___
6.	Is coding schedule maintained - no fresh meat over two days, no packaged deli items over 10 days?	___	___
7.	Are advertised items displayed and identified correctly?	___	___
8.	Is temperature in the display cases between 32° and 35°F?	___	___
9.	Is sales area presentable - clean cases, glass, wrapping stations, floor?	___	___
10.	Is frozen meat and poultry display satisfactory - adequate selection, no freezer burned merchandise?	___	___
11.	Are all salads and cold cuts fresh and appealing, not dried out?	___	___
12.	Is deli equipment clean - spoons, pans, slicer, Bar-B-Que?	___	___
13.	Are trash containers covered?	___	___
14.	Are all employees presentable - clean coats and aprons, girls with hairnets?	___	___

STORAGE AND WORK AREAS

		YES	NO
1.	Is all merchandise checked and weighed when received?	___	___
2.	Is all boxed merchandise dated and rotated?	___	___
3.	Is merchandise kept under refrigeration until processed?	___	___
4.	Is merchandise needed for display being processed first?	___	___
5.	Are rewraps processed promptly?	___	___
6.	Are safety rules being observed - cutters with aprons, guards on machines, etc.?	___	___
7.	Are equipment and tools in good working order?	___	___
8.	Are floors, blocks, equipment and tools clean?	___	___
9.	Is merchandise returned for credit handled promptly?	___	___
10.	Are bulk salads covered and not over four days old?	___	___
11.	Is all sliced and wrapped merchandise in the cooler not over five days old?	___	___

OVERALL DEPARTMENT EVALUATION

GOOD	Minor Improvements Needed.	_____
FAIR	Major Improvements Needed.	_____
VERY GOOD	Department Well Organized.	_____

Please indicate reasons for negative checks by number on back of sheet.

FIGURE 8-11   Meat department evaluation report. Courtesy of Food Marts, Inc., Holyoke, Massachusetts.

Figure 8-12 shows an example of a single checklist that can be used for all departments. This checklist lists points that must be evaluated according to merchandising objectives and given a score of zero to two. It is designed for use by merchandisers with specific departmental responsibilities

FERNANDES SUPER MARKETS, INC.
MERCHANDISER'S REPORT
KITCHENS - DELICATESSENS - SNACK BARS

Good - 2
Fair - 1
Poor - 0

KITCHEN — DELI — SNACK BAR

STORE: _____ DATE: _____
TIME ARRIVED: _____
TIME DEPARTED: _____ SIGNATURE: _____

1. Cooperation of Personnel in observing rules of personal health and cleanliness☐
   Unclean Hands☐   Hair Nets☐
   REMARKS: _____   ☐ ☐ ☐

2. Washing and Sanitizing of eating and cooking utensils☐   Proper disposal of wastes☐
   Waste containers covered at all times☐   Floors and equipment clean☐
   REMARKS: _____   ☐ ☐ ☐

3. Proper storage of Foods☐   Drinks☐   Containers☐   Utensils☐   Dishes☐
   Silverware☐   Ice Cream Dippers in running water☐
   REMARKS: _____   ☐ ☐ ☐

4. Foods properly refrigerated☐   Foods in Steam Table kept HOT☐
   Displayed foods kept covered☐
   REMARKS _____   ☐ ☐ ☐

5. Personnel trained in food handling☐   Food contamination precautions☐
   REMARKS: _____   ☐ ☐ ☐

6. Appearance of Preparation Areas☐   Coolers☐   Freezers☐   Refuse Areas☐
   Fountain Area☐
   REMARKS: _____   ☐ ☐ ☐

7. Safety principles observed☐   Use of all supplies☐   Supply Inventory☐
   Effective salvage use☐
   REMARKS: _____   ☐ ☐ ☐

8. Uniforms☐   Badges☐
   REMARKS: _____   ☐ ☐ ☐

9. Merchandising: Quality and taste☐   Freshness☐   Prices Correct☐
   Unauthorized items☐   Portion control☐
   REMARKS: _____   ☐ ☐ ☐

10. Work schedule posted☐   Efficient manpower use☐
    REMARKS: _____   ☐ ☐ ☐

                                          TOTAL SCORES _____

THE FOLLOWING MUST BE FILLED IN

A. Cleanliness of Store in General☐   Parking Lot☐   Rest Rooms☐   Personnel
   Appearance☐   Sales Floor Areas☐   Windows, Walls, Doors, Cases☐   Back Room☐   ☐ ☐ ☐
B. Courtesy: Thank you☐   Hello☐   Smile☐   Helpfulness☐   ☐ ☐ ☐
C. Service: Courtesy☐   Speedy Checkouts☐   Carry Out☐   ☐ ☐ ☐
   Any Customers Waiting for service at: Courtesy Booth☐   Checkouts☐
   Meat Case☐   Deli☐   Bakery☐   Snack Bar☐   ☐ ☐ ☐
D. Other Depts. (besides your own). How do you rate them on Merchandising,
   Service, Cleanliness: (Be critical & constructive - explain Fair & Poor ratings)

DEPARTMENT	GOOD	FAIR	POOR	EXPLAIN
Grocery	☐	☐	☐	_____
Front End	☐	☐	☐	_____
Meat	☐	☐	☐	_____
Deli	☐	☐	☐	_____
Produce	☐	☐	☐	_____
Dairy & F.F.	☐	☐	☐	_____
Snack Bar	☐	☐	☐	_____
Bakery	☐	☐	☐	_____

COMMENTS: _____

FIGURE 8-12   Food store merchandiser's report. Courtesy of Fernandes Super Markets, Inc., Norton, Massachusetts.

and requires each merchandiser to rate departments other than the one for which he is primarily responsible as well as overall cleanliness and customer service in the store.

There are many variations in the preparation of checklists depending upon the organization of the retail firm, the number of stores, and the amount of detail desired in evaluation. There is also considerable variation in how checklists are used in terms of who completes them and the frequency of completion.

For maximum effectiveness, everyone with managerial responsibilities should be involved in the use of checklists. Merchandisers, specialists, or supervisors in multi-unit firms should be required to complete or verify checklists for their respective departments or the entire store if total store supervision is employed. Store managers and department managers should be required to complete or verify the checklists. This procedure requires everyone with management responsibilities to review periodically the actual merchandising conditions with respect to expected conditions as defined by merchandising objectives. Even when the merchandising objectives are only observable and subject to differences of judgment, the checklist system at least requires that a judgment be made so that differences will be identified and can be resolved. The use of a uniform checklist insures that attention will be focused on the important merchandising conditions and that all concerned will have an objecitve basis for communicating. The checklist system identifies problems by exception and, together with merchandising objectives, provides a basis for a teamwork approach to identifying and solving the cause of problems.

The frequency with which checklists are completed depends upon the degree of control desired and the rapidity with which merchandising conditions are likely to change. For instance, the frequency of evaluation needs to be greater in departments with highly perishable merchandise, like delicatessen items, than in departments where perishability is less of a factor, like dry groceries. One procedure that has been used with good results in a small chain is to require the store manager, or assistant manager in the manager's absence, to complete a checklist for each department twice a day and review them with the respective department managers. The supervisors fill out the same checklists at least twice a week and review them with the store manager. The supervisors' and store managers' checklists are then forwarded to the general manager, who is afforded a concise summary of merchandising conditions in each store.

An incentive system based on the use of checklists was utilized by one firm, and it was successful in bringing about greater teamwork among all levels of management and in improving contribution to overhead and profit in all stores.[5]

---

[5]Theodore W. Leed and Kenneth G. Abrahams, *Improving the Performance of Retail Food Store Managers,* Management Information Series, Food Distribution Program, University of Massachusetts, September, 1964.

SUMMARY

It is important to plan both annual and short-term financial objectives and merchandising objectives and to establish a systematic procedure for evaluating results in order to identify and correct problems before they become more serious.

Sales, gross-margin, and controllable expense objectives should be established on a weekly and/or quarterly or four-week basis so that progress toward the annual net-profit objective can be evaluated and controlled.

Merchandising objectives describe the conditions that are considered acceptable when value to the customer is being provided adequately. Merchandising objectives define the conditions necessary to reach the financial objectives in terms of quality, selection, customer service, and other elements of value to the customer.

Some financial objectives should be evaluated weekly because of the dynamic nature of the retail food business. Quarterly or semiannual analysis based upon physical inventories in all departments will permit a complete financial analysis based upon accurate gross margins. The weekly and other short-term financial analysis should be based upon a comparison of planned objectives with actual results, and failure to achieve any of the planned objectives should be followed by subsequent analysis to determine the cause of the problem so that corrective action can be taken.

Merchandising objectives can be evaluated on a day-to-day basis through the use of a checklist system. The checklist system requires an evaluation of important merchandising conditions based upon merchandising objectives that describe acceptable conditions necessary for providing the desired value to the customer.

The planning and control of financial and merchandising objectives on a short term basis is essential to continued success in the retail food business.

9

Regulations Affecting Food Merchandising

GOVERNMENT AND BUSINESS[1]

Introduction

Although food merchandising is conducted within the framework of "free enterprise," there is a substantial body of regulations that govern or control many activities of food merchandising firms. As the food distribution system has become more complex and as the consumerism movement has grown, government economic regulation of food business activities has increased at the federal, state, and local levels.

Federal and state regulations governing food merchandising are usually similar and, in many cases, identical. Federal regulations normally apply to interstate commerce only, and state and local regulations apply to intrastate commerce only.

Government regulation of business seeks to serve a number of general purposes. Among these purposes are:

1. Maintenance of uniform standards of exchange, courts for enforcement of business arrangements, laws for establishing business enterprises, and general laws of commerce and industry.
2. Protection of public health and safety.
3. Establishment of policies to maintain a competitive system and to guarantee to the consumer the benefits of competition.

Although most would agree with the objectives of government regulations, there is substantial disagreement on how the objectives can best be achieved. The proper role of government in regulating business in order

---

[1]Adapted from James F. Rill, *Government Regulations of Business* (Washington, D.C.: National Association of Food Chains, 1966).

that the interests of the consumer be best served is difficult to define and will continue to be debated. This issue will not be resolved in this chapter. However, it is the purpose of this chapter to identify the primary intent and basic requirements of the most important types of regulations affecting food merchandising at the federal, state, and local levels. It should be kept in mind that state and local regulations may differ widely from state to state and locality to locality.

The chapter will also include a more detailed discussion of some of the most recent regulations, especially those dealing with consumer protection.

Types of Government Regulations

Government regulation provides for maintenance of uniform standards of exchange, courts for enforcement of business arrangements, laws for establishing business enterprises, and general laws of commerce and industry.

Our uniform monetary system permits a common medium of exchange for goods and services. This is an extremely important function of government without which our modern system of food merchandising could not operate. Similarly, uniform weights and measures developed by industry and government make a vital contribution to the food merchandising process. Most states and many municipalities have regulations that require the accuracy of devices used to weigh or measure commodities as well as the accurate representation of the quantity offered for sale to consumers. These regulations are intended to assure equity for all parties engaged in buying and selling goods and usually require periodic inspection for accuracy of all scales and other weighing and measuring devices used in wholesale and retail trade. The devices must be approved by an authority of the state or municipality (commonly known as the Sealer of Weights and Measures) after inspection and testing. The Sealer of Weights and Measures or other designated official also may spot check the weight or measure of commodities offered for sale to make certain that they provide the full net weight or quantity indicated on the package at the time of purchase by the consumer. It is the responsibility of the food retailer to see that the consumer receives the full weight or measure indicated on each package of merchandise offered for sale.

There are agencies responsible for the enforcement of the regulations that affect food merchandising, and courts have been established for the resolution of disputes, interpretation of agreements, and the provision of remedies for their breach. The Food and Drug Administration, the United States Department of Agriculture, the Federal Trade Commission, and the Justice Department are the agencies that are responsible for the enforcement of most of the federal laws that affect food distribution. The agencies responsible for the enforcement of state and local regulations vary among states and localities but often include Public Health Departments, the Attorney General, the Department of Agriculture, and the Department of Standards or Weights and Measures.

Basic rules for the creation of business relationships relating to the nature of corporations, partnerships, and other forms of enterprise have been set up by federal and state governments. These rules spell out in great detail the duties, rights, and remedies of those who make up business organizations and of those outsiders who have business dealings with them.

Government Regulation for Protection of Public Health and Safety

There have been enacted since the beginning of the century a number of federal laws that seek to prevent the shipment of adulterated or unsafe foods, drugs, and cosmetics in interstate commerce or the receipt or acceptance of such articles by the purchaser (dealer) or his agent. The objective of such legislation is to protect the consumer under circumstances in which self-protection is difficult if not impossible. Some of these regulatory acts are explained in the sections that follow.

The Food, Drug, and Cosmetic Act of 1938—a comprehensive revision of the Pure Food and Drug Act of 1906—prohibits the shipment and receipt in commerce of foods, drugs, devices, or cosmetics that are adulterated or misbranded. An *adulterated* food is one that contains any poisonous or harmful substance that may make it injurious to health, and a *misbranded* food is one whose labeling or packaging is false or misleading in any particular. Although the statute contains numerous additional refinements, basically a food is classified as adulterated if " ... it has been prepared, packaged, or held under unsanitary conditions whereby it may have been contaminated with filth." Under this section, the Food and Drug Administration in the Department of Health, Education, and Welfare has authority to inspect wholesale and retail food distribution centers as well as manufacturing plants to investigate whether or not sanitary conditions are maintained.

The law imposes criminal penalties on firms and individuals responsible for a violation without regard to their knowledge of the adulterated or misbranded character of the goods involved.

No person, firm, or corporation may be punished for having received adulterated or misbranded foods, drugs, devices, or cosmetics in commerce if it can be shown that he received in good faith a guarantee in writing from his supplier that the article involved was not adulterated or misbranded.

The Food, Drug, and Cosmetic Act also requires that receivers of foods, drugs, devices, or cosmetics permit the Food and Drug Administration access to records of such receipts and to warehouses and establishments where such merchandise is held after receipt in commerce. Failure to permit access to records or inspection makes the offender subject to prosecution.

The meat and poultry inspection acts are similar in purpose to the Food, Drug, and Cosmetic Act. The Meat Inspection Act of 1907 and the Poultry Products Inspection Act of 1957 established procedures for the inspection of red meats and poultry products by the Department of Agriculture prior to shipment in interstate or foreign commerce. The Wholesome Meat Act of 1967 and the Wholesome Poultry Act of 1968 provide for the mandatory inspection of meat and poultry that does not enter into interstate or foreign commerce.

In addition to the inspection for wholesomeness of meat and poultry products, federal, state, and local regulations also govern the conditions under which food products are processed, stored, and distributed. In general, food must be processed, handled, stored, and sold in a sanitary manner. Here again, state and local regulations on food sanitation vary, but in most instances food processing plants, wholesale warehouses, food service establishments, and retail food stores must conform to state and local sanitary codes as well as federal regulations if engaged in interstate commerce.

Although inspection is intended to assure the wholesomeness of food products, there is a system of grades that relates to standards of quality for some food products. Federal grades exist for fruits and vegetables, meat, fish, poultry, and eggs and dairy products. The use of federal grades is voluntary. Some states require the use of grades for certain food products, usually fruits and vegetables such as apples, peaches, and potatoes. The grades required by states are very similar or identical to the federal grades.

In addition to the foregoing statutes, the federal government employs a variety of controls designed to restrain, discourage, or penalize the sale of certain commodities thought to be harmful to health or morals. These controls may take the form of unusually high taxes, as in the case of the special excise taxes on liquor and tobacco. They may take the form of labeling requirements, as in the marketing of cigarettes. This law requires that the label on each pack and all related advertising warn the public of the alleged health hazards in smoking, or the control may take the form of outright prohibition, as for example, the Consumer Product Safety Commission's power to ban a consumer product that presents an unreasonable risk of injury when there is no product safety standard that would adequately protect the public.

Government Regulation Concerning Competition

It is generally recognized that the federal government is acting within its authority when it seeks to promote conditions essential to the competitive functioning of business. The federal antitrust laws are outstanding among the laws that seek to promote competition in business.

The Sherman Act, the first of the antitrust laws, prohibits contracts, combinations, and conspiracies that restrain interstate or foreign commerce. It is a criminal statute under which fines and jail sentences may be imposed.

Although the Sherman Act does not mention the word *competition,* it has been interpreted as prohibiting certain anticompetitive practices, such as price fixing by competitors, market-division agreements, agreements limiting supply, group boycotts, and resale price maintenance unprotected by fair trade. These practices are condemned because of their harmful effect on free competition.

Fair trade laws is a term applied to a body of state laws that permits sellers to establish by contract the price at which customers may resell their branded articles. These price-maintenance agreements under state law were made generally permissible by Congress in 1938, and enforcement against nonsigners was sanctioned in 1952, where permissible under state law. Two important conditions were attached by Congress to its legislation: (1) the branded article must be in free and open competition with similar articles where fair trade is in force; (2) the seller must not be in competition with his customers upon whom he seeks to impose fair trade.

There are other arrangements falling within the scope of the Sherman Act that restrain trade to some degree. However, these arrangements are not considered so harmful as to be unlawful without regard to their reasonableness and their effects on competition. These arrangements include limited agreements not to compete given by a seller of a business to its buyer, exclusive franchise contracts, agreements limiting territory within which dealers may operate, and exclusive dealing agreements and mergers not covered by the Clayton Act (as explained in the following sections).

Consideration of the volume of business affected, the duration of the retraint, and the legitimate business objectives to be served are factors considered in determining the validity of these practices.

Monopolies and Attempts to Monopolize. Generally, a *monopoly* exists when a firm has the unrestricted power to set the price of a product together with the power to exclude competition. Actually, such a condition can rarely be found. The mere existence of a monopoly in itself does not mean that an unlawful condition exists. The courts have recognized that monopoly may be the result of superior efficiency, the development of a new product, proximity to supplies or outlet, and other similar factors. A monopoly (monopolization) is said to have been established when the firm involved exercises its control and power over a product in such a way that the natural result of the practice is to strengthen and perpetuate their monopoly position.

The Clayton Act. The Sherman Act was supplemented in 1914 by the passage of the Clayton Act, designed to make more explicit the types of practices forbidden as anticompetitive. Under the Clayton Act, practices are disapproved without regard to competitive effect or "reasonableness." The issue is whether a specified practice "may be substantially to lessen competition or tend to create a monopoly." The Department of Justice and the Federal Trade Commission have joint responsibility for the administration of the Clayton Act. Relief in the form of injunctions is granted in Justice Department cases; "cease and desist" orders are issued in cases initiated by the Federal Trade Commission.

Exclusive dealing and tie-in agreements. Under Section 3 of the Clayton Act, two types of practices are prohibited: exclusive dealing and tie-in agreements.

> The Murry Bread Company agreed to sell their products at a special discount to Ace Supermarkets if Ace would carry their complete line of baked goods.

Such an agreement is not unlawful because it does not specifically exclude other competitors. If the Murry Bread Company had offered this special discount on the condition that Ace handle their line exclusively, the agreement would have been in violation of the Clayton Act. This would have been considered an *exclusive dealing* agreement.

If Ace Supermarkets had accepted the special discount on the basis that they would not handle any fancy cakes or pies from other competitors, the Clayton Act would have been violated. This would have been considered an unlawful *tie-in* agreement.

Such agreements are usually considered unlawful if a substantial volume of business is denied to competing suppliers and if there are no valid, legitimate business reasons supporting them.

Mergers and acquisitions. Under Section 7 of the Clayton Act, a corporation engaged in interstate or foreign commerce may not acquire all or part of the stock or assets of another corporation engaged in interstate or foreign commerce where the effect may be to substantially lessen competition or tend to create a monopoly in any line of commerce or any section of the country. As amended in 1950, Section 7 applies to three types of mergers and acquisitions: horizontal, vertical, and conglomerate. A horizontal acquisition occurs when the acquiring and acquired firms are competitors.

> The Ardene Wholesale Grocery Company acquired all the stock of the Sardis Grocery Wholesalers, each selling to stores in the same market area prior to the acquisition. This is a horizontal acquisition.

A vertical acquisition occurs when the acquiring and acquired firms are in a supplier-customer relationship.

> The Newton Supermarket Company acquired all the assets of the Larncy Produce Company, who was a former supplier. This is a vertical acquisition.

A conglomerate embraces all types not included in the other two categories.

> The Northwoods Paper Company acquired all the stock of the Big Bag Supermarket Company. This is a conglomerate acquisition.

Acquisitions are neither lawful nor unlawful in themselves. A merger as such does not necessarily imply that force, control, or the stifling of competition is an outgrowth of the merger. Mergers may actually remove from the market companies that are on the verge of failing because they cannot meet the competition and thus prevent potential bankruptcies. They may also effect economics by spreading overhead costs. Determining the validity of a merger involves the analysis of a variety of market factors including the share of the market held by the acquiring and acquired firms, the degree of concentration in the industry, the efficiencies produced by the acquisition, the financial condition of the acquired firm, and other factors bearing on the structure, behavior, and performance of the market.

The Robinson-Patman Act thoroughly revised Section 2 of the Clayton Act in 1936 so as to substantially broaden its affect. As amended, the legislation relates to discriminations in price, brokerage payments, promotional and advertising allowances and services, and buyer liability. It is one of the most important pieces of legislation affecting food merchandising, and anyone engaged in food merchandising should be familiar with its basic requirements.

Discriminations in price. An unlawful discrimination in price is a price difference between purchasers of goods of like grade and quality where the effect may be to substantially lessen competition or tend to create a monopoly. Price discrimination is also considered unlawful if it tends to injure, prevent, or destroy competition at either the seller or customer levels. However, there are several ways in which price discrimination may be justified. One of these is savings to the seller in cost of manufacture, sale, or delivery to different customers. For example, a truckload of canned goods might be priced higher than a shipment of the same merchandise in a full rail car. Price discrimination may also be justified by proving that it was a result of a good faith attempt to meet the lower lawful price of a competitor. For example, if a competitor lowers a price on a competing item in a certain geographic area, a manufacturer may also be justified in lowering prices in this same area. A third jurisdiction involves showing that the price discrimination reflected factors affecting the marketability of the goods involved, such as deterioration of perishables or obsolescence of seasonal goods. For example, two retailers may be charged different prices for the same merchandise if one buys seasonal merchandise at the end of the season. Also, Retailer A may buy a carload of lettuce for $4.80 per case from the same grower as Retailer B, who pays only $4.00 per case. Here price discrimination could be justified if the grower could show that the merchandise purchased by Retailer B was of poorer quality or could *not* be sold at a higher price. Perishable merchandise may be sold at a lower-than-market value in order to dispose of it.

Whenever a complaint of price discrimination is made, it becomes the subject of careful study and judgment by the courts and the Federal Trade Commission.

Brokerage payments. The Robinson-Patman Act also prohibits the payment or receipt of brokerage fees or commissions, directly or indirectly, by the buyer from the seller, by the seller from the buyer, or by the agent of either from the other party to a sales transaction. This provision does not require proof that the brokerage or commission payment may have an adverse effect on competition to establish a violation, nor may the cost-justification or meeting-competition defenses be used. Brokerage payments from seller to buyer are unlawful under the provisions of this act.

Promotional and advertising allowances. Section 2(d) of the Clayton Act as amended by the Robinson-Patman Act prohibits the payment of allowances by a seller to a customer for services in connection with the processing, handling, sale, or offering for sale of products unless the payment is made available on proportionally equal terms to all other customers competing in the resale of the products involved. As in the case of the brokerage provision, potential competitive injury is not an element of the offense, nor is the cost-justification defense available; but the meeting-of-competition defense does apply. This section applies to the payment of discriminatory advertising and promotional allowances.

> The Dalton Baking Company grants one retailer an allowance equal to one-half the cost of a newspaper advertisement placed in a local paper, promoting the sale of Dalton's bakery products. The supplier does not make a similar offer to another retailer who sells Dalton's bread in the same market area.

This is clearly a violation of Section 2(d) of the Clayton Act as amended by the Robinson-Patman Act. This provision of the act only applies if the customers involved are competing in the resale of the supplier's product in the market area where the sale of the product is being promoted. Moreover, a supplier need not promote his full line of products but may limit the allowance to selected items.

It is not essential that each retailer perform the same service, but an allowance plan may permit retailers to select from a variety of services to be performed with varying degrees of compensation. In the event that certain equivalent services cannot be performed by some competing retailers, the supplier must afford such customers alternative forms of promotional assistance of equal value, such as radio, newspaper, or television advertising.

It is the supplier's duty to ensure that the retailer performs the agreed-upon services; allowances granted for no services are the same as a price discount. Similarly, the retailer is obliged to perform the equivalent services called for and would himself be in violation if he does not.

Promotional services. Similar to the promotional allowances provisions, Section 2(e) of the Clayton Act as amended by the Robinson-Patman Act requires sellers to make their promotional services available on proportionally equal terms to competing customers. Promotional services include such activities as assistance in display arrangement, shelf-stocking, and demonstrator services.

Buyer liability. Section 2(f) of the Clayton Act as amended by the Robinson-Patman Act provides that it is unlawful for a customer (buyer for a food chain or wholesaler) knowingly to induce and receive an unlawful discrimination in price. The "knowledge" elements of the offense includes knowledge or reason to believe on the part of the buyer that the cost-justification and meeting-competition defenses may not be used by the seller.

Although the promotional-allowance and services sections speak only in terms of seller violation, the Federal Trade Commission has successfully used Section 5 of the Federal Trade Commission Act that follows to attack buyers who knowingly induce and receive disproportionate allowances.

The Packers and Stockyards Act of 1921.   In addition to the general antitrust laws, there are some laws that apply to specific industries that prohibit many of the practices condemned by the Sherman and Clayton

Acts. Among them is the Packers and Stockyards Act, administered by the Department of Agriculture, that prohibits meat and poultry packers from engaging in practices similar to those covered by the antitrust laws.

Statutes to Provide Benefits of Competition to the Consumer

One of the conditions of a competitive system is the full knowledge of market conditions by buyers and sellers. Some sellers, however, over-describe their merchandise in such a manner as to mislead buyers. Several federal statutes attempt to prevent this practice in interstate or foreign commerce.

The Federal Trade Commission Act of 1914 prohibits not only unfair methods of competition but unfair and deceptive acts and practices as well. False and misleading advertising and labeling practices are within the scope of this act. For example, a toothpaste is advertised as preventing cavities, when, in fact, it has no preventive power. This would be in clear violation of the Federal Trade Commission Act.

Unlike the common-law tort of deceit, a false or misleading practice can be committed even if the one making the representation did not intend to be misleading. Proof of actual deception need not be obtained if, in the Commission's judgment, the representation would tend to deceive the consumer. A material omission as well as an actual misrepresentation may constitute a deceptive practice under the Federal Trade Commission Act as it does under the common law. Familiar misrepresentations relate to the quality, performance, and price of the merchandise involved. They must be sufficiently material to warrant Commission action in the public interest.

> A tea is advertised as possessing a rich, deep appearance, which, in fact, it has. When the product is advertised on television, however, colored water is used to simulate the appearance of the tea. Is this in violation of the Federal Trade Commission Act?

Under the Federal Trade Commission Act this is not considered a deceptive practice because the advertising claims did not mislead the buying public about the quality or appearance of the tea.

> The Modern Drug Company ships Snake Oil Elixir in interstate commerce. It advertises it on national television as a cure for arthritis in humans. Each package contains a pamphlet giving directions for use and indicating the product's purported curative powers. The label attached to each bottle sets forth in addition to required information only the words "Snake Oil Elixir." The Snake Oil Elixir does not in fact cure arthritis in humans.

This is a violation of the Federal Trade Commission Act because the advertising is misleading and deceptive. Since 1938, however, the Food and Drug Administration has had primary jurisdiction over the labeling of food, drugs, and cosmetics; and the Federal Trade Commission has had primary jurisdiction over the advertising of these products. Thus, there is a dual violation, but prosecution would probably emanate from the Food and Drug Administration.

Unfair methods of competition, which include deceptive practices that injure a competitor or the consumer, are also illegal under the Federal Trade Commission Act. What constitutes deceptive practices depends upon the circumstances, but the Federal Trade Commission does issue rules from time to time that define illegal practices.

For example, in 1971 the Federal Trade Commission issued a rule that required that sufficient quantities of advertised food and grocery specials be available and accessible at the retail store level and that they be sold at advertised prices or less. Failure of any retailer to take the steps necessary to make reasonably certain that advertised specials are actually available at the advertised prices during the effective period of the advertisement could result in a charge of an unfair method of competition and/or an unfair or deceptive act or practice.

The jurisdictional reach of the Federal Trade Commission has recently been expanded by a Supreme Court decision. Known as the *S & H* case, which dealt with practices in the trading-stamp industry, the Supreme Court expanded the definition of the term *unfair* to trade practices that do not violate either the spirit or the letter of the antitrust laws. The court, in reaching its result, pointed out that the effect of a trade practice on *consumers* regardless of its impact on competition is a permissible area for FTC regulation. The Court concluded that the commission can act like a court of equity and weigh "public values beyond simply those enshrined in the letter or encompassed in the spirit of the antitrust laws." Thus, if a trade practice offends public policy or if it is immoral or if it causes substantial injury to consumers, then the Federal Trade Commission may prohibit the practice. It is too early to predict how the commission will choose to exercise its powers under the "unfairness doctrine." However, the commission is likely to scrutinize all unconscionable trade practices in addition to antitrust violations and deceptive practices.

Many states have enacted laws dealing with fair trade practices. These laws are intended to encourage and maintain fair competition and protect the consumer. In addition to the state fair trade laws mentioned previously, the state fair trade practice statutes often prescribe minimum markups or resale prices for some food and grocery products, most frequently such products as milk, alcoholic beverages, and tobacco products.

Packaging and Labeling. Federal and state laws include labeling requirements for food products, both fresh and processed. Normally, a food package must show on its label the name and address of the manufacturer or packer, the name of the food, the ingredients listed in descending order by weight, and the weight and measure or count of the package contents. The design of package display panels including the size, color, illustrations, and style of type used for presenting information is also controlled by federal and state laws. The Fair Packaging and Labeling Act of 1966 is the most recent federal legislation concerning the packaging and labeling of food products, and it prescribes mandatory labeling requirements along with voluntary standardization of package sizes. It supplements existing labeling requirements of the Food, Drug, and Cosmetic Act and the Federal Trade Commission Act.

The Perishable Agricultural Commodities Act of 1930. From time to time, special legislation to control deceptive practices in a particular industry or with respect to specific commodities has been enacted. Among these special laws is the Perishables Agricultural Commodities Act, which is intended to prevent unfair practices in the marketing of fresh and frozen fruits and vegetables. This act, which is administered by the Department of Agriculture, also provides for the licensing of brokers, dealers, and certain retailers who buy, sell, or handle fresh or frozen fruits and vegetables in interstate commerce.

Consumer Protection Developments[2]

In recent years, pressures have increased for regulations that go beyond the requirements of existing federal, state, and local laws that relate to food merchandising. These pressures are due to the increasing complexity of consumer decision-making in the marketplace, greater concern for nutrition and safety of the food supply, and the more effective organization of consumers in influencing both industry and government actions. As a result, the food industry and government agencies have responded with new practices and regulations to meet the demands of consumer protection, especially those that relate to providing the consumer with more complete information upon which to base buying decisions.

The consumer protection movement has generated legal innovations by the Federal Trade Commission, the Food and Drug Administration, the Congress, state legislatures, and local governments. In addition to these regulatory developments, the demand for consumer protection has led businessmen to voluntarily adopt practices responsive to consumers' interests. Hence, a significant element of competition today is the ability of stores to provide information to consumers—data upon which shoppers can make sound, logical decisions between Brand A and B and package X and package Y. Shoppers want and today are demanding information that is clear and reliable.

Among recent regulations and proposals affecting the retail food industry are unit pricing, open dating, nutritional labeling, and ingredient labeling. In a number of these areas, retailers have voluntarily entered the field. It is estimated that approximately 50 percent of the food industry now uses some form of unit pricing. Further, approximately two-thirds of the industry "open dates" some of their items, and at least one food processor is experimenting with nutritional labeling. In short, whether the impetus to incor-

[2]This and the following sections adapted from Barton J. Menitove, Esq., *Business Law, Study Guide* (Ithaca, N.Y.: Cornell University Home Study Program, 1973).

porate all or some of these developments stems from the desire to aid the consumer, meet competition, or comply with a statute, food retailers would be remiss if they did not understand these merchandising developments.

Unit Pricing. There has been much concern in recent years about the lack of standardization in food packaging and the difficulty that consumers face in making meaningful price comparisons. This concern on the part of legislators, individuals, and public and private agencies became intensified when the Fair Packaging and Labeling Act of 1966 (Truth in Packaging) failed to bring about an appreciable increase in standardization of food packaging.

As a result of this concern, legislation was enacted in Massachusetts that went into effect in January, 1971, requiring the marking or posting of the total price and the price per unit for specified food and nonfood products sold at retail.[3] The intent of the legislation is to enable consumers to make price comparisons among brands and sizes of commodities sold in retail food stores based upon standard units of weight or measure. The legislation requires a dual pricing system that includes the posting or marking of both a total price per package and a unit price. Similar legislation subsequently was enacted in Connecticut, Maryland, Rhode Island, Vermont, and the City of New York and is under consideration in several other states as well as in the U.S. Congress.

In addition to legislated unit pricing, more than 100 food chains were voluntarily unit pricing some products in 1972, according to the National Association of Food Chains. Some independent food stores were also unit pricing, although there is no indication of the number of stores involved.

The Massachusetts law, which is similar to the laws in other states and in New York City, requires that an orange stamp, tag, or label be used on the item or on the shelf directly under or over the item to designate the unit price to the nearest full cent if the price is over $1.00, or to the nearest one-tenth of one cent if the price per unit is less than $1.00. If the packaged commodity is not conspicuously visible to the consumer, such as frozen-food items in a chest-type display case, then the unit price may be indicated on a list placed near the point of purchase. The law specifies a minimum size of type for the unit price.

The unit price must be expressed as price per pound, pint, quart or gallon, 50 feet or square feet, or per 100 units depending upon the type of commodity and the customary method of expressing quantity. More than 4,500 commodities are included under the regulations, and many retailers provide unit price information for commodities not included in the regulations.

Massachusetts has had a law since 1960 that requires the identification of the price per pound and total selling price for packaged meat, poultry,

---

[3]Unit Pricing Law, Chapter 885, Acts of 1970, Commonwealth of Massachusetts General Laws, Chapter 38.

and fish sold at retail, and, therefore, these commodities were not included in the list of commodities subject to unit pricing under the 1970 legislation.[4]

Figure 9-1 illustrates a shelf tag used to indicate the unit price, total selling price, item description, and code and number of facings. The item description and code and number of facings are for inventory control purposes and are not required for consumer information.

FIGURE 9-1   Retail shelf tag showing unit price, total selling price, and merchandising information.

The nature of food and grocery products, packaging requirements, and the efforts of manufacturers to gain a competitive edge have contributed to a growing abundance of sizes and shapes of packages. The variety of choices has created display and inventory problems for retailers as well as value comparison difficulties for the consumer.

It should be possible for the consumer to make value judgments based, at least in part, upon the cost per standard unit of measure of each item. Standardization of packages would be one way of enabling consumers to make unit cost comparisons quickly and easily. If all merchandise were packaged in standard sizes such as pounds, quarts, and square feet or multiples and fractions thereof, the comparison of unit prices would be relatively simple depending upon how many sizes were available. However, this kind of standardization poses a real problem where products differ substantially in composition, density, or yield such as breakfast cereals, baking mixes, and dry detergents. However, for commodities where product characteristics are similar, a substantial number of odd sizes could be eliminated, particularly when they serve no real purpose except to gain additional shelf space or make it difficult for the consumer to make unit price comparisons both within and among brands. Until greater standardization is achieved in the packaging of food and grocery products, unit pricing appears to be the most practical means for enabling consumers to make meaningful price and value comparisons quickly and easily.

Although lowest price per standard unit of measure is not necessarily the best value because of personal tastes and preferences, quality, conveni-

---

[4]Section 181, Chapter 261 of the Acts of 1939, Commonwealth of Massachusetts General Laws, Chapter 94.

ence and brand confidence factors, unit pricing enables the consumer to make a better informed decision concerning relative values. In the long run, informed consumer choice contributes to a more efficient marketing system. It is also likely that unit pricing might lead to the elimination of some package sizes, which will contribute to a more efficient marketing system.

From the retailer's point of view, unit pricing is consistent with providing maximum value to the customer, since the customer needs full and complete information about product cost and quality in order to obtain the greatest possible value for her dollar.

The critical question regarding unit pricing concerns the costs compared with the benefits. Both are difficult to evaluate. The cost depends primarily upon the method of marking or posting the unit prices in the retail store. Consumer benefits depend upon the savings available and the extent of the consumer use of unit prices in making buying decisions. A study conducted in Toledo, Ohio, showed that the cost of implementing and maintaining a shelf tag unit pricing system is mostly fixed so that the cost per dollar of sales depends upon the sales volume of the store, and the number of stores served by the chain or affiliated distribution center.[5] The larger the sales volume per store and the greater the number of stores supplied by the distribution center, the lower the cost per dollar of sales.

The estimated cost of unit pricing for the entire retail industry was 0.59 percent of sales. The estimated average cost for stores with annual sales over $500,000 annually was 0.17 percent of sales, and these stores account for 76 percent of food store sales. The average cost estimate of 0.17 percent for larger stores is about one-tenth the cost of trading stamps according to the McCullough-Padberg study. The cost of unit pricing may be more or less than the estimates in this study depending upon the method used and the number of items included. If unit pricing is required through legislation, there is also an enforcement cost which must be considered.

The benefits of unit pricing are difficult to measure, especially over a short period of time. The McCullough-Padberg study indicated there were no significant shifts in consumer purchasing patterns for 326 items as a result of unit pricing but there were some tendencies for consumers to shift purchases within some individual product families. These results were based upon a sixteen-week test period in eight food stores.

Interviews of 1,600 customers in the McCullough-Padberg study showed that 769 or 48.5 percent saw and understood the unit price labels. Of the 769 shoppers who saw and understood the labels, 469 (64.2 percent of 769) indicated that the labels had been of use to them in their shopping.

Neither analysis of product sales or consumer interviews are likely to give fully satisfactory answers as to the usefulness of unit pricing to consumers. The use of unit pricing in making buying decisions may not

---

[5]T. David McCullough and Daniel I. Padberg, "Unit Pricing in Supermarkets, Alternatives, Costs, and Consumer Reaction," *Search,* Cornell University Agricultural Experiment Station, Ithaca, N.Y., Vol. 1, No. 6 (January 1971).

be reflected in changed buying patterns. For example, consumers may continue to buy their favorite brand or size of product even though it costs more per unit. The unit price may actually reinforce consumer preferences if the differences in unit prices between the favorite brand or size and alternative choices are the same or less than the consumer had believed. Interviews are not likely to give a complete appraisal of the usefulness of unit pricing to consumers, especially until it has been in effect for a longer period of time so that the awareness and understanding are greater. A uniform method of presenting unit prices along with an educational effort, especially among low-income consumers, are likely to increase consumer awareness and understanding. The use of unit pricing by consumers is likely to increase as awareness and understanding improve, but even the proportion of shoppers who use unit pricing in making buying decisions is only one indication of benefit. The extent to which unit pricing helps consumers to achieve their needs and preferences (value sets) at the lowest cost is the true test of the benefits received and this is difficult to measure.

Imperfect as the measurements of costs and benefits may be, however, retail food firms and government agencies should consider both in deciding whether to implement unit pricing on either a voluntary or compulsory basis.

Open dating. Another practice that will continue to increase in usage, both on a voluntary and mandatory basis, is the open dating of many food products. The phrase open dating generally refers to any date on a packaged food product that can be read and understood by the shopper. The date may be shown alpha-numerically, FEB 23, or in numbers only, 2-23, or 0223. It may or may not include the year.[6]

The main purpose of open dating is to provide the consumer with information concerning the freshness of food products at the point of sale. The date on the package may represent the *pack date,* the *pull date,* the *quality assurance date,* the *expiration date* or the *display date.*

The *pack date* refers to the date of manufacture or processing or final packaging. The *pull date* indicates the last day that product may be offered for sale in a retail store. The pull date is designed to allow the consumer a reasonable amount of time to store and use the product at home even if she bought it on the pull date. The *quality assurance date* indicates the date beyond which the product will not be of the same quality as when it left the processing plant. The *expiration date* generally means "do not use after the date shown" and indicates that the quality is likely to be unacceptable beyond that date. The *display date* refers to the date on which the product was placed on display, or first offered for sale in the retail store.[7]

---

[6]"Unit Pricing and Open Dating Today and Tomorrow," a talk by Eileen F. Taylor, Marketing Economics Division, Economic Research Service, United States Department of Agriculture, at the 1972 National Agricultural Outlook Conference, Washington, D.C., February 23, 1972.

[7]"Unit Pricing and Open Dating Today and Tomorrow."

Until recently, nearly all processed food products were coded, either by the manufacturer or retailer, and the codes usually included information like the plant location, the production shift, and perhaps the date and time that the item was produced, the pull date, or the expiration date. The codes involve the ingenious use of letters, numbers, symbols or some combination thereof. Sometimes a color system is used or a key word or phrase is the basis for the code. The codes are often complicated, although some manufacturers and distributors use a relatively simple code such as a numerical pull date. Codes vary widely among manufacturers and distributors so that it would be practically impossible for the consumer to translate many of them readily even with the assistance of a code book that provided the keys for code translations.

Since 1970, many food retailers have been dating highly perishable items including bakery products, milk and other dairy products, and fresh hamburger. A few manufacturers are moving in the direction of open dating processed foods.

The use of open dating as a guide to quality has some serious limitations. The length of time that a product retains its original level of quality or even an acceptable level of quality can be estimated reasonably accurately only if the conditions of handling and storage are known. The use of pull, quality assurance, or expiration dates are based upon the assumption that the product will be handled properly. Many factors influence the quality of foods and time is only one of them. Temperature is a primary factor and time is subordinate to temperature.[8] Thus, dating may or may not indicate freshness and quality depending upon the handling, storage, and display conditions.

Another problem associated with the use of open dating is the interpretation of the dates by consumers. A study of 1,700 female shoppers in 18 food stores in Chicago showed that shoppers' interpretations of the dates varied widely. Only 20 percent of those interviewed correctly interpreted the pull date. The study also indicated that more than half the shoppers were aware of the open dating program and that the in-store effects were generally favorable.[9]

Another problem concerns the storage and handling of food products in the home. Pull dates allow for a "reasonable" amount of time to store and use the product at home. However, the amount of time that the product is kept in the home before use, and the temperature of home storage may vary widely among consumers. Expiration and quality assurance dates must also be based upon assumed or ideal temperature conditions which may not exist in many homes.

Another concern is the possibility of higher operating costs and, consequently, higher food prices as a result of open dating, due to implementation

---

[8] *Food Stability Survey,* Volume 1, Rutgers University in cooperation with the Economic Research Service, United States Department of Agriculture, February 1971.

[9] *A Case Study of Food Dating in Selected Chicago Supermarkets,* Marketing Research Report No. 943, Economic Research Service, United States Department of Agriculture, Washington, D.C., November 1971.

costs and greater product losses from more selective buying by consumers. Preliminary findings of a study in Ohio showed that the introduction of open dating did not increase loss in the test stores and, in fact, decreased product losses possibly because of more efficient practices encouraged by the open dating experiment.[10]

Food Labeling. The Food and Drug Administration of the Department of Health, Education and Welfare published a new 12-part program in 1973 that established far-reaching changes in the labeling of foods. FDA directed its attention to food nutritional claims including fat and cholesterol content, calories, vitamins, proteins, minerals, and "imitation foods." The FDA standard is essentially voluntary. But once manufacturers assert "fortified" or "nutritional" claims on food packages, the FDA regulations, which require uniform labeling in conformance with the specific requirements of the regulations, are triggered.[11]

The reason underlying nutritional labeling is to furnish consumers with reliable information on nutritional values. Thus, not unlike open dating and unit pricing, information dissemination is the rationale for requiring nutritional labeling. The FDA regulation is aimed at providing consumers with basic nutritional data for certain classes of foods. For example, low calorie or dietetic foods fall within the FDA regulation. Criticism has been directed at some dietetic foods that contained low nutritional value or that provided relatively high caloric content. The consumer had no basis for intelligently comparing such items.

The FDA regulations are essentially voluntary—that is, only if a producer chooses to assert nutritional information or "fortified" claims are the FDA standards invoked. Greater controversy surrounds mandatory nutritional labeling for all foods as opposed to those that assert nutritional claims. Proponents of full labeling argue that consumers should be provided with nutritional information on all food labels. At the present time, no statute or regulation requires full nutritional labeling.

The FDA regulations change the old Minimum Daily Requirement to a new standard—U.S. Recommended Daily Allowances (U.S. RDA). Other changes include listing of seven minerals and vitamins, protein-content labels, cholesterol labeling, and specialty dietary-use statements. Figure 9-2 is an example of the standard format required if a product is fortified or if a nutritional claim is made.

Nutritional labeling represents another innovative development in consumer protection. It remains to be seen how consumers will utilize this information.

Percentage ingredient labeling, which would require food marketers to list the percentage of at least each major ingredient on the package, bottle, or can, is currently under active consideration at the Food and Drug Administration. The purpose of ingredient labeling is to inform shoppers

---

[10]"Unit Pricing and Open Dating Today and Tomorrow."

[11]*Federal Register,* Department of Health, Education and Welfare, Food and Drug Administration, Volume 38, Number 13, Part 3, Washington, D.C., Friday, January 19, 1973.

FIGURE 9-2   Nutritional Information (Beef Pot Pie) Contains
One 8 oz. Serving

Calories	560
Protein	23 gram
Carbohydrate	43 gram
Fat (53% of calories)	33 gram
Fatty acids:	
saturated	9 gram
polyunsaturated	22 gram
other	2 gram
Cholesterol (18 mg/100 gm)	40 mg
Sodium (365 mg/100 gm)	810 gram

Percentage of U.S. Recommended
Daily
Allowable (U.S. RDA)

protein	35	riboflavin	15
vitamin A	35	niacin	25
vitamin C	10	calcium	2
thiamin	15	iron	25

Source: Food and Drug Administration

of the true contents of packaged foods. For example, producers of beef pies would be required to disclose the percent of beef, peas, carrots, water, and so on, on the package.

Conflicting State and Federal Laws.   Problems have arisen because adjoining states have adopted different consumer protection standards on the same matter. For example, if state X requires that all unit prices be printed in cents per pound and state Y requires cents per ounce labeling, then retailers that operate in both states must comply with two different standards. Even minor deviations enacted in different jurisdictions may lead to burdensome problems for retailers.

The ultimate response to multiple conflicting state legislation is for the federal government to enact legislation that supercedes the states' actions. This approach has its roots in the Supremacy Clause of the Constitution, which raises federal law above the states. But state statutes and regulations are not lightly overruled even in the face of federal legislation covering the same field. This is particularly true with respect to legislation involving health and safety standards (the police power) including consumer protection, which has constitutionally and traditionally been reserved to the states. Thus, as a general rule, state laws are not superseded by federal laws unless there is a clear Congressional intent to preempt the state law.

Franchising

Franchising has steadily grown in recent years. Fast-food outlets have perhaps shown the greatest growth. But franchising has proliferated in other retailing fields as well, including convenience food stores. Usually, the franchisor provides a trademark, advertising, often building plans, and a product. In conjunction with these benefits, the franchisee receives management support, experience, and instant recognition.

However, the franchisee usually gives up a good deal of freedom in entering a franchise agreement. For example, franchisors have obtained clauses in these agreements that require the franchisee to purchase equipment, packaging products, and product supply as a condition of obtaining a trademark license.

Other limitations on the franchise may include agreements to purchase solely from the franchisor, agreements to operate certain hours, or agreements specifying the number of employees. In addition, the franchisor usually may terminate dealership of franchise annually or at other intervals notwithstanding the diligent work and investment of the franchisee. These provisions have been scrutinized under the antitrust laws. Generally, most dealership agreements have been upheld as reasonable. But, tying arrangements operate whereby one product may not be purchased unless another less-desirable product is also purchased. In *Siegel v Chicken Delight, Inc.,* 448 F. 2d (9th Cir., 1971,) the Ninth Circuit Court of Appeals found that the trademark and franchise license of Chicken Delight were separate products and distinct from the packaging, mixes, and equipment sold by the franchisor. The court held that the Chicken Delight franchise agreement, which required franchisees to purchase Chicken Delight products, constituted an illegal tying arrangement. Thus, if Alpha Food Stores gives a license to another food store to use the Alpha name, the franchisee cannot be required to purchase solely Alpha products.

The Federal Trade Commission is presently undergoing a review of franchising practices. The Commission is acting in response to numerous complaints of alleged misrepresentation by franchisors including promotional materials and selling practices. The proposed trade regulation rule would require franchisors to disclose certain financial information and detailed information concerning terms and conditions of franchise agreements and data.

Franchising in food retailing and elsewhere will undoubtedly continue to grow. But, franchisees should carefully study the agreements that they enter in order to avoid or at least understand potential pitfalls.

COOPERATIVE PURCHASING AND SELLING

Smaller food chains and independents by virtue of their size have generally been unable to market private-label items alone. By joint or cooperative purchasing, however, such supermarkets have been able to create their own private brands to compete with the larger chains.

The Supreme Court focused on the selling practices of such a group of affiliated food retailers in *U.S. v. Topco Associates, Inc.,* 405 U.S. 596 (1972). The court held that it was an illegal restraint of trade to allocate territories among association members even if competition between the large national and regional chains and the smaller chains and independents was enhanced by the Topco program. Topco Associates was a cooperative association wholly owned by 25 small and medium-size grocery chains.

Topco, which served as a purchasing agent for its members, did not manufacture, produce, or warehouse goods. Products purchased by Topco were shipped directly to its members from manufacturers or wholesalers. The Topco program was designed to offer a strong private label to small and medium-size chains in order to compete better with the private labels of national and regional chains. The bylaws of the association contained licensing provisions whereby each member was assigned a specific exclusive sales territory. Members eliminated, in effect, brand competition among members of the association.

The Justice Department sought an injunction against Topco and its members, charging a violation of the Sherman Act. The lower court ruled against the government and found that any intrabrand anticompetitive effects were outweighed by the procompetitive effects, which were generated by competition with the larger national chains. The lower court emphasized the benefits of an alternative label available to consumers, the increased ability of smaller chains and independents to compete with large national chains, and benefits to small producers who serviced the Topco system. The Supreme Court, in rejecting this analysis, pointed out that even if the Topco plan was intended to increase competition, allocation of retail markets constituted a horizontal restraint of trade and furthermore violated Section 1 of the Sherman Act. The Supreme Court refused to inquire into the competitive impact of the Topco program because division of markets by competitors represents an illegal practice regardless of its overall effect on competition.

The Topco decision is significant from the standpoint of small chains, independent grocers, and cooperatives. It is clear that today cooperative associations may jointly market private-label products so long as members are free to resell such products as they choose.

SUMMARY

Food merchandising is conducted within a framework of federal, state, and local rules and regulations. The basic intent of the regulations is to facilitate orderly business transactions, protect public health and safety, and to insure that consumers receive the full benefits of competition. Many regulations protect not only the consumer, but legitimate business firms as well.

The intent of government regulations is implemented through regulations that control the processing, handling, packaging, labeling, advertising, and business practices utilized in buying and selling food and grocery products.

The role of government in food merchandising is taking on increased importance, especially with respect to the amount and kind of information that must be provided on food packages or at the point of sale. As government activity in the merchandising process grows, the question of just how far government should go in protecting consumer interests will be more of an issue. It is a difficult question to resolve because of the extreme difficulty in measuring both the costs and benefits of a particular piece of legislation to the consumer.

However, the expanding role of government in food merchandising is a fact of life that must be recognized, and those engaged in the merchandising process will have to understand and adapt to the new "rules of the game."

It also seems clear that food retailers and others concerned with food merchandising must become involved in the political process in order that the role of government represent the best interests of consumers.

10

Merchandising Trends and the Future

THE CONDITIONS OF CHANGE

Truly remarkable changes have taken place in food merchandising during the past 50 years in the United States. Today's consumer has a choice of thousands of items that were not even available 50 years ago, and many of these items are in the form of partly or completely prepared dishes.

Foods are attractively packaged in materials that protect appearance and quality. Most highly perishable foods are now available during most of the year or all year instead of only during a short season. Citrus fruit, strawberries, and watermelons are examples of foods that have become available on nearly a year-round basis.

A wide selection of frozen foods is now commonplace, whereas 25 years ago few if any frozen foods were available to most consumers.

Certainly one of the most important developments in food merchandising during the last 50 years was self-service retailing as introduced and developed by the supermarket. Self-service made a wider variety of products available to the consumer at lower cost, and it revolutionized existing methods and concepts of merchandising, including packaging, pricing, and presentation of product.

Self-service retailing and the changes in food distribution methods that it encompassed were primarily a response to the changing economic and social conditions that were brought about by the advancing state of technology. The conditions that led to the development of the self-service supermarket included the following:

1. Urbanization of the population
2. An economic depression
3. The mass-produced automobile
4. Modern processing and packaging
5. Low-cost commercial and home refrigeration

The lower prices offered by the self-service supermarkets in comparison with the small, neighborhood stores were especially effective in building consumer acceptance because of the economic conditions that prevailed during the early 1930s when the first supermarkets were opened. Consumers were attracted by lower prices due to the extreme hardship brought about by the depressed economic conditions.

However, in order for the supermarket to offer lower prices than existing neighborhood stores, relatively high weekly sales volumes were required. This meant that the trading area of the supermarket had to be extended beyond the neighborhood boundaries. The social and technological conditions of the times were such that larger, more densely populated trading areas were prevalent because of the movement of a growing population from rural areas to the city and because the automobile provided a practical and convenient means for consumers to travel greater distances to do their shopping. The widespread availability of refrigeration made it possible for the supermarket to offer a wider selection of perishable merchandise and enabled the consumer to purchase food less frequently and store it for longer periods in the home.

At the same time, improved processing and packaging methods made it possible to display processed foods and eliminate the need for clerks to package and weigh the product. The customer could make his own selections, and by performing this service obtain his food needs at lower cost than in a clerk-service neighborhood store.

Thus, the development of the self-service supermarket was largerly a reflection of the social, economic, and technological conditions that prevailed. In order to identify important developments that are likely to occur in food merchandising during the next 50 years, it is first necessary to project social, economic, and technological changes and then relate those changes to food merchandising.

POPULATION CHARACTERISTICS[1]

Of primary importance in shaping food merchandising in the future are consumers—how many will there be, where and how will they live, what level of education will they achieve, where will they work, and what income will they have? If these questions can be answered, it will provide a basis for estimating consumer needs and preferences with respect to food and food-shopping facilities and indicate what changes might be expected in food merchandising.

Population Size and Composition

The population of the United States has been growing steadily during the

---

[1]The projections in this section are based upon information from *200 Million Americans,* United States Department of Commerce, Washington, D.C., November 1967.

last 50 years, but the rate of growth has been declining since 1960 due to a lower birth rate. However, by about 1975 a rise in the birth rate is anticipated because there will be more women in the fruitful 20 to 24 age group—those who were born during the "baby boom" of the early 1950s.

It is a foregone conclusion that the population will increase during the next 50 years, now it is simply a question of how great the increase will be. Table 10-1 includes population estimates based upon four fertility or birth rates. The *Series B* fertility rate is only slightly above the average number of children expected by young married women as determined by national surveys, and would result in a population by the year 2020 that would be more than double the population of 1970.

TABLE 10-1   Projections of Total Population in the United States, 1975 to 2020
Based upon Four Fertility Rates [a]

Year	Fertility Rates			
	Series B	Series C	Series D	Series E
	(population in thousands)			
1970	205,456	205,357	205,167	205,070
1975	219,101	217,557	215,588	214,735
1980	236,797	232,412	227,510	225,510
1985	256,980	249,248	240,925	236,918
1990	277,286	266,319	254,720	247,726
1995	297,884	283,180	267,951	257,345
2000	320,780	300,789	280,740	266,281
2005	347,073	320,055	293,751	275,066
2010	376,249	341,033	307,436	283,711
2015	407,379	363,191	321,683	291,893
2020	440,253	385,959	335,869	299,177

[a] *Assumed fertility rates for Series B, C, D and E are 3.10, 2.78, 2.45, and 2.11, respectively. The fertility rate is an estimate of the average number of children that women will bear during their life time.*

Source: "Population Estimates and Projections," *Current Population Reports*, Series P-25, No. 448, August 1970, United States Department of Commerce, Bureau of the Census.

On the low side, some demographers believe that the birth rate could drop to the replacement rate of 2.11 assumed for *Series E*, or below, in view of the current concern with population growth and its effect on the environment and changes in the state laws on abortion.

Estimates *C* and *D* are based upon fertility rates that are less than the rate indicated by surveys of young married women but greater than the replacement birth rate that would eventually stabilize the population.

Regardless of the exact rate of population growth, there are going to be many more consumers in the next 50 years who will place increased demands on the food distribution system.

In terms of shaping food merchandising in the future, the number of consumers is probably less important than the composition and life styles of the population, which influence needs and preferences for food and food-shopping facilities.

A relatively large increase in the 20 to 34 age group is being experienced between 1966 and 1975. By 1975, the 20 to 24 age group will increase by 37 percent, the 25 to 29 age group will increase by 50 percent, and the 30 to 34 group will undergo a 27 percent increase. In conjunction with the increasing total population and composition by age groups, the marriage rate is increasing after a post-1950 slowdown. The marriage rate will continue to rise and will show a sharper increase beginning in 1975 and continuing into the 1980s as the ratio of men to women in the most marriageable ages increases. This will mean an increase in the number of young married couples and new families.

Urbanization and Housing

The American people are metropolitan dwellers. Two out of every three of us now live in a metropolitan area, and between 70 and 75 percent of the population will live in or around the cities by 1975 to 1980.

The metropolitan suburbs are growing five times as fast as the central cities. Many people leave the central cities for the suburbs so that many central cities are shrinking. The bulk of the people moving out of central cities into the suburbs are white; the bulk of people moving into the central cities are nonwhites.

It appears that the central city of the metropolitan area will be inhabited by low-income families to an increasing extent. Today, one-half of U.S. blacks live in central cities, among them many disadvantaged. This situation poses a real challenge for food merchandisers in the future if we are to provide an adequate selection of food, services, and shopping facilities to low-income consumers at prices that are no greater or even less than those paid by more affluent citizens.

In addition to a liking for metropolitan areas, Americans have a definite preference for the seacoasts—the Atlantic, the Pacific, and the Gulf—and the southern shores of the Great Lakes. As the population tends to become concentrated more and more into these areas, small communities will be swallowed up into a megalopolis, which is one vast metropolis extending over a relatively large geographical area. One such megalopolis extends from Boston down the eastern seaboard to Washington, D.C. Other megalopolis areas will include the Pittsburgh to Milwaukee industrial empire and the San Francisco to Los Angeles belt.[2]

A rapid upgrading of houses and apartments has been going on during the last 25 years and will continue into the future. In 1967, over 90 percent of our housing offered satisfactory and reasonably up-to-date living accommodations. More than 62 percent of occupied homes were lived in by their owners in 1967 compared to only 44 percent of occupied houses in 1942.[3]

Household formation will increase at the rate of about one million a year well into the 1980s. By about 1985, there will be 82 to 83 million

---

[2]*200 Million Americans*, pp. 25-26.
[3]*200 Million Americans*, pp. 37-38.

U.S. households—there were 59 million in 1965. The average household size will be smaller, however, due to separate housing for more of our older citizens who will no longer live "doubled up" with newly married couples or with their children.[4]

Education, Employment, and Income

We are rapidly becoming a better-educated people as indicated by the fact that a higher proportion of the population is staying in school longer, and this trend will continue according to the Bureau of Census projections. By 1985, two-thirds those over 25 will have completed high school compared to about one-half of those over 25 in 1967. There will be a 40 percent increase in college enrollment by 1975, and in the ten-year period ending in 1975, more doctor's and master's degrees will have been granted than during the preceding 50 years.[5]

Our technological economy is resulting in an increasing need for more highly skilled workers, especially white-collar workers. The future will probably see a continuation of the shift of workers from production lines to service occupations. The demand for many technicians will rise swiftly because the demand for such people as physicians and dentists cannot be filled; more things will be turned over to paraprofessionals to free the professionals for work that they alone can perform.

The big growth in government employment will be largely in state and local governments, resulting from expanding services such as education, police, and fire protection.

Older workers, especially men, are retiring earlier, and together with the trend toward a shorter work week, an increasing proportion of the population will be realizing more leisure time. The recreation business, which already is booming, will grow even more, offering both business and job opportunities.

Another important trend is the increase in the number of women working. Over 40 percent of the women in the country are now in the work force.

The real income or purchasing power of most American families has increased dramatically during the last 20 years and will continue to increase. Although we will still have the problem of upgrading the incomes of families below the poverty income level, the proportion of families achieving middle income status will increase.

Family incomes and purchasing power will increase primarily because of the general growth and expansion of the economy and the probability that more family members will be working. Advances in technology and a more highly educated population will contribute to an increase in productivity and an unprecedented level of living for most Americans.

---

[4] *200 Million Americans*, pp. 41-42.
[5] *200 Million Americans*, pp. 56, 75.

Consumer Needs and Preferences

What are the implications of the economic and social changes that we can anticipate during the next 50 years? The changes in food merchandising will depend primarily upon how the needs and preferences of consumers are influenced by the changing economic and social environment.

The consumer of the future will be highly urbanized, well educated, more affluent, and more discriminating. The life style wll encompass a higher proportion of married women either in the labor force or involved in activities outside the home and more leisure time in which families can travel and participate in other recreational activities.

Consumers will desire more convenience in both obtaining and preparing food without sacrificing quality, and they will be less tolerant of advertising, packaging, and labeling that is misleading or in poor taste.

What then, specifically, are some of the important developments that we can expect in food merchandising in the future?

FOOD PRODUCTS

There are likely to be some important changes in the types of food products marketed in order to meet the demand of the consumer for nutritious, tasty meals that offer greater convenience in preparation. The housewife of the future is likely to think more in terms of purchasing complete meals that are either fully or partially prepared but that satisfy the nutritional needs as well as the tastes and preferences of the family.

The prepared foods of the future will be ready-to-cook or ready-to-serve and will lend themselves to variety and individuality. One professor visualizes it as follows:

> The housewife of 2000 A.D. will have available to her a complete line of fresh items, condiments and specialty items in addition to completely prepared meals. Individuality of expression may indeed be enhanced due to improvement in the quality of meal components and condiments and to concentration of creativity on a few meals instead of all meals.[6]

He believes that the desire for convenience will result in housewives utilizing ready-to-serve meals most of the time but devoting more time and effort to the occasional creation of more original meals. Even the ready-to-serve meals, however, will provide the consumer with opportunities for more variety and originality than the standard TV dinner through the use of special seasonings and meal components that can be combined in different ways.

In addition to supplying the components for the home preparation of original meals, the supermarket may cash in on the opportunity provided

---

[6]*The Food Industry–2000 A.D.*, Mimeographed paper by Jarvis L. Cain, Associate Professor of Agricultural Economics, University of Maryland, College Park, Maryland.

by the \$44.1 billion away-from-home food business, which is growing at an estimated 8 to 10 percent yearly. Latest estimates are that the American consumer eats out or carries away nearly one out of three meals, and that figure might reach one out of two between 1975 and 1980. Large supermarket chains like Acme, Jewel Food Stores, Grand Union, and Schnuck's have been operating successfully in the food service area. Food services have also been made available to the public through wholesaler-sponsored independent stores served by Super-Valu in Minnesota, Wisconsin, and Ohio, and the wide array of deli modules in stores operated by Foodland-Clover Farm franchisees.[7]

Fresh fruits, vegetables and meats will become more highly standardized and selling by brand will become more common especially for fresh fruits and vegetables, which will be produced, packaged, and marketed by fewer, more highly integrated organizations that will control quality in order to build brand acceptance. "Perdue" chickens and "Chiquita" bananas, lettuce, and other vegetables are examples of this trend.

Centralized cutting and packaging along with better control of temperature and sanitation will result in more uniform and higher quality fresh meats. The Stop and Shop meat-cutting and distribution facility in Marlborough, Massachusetts, may well be the prototype of future meat operations. This plant, opened in 1972, employs the latest methods and equipment for controlling the quality and uniformity of fresh beef from the time it is received in carcass form until it is shipped to retail stores. Because of improved technology and for economic considerations, an increasing quantity of of meat may be merchandised as boneless, trimmed, uniform frozen portions if adequate consumer acceptance can be achieved.

RETAIL MERCHANDISING METHODS

Food merchandising is likely to undergo some fundamental changes in the future in order to meet the changes in consumer demand shaped by the economic and social environment. The changes in food merchandising will also reflect the new technology.

First of all, the extensive use of land required for the present-day food store and parking area will become more prohibitive, especially in high-density population areas. Second, there will be less of a need and desire on the part of consumers to buy all their food on a personal inspection basis. As products become more highly standardized, a greater degree of uniformity and consistency of quality will be achieved so that the consumer will be much less inclined to inspect each item before making a buying decision. Third, many consumers, especially the working women, will regard the weekly shopping trip to a large food store in order to select each item

---

[7] "Prepared Foods Served In-store or at Home," *Chain Store Age Supermarket Headquarters Edition*, March 1973, pp. 91-95.

from display an inconvenience and will be increasingly responsive to new food retailing methods that are more convenient.

One group of researchers visualizes the evolution of the "super store" that is aimed at serving the consumer's total needs for all types of routine purchases, including those now served by the supermarket and an extensive range of other products and services. The concept of the super store will be enhanced by increasing problems in achieving growth and profits due to restrictive public policies and government regulations that affect food retailing costs. The super stores are visualized as offering a broader nonfood assortment than the conventional supermarket offers by utilizing a selling space on the order of 30,000 square feet. Foods and nonfoods will be integrated in the building layout. Consumers will want the ever-expanding variety of products and services in both foods and nonfoods as their education and income levels rise. As incomes rise, a wider and wider range of products and services will be regarded as "routine purchases." The super-store concept will provide for convenient, one-stop shopping for a wide range of routine shopping needs.[8]

Another researcher also believes that the supermarket as we know it today will not be adequate to serve the needs of tomorrow's consumer and will be replaced by the "ultramarket." He provides the following description of the ultramarket:

> While it is hard to define the ultramarket precisely, we may begin by identifying some things it is not. *It is not a shopping place* as a supermarket was, involving a parking lot, where people go to buy food. We do not have the space in the urban high density setting to accommodate this. The cost of space for moving that many automobiles through any arrangement is prohibitive. *It is not a self-service operation.* The present food retailing arrangement involves assembling tons and tons of food which must be heated, cooled, graded, cleaned and financed—simply to stimulate purchase decisions. We must find a way to make the purchase decision independent of physical goods handling. Until this is done neither of these functions can be automated.[9]

He also visualizes that the ultramarket will involve the delivery of the consumers' purchases from distribution points where orders will be assembled from ordering points. He assumes that purchase decisions will be made where people are, perhaps in office and apartment buildings, while the order-filling or goods-handling functions will occur where the products and delivery trucks are located.

Although it appears that changes in food merchandising methods along the lines suggested by Padberg are likely, it is unclear at this point as to when they will occur and precisely what they will be. The possibilities

---

[8]Walter J. Salmon and others, *The Super-Store–Strategic Implications for the Seventies* (New York: Family Circle Magazine, 1972), pp. 2-21.

[9]Daniel I. Padberg, "Food Retailing Beyond the Supermarket," *Journal of Food Distribution Research,* Proceedings Issue, Vol. 1, No. 1 (1970).

are many. Shopping from a catalog and placing orders by mail or telephone with once- or twice-a-week delivery to the home or a central pickup point is one possibility. The use of closed-circuit or cable television as a means for in-home viewing of the selection of merchandise offers interesting possibilities. This might be an effective method for providing the prospective customer with a look at specials, new items, and highly perishable items that would not otherwise be possible when shopping at home. The combination of telephone and television into a videophone arrangement is already in limited use and may soon be available to consumers at a reasonable cost. This arrangement would make it possible for the consumer to simultaneously view and order merchandise in the comfort of home or apartment.

The availability of closed-circuit television and videophones also offers some exciting possibilities with respect to consumer education in the selection, handling and preparation of food. The consumer could submit inquiries via telephone and, with the assistance of computers, receive audio-visual replies concerning an endless variety of topics, including recipes, nutrition, product characteristics, cooking and serving, storage, tips on selection, and quantities required. The replies could be tailored to meet the needs of the consumer with respect to size of family, food budget, and tastes and preferences. The use of computers in preparing shopping lists for individual families based upon tastes and preferences, nutrition requirements, and budget limitations is already being tested.

Along with changes in merchandising methods, the use of credit will very likely become as commonplace in buying food as it is and will be in other retail fields. It will be much more convenient to use credit, especially if home delivery or pickup points are involved. Also, the use of credit practically eliminates the possibility of loss of cash through theft, both for the consumer and the retailer. The credit arrangement will probably involve the conventional credit card or instantaneous adjustment of checking accounts upon validation by customer identification card or code number.

The "cashless society" may be closer than most realize. A cashless system was tested in a well-to-do suburb of Columbus, Ohio, in 1972 by The City National Bank and Trust Company (of Columbus). The retailer bank-card credit sales are electronically cleared through the bank's computer credit-card file using a point-of-sale terminal on-line to the computer. At day's end, credit sales are electronically credited directly to the merchant's bank account. The test was so successful that only about 1 percent of the transactions and only 2.8 percent of total sales were declined. Based upon these test results, the system is being extended to include 60 stores in Columbus.[10]

Regardless of the particular form that food merchandising in the future assumes, it is quite possible that there will evolve a method of retail merchandising that eliminates much of the physical handling that is characteristic

---

[10]"Cashless Society Expanding." *Chain Store Age Executives Edition,* March 1973, p. E19.

of our present system. It seems strange that in today's space age nearly every package on display in a food store has been placed there individually by hand, to say nothing of the number of times that each package is handled before it reaches the retail display floor. This method appears particularly wasteful when one realizes that the consumer simply removes the package from the shelf, often without physical inspection. Thus, it would seem that a more efficient method of merchandising could be developed that would eliminate much of the physical handling of products while satisfying consumer needs and preferences adequately.

Current technological advances will be developed to the point where they will substantially increase the efficiency of food merchandising. Electronic data processing has already reduced the time required to replenish retail shelves and wholesale warehouse stocks while providing more instantaneous and complete information upon which to base merchandising decisions. Perhaps the most significant technological breakthrough in many decades is the computerized checkout. Once the process of identifying each item through the assignment of a universal product code is completed, the computerized checkout system can be utilized effectively. It will enable food retailers to eliminate checker errors in ringing prices, provide accurate, instantaneous information on inventory levels of each and every item, and expedite the checkout procedure, which has been a bottleneck in the food retailing process every since the advent of self-service merchandising. (See Chapter 2.)

Another technological development that will have an important impact upon food distribution in the future is the mechanized distribution warehouse. The mechanized warehouse promises to eliminate most of the costly hand labor that for years has been required to receive, store, select, and ship grocery items to retail stores. Although the initial cost is quite high—at least $1 million—the partially or fully mechanized warehouse offers substantial productivity gains that can be expected to be reflected in cost savings to retailers and consumers. The Kroger Company was the first food distribution firm to develop and test a highly mechanized warehouse. Now, A&P, Springfield Sugar and Products Company, Giant Food, Wakefern Food Corporation, Meijer, Lucky Stores, and Steinbergs (Canada) have either built or are studying sophisticated mechanized distribution depots. In addition to grocery items, it is likely that mechanization may follow quickly in the distribution of frozen foods, produce, and other categories.[11]

THE ROLE OF GOVERNMENT

Federal, state, and local governments have always played a role in food merchandising, essentially that of maintaining healthy competition free of exclusion and deception so that the free market can operate effectively

---

[11]*Supermarket News*, April 2, 1973, pp. 4-5.

in serving the consumer. During the late 1960s and early 1970s, there has been an upsurge in legislation, both enacted and proposed, concerning the protection of the consumer in the marketplace for food (see Chapter 9). It appears as if the role of government in the future will continue to expand in order to meet increased pressure from consumer organizations and legislators for more regulation of food merchandising in the consumer's behalf. At the same time, business firms have become more responsive to the needs and desires of consumers in the marketplace and in the future will probably anticipate and act rather than react to legitimate consumer concerns.

Consumerism

The term *consumerism* has been coined to describe "the widening range of activities of government, business, and independent organizations that are designed to protect individuals from practices (of both business and government) that infringe upon their rights as consumers."[12] Although consumerism refers to all types of business activity, much of the activity has centered on the food industry, especially in the area of information.

Many in the consumer movement believe that the major problem is that of imperfections in the marketplace and that competition will serve consumer interests only if they can learn quickly and accurately about available brands and their prices and characteristics. However, as products and ingredients proliferate, each consumer is less and less able to make useful price and quality comparisons.

The increasing concern for better information on food prices and quality in the marketplace to facilitate consumer choice making has led to several important legislative enactments and proposals and to voluntary action by industry. These programs and proposals contain important implications for food merchandising in the future.

Sanitation Regulations

An area of increased activity on the part of business firms and federal, state, and local government agencies is that of sanitation practices in the processing, handling, and distribution of foods. Food distribution firms are placing greater emphasis on improved sanitation in order to provide the consumer with more wholesome food as well as to reduce spoilage and increase shelf life. For example, meat-cutting and packaging facilities and methods, both in the store and in central locations, have been greatly improved in recent years and will continue to be upgraded in the future. Meat cutting and packaging will be done to an increasing extent under near-sterile conditions, which will reduce the bacterial count on the retail cuts and result in a higher quality, more wholesome product for the consumer

---

[12]George S. Day and David A. Aaker, "A Guide to Consumerism," *Journal of Marketing,* Vol. 34, (July 1970), pp. 12-19.

while increasing the shelf life and reducing product spoilage losses for the retailer.

General sanitation regulations concerning the handling and distribution of foods are becoming more stringent and more strictly enforced, and food retailers will have to pay greater attention to the cleanliness of facilities, equipment, and personnel involved in the storage, handling, and selling of food products.

Economic Controls

Along with increasing concern for more consumer information and more wholesome foods is the concern for the cost of food to the consumer. Constant inflation led to peace-time wage and price controls beginning in 1971 that included most food prices. Because a major objective of both political parties is to stem or control inflation, it is not unlikely that the retail food industry will be subject to some degree of continuing control in establishing selling prices and margins.

The Metric System

It is quite likely that in the future federal legislation will require conversion from our present system of weights and measures to the metric system. The metric system, unlike our present system, is a decimal system based upon the kilogram as the basic unit of weight and the meter as the basic unit of measure. The metric system has many advantages, and, once consumers become accustomed to it, it will be easier to use in making purchasing decisions than our present system, which includes many nondecimal units to indicate weight and measure. An important advantage of the metric system is the fact that the vast majority of nations are using it as their official system of weights and measures.

If and when the conversion to the metric system occurs, it will require extensive changes in the packaging and labeling of food and grocery products as well as the intensive education of consumers who are accustomed to the U.S. system.

The adoption of the metric system would be a very significant development with respect to food merchandising because a system of weights and measures is essential to the merchandising process. In the long run, it is very likely that the metric system will be of great benefit because it will facilitate the consumer decision-making process involving the comparison and purchase of food and grocery products.

SOCIAL AND ENVIRONMENTAL CONCERNS

Two issues have emerged during recent years that will influence food merchandising in the future. These issues are partly economic in nature but are more closely associated with concerns for the well being of our fellow man and for the condition of our environment, the air we breathe, the water we drink, and the landscape we see.

Social Concerns

In spite of the unprecedented prosperity in the United States, a sizable segment of the population remains disadvantaged in terms of the ability to earn enough income to purchase an adequate diet. It is estimated that nearly 25 million Americans are living on incomes that are below the level required for an adequate standard of living.

In recent years, several food assistance programs have been expanded in order to achieve a national policy of eliminating hunger and malnutrition. Included in these programs are the food-stamp plan, commodity distribution, the school lunch program, and special programs designed to supplement the dietary needs of the elderly, expectant and recent mothers, and young children. Most of these programs are financed mostly by the federal government with state, county, and local governments sharing in the administrative costs and determining who is eligible to participate.

The food-stamp plan is the only food assistance program that involves the food retailer directly. It involves the redemption of coupons, which are purchased by eligible persons for less than their redemption value, for food at retail stores that participate in the program. A few imported foods, as well as nonfood products, tobacco, and alcoholic beverages are ineligible for purchase with stamps. Retailers must be certified by the USDA in order to participate in the program.

The retail food stores redeem the food coupons through a bank just as they do cash receipts and checks. Or the store may redeem the coupons through an authorized wholesaler who deposits them at a bank. The bank then redeems the coupons through a Federal Reserve Bank that is, in turn, reimbursed out of a special account maintained in the U.S. Treasury. The USDA also has the responsibility of enforcing the rules that retailers must follow in redeeming food stamps for consumers. It is possible that the food-stamp plan will continue to be expanded as the major means for eliminating hunger and malnutrition among the needy.

Another aspect of the problem of providing an adequate diet to low-income consumers is that of food shopping facilities and prices. There has been much concern on the part of public officials and consumer groups that higher prices are charged in low-income area stores than in stores located in other income areas.

Various studies and investigations have been made in an attempt to ascertain whether or not price discrimination is practiced to the disadvantage of consumers living in low-income areas. Although the results of these studies and investigations have sometimes been conflicting, the weight of evidence indicates that food retailing firms do not deliberately establish higher price structures in low-income area stores.

Two studies conducted by U.S. government agencies showed that there were no significant differences in prices charged by food stores located in low-income areas as compared to prices charged by stores in higher income areas. The first of these studies was conducted by the Bureau of Labor Statistics for the National Commission on Food Marketing; the second study was conducted by the U.S. Department of Agriculture.[13]

The BLS study included chain, large independent, and small independent stores in lower and higher income areas of six cities in the United States. The conclusions indicated that although prices charged by food stores in low-income areas versus those charged by stores in higher income areas were not significantly different when the same types of stores were compared, prices were usually higher in small independent stores than in large independents and chain stores.[14] The small independent stores were most common to low-income neighborhoods. The study further indicated that stores located in low-income areas tended to be somewhat less orderly and clean than those located in higher income areas and that meats and produce did not appear as fresh.[15]

The U.S. Department of Agriculture Study included selected chain stores operating in low- and high-income areas in six cities. The results indicated that prices charged for food items purchased in stores of two chains in each of six cities showed no identifiable pattern of differences between sample stores of the same chain operating in high- and low-income areas. Though uniform prices were the rule, there was some variation from store to store in prices of individual items. The prices of 17 kinds of foods were included in the study, which was conducted during a two-day period when relatively high rates of food-stamp redemption and issuance of welfare assistance checks were anticipated.[16]

It appears that the greatest problem facing the residents of low-income areas is not a discriminatory pricing policy followed by chain and independent stores, but rather the absence of opportunity to shop in large stores such as those available to residents of higher income areas. Many residents of low-income areas may be forced to shop in small stores where prices are higher, and the store conditions, services, selection, and quality of merchandise may be inferior to those provided in supermarkets.

The scarcity of supermarkets in low-income areas may be due to higher operating costs and lower profits associated with low-income area supermarkets. If this is true, chain and independent firms might tend to avoid operating supermarkets in low-income areas.

---

[13]In the BLS study, low-income areas were those census tracts in which annual median family income was in the lowest quartile (one-fourth) for the city based upon census data. The USDA study also used census income data as well as food-stamp redemption rates in selecting low-income areas and the sample of stores.

[14]*Small independents* were defined as those independent stores having an annual sales volume of less than $300,000.

[15]"Retail Food Prices in Low and Higher Income Areas," *Special Studies in Food Marketing,* Technical Study No. 10, National Commission on Food Marketing, USDA, Washington, D.C., June 1966.

[16]*Comparison of Prices Paid for Selected Foods in Chain Stores in High and Low Income Areas of Six Cities,* United States Department of Agriculture, Washington, D.C., June 1968.

The National Commission on Food Marketing, in a study of five food chains in two Midwestern cities, reported that " . . . chain stores in the poorer neighborhoods were older, smaller, did less business per square foot, had greater inventory shrinkage (which includes pilferage and waste), had lower sales volume per store, and had lower average purchases per customer than did stores of the same chain in higher income areas. The average gross margins in the low-income and other neighborhoods were almost identical. Average store expense was considerably higher in the low-income areas, however, leaving net margin substantially lower for the stores in the low-income neighborhoods. These circumstances help to explain why chain building and expansion efforts have been directed mainly to higher income suburban areas."[17]

Similar results were found when the data were analyzed on the basis of racial composition of the neighborhoods in which the stores were located. This was probably because of the high correlation between racial balance and income, according to the commission study.

A more recent study conducted in five metropolitan areas in New England compared operating results of 35 chain food stores in low-income and

TABLE 10-2   Operating Results for Chain Food Stores in Low-income Areas as a Percentage of Operating Results in Non-low-income Areas, Five New England Metropolitan Areas

	Low-income Area Stores as a Percentage of Non-low-income Area Stores		
Item	*Predominantly White Areas (6)*	*Predominantly Black Areas (13)*	*All Low-Income Areas (19)*
Total Annual Sales	62.7%	61.5%	61.8%
Gross Margin	101.6	98.5	99.5
Expenses			
Labor	107.7	111.2	110.1
Rent	106.0	134.0	125.3
Advertising	110.3	121.8	117.2
Insurance	107.1	103.6	103.6
Security	152.6	326.3	268.4
Bad Checks	300.0	520.0	440.0
Total Expenses	108.6	120.9	116.9
Net profit (before taxes)	19.7	-82.8	-50.0
Inventory shrinkage	151.2	544.2	414.0

Source: Donald R. Marion, Assistant Professor of Food Marketing, *Operating Problems of Marketing Firms in Low-Income Areas — The Food Retailing Case*, Department of Agricultural and Food Economics, University of Massachusetts. Background paper prepared for Inner City Marketing Symposium, University of Buffalo, June 4-6, 1970, p. 12.

---

[17]*Organization and Competition in Food Retailing*, Technical Study No. 7, National Commission on Food Marketing, Washington, D.C., June 1966, p. 339.

non-low-income areas. The low-income area stores were divided into predominantly white and predominantly black neighborhood stores.[18]

The results indicated that annual sales were lower in low-income area stores than in stores in other areas, inventory shrinkage and expenses were higher in low-income area stores, and net profits in low-income area stores were far below those in non-low-income area stores. The stores in predominantly black neighborhoods showed an average net loss as compared with an average net profit in non-low-income area stores (Table 10-2).

The study revealed that there was relatively little difference in gross margins between low-income and non-low-income area stores, so that higher expenses and inventory shrinkage were primarily responsible for the lower net earnings in the low-income area stores. Labor, security, and bad-check expenses in addition to inventory shrinkage were responsible for a large part of the differences in net profit between low- and non-low-income area stores. The predominantly black neighborhood stores showed a much higher inventory shrinkage, and total expenses, especially rent, insurance, security, and bad checks, were higher than in stores in predominantly white, low-income areas.

Although there were wide variations in the data, operating results from eleven low-income independent stores indicated that sales were lower and gross margins higher than in low-income area chain stores. Net profits were not really comparable because the owner's salary was included in net profit in some of the independent store data.

Both chain and independent food merchants operating in low-income areas cited pilferage, labor, vandalism, occupancy, insurance costs, and bad-check losses as major operating problems. Interest in moving out of the inner-city, low-income areas was more evident than interest in expanding food businesses there.

The study concludes that the food marketing situation in inner cities is quite dismal and that poverty, racial, and crime problems are largely at the root of the marketing problems. It also raises some questions concerning possible solutions to inner-city food marketing problems. These include the possibilities of additional police protection, government-sponsored insurance protection at rates comparable to those outside the inner-city, tax advantages to spur investment in inner-city food marketing facilities, and the encouragement of minority operated businesses.

It is clear that food retailing in low-income areas poses some unique problems, and that business and government will need to work together in order to find solutions so that the benefits of modern food merchandising can be made available to all.

[18]Donald R. Marion, Assistant Professor of Food Marketing, *Operating Problems of Marketing Firms in Low-Income Areas—The Food Retailing Case,* Department of Agricultural and Food Economics, University of Massachusetts. Background paper prepared for Inner City Marketing Symposium, University of Buffalo, June 4-6, 1970.

Environmental Concerns

Perhaps the issue of greatest importance to food merchandising in the future is that of the quality of the environment. Efforts to purify our air and water and to preserve the natural beauty of our landscape have just begun in earnest and will accelerate as public awareness and effective enforcement of legislation increases.

The packaging of food and nonfood supermarket products will come under increasing scrutiny because of problems of littering and solid waste disposal. The growing accumulation of used glass, aluminum, and plastic containers is becoming especially troublesome because of the nonbiodegradable characteristics of these containers.[19]

In some municipalities and states, legislation has been proposed or already enacted that places a tax upon containers that create problems in an attempt to discourage the use of these containers and to help offset the costs of disposal. Legislation has also been proposed that would prohibit the use of nonreturnable glass and metal containers for beverages.

The disposal of garbage and trash at the food store is also becoming a greater problem, especially where ordinances restrict or prevent the use of incinerators in order to reduce air pollution.

In addition to these solid-waste disposal problems, the pollution of fresh bodies of water by detergents containing phosphate is of concern to the retail food industry. Although there is controversy concerning the role of phosphates in the deterioration of fresh-water bodies, manufacturers and retailers have assumed responsibility for informing consumers of the phosphate content of detergents available in the retail food store. The state of New York has established a maximum level for the legal phosphate content of detergents. There is the possibility that the sale of phosphate-bearing detergents will be controlled or prohibited by law in other states.

The problems of improving the quality of the environment are quite complicated, and it will be some time before adequate solutions are found. One thing seems certain, however — the critical importance of the issue during the years ahead. The task of cleaning up our environment is likely to foreshadow all other problems in our society for some time to come. The retail food industry will be called upon to assume an important share of the responsibility for achieving a clean, attractive environment. In order to fulfill this responsibility, decisions made concerning retail operations and merchandising must take into consideration the relationships between those decisions and the effect upon the environment.

---

[19]The term *biodegradable* refers to the modification or alteration of certain properties of a substance by the effects of a biological system. With respect to glass and some metal and plastic packaging materials, that are not biodegradable, this means that they will not break down or decompose when subjected to natural biological processes occurring in dumpsites or sanitary landfills.

SUMMARY

We have seen food merchandising develop from the "Mom and Pop" neighborhood store of the early 1900s with several hundred items to the large, self-service supermarket with many thousand items in the 1970s. As consumer's income and purchasing power has increased and tastes and preferences have changed, food distribution firms have sought new ways to meet consumer demand and to gain an advantage in a highly competitive industry.

Discounting, warehouse markets, 24-hour openings, convenience stores, and a wider selection of nonfoods are a few examples of new directions in food retailing. As consumers become better educated, more affluent, and more discriminatory and vocal, the food industry will need to become even more responsive to changing needs and preferences. New technology will make possible many new and exciting ways for food merchandising to meet the challenges of the future. And, if the past is a true indicator of the future, our food industry will meet the challenges successfully.

Index